When Did We See You Naked?

Jesus as a Victim of Sexual Abuse

Edited by

Jayme R. Reaves, David Tombs
and Rocío Figueroa

scm press

© The Editors and Contributors 2021

Published in 2021 by SCM Press
Editorial office
3rd Floor, Invicta House,
108–114 Golden Lane,
London EC1Y 0TG, UK
www.scmpress.co.uk

SCM Press is an imprint of Hymns Ancient & Modern Ltd
(a registered charity)

Hymns Ancient & Modern® is a registered trademark of
Hymns Ancient & Modern Ltd
13A Hellesdon Park Road, Norwich,
Norfolk NR6 5DR, UK

British Library Cataloguing in Publication data

A catalogue record for this book is available
from the British Library

978-0-334-06032-1

Typeset by Regent Typesetting
Printed and bound by
CPI Group (UK) Ltd

'come celebrate
with me that everyday
something has tried to kill me
and has failed.'

excerpt from 'won't you celebrate with me?' by Lucille Clifton,
from *The Book of Light* (Copper Canyon Press, 1993)

For those who have found a way to survive, in life or in death,
and for those who bear witness to their stories

Contents

Part 3: Parsing Culture, Context and Perspectives

Part 4: Sexual Abuse, Trauma and the Personal

List of Contributors

Beth R. Crisp is Professor and Discipline Leader for Social Work at Deakin University in Australia. Working at the interface between religion and social welfare practice, she explores how faith-based responses can address social exclusion for people who find themselves on the margins of the Church or wider society. Beth is the author or editor of 12 books including *Re-imagining Religion and Belief: 21st Century Policy and Practice* (Policy Press), *Eliminating Gender-Based Violence* (Routledge) and *Sustaining Social Inclusion* (Routledge), as well as more than 120 major articles in peer academic journals and numerous book chapters.

Rocío Figueroa is a Peruvian theologian, Lecturer in Systematic Theology at the Te Kupenga Catholic Theological College in Auckland and an External Researcher at the Centre for Theology and Public Issues at Otago University, New Zealand. She has a bachelor's degree and licence in theology from the Pontifical Faculty of Theology in Lima and her doctorate in theology from the Pontifical Gregorian University in Rome. She has previously lectured and worked in Peru, Italy and Mexico and worked in the Holy See as head of the Women's section in the Pontifical Council for the Laity. Figueroa's present research focus is theological and pastoral responses for survivors of Church sexual abuse.

Ruard Ganzevoort is Professor of Practical Theology and Dean of the Faculty of Religion and Theology at Vrije Universiteit Amsterdam. He has published extensively in the field of religion and sexual abuse. For more information, visit www.ruardganzevoort.nl/.

Mmapula Diana Kebaneilwe is a Senior Lecturer in Hebrew and Biblical Studies at the University of Botswana. She is a Womanist Scholar. She obtained her PhD in Old Testament Studies from the University of Murdoch in Perth, Australia in 2012. The title of her PhD thesis was *This Courageous Woman: A Socio-rhetorical Womanist Reading of Proverbs 31:10–31*. She is a member of the Old Testament Society of South Africa (OTSSA), the African Consortium for Law and Religion Studies (ACLARS) and the Circle of Concerned African Women Theologians. Her research focus is on the Bible, women, gender and environment.

Elisabet le Roux is Research Director of the Unit for Religion and Development Research at Stellenbosch University, South Africa. She has a proven track record in mixed methodology research on religion and gender-based violence, with a focus on qualitative research especially in conflict and post-conflict settings. Over the past ten years she has secured funding and delivered a range of evaluation and formative research projects in 22 countries across four continents, with a particular focus on gender equality, gender-based violence, women's participation, and a critical lens on the important roles of religion and culture.

Karen O'Donnell leads the programmes in Christian Spirituality at Sarum College, Salisbury, UK. In her most recent publications – *Broken Bodies: The Eucharist, Mary, and the Body in Trauma Theology* (SCM Press, 2018) and *Feminist Trauma Theologies: Body, Scripture and Church in Critical Perspective* (SCM Press, 2020) – her research is particularly focused on the places where bodies intersect with theology.

Pádraig Ó Tuama is a poet and theologian from Ireland whose work centres around themes of conflict, language and religion. His poetry has been featured in *Poetry Ireland Review*, the *Harvard Review*, AAP's *Poem A Day*, BBC, RTÉ, NPR, ABC and others. He presents *Poetry Unbound* from On Being Studios. He is the former leader of the Corrymeela Community and the co-founder, together with Paul Doran, of the Tenx9 storytelling movement. His poetry and prose have been published by Canterbury Press, Hodder and Broadleaf. For more information, visit padraigotuama.com.

Monica Poole serves as Professor of Philosophy and Religious Studies at Bunker Hill Community College in Boston, Massachusetts, USA. Current projects include a chapter for an open textbook on epistemology, a series of adaptations of biblical texts and an article about wrongful forgiveness.

Jeremy Punt is Professor of New Testament in the Theology Faculty at Stellenbosch University, South Africa. His work focuses on biblical hermeneutics past and present, including critical theory in interpretation, the intersection of biblical and cultural studies, and on the significance of contextual configurations of power and gender, and social systems and identifications for biblical interpretation. He has recently published *Postcolonial Biblical Interpretation: Reframing Paul* (Brill) and regularly contributes to academic journals and book publications.

Jayme R. Reaves is a public theologian and her research focuses on the intersections between theology, peace/conflict, trauma, interfaith cooperation, memory, gender and stories. She is the Director of Academic Development and lecturer in theology and biblical studies at Sarum College (UK) and has an M.Div from Baptist Theological Seminary in Richmond, Virginia (USA) as well as an M.Phil in Reconciliation Studies and a PhD in Theology from Trinity College, University of Dublin (Ireland).

Nicola Slee is Director of Research at the Queen's Foundation, Birmingham, and Professor of Feminist Practical Theology at Vrije Universiteit, Amsterdam. Her most recent publications are *Fragments for Fractured Times: What Feminist Practical Theology Brings to the Table* (SCM Press, 2020) and *Abba, Amma: Improvisations on the Lord's Prayer* (Canterbury Press, 2021, forthcoming).

Mitzi J. Smith PhD is the J. Davison Philips Professor of New Testament at Columbia Theological Seminary, Decatur, Georgia (USA). Her research interests are Womanist and African American Interpretation with an emphasis on systemic injustice, ancient and modern slavery and biblical interpretation more broadly. Her latest book, co-edited with Jin Young Choi, is *Minoritized Women Reading Race and Ethnicity: Intersectional Approaches to Constructed Identity and Early Christian Texts* (Lexington, 2020).

Shanell T. Smith PhD is a New Testament and early Christianity scholar and an ordained Teaching Elder in the Presbyterian Church (USA). She is also a doctoral coach and keynote speaker. Her scholarly interests include Feminist and Womanist Biblical Interpretation, Gender and Sexuality in the New Testament, and the intersections of Post-colonial, African American and New Testament Studies, particularly with regard to the book of Revelation. She is the author of several works, including: *touched: For Survivors of Sexual Assault Like Me Who Have Been Hurt by Church Folk and for Those Who Will Care* (Fortress Press, 2020) and *The Woman Babylon and the Marks of Empire: Reading Revelation with a Postcolonial Womanist Hermeneutics of Ambivalence* (Fortress Press, 2014). Smith continually works to enhance the status of women in the profession, mentors students so they can reach their greatest potential, and publishes works that will further New Testament scholarship by inciting others to engage.

Srdjan Sremac is Assistant Professor in the Faculty of Religion and Theology at Vrije Universiteit, Amsterdam, and Co-Director of the Amsterdam Center for the Study of Lived Religion, The Netherlands. His interdisciplinary research interests include religion and sexuality, war-related trauma, the lived religion of marginalized groups, material non-Western culture/religion and post-conflict reconciliation studies.

Rachel Starr is Director of Studies (undergraduate programmes) at the Queen's Foundation for Ecumenical Theological Education, Birmingham. She completed her doctorate at Instituto Superior Evangélico de Estudios Teológicos in Buenos Aires, Argentina. Recent publications include *Reimagining Theologies of Marriage in Contexts of Domestic Violence: When Salvation is Survival* (Routledge, 2018) and *SCM Studyguide: Biblical Hermeneutics, 2nd edition* (SCM Press, 2019).

David Tombs is a lay Anglican theologian and the Howard Paterson Chair Professor of Theology and Public Issues at the University of Otago, Aotearoa New Zealand. His work addresses religion, society and ethics, and he has a longstanding interest in contextual and liberation theologies. Originally from the United Kingdom, David previously worked at the University of Roehampton, London, and at the Irish School of Ecumenics, Trinity College Dublin, Ireland.

Michael Trainor is Senior Lecturer in Biblical Studies at the Australian Catholic University. His monograph, *The Body of Jesus and Sexual Abuse* (Wipf and Stock, 2015), offers a way of engaging with the gospel stories of Jesus' passion and death in the light of institutional sexual abuse.

Carlton Turner is a Bahamian Anglican Priest and Caribbean Contextual Theologian working as a theological educator at the Queen's Foundation, Birmingham, UK. He teaches Mission Studies and Contextual Theology, supervises research and publishes in the areas of global Christianity, colonialism, mission and inculturation.

Gerald O. West is Professor Emeritus in the School of Religion, Philosophy and Classics at the University of KwaZulu-Natal, South Africa. He serves on the Advisory Board and continues to do Contextual Bible Study work with the Ujamaa Centre for Community Development and Research. Among his activist and research interests is how an understanding of the Bible as a site of struggle might offer resources for social transformation to faith-based communities.

Teguh Wijaya Mulya is a lecturer in the Faculty of Psychology, the University of Surabaya, Indonesia. He specializes in research in the areas of sexuality, gender and religion. His work is inspired by the work of Michel Foucault, post-structuralist feminism and queer theology.

Foreword

RIGHT REVEREND DR ELEANOR SANDERSON

Assistant Bishop of Wellington, New Zealand

The crucifixion of Jesus is confrontational. According to Jürgen Moltmann it is impossible to speak of Christian eschatological hope without being in conversation with the cross and all that the cross offends in our sensibilities.[1] Yet, as this body of work contends, there have been pejorative limits to the confrontation of the cross and recognizing Jesus as a victim of sexual abuse has often felt beyond those limits. Having this important conversation, which recognizes the extent of violence and abuse that Jesus endured, requires us to have a deep level of vulnerability, rawness and honesty. This is because it is an active and real conversation about historic and contemporary divine and human suffering.

As an Anglican priest, I have guided Christian communities through the passion narratives of Holy Week over many years. Now, as a bishop, my identity and my life are connected to the cross in new ways. When I sign my name, I first mark the paper with the sign of the cross, the traditional signature of a bishop. I am called to be a bearer of blessing among my communities, using the outstretched arm of my own body to make the sign of the cross over our people. In all these bodily actions I must choose to walk with Jesus to the cross and beyond the cross. In my and Jesus' walking together, in our spiritual intimacy, in the physicality of all mystical encounter, there is always a holding of each other's trauma and the choice to be ministers of reconciliation in this world in which trauma abounds. Journeying with people who have experienced, or perpetrated, sexual trauma has been a consistent part of my life as a minister in the Church and I welcome a fresh sensibility of the way that Jesus' own earthly experiences speak into a world so deeply affected by sexualized trauma.[2] Even though, in doing so, we expose ourselves and each other to the pain of trying to have this conversation well: a call to speak reverently and responsibly.

Suffering, albeit in diversity, has been a global experience characterizing our current epoch. A global pandemic, interspersed with present-day violence and, sometimes, painful protest to highlight historic and enduring violence and injustice, has shaped our global consciousness. These experiences intertwine the local/embodied specific and the global cultivation of our shared humanity. The paschal mystery is potent and important for both this cultivation of our human society and for our deeply personal experiences of being human. Journeying with Jesus' passion and trauma in New Zealand in Holy Week in 2019 required exceptional reverence and responsibility. The horrific and violent deaths of 52 men, women and children while at prayer in mosques in Christchurch on 15 March were very present in our country's consciousness at Eastertide. The Royal Commission into historic abuse in state care and institutions, including the Church, also began in 2019 in Aotearoa New Zealand. The phrase, 'you should have been safe here', first spoken by Prime Minister Jacinda Ardern in response to the mosque attacks, became a strong lament in our society. It was a phrase that confronted me as I came to write to our diocese in our Bishops' Easter message in 2019, when the violence of the mosque attacks was so recent:

You should have been safe here

Those haunting words which have been spoken out over our nation in these recent weeks keep resounding in my heart. As I have moved between our churches, week by week, and as we have gathered day by day in the deep tradition of our Holy Week, my mind has become stuck on that phrase. *You should have been safe here.* The grief of my heart for our world at this time is ripe, as is my grief for the people about whom those words were rightly spoken. Yet I find myself repeating them under my breath to someone else: to Christ. To my friend Jesus those words also seem so painfully real. *You should have been safe here.* You came to that which was your own, but your own didn't recognise you. All things came into being through you and what came into being was light and life (as proclaimed in the beginning of John's Gospel). You, friend, bringing your light and life, should have been safe here. But you weren't … You gave life to people. You loved people. You who are one with the God who is love. You who are one with the source of life. Yet, in response to your gift of love and life to this world, you were given death. You were given hate.

You knew all those things, and in the agony of your heart you still accepted that, and so you said, 'this is my body given for you'.

One physical body was destroyed by fear, by hate, by human power. Unless a grain of wheat falls to the ground and dies, it remains but a seed, but if it dies it produces many seeds (John 12.24). Our lips now confess that we are the body of Christ, we are those many seeds. That you are with us. That we get to proclaim that you are here, that you are risen, that in you nothing can separate us from the love and life of God.

Asking us to have a conversation *about* Jesus as a victim of sexual abuse and inviting us to have a conversation *with* Jesus as a victim of sexual abuse can have powerful consequences. These consequences can be deeply personal, institutionally transformative and also profoundly significant for societies and cultures that have been so influenced by interpreting the historical life, death and resurrection of Jesus Christ.

I am therefore thankful for the courage of those initiating these conversations. I am also thankful for the Christian theological posture of hope. I therefore offer into the beginning of these conversations two things: the first, words spoken between some of the earliest followers of Jesus, from the Letter to the Hebrews 12.1–3; the second, a poem written many years ago, which was my personal response to Christ's solidarity with those who experience sexual violation.

Therefore, since we are surrounded by so great a cloud of witnesses, let us also lay aside every weight and the sin that clings so closely, and let us run with perseverance the race that is set before us, looking to Jesus the pioneer and perfecter of our faith, who for the sake of the joy that was set before him endured the cross, disregarding its shame, and has taken his seat at the right hand of the throne of God. Consider him who endured such hostility against himself from sinners, so that you may not grow weary or lose heart.

Love is vulnerability
Strength didn't come in the shape
I painted and pursued,
but in the form of a humiliated man
stretched out to die
upon a splintered tree,
Whose tears of love;
pure vulnerability,
flow endlessly and endlessly.
In his outstretched, bruised
and beaten embrace,
that dusty cheek
against my face
is freedom.
Freedom that no pain or shame
needs to be explained or named
to this friend who shaped them not,
but wore them as his only clothes
then shook them off
to rise and dress us all in joy

Notes

1 Jürgen Moltmann, *Theology of Hope* (London: SCM Press, 1967) and *The Crucified God: The Cross of Christ as the Foundation and Criticism of Christian Theology* (London: SCM Press, 1973).

2 For a fuller exploration of this journey see Eleanor Sanderson, 'Embodying Freedom and Truth Within the Compass Rose: Spiritual Leadership in the Revolution of Love', in *Shame, Gender Violence and Ethics: Terrors of Injustice*, eds Lenart Skof and Shé Hawke (Lanham, MD: Lexington Press, 2021).

Introduction
Acknowledging Jesus as a Victim of Sexual Abuse

JAYME R. REAVES AND DAVID TOMBS

At the heart of this book is a surprising, even scandalous, claim: that Jesus was a victim of sexual abuse. It may seem a strange and implausible idea at first. This initial puzzlement is to be expected; the starting point and central focus of the book is both unusual and confronting. As the following chapters will highlight, there is significant evidence that, at the very least, the forced stripping and naked exposure of Jesus on the cross should be acknowledged as sexual abuse.[1] The acknowledgement of this truth has the potential for positive consequences, but we also acknowledge it is a difficult and disturbing subject to address. Sexual abuse points to what is speakable – and what is unspeakable – in the suffering Jesus experienced.

To say that Jesus suffered, even suffered greatly, is uncontentious. Jesus' suffering is firmly attested in Christian faith as we know it. The Apostles' Creed explicitly acknowledges Jesus' suffering with the phrase 'suffered under Pontius Pilate' (*passus sub Pontio Pilato*). The word excruciating (derived from the Latin *crux*) connects the cross (*crux*) with acute suffering in the passion narratives. The early Church at the Council of Chalcedon (451 CE) firmly condemned the Docetic heresy, which denied the reality of Jesus' suffering. The ruling established that Christian orthodoxy included an acknowledgement of the reality of suffering on the cross.

A number of works have also spoken of Jesus' suffering as torture.[2] Naming Jesus' ordeal as torture underlines the intentional cruelty and violence in his mistreatment. The term 'torture' is not used in the Gospel texts to describe Jesus' experience. However, a close reading of the passion narratives provides a strong argument for seeing Jesus' experience in this way. Although some might prefer not to use the word 'torture' for Jesus' experience, there are few Christians likely to see the use of the term as morally shocking or theologically objectionable. To acknowledge Jesus' suffering as torture does not create new theological difficulties.

To acknowledge Jesus as a victim of sexual abuse, however, typically prompts a very different reaction: blank surprise, stony silence, scepticism, correction, or even offence. Some ask questions like, 'Do you really mean that?' Others say there is no evidence in the Bible to support such a claim. Some flatly declare, 'You can't say this.' Jesus is readily spoken of as a victim of suffering, and there is little problem in describing his suffering as torture. But to speak of him as a victim of sexual abuse is shocking and meets resistance. Why? We have come to see the *resistance* to the idea of Jesus as a victim of sexual abuse as part of the key to understanding what sexual abuse means and why it could be so important to our understanding of both Jesus' experience and our contemporary context.

If our experiences over years of work with church and academic groups are an indication, there are often several stages that people go through as they consider this proposal. At first, it is likely to be viewed as speculative conjecture, without biblical or historical evidence to support it. Or it might be seen as a subjective reading imposed on the text and drawing on an agenda from a very different time and place, rather than being supported by the text itself. Why, people may ask, if Jesus suffered sexual abuse, has this not been recognized in 2,000 years of Christian history? If it were in the Bible, they may continue, surely it would have been more openly acknowledged before now? This stage is marked by a sense of the novelty of the claim, and the lack of familiarity with the biblical evidence that supports it.

Deeper dynamics are also often at work. The resistance to this suggestion also takes the form that it is absurd, insulting, offensive, and even blasphemous. Those who oppose it claim that it conflicts with both the historical record and the theological understanding of who Jesus was. The chapters in Part 1 of this volume will show that evidence of the sexual abuse of Jesus is clear in the biblical text but is rarely noticed or discussed. The failure to notice this abuse in the Gospel texts is linked to how the texts are usually read.[3] Some chapters in this volume mention the limited scholarship in this area, and it is important to register both this silence and the reasons for it at the outset. The paucity of work on Jesus and any sexual topics makes an open discussion on Jesus and sexual abuse very difficult.

It is hardly surprising, then, that the suggestion that Jesus should be acknowledged as a victim of sexual abuse at first seems to be absurd. When most people think of the crucifixion, they think of visual representations in Christian art, often explicitly regulated by the Church. For example, the final session of the Council of Trent (1545–1563) set down requirements on holiness and devotion in religious art. The Council's 25th Decree stipulated that 'all lasciviousness be avoided' and nothing be seen that is disorderly or unbecoming.[4] Although the convention of a loincloth was already established in practice, this ruling explicitly increased the pressure to conform to such conventions, with those who flouted it at risk of being declared anathema. As a result, there are few visual images which illustrate the reality of Jesus' naked exposure. The number started to increase in the twentieth century, but these are still a small minority. In the common visual imagination of crucifixion, both in churches and in wider society, a modest loincloth obscures the clear historical record of the nature of crucifixion.

Despite the fact that a fully naked Jesus is only rarely depicted, the historical reality is nonetheless quite widely known. Historians and biblical scholars believe that Jesus was fully naked on the cross even though it is rarely discussed in detail. Similarly, many churchgoers are familiar with this reality and so describing Jesus as naked on the cross is not new.

Over the years, our experience has been that it is the naming of the stripping and nakedness as sexual abuse that is new to people, rather than the nakedness itself. And it is here that we come to a strange mismatch between what we know and what we acknowledge. It seems it is possible to know about the nakedness of Jesus on the cross, and even see this depicted in some artistic works, and yet still not describe or name his stripping and forced naked exposure as sexual abuse. This reticence becomes more obvious if we contrast it with contemporary examples of prisoners who have been stripped naked in detention, such as, for example, the prisoner abuse at Abu Ghraib in Iraq in the early 2000s.[5] There was no reticence in the wide coverage of this scandal or in describing the stripped and humiliated detainees at Abu Ghraib prison as victims of sexual abuse. Indeed, it was so obvious that a reluctance to describe it in such a way would be seen as dishonest.

Some have suggested that Jesus suffered abuse, but that stripping and exposure are not really sexual. This raises questions about when abuse should be recognized or qualified as sexual abuse. To believe that the more generic term of 'abuse' (instead of 'sexual abuse') would be preferable is problematic. What sort of abuse is stripping and forced exposure if it is not sexual abuse? Public stripping, enforced nakedness and sexual humiliation constitute sexual abuse because they are attacks on sexual identity and sexual vulnerability. They have a specifically sexual meaning. They derive their power and impact because they were understood – and still are understood – to have a sexual dimension. To name them only as abuse is to mischaracterize what has happened, which serves to distort the reality of Jesus' experience.

When the initial surprise has passed, many people find it difficult to understand why it has taken them so long to see what is obvious, something that seems, in fact, to have been hidden in plain sight. They ask questions about what might have prevented them from seeing this before, and they often wonder why it is never mentioned in sermons. These questions should be taken seriously. Unspoken reasons behind the reluctance to notice and name Jesus' experience as sexual abuse need to be recognized. Deeper conversations on the subject often reveal that assumptions about stigma are a critical factor in people's attitudes. Most frequently, the resistance comes from the sense that Jesus would be somehow demeaned and less worthy as a saviour if he were a victim of sexual abuse.

The stigma and shame that comes with being named as a victim of sexual abuse is one of the central concerns that we want to identify and explore in this volume. The early Church spoke of the immense shame Jesus endured in his trial, torture and execution. Indeed, in this light the profound shame

3

may be the key to the offence and scandal of the cross acknowledged by the apostle Paul in 1 Corinthians 1.23. However, over the centuries the memory of this shame has been lost. Despite the display of so many images of Jesus' body hanging from a cross, we are unable to see what is right in front of us. When it is named in ways that make the shame and humiliation more explicit, this naming is often resisted.

We see the resistance to the idea as at least as important as the idea itself. It is because of the resistance that we as editors felt it important to put this collection together. A question articulated by a respondent to a recent presentation captured this issue succinctly: 'If it is acceptable to say that Jesus suffered torture and crucifixion, why is it not acceptable to say that he was the victim of sexual abuse as well?'[6]

There are several levels to this discussion: what happened, why people resist this idea, and why these both matter. The issues are closely linked to the importance of acknowledging that Jesus was a victim of sexual abuse. We believe that appropriately exploring these painful and difficult issues can lead to positive consequences for survivors of abuse, those who love them, for the Church as the body of Christ, and for the wider society in which silence about sexual violence has been accepted as the norm. We hope to provoke a longer-term conversation.

A starting point for this volume is the work by David Tombs from over 20 years ago. In his 1999 article 'Crucifixion, State Terror, and Sexual Abuse', Tombs drew on Latin American liberationist hermeneutics for a reading of biblical texts with attention to both past and present contexts.[7] He described the dynamics of state terror and sexual abuse in the torture practices of the regimes of Brazil, Chile, Argentina, Guatemala and El Salvador in the 1970s and 1980s. He then used this historical reality as a vantage point from which to re-examine Roman crucifixion practices that might shed light on the biblical narratives. A guiding hermeneutical principle was that those reports on torture provided a lens through which to see the first-century context and the biblical text in new ways.

Understanding the use of torture for state terror – and the prevalence of sexual abuse in torture practices – provides insights into what is clearly present within the texts but is often unrecognized or ignored. Torture reports also raise the possibility of further sexual assault that may have taken place in the praetorium. Since this article was first published in 1999, reports from Sri Lanka, Libya, Syria, Democratic Republic of Congo, South Sudan, Myanmar and other contexts have attested to a range of sexual abuses being a feature of the mistreatment of prisoners in detention and a global issue.

Tombs' article focused primarily on a historical rereading and the hermeneutical approach that might support this. However, in a short final section it offered a brief reflection on some of the theological and pastoral implications of this recognition prompted by the parable of judgement (Matt. 25.31–46). Matthew 25.40 provides a clear theological basis for affirming that Christ shares in the suffering of others: 'Truly I tell you, just as you did it to one of the least of these who are members of my family, you did it to me.'[8]

We have taken the words 'When did we see you naked?' (Matt. 25.38–40) from the parable as the title for this book. The parable of judgement does not suggest that Jesus was himself naked, nor did he need to be for his teaching to convey his message. However, the words capture a question that needs to be asked. Later, in Matthew 27, as the passion story unfolds, this question, 'When did we see you naked?' becomes more urgent and immediately relevant. The book title is intended to raise the question as to whether we see the naked Jesus in Matthew 27 and other texts or avoid what is in front of us. It is an invitation to reflect back during the passion narratives to the question asked in Matthew 25.38–40 with a new awareness of what was actually done to Jesus and a new sense of what he might fully share with others.

In this book we explore both Jesus' historical experience of sexual abuse and the theological and pastoral significance that this might have today. We are not saying that sexual abuse is the only form of suffering that Jesus experienced in his trial, torture and execution. It is not our intention to limit understandings of Jesus' crucifixion in any way. Instead, our aim is to broaden the established narrative and to notice the gaps in the story that have heretofore been untold and/or unacknowledged.

Sexual violence and sexual abuse have been a part of lived experience for millennia, and its presence is shockingly prevalent in the biblical text as well. Nevertheless, one of the prevailing characteristics of sexual violence is that it can be hidden in plain sight. Either by commission or omission, it is often unseen and rarely discussed outside of specialist scholarship or within victim/survivor support groups. Often we need a catalyst – something outside the norm of what we think and how we do things – to push us to see something differently and to give us new ways of knowing. In recent years, revelations of clergy sexual abuse and sexual harassment cover-ups, and the corresponding #MeToo and #ChurchToo movements, have shone light into some of the most shame-filled experiences of society. As much as ever, we need theologies and biblical interpretations that offer tools that address issues related to sexual violence and abuse in a way that can lead to liberation rather than continued stigma, silence and despair.

The chapters in this book take up the questions and challenges of understanding Jesus' experience in a way that may at first seem unimaginable. What is presented here is not intended to shock. It is offered with a serious historical, theological and pastoral concern. Many contributors write not just as scholars but as people deeply committed to the Church in a variety of ways. They write with an awareness that the topic is sensitive. Breaking the silence around the unspeakable is fraught with risk of offence. However, keeping silent involves risk of a different sort. As Sara Ahmed says, 'Silence about violence is violence.'[9] Silence risks acceptance of the status quo and complicity with how things are. Sexual abuse and sexual violence demand a response beyond silence. As survivors and people who work with them attest, breaking silence can be a first step to transformation.

How to discuss Jesus as victim of sexual abuse is a question that has to be opened up, not a provocation that must be closed down. But of course this raises ethical concerns. As Roxane Gay asks: 'How do you write violence authentically without making it exploitative? ... [W]e need to be vigilant not only in what we say but also in how we express ourselves.'[10] The question is not whether unspeakable abuse should or should not be addressed, but how it can be addressed in an appropriate way.

Here, authors take a number of theological approaches: feminist, womanist and post-colonial hermeneutics; discourse analysis; constructive and practical theology; memoir and reflection; poetry; and qualitative research drawing on victim/survivor testimony and faith community response. These chapters reflect a variety of opinions and starting points. There is a range of emotions also at play within these pages: curiosity, pain, hope, rage, courage, disgust, healing, anger, as well as resolve to create a better world. For some, there is hope and redemption to be found in the acknowledgement of Jesus as a victim of sexual abuse, and in the belief that recognition of shared experience has value and meaning. For others, there is more attention to the pain and the harm, including a charge to the reader that there are no easy answers.

The work is divided up into four main sections. We are grateful for the authors' insights and their courageous commitment in this volume to build a framework for our exploration.

Part 1: Biblical and Textual Studies introduces the topic with an exploration of the biblical text and historical sources related to Jesus' crucifixion. This part starts with an abbreviated version of David Tombs' 1999 article, entitled here 'Crucifixion and Sexual Abuse'. The original article is now readily available and offers greater detail on the politics of 'state terror', exploring the torture practices of the Roman Empire in comparison to Latin American regimes in the 1970s and 1980s. The chapter included here focuses on connections between sexual violence and torture and gives perspective on the sexual humiliation, violence and abuse involved in crucifixion.

Michael Trainor's chapter, 'Covering Up Sexual Abuse: An Ecclesial Tendency from the Earliest Years of the Jesus Movement?', provides a comparative analysis of the passion accounts in Mark and Luke. Trainor takes into account narrative choices made in each Gospel that reflect early Church sensibilities and what the Gospel audience(s) would have heard and understood. Trainor's work reads the gospel tradition in the light of the cover-ups conducted within the clergy sexual abuse scandals in Australia, drawing parallels between the two.

Mitzi J. Smith explores the crucifixion narratives in the Gospels from a womanist lens with her chapter '"He Never Said a Mumbalin' Word": A Womanist Perspective of Crucifixion, Sexual Violence and Sacralized Silence'. Smith explores the parallels in black hymnody, the reality of lynching and racialized sexual violence by building on the notable work of James Cone and Angela Sims, and considers how the black church in the US has historically made meaning from Jesus' 'silent suffering' in New Testament accounts.

Monica Poole introduces three biblical texts in her chapter 'Family Resemblance: Reading Post-Crucifixion Encounters as Community Responses to Sexual Violence'. Through a lens of feminist biblical studies, Poole takes on Thomas's doubting demands (John 20.24–25), the centurion's declaration of belief (Luke 23.46–49) and Jesus' words 'Don't touch me' (*noli me tangere*; John 20.17). In these three texts, Poole takes consent and believing victims/survivors of sexual violence seriously. She also compares acts of sexual violence to a bomb blast with wide area effects, arguing that the 'blast radius' includes not only the victim's own trauma, but how the community members respond, including in ways that may compound the harm.

In Jeremy Punt's chapter 'Knowing Christ Crucified (1 Corinthians 2.2): Cross, Humiliation and Humility', the focus shifts into the Pauline New Testament. Punt explores the concern for Jesus' body in Pauline literature and Paul's emphasis on the humiliation of the cross. In this chapter, Punt addresses gender, body, shame and honour, and what it meant for the church in Corinth to follow a shamed and crucified Christ.

In the final chapter in Part 1, there is a comparative analysis from Gerald O. West entitled 'Jesus, Joseph, and Tamar Stripped: Trans-textual and Intertextual Resources for Engaging Sexual Violence Against Men'. West draws links between the Hebrew Bible and New Testament to illuminate sexual violence through forced stripping. He explores the Joseph narrative in Genesis 37—46, the Tamar narrative in 2 Samuel 13, and the gospel texts Mark 15 and Matthew 27. West also describes a contextual Bible study methodology developed at the Ujamaa Centre in South Africa to take this further. In this work, West and colleagues focus on contextual readings that consider the specific experience of men who have been victims of sexual violence and abuse.

Part 2: Stations of the Cross comprises 14 poems entitled 'This is M̶y̶ A Body' from Irish poet and theologian Pádraig Ó Tuama. These serve as a meditation on the 14 Stations of the Cross observed mainly within the Roman Catholic tradition. Ó Tuama's wider work in the areas of peace, conflict, queerness, biblical studies, stories and the body provide a rich range of resources to encourage new thinking. The moving reflections presented here give space for a different type of creativity which, in turn, enables a different type of engagement with the material. The content of this volume is difficult and we hope to provide multiple entry points for engagement, from biblical studies into cultural analysis, and on to lived experience in the later chapters.

Part 3: Parsing Culture, Context and Perspectives starts with the chapter 'Conceal to Reveal: Reflections on Sexual Violence and Theological Discourses in the African Caribbean' by Carlton Turner. Turner uses post-colonial hermeneutics and socio-historical analysis in order to address the legacies of shame and the systemic consequences of sexual violence in the Caribbean that are 'hidden in plain sight'. Looking specifically at the legacy of slavery and colonialism and then considering its effect on African Caribbean culture and dance hall music, Turner's work connects these strands to build a painful picture of a violent past and present that still offers hope and scope for resistance and healing.

Rachel Starr invites us to consider culture via the television show *Veronica Mars* with her chapter '"Not pictured": What *Veronica Mars* Can Teach Us About the Crucifixion'. Continuing a 'hidden in plain sight' theme, Starr uses storytelling and references in *Veronica Mars* and pop culture to explore bigger questions. She asks what exactly it is in the torture and sexual violence experienced by Jesus – if anything – that saves us. In true feminist fashion, Starr reads the gaps in the stories, considering who is left out, whose story is not told, and why.

In 'Jesus is a Survivor: Sexual Violence and Stigma Within Faith Communities', Elisabet le Roux builds upon qualitative research based on the lived experiences of survivors of sexual violence in various African countries undertaken by faith-based organizations. In this chapter, Le Roux considers the cultural contexts and perspectives that inform understandings and responses from individuals and faith communities that lead to stigmatization and pressure to conform and/or stay silent.

Ruard Ganzevoort, Srdjan Sremac and Teghu Wijaya Mulya creatively tweak the words of Matthew 25.40 in their title 'Why Do We See Him Naked?: Politicized, Spiritualized and Sexualized Gazes at Violence'. They offer a critical perspective on the differing ways in which we see, understand and make meaning of sexual violence, and explore how this applies to Jesus' crucifixion. Drawing on academic conversations between sadomasochism and Christian theology, they ask how the torture practices of the cross can be seen by a Christian audience as both sexual and spiritual.

In 'The Crucified Christa: A Re-evaluation', Nicola Slee critiques the representation of the abuse and humiliation of women in Christa figures and discusses how Christa figures might bring the nakedness, sexual humiliation and abuse of Jesus into clearer public view. From a feminist and practical theology perspective, Slee argues that the gendering of nakedness as female in Christian thought and representation may act as a further barrier to recognizing the significance of Jesus being naked on the cross.

Writing from Botswana, Mmapula Diana Kebaneilwe combines womanist theology and critical discourse analysis methodology in 'Jesus as a Victim of Sexual Abuse: A Womanist Critical Discourse Analysis of the Crucifixion'. In this chapter, Kebaneilwe draws on the lived experiences of women in Botswana and explores how the stripping of women as an act of public sexual humiliation and abuse in Botswana can inform a reading of the stripping of Jesus and vice versa.

Finally, with Part 4: Sexual Abuse, Trauma and the Personal, we gather together stories and reactions from survivors and those close to them. They consider the legacy of sexual abuse and the ways in which victims, survivors and the ones who love them make meaning of the experience. They ask searching questions for which there are no easy answers.

The chapter from Beth R. Crisp entitled 'Jesus: A Critical Companion in the Journey to Moving On From Sexual Abuse' begins this final section. Crisp provides a personal victim/survivor account, considering the various tools and resources available within the Christian tradition and her personal faith that enabled her to reclaim her experience. She then explores issues related to communal responsibility and solidarity.

From the perspective of those who bore witness to Jesus' abuse, Karen O'Donnell explores what bystanders and witnesses are called to do in her chapter 'Surviving Trauma at the Foot of the Cross'. O'Donnell calls us to an ethical activism that is informed not just by solidarity, but also by bearing witness and embodying a love that prioritizes survival out from the depths of fragmentation and death, and into life. Moreover she also constructs and includes a liturgical resource based in the Church of England (Anglican) tradition that takes the needs of victims/survivors and their community to heart.

Shanell T. Smith writes a raw and powerful account entitled '"This is My Body": A Womanist Reflection on Jesus' Sexualized Trauma During His Crucifixion from a Survivor of Sexual Assault'. Smith is a womanist New Testament scholar and writes a personal reflection on the ongoing legacy and pain of sexual abuse and the questions that remain in relation to Jesus' experience in the light of her own. This chapter reflects Smith's 2020 publication *touched: For Survivors of Sexual Assault Like Me Who Have Been Hurt by Church Folk and for Those Who Will Care*.

The volume concludes with 'Seeing His Innocence, I See My Innocence', written by Rocío Figueroa and David Tombs, who are fellow co-editors for this volume. Their chapter reflects the findings from a qualitative research project with women who served in religious orders and were victims/survivors of clergy sexual abuse. Figueroa and Tombs present responses from several women as to what acknowledging Jesus as a victim of sexual abuse means for them and how helpful that acknowledgement may or may not be in relation to their own personal experience.

We have formatted the notes and referencing in a way that makes the scholarship as accessible as possible in order to facilitate further learning and research. Readers will note a diversity of sources. The work here is not limited to academic and biblical scholarship but also takes into account public sources such as news media, podcasts, TV series, poetry, fiction and other 'everyday' sources that help us make sense of what we encounter on a daily basis.

We believe that understanding Jesus as a victim of sexual abuse matters in ways that might not be obvious at first. This is partly because truth matters, and this truth has been hidden for too long. It is important to be honest in naming the things that over 2,000 years of Christian tradition have largely not been named. However, we believe that naming this truth does more than just correct a historical record about the past. It is a truth that matters in the present because it can make a practical difference. For the wider Church, it can help to expose and challenge the stigma that many in the churches mistakenly impose on survivors of abuse. Some survivors feel a personal sense of solidarity and practical support in seeing that Jesus experienced sexual abuse. Other survivors report that Jesus' experience should be acknowledged as historical fact but they do not take comfort in this as survivors. They say the concern for practical consequence should be directed at the wider Church rather than being seen as a help to survivors. It is important to hear these different responses and understand the experiences behind them. Understanding Jesus as a victim of sexual abuse will mean different things to different people. Diverse voices need to be heard and we hope this volume will lead to a deeper understanding of Jesus' experience and further conversation on how and why this experience matters.

Our hope is that with this volume the reader is challenged, encouraged and given tools to reconsider the story of the cross and what these reconsiderations mean not only for victims and survivors of sexual violence but also the Church as a whole. Ultimately, what makes this work distinctive and constructive is its commitment to testing whatever theological constructions and new forms of knowledge are made by setting them alongside the lived experiences of victims and survivors of sexual violence and abuse. The following chapters offer new opportunities to question assumptions in received traditions and to think anew about the passion story, and they provide new tools and reading practices that work toward liberation, justice, healing and life.

Notes

1 See also David Tombs, 'Crucifixion, State Terror, and Sexual Abuse', *Union Seminary Quarterly Review* 53:1–2 (Autumn 1999), pp. 89–109; Elaine A. Heath, *We Were the Least of These: Reading the Bible with Survivors of Sexual Abuse* (Grand Rapids, MI: Brazos, 2011); Wil Gafney, 'Crucifixion and Sexual Violence', *HuffPost*, 28 March 2013, www.huffingtonpost.com/rev-wil-gafney-phd/crucifixion-and-sexual-violence_b_2965369.html; Michael Trainor, *The Body of Jesus and Sexual Abuse: How the Gospel Passion Narrative Informs a Pastoral Approach* (Eugene, OR: Wipf & Stock Publishers, 2014); Chris Greenough, *The Bible and Sexual Violence Against Men* (London: Routledge, 2020).

2 See especially John Neafsey, *Crucified People: The Suffering of the Tortured in Today's World* (Maryknoll, NY: Orbis, 2014).

3 Indeed there has been very little serious discussion of the historical Jesus in relation to any form of sex and sexuality. Church traditions have sustained an association of sex with impurity, maintained a long-standing taboo around Jesus and sex, and implied Jesus had no sexuality. See William E. Phipps, *The Sexuality of Jesus: Theological and Literary Perspectives* (New York: Harper & Row, 1973); Leo Steinberg, *The Sexuality of Christ in Renaissance Art and in Modern Oblivion* (New York: Pantheon Books, 1983); Robert Beckford, 'Does Jesus have a Penis?

Black Male Sexual Representation and Christology', *Theology & Sexuality* 5 (1996), pp. 10–21.

4 *The Canons and Decrees of the Sacred and Oecumenical Council of Trent*, ed. and trans. J. Waterworth (London: Dolman, 1848), pp. 235–6.

5 Mark Danner, *Torture and Truth: America, Abu Ghraib, and the War on Terror* (New York: Review Books, 2004).

6 Jessica Delgado, 'Response to Papers on Sexual Violence and Religion', Joint Symposium of the Center of Theological Inquiry and Center for the Study of Religion, Princeton, NJ, 7 December 2018.

7 Tombs, 'Crucifixion, State Terror, and Sexual Abuse', pp. 89–109. See also Fernando F. Segovia, 'Jesus as Victim of State Terror: A Critical Reflection Twenty Years Later' in *Crucifixion, State Terror, and Sexual Abuse: Text and Context*, ed. David Tombs (Dunedin: Centre for Theology and Public Issues, University of Otago, 2018), http://hdl.handle.net/10523/8558.

8 Jayme R. Reaves and David Tombs, '#MeToo Jesus: Naming Jesus as a Victim of Sexual Abuse', *International Journal of Public Theology* 13:4 (2019), pp. 387–412.

9 Sara Ahmed, *Living a Feminist Life* (Durham, NC: Duke University Press, 2017), pp. 260–1.

10 Roxanne Gay, *Bad Feminist* (New York: HarperCollins, 2014), p. 135.

PART I

Biblical and Textual Studies

I

Crucifixion and Sexual Abuse[1]

DAVID TOMBS

Introduction

The Bible is always read with a context in mind. Assumptions are made about the original social context of the text and these are most often derived – consciously or otherwise – from the current social context of the reader or critic.[2] In recent decades the positive value of recognizing these connections has been advocated by contextual theologies in Latin America and elsewhere. Although some critics have rightly cautioned against temptations to superficially equate contemporary social contexts and the biblical world, those committed to a contextual approach have maintained that, when used appropriately, a serious engagement with current social contexts can offer insights into the biblical context and hence into neglected aspects of the biblical text.[3]

One area where I believe that shared similarities between past and present contexts can be most usefully investigated is the political arena of state terror and its use of torture. Latin American military regimes used terror in the 1970s and 1980s to create fear and promote fatalism throughout the whole of society. An understanding of this provides a context to recognize Roman crucifixions as instruments of state terror. Furthermore, Latin American torture practices involved deliberate attempts to shame the victims and undermine their sense of dignity. Physical torture and assaults were often coupled with psychological humiliation in attempts to end the victim's will to resist, or even to live. Sexual assaults and sexual humiliation are a particularly effective way to do this, and are commonplace in torture practices past and present.[4]

This chapter argues that torture practices can offer a deeper understanding of Roman crucifixion as a form of state terror that included sexual abuse. The analysis below draws on Latin American reports, but a similar reading could be offered through attention to torture in many other contexts, including torture and prisoner abuse at Abu Ghraib.[5]

To raise the question of sexual abuse in relation to Jesus may at first seem inappropriate. However, the Gospel accounts indicate a striking level of public sexual humiliation in the treatment of Jesus, and even this may not disclose the full horror of Jesus' torture before his death. Although this may be a very disturbing suggestion at first, at a theological level a God who has identified with the victims of sexual abuse can be recognized as a positive challenge for contemporary Christian understanding and response. At a pastoral level it could help sensitize people to the experiences of those who have suffered sexual abuse and, in some cases, might even become a healing step for the victims themselves.

Crucifixion and state terror

Military coups in the 1960s and 1970s installed military regimes in Brazil (1964–85) and throughout the Southern Cone of Latin America (Chile 1973–89; Uruguay 1973–85; and Argentina 1976–83). During these years state-sanctioned human rights abuses, including torture, assassinations and disappearances, were commonplace. Likewise, in the 1980s the authoritarian governments in Guatemala and El Salvador were involved in some of the most brutal campaigns of repression the region has known. The transition to democracy in Brazil and the Southern Cone countries and the peace treaties in El Salvador (1992) and Guatemala (1996) have prompted official investigations into human rights abuses during the repression. Published reports from these countries offer detailed documentation that make grim reading on the years of terror endured by the civilian populations.[6]

Any understanding of the political and social dynamics of the countries during this time must address the widespread use of state terror to support and enforce the illegitimate power of military regimes. Terror was an effective means of enforcing brutal authoritarianism through a culture of fear.[7] Fear 'persuades' people that it is better to endure injustices fatalistically rather than to resist them. The arrest and torture of 'suspects' by the police and military in Latin America cannot be adequately explained in terms of the threat they might have posed or the need to elicit information from them. Rather they should be understood as intended to paralyse a society's willingness to resist. In addition to targeting the victims themselves, disappearances, torture and executions were intended to terrorize a public audience.

In a similar way, Roman crucifixion was more than the punishment of an individual. Crucifixions were instruments within state terror policies directed at a wider population in the ancient world.[8] As acts of terror against potentially rebellious people, the Romans principally used crucifixion against slaves and other subjected peoples who might challenge Roman authority.[9] One of the clearest illustrations of the use of crucifixion to inspire terror is provided by Josephus' description of the treatment of those who attempted to flee Jerusalem during the siege by Titus in 70 CE:

> Scourged and subjected before death to every torture, they were finally crucified in view of the wall. Titus indeed realised the horror of what was happening, for every day 500 – sometimes even more – fell into his hands ... But his chief reason for not stopping the slaughter was the hope that

the sight of it would perhaps induce the Jews to surrender in order to avoid the same fate. The soldiers themselves through rage and bitterness nailed up their victims in various attitudes as a grim joke, till owing to the vast numbers there was no room for the crosses, and no crosses for the bodies. (*War*, V. 446–52)[10]

The effectiveness and security of the Roman troops in Palestine was ultimately based on the legions in Syria and – if necessary – elsewhere in the Empire. The relatively small force in Palestine was able to maintain order because it was backed by an assurance of severe reprisals if serious rebellion broke out. The combination of moderate presence and massive threat was usually enough to preserve the so-called 'peace' of the *pax Romana*.

The mass crucifixions with which the Romans responded to major incidents conveyed the message of fearful retaliation with a terrifying clarity. Josephus describes how in 4 BCE Varus (governor of Syria) responded to the upheaval caused by the inept rule of Herod's son Archelaus with the crucifixion of 2,000 'ringleaders' of the troubles (*War* II. 69–79 [75]). The census revolt when Quirinius was governor of Syria (6–7 CE) and Coponius procurator of Judea (6–9 CE) also met with widespread reprisals (*Ant.* 18.1–10; *War* II. 117–18). Josephus also records that when Cumanus (procurator of Judea 48–52 CE) took a number of prisoners involved in a dispute, Quadratus (governor of Syria) ordered them all crucified (*War* II. 241). Likewise, when Felix (procurator of Judea, 52–60 CE) set out to clear the country of banditry, the number that were crucified 'were too many to count' (*War* II. 253). Josephus also records how, in the build-up to the revolt of 66 CE, Florus (procurator 64–66 CE) raided the Temple treasury and then – because of the disturbance that followed – scourged and crucified men, women and children until the day's death toll was 3,600 (*War* II. 305–08).

Individual crucifixions should be understood within this political context. Even if only one victim was crucified, the execution had more significance than the punishment of an individual victim. Crucifixion was an important way in which the dire consequences of rebellion could be kept before the public eye. Individual crucifixions served to remind people of the mass crucifixions and other reprisals that the Romans were all too ready to use if their power was challenged.

There are few detailed descriptions of how crucifixion took place – the Gospels provide the fullest description in ancient literature – but the picture that emerges fits the profile of public state torture very well.[11] The victim was tied or nailed to a wooden cross to maximize their public humiliation: a contrast of the shame of the victim with the might of imperial power. The Romans displayed the victim on a roadside or similar public place. Crucifixion was a protracted ordeal that might last a number of days, a sustained attack on the dignity of the human spirit as well as the physical body.[12] The shame for Jews was further heightened by the belief that 'anyone hung on a tree is under a curse' (Deut. 21.23), a curse that Paul refers to in relation to Jesus' crucifixion in Galatians 3.13.

Crucifixion and sexual abuse

Testimonies to torture in Brazil, Argentina, Chile, Central America and elsewhere consistently report stripping and sexual abuse as part of torture.[13] In Brazil torture by electric shock invariably included shocks to the genitals.[14] The same focus on the genitals was shown in Argentina. The preferred instrument for administering electric shocks in Argentina, *la picana* (a small electrified prod), is itself highly suggestive of the sexual element in this torture.[15] Its use in the rape and sexual abuse of women has been well documented and at least two Argentinean male victims also witness to how this abuse eventually led to anal rape.[16]

For a reading of crucifixion, two elements of these torture practices deserve particular attention. First, sexual assault and humiliation were standard practices in state torture practices; sexual abuse was standard rather than unusual or exceptional. Second, the awareness among a wider public of a victim's sexual humiliation was often an important part of this humiliation.

Against this background, the crucifixion of Jesus may be viewed with a disturbing question in mind: to what extent did the torture and crucifixion of Jesus involve some form of sexual abuse? The testimonies from twentieth-century Latin America create hermeneutical suspicions that merit careful examination of the Gospels to see whether there is any evidence that this was the case.

To explore this question further, it is helpful to distinguish between sexual abuse that involves only sexual humiliation (such as enforced nudity, sexual mockery and sexual insults) and sexual abuse that extends to sexual assault (which involves forced sexual contact, and ranges from molestation to penetration, injury or mutilation). The Gospels clearly indicate that sexual humiliation was a prominent trait in the mistreatment of Jesus and that sexual humiliation was an important aspect of crucifixion. If this is the case, the possibility of sexual assaults against Jesus will also need to be considered. In the absence of clear evidence to decide this one way or another, I will suggest that what has proved so common in recent torture practices cannot be entirely ruled out in the treatment of Jesus.

Crucifixion in the ancient world appears to have carried a strongly sexual element and should be understood as a form of sexual abuse that involved sexual humiliation and sometimes sexual assault. Crucifixion was intended to be more than the ending of life; prior to actual death it sought to reduce the victim to something less than human in the eyes of society. Victims were crucified naked in what amounted to a ritualized form of public sexual humiliation. In a patriarchal society, where men competed against each other to display virility in terms of sexual power over others, the public display of the naked victim by the 'victors' in front of onlookers and passers-by carried the message of sexual domination. The cross held up the victim for display as someone who had been – at least metaphorically – emasculated.[17] Depending on the position in which the victim was crucified, the display of the genitals could be specially emphasized. Both Josephus and the Roman historian Seneca the Younger attest to the Romans' enthusiasm for experimentation with different positions of crucifixion.[18] Furthermore, Seneca's description suggests that the sexual violence against the victim was sometimes taken to the most brutal extreme with crosses that impaled the genitals of the victim. This practice might never have been the case in Palestine – and there is no evidence that suggests it happened to Jesus – but at the very least it suggests the highly sexualized context of violence in which Roman crucifixions sometimes took place.

The sexual element in Roman practices was part of their message of terror. Anyone who opposed the Romans would not only lose their life but also be stripped of all personal honour and human dignity. It is therefore not surprising that the Gospels themselves indicate that there was a high level of sexual humiliation in the way that Jesus was flogged, insulted and then crucified. From evidence of the ancient world it seems that flogging the victim in public while naked was routine. Mark, Matthew and John all imply that this was also the case with the flogging of Jesus.[19] Likewise, as noted above, crucifixion usually took place while the victim was naked and there is little reason to think that Jesus or other Jews would have been an exception to this.[20] If the purpose was to humiliate the victim, full nakedness would have been particularly shameful in the Jewish context.[21] Furthermore, prior to crucifixion, Jesus was handed over to a cohort of Roman soldiers to be further humiliated (Mark 15.16–20; Matt. 27.27–31; John 19.1–5).[22] All the Gospels apart from Luke report that the Roman soldiers mocked Jesus by placing a crown of thorns on his head (Mark 15.17; Matt. 27.29; John 19.2) and clothing him in a purple (Mark 15.17; John 19.2) or scarlet garment (Matt. 27.28).[23] The texts also mention that the soldiers spat at Jesus (Mark 15.19; Matt. 27.30), struck him with a reed (Mark 15.19; Matt. 27.30), and mocked him with verbal taunts (calling him king: Mark 15.18; Matt. 27.29; John 19.3) and symbolic homage (kneeling before him, Mark 15.19; Matt. 27.29).[24]

Based on what the Gospel texts themselves indicate, the sexual element in the abuse is unavoidable. An adult man was stripped naked for flogging, then dressed in an insulting way to be mocked, struck and spat at by a multitude of soldiers before being stripped again (at least in Mark 15.20 and Matt. 27.31) and reclothed for his journey through the city – already too weak to carry his own cross – only to be stripped again (a third time) and displayed to a mocking crowd to die while naked. When the textual presentation is stated like this, the sexual element of the abuse becomes clear: the assertion is controversial only in so far as it seems startling in view of usual presentations.[25] The sexual element to the torture is downplayed in artistic representations of the crucifixion that show Jesus wearing a loincloth. These images distance us from the biblical text, perhaps because the sexual element has been too disturbing to confront.

Although it is vital to acknowledge the sexual humiliation that is revealed in the text, what the texts might conceal may also be significant.

There may have been a level of sexual abuse in the praetorium that none of the Gospels immediately discloses. This suspicion is prompted by the testimonies from Latin America presented earlier. While the testimonies from Latin America do nothing to directly establish the historical facts of crucifixion in Palestine, they are highly suggestive for what may have happened within the closed walls of the praetorium.[26]

Both Matthew and Mark describe Jesus as being handed over weakened and naked – already a condemned man without any recourse to justice – to soldiers who took him inside the praetorium and assembled the other troops.[27] Both Gospels explicitly state that it was the *whole cohort* (*holēn speira*) of Roman soldiers – about 500 men – that was assembled together to witness and participate in the 'mockery'. This probably included a significant number of Syrian auxiliaries who might have viewed their Jewish neighbours with particular hostility.[28] In view of the testimonies to gang rape that are given by victims detained by security forces in the clandestine torture centres of Latin America, this detail of overwhelming and hostile military power sounds a particularly disturbing note.

Many in the Roman cohort would have experienced the fears and frustrations of military life in an occupied country, which could have generated an awkward inner tension of omnipotence and powerlessness. As representatives of imperial Rome, the soldiers collectively exercised almost unlimited power. On the other hand, each individual soldier was at the bottom of a long chain of Roman hierarchical command and would also have felt their individual powerlessness on a daily basis. The instinctive response to such powerlessness is often to impose one's own power forcefully on those who are even less powerful. Individual soldiers had very little freedom or personal choice to act on this, however, and often their interactions with local people would reinforce their feelings of powerlessness and frustration. The common soldier would often have to suffer without taking immediate revenge when faced by lack of co-operation, disrespect or barely concealed hostility. The resentment created by this situation would normally have been held in check by military discipline and the fear of military superiors who wished to avoid unnecessary trouble wherever possible. Nonetheless the aggressive urge to vengeance would remain close to the surface and could give rise to extreme violence when superiors were willing to turn a blind eye or sanction its expression on a sacrificial victim. The desire to take out the frustrations and brutalities of military life through sexual violence has given rise to atrocities throughout history.

Josephus' account of the Siege of Jerusalem (*War*, V. 420–572) suggests that the comparisons between the ancient world and twentieth-century Latin American torture practices may be appropriate. Josephus' description of how the Jewish militants inside Jerusalem tortured the civilian population in the search for food provides a graphic insight into sexual tortures at the time: 'Terrible were the methods of torture they devised in their quest for food. They stuffed bitter vetch up the genital passages of their victims, and drove sharp stakes into their seats' (*War*, V. 435).

Although the actual historicity of Josephus' claims can hardly be taken for granted (since Josephus was writing for a Roman audience and his exaggerations and vested interest in casting the Jewish rebels in a poor light affects his testimony throughout his account), it nonetheless suggests that the sexualized tortures of twentieth-century Latin America might correspond quite closely to their first-century Mediterranean equivalents. Likewise, Plato's description in the *Gorgias* of a hypothetical crucifixion (preceded by torture and castration while on the rack) indicates that castration might have taken place prior to crucifixion in at least some parts of the ancient world.[29] Furthermore, the historian Richard Trexler has claimed that the anal rape of male captives was 'a practice notoriously rife in the ancient world'.[30] In view of this background it is important to ask whether the fraternal and respectful kiss of greeting in the Garden of Gethsemane might have set events in motion that led to some form of sexual assault in the praetorium of Pilate.[31]

The privacy of the praetorium makes it unrealistic to expect a definitive answer on what exactly happened inside. Nonetheless, the suspicions raised by the experiences of those who have suffered under recent Latin American regimes suggest that a question mark needs to be put against the completeness of the Gospel narratives at this point. There is a possibility that the full details of Jesus' suffering are missing from the Gospel accounts. Whereas the texts offer clear indications of sexual humiliation, the possibility of sexual assault can only be based on silence and circumstance. However, it should be remembered that although a distinction in sexual abuse between humiliation and assault is helpful, there can also be considerable overlap between them and the two tend to go together. In sexual torture, sexual assault is a form of sexual humiliation par excellence and sexual humiliation often rests on the threat of physical or sexual assault. What form of sexual assault – if any – might actually have taken place may be impossible to determine but the possibility needs to be recognized and confronted more honestly than has happened so far. To shed light on this, further historical investigation into the treatment of condemned prisoners by Roman soldiers and the treatment of Jesus in particular is obviously required. If this is to happen, however, it is appropriate to pause and ask what positive purpose these lines of enquiry will serve.

Theological and pastoral perspectives

I have found the direction my research has taken me to be very disturbing and I realize that others will feel the same way. I believe, however, that for Christians today these issues might serve constructive purposes in the theological and pastoral fields. Both our resistance and our openness to this line of enquiry might lead to insights and discoveries.

First, at a theological level, confronting the possibility of sexual abuse in the passion of Christ might deepen Christian understanding of God's solidarity with the powerless. Sexual abuse is a destructive assertion of power. It shows the degrading consequences that distorted power can generate in human society. An important element in Christian doctrine has been that Jesus confronted the power of evil and suffered death on the cross as a result. The views presented here – that Jesus was a victim of sexual abuse in the sexual humiliation he underwent and he may even have been a victim of sexual assault – are deeply distressing. They may, however, offer insights into a fuller Christian understanding of a God who is in real solidarity with the powerless and suffers the worst evils of the world. An a priori judgement that Jesus did not and could not suffer sexual abuse may accompany an unexamined assumption that Jesus was not in fact fully human, a form of the Docetic heresy which denies the real form of Jesus' physical suffering. Refusal to accept that Jesus *could* have been sexually abused suggests a refusal to accept Christ's full incarnation into human history. To say that Jesus could not have been vulnerable to the worst abuses of human power is to deny that he was truly human at all.

At the pastoral level, confronting the possibility of sexual abuse in the passion of Christ could provide practical help to contemporary victims of torture and sexual abuse. Recognition of sexual abuse in the treatment of Jesus could bring a liberating and healing message to the women, children and men of Latin America, and elsewhere, who have also been abused. The acceptance that even Jesus may have suffered evil in this way can give new dignity and self-respect to those who continue to struggle with the stigma and other consequences of sexual abuse. A God who through Christ is to be identified with the hungry, the thirsty, the stranger, the naked, the sick and the imprisoned (Matt. 25.31–46) is also to be identified with those suffering abuse and torture in the contemporary world.

Conclusion

Despite the potential pitfalls, the dynamics of state terror in Latin America and other countries can be a fruitful starting point for insights into the Gospels. An awareness of human rights abuses in Latin America can yield important insights into the political context and full horror of Jesus' crucifixion. The role of crucifixions in the production and maintenance of state terror and the element of sexual abuse in Roman practices require further investigation. The Gospels indicate a high level of public sexual humiliation in the treatment of Jesus and the closed walls of the praetorium present a disturbing question about what else might have happened inside.

References

Archdiocese of Sao Paulo, *Torture in Brazil: A Report by the Archdiocese of São Paulo*, New York: Vintage Books, 1986.

Boff, Clodovis, *Theology and Praxis: Epistemological Foundations*, Maryknoll, NY: Orbis Books, 1987.

Brown, Raymond E., *Death of the Messiah*, New York: Doubleday, 1994.

Corradi, Juan E., Patricia W. Fagen and Manuel A. Garretón, eds, *Fear at the Edge: State Terror and Resistance in Latin America*, Berkeley and Los Angeles, CA: University of California Press, 1992.

Graziano, Francisco, *Divine Violence: Spectacle, Psychosexuality, and Radical Christianity in the Argentine 'Dirty War'*, Oxford: Westview Press, 1992.

Hengel, Martin, *Crucifixion in the Ancient World and the Folly of the Cross*, Philadelphia, PA: Fortress Press; London: SCM Press, 1977.

Josephus, *The Jewish War*, trans. G. A. Willon, revised ed., Harmondsworth: Penguin Books, 1970.

Moore, Stephen D., *God's Gym: Divine Male Bodies of the Bible*, New York: Routledge, 1996.

National Commission on Disappeared People, *Nunca Más: A Report by Argentina's National Commission on Disappeared People*, Boston, MA, and London: Faber and Faber, 1986.

National Commission on Truth and Reconciliation, *Report of the Chilean National Commission on Truth and Reconciliation*, Notre Dame, IN: Centre for Civil and Human Rights, Notre Dame Law School, 1993.

Scarry, Elaine, *The Body in Pain: The Making and Unmaking of the World*, Oxford: Oxford University Press, 1985.

Segovia, Fernando F., 'Jesus as Victim of State Terror: A Critical Reflection Twenty Years Later', in *Crucifixion, State Terror, and Sexual Abuse: Text and Context*, ed. David Tombs, Dunedin: Centre for Theology and Public Issues, University of Otago, 2018; http://hdl.handle.net/10523/8558.

Sloyan, Gerard S., *The Crucifixion of Jesus: History, Myth, Faith*, Minneapolis, MN: Fortress Press, 1995.

Tombs, David, 'Crucifixion, State Terror, and Sexual Abuse', *Union Seminary Quarterly Review* 53:1–2 (1999), pp. 89–109.

——, 'Prisoner Abuse: From Abu Ghraib to The Passion of The Christ', in *Religion and the Politics of Peace and Conflict*, eds Linda Hogan and Dylan Lee Lehrke, Princeton, NJ: Princeton Theological Monograph Series, 2009, pp. 179–205.

——, 'Silent No More: Sexual Violence in Conflict as a Challenge to the Worldwide Church', *Acta Theologica* 34:2 (December 2014), pp. 142–60.

——, 'Crucificação e abuso sexual', *Estudos Teológicos* 59:1 (July 2019), pp. 119–32.

Trexler, Richard, *Sex and Conquest: Gendered Violence, Political Order, and the European Conquest of the Americas*, Cambridge: Polity Press, 1995.

United Nations Commission on Truth for El Salvador, *From Madness to Hope: The Twelve Years War in El Salvador: Report of the Commission on Truth for El Salvador, 1992–93*, New York: United Nations, 1993.

Notes

1 This chapter is an abridged version of David Tombs, 'Crucifixion, State Terror, and Sexual Abuse', *Union Seminary Quarterly Review*, 53:1–2 (Autumn 1999), pp. 89–109. The central argument was first presented as David Tombs,

'Biblical Interpretation in Latin America: Crucifixion, State Terror, and Sexual Abuse' in the Biblical Hermeneutics Section at the Society of Biblical Literature International Conference, 20 July 1998, Krakow, Poland. An abridgement was first published in Portuguese as David Tombs, 'Crucificação e abuso sexual', *Estudos Teológicos* 59:1 (July 2019), pp. 119–32, and republished as *Crucifixion and Sexual Abuse* (Dunedin: Centre for Theology and Public Issues, University of Otago, 2019), http://hdl.handle.net/10523/9834 (English); http://hdl.handle.net/10523/9843 (Spanish); http://hdl.handle.net/10523/9846 (French); http://hdl.handle.net/10523/9924 (German). This chapter version includes a few further minor amendments to the 2019 versions but the text is primarily intended to summarize the 1999 article rather than to reflect further developments since then. I hope to address further developments in David Tombs, *The Crucifixion of Jesus: Torture, Sexual Abuse, and the Scandal of the Cross* (London: Routledge, forthcoming).

2 See Fernando F. Segovia, 'Jesus as Victim of State Terror: A Critical Reflection Twenty Years Later', in David Tombs, *Crucifixion, State Terror, and Sexual Abuse: Text and Context* (Dunedin: Centre for Theology and Public Issues, University of Otago, 2018); http://hdl.handle.net/10523/8558.

3 For one of the most sophisticated and sustained developments of a contextual hermeneutic, see Clodovis Boff, *Theology and Praxis: Epistemological Foundations* (Maryknoll, NY: Orbis Books, 1987). Boff's approach recognizes both the similarities and differences between the contemporary Latin American context and the biblical world.

4 David Tombs, 'Silent No More: Sexual Violence in Conflict as a Challenge to the Worldwide Church', *Acta Theologica* 34:2 (2014), pp. 142–60.

5 On state terror and sexual abuses in Latin American torture in the 1970s and 1980s, see further discussion in Tombs, *Crucifixion, State Terror, and Sexual Abuse*. On reading crucifixion in the light of the torture at Abu Ghraib, see David Tombs, 'Prisoner Abuse: From Abu Ghraib to The Passion of The Christ', in *Religions and the Politics of Peace and Conflict*, eds Linda Hogan and Dylan Lee Lehrke (Princeton, NJ: Princeton Theological Monograph Series, 2009), pp. 179–205.

6 These include: Archdiocese of Sao Paulo, *Torture in Brazil: A Report by the Archdiocese of São Paulo* (New York: Vintage Books, 1986); National Commission on Disappeared People, *Nunca Más: A Report by Argentina's National Commission on Disappeared People* (Boston, MA, and London: Faber and Faber, 1986); National Commission on Truth and Reconciliation, *Report of the Chilean National Commission on Truth and Reconciliation* (Notre Dame, IN: Centre for Civil and Human Rights, Notre Dame Law School, 1993); United Nations Commission on Truth for El Salvador, *From Madness to Hope: The Twelve Years War in El Salvador: Report of the Commission on Truth for El Salvador, 1992–93* (New York: United Nations, 1993).

7 See the collection of essays that explore this from different disciplines in Juan E. Corradi, Patricia W. Fagen and Manuel A. Garretón, eds, *Fear at the Edge: State Terror and Resistance in Latin America* (Berkeley and Los Angeles, CA: University of California Press, 1992). On the use of torture to promote terror, see Elaine Scarry, *The Body in Pain: The Making and Unmaking of the World* (Oxford: Oxford University Press, 1985).

8 For a brief history of crucifixion, see the classic work by Martin Hengel, *Crucifixion in the Ancient World and the Folly of the Cross* (Philadelphia, PA: Fortress Press; London: SCM Press, 1977).

9 Crucifixion was rarely used against Roman citizens and even these infrequent occasions were to punish lower classes rather than the aristocracy. On the use of crucifixion by the Romans, see the classic work by Hengel, *Crucifixion*. For recent treatments, see Raymond E. Brown, *Death of the Messiah* (New York: Doubleday, 1994), pp. 945–52, and the exhaustive bibliography, pp. 885–7; Stephen D. Moore, *God's Gym: Divine Male Bodies of the Bible* (New York: Routledge, 1996); and Gerard S. Sloyan, *The Crucifixion of Jesus: History, Myth, Faith* (Minneapolis, MN: Fortress Press, 1995).

10 The English translation, Josephus, *The Jewish War*, trans., G. A. Willon, revised edn (Harmondsworth: Penguin Books, 1970) is used here and for all other passages cited below.

11 Analysis of how crucifixion was used in the ancient world is complicated by the close relationship between crucifixion, impalement and the hanging of bodies (which might be carried out either before or after death). That the New Testament writers can move easily between crucifixion and hanging on a tree is shown in Galatians 3.13; Acts 5.30; 10.39.

12 During crucifixion it is likely that all control over many body functions would have failed. The following account of electric shock torture in Argentina by Nélson Eduardo Dean suggests how humiliating the consequences of this would be: 'During the application of electricity, one would lose all control over one's senses, such torture provoking permanent vomiting, almost constant defecation, etc.' National Commission of Disappeared People, *Nunca Más*, p. 39.

13 Further examples are included in Tombs, *Crucifixion, State Terror, and Sexual Abuse*.

14 '[H]e was tortured naked, after taking a bath, while hanging on the parrot's perch where he received electric shocks from a magneto [small electric generator] to his genital organs and over his whole body.' Quoting José Milton Ferreira de Almeida in Archdiocese of Sao Paulo, *Torture in Brazil*, p. 17.

15 On the sexualized use of the *picana* and other sexual aspects in Argentinean torture, see Francisco Graziano, *Divine Violence: Spectacle, Psychosexuality, and Radical Christianity in the Argentine 'Dirty War'* (Boulder, CO, and Oxford: Westview Press, 1992), especially pp. 153–8.

16 The rape of women during torture has been well documented but recorded instances of the rape of men are less frequent. The frequency with which male prisoners were subjected to some form of rape is hard to determine. However, it is clear that rape was sometimes used to torture men as well as women. Dr Norberto Liwski, whose extended testimony starts the *Nunca Más* report, describes his treatment in detail: 'Another day they took me out of my cell and, despite my [previously tortured] swollen testicles, placed me face-down again. They tied me up and raped me slowly and deliberately by introducing a metal object into my anus. They then passed an electric current through the object. I cannot describe how everything inside me felt as though it were on fire.' Quoting Dr Liwski in *Nunca Más*, p. 24.

17 1 Samuel suggests that emasculation and sexual assault were also recognized practices at an earlier time in Israel's history. On emasculation, see 1 Samuel 18.27: 'David rose and went along with his men, and killed one hundred of the Philistines; and David brought their foreskins, which were given in full number to the king, that he might become the king's son-in-law.' On the fear of sexual assault, see 1 Samuel 31.4: 'Then Saul said to his armour-bearer, "Draw your sword and thrust me through me with it, so that these uncircumcised may not come and thrust me

through, and make sport of me".' I am grateful to John Jarick for pointing these out to me.

18 Josephus, *War*, V. 452 (see above); Seneca, *To Marcia on Consolation* 20:3, records: 'I see crosses there, not just of one kind but fashioned in many ways: some have their victims with head down toward the ground; some impale their private parts; others stretch out their arms on their crossbeam.' Cited in Hengel, *Crucifixion*, p. 25.

19 Although Mark 15.15, Matthew 27.26 and John 19.1 are not explicit on this (and Luke does not mention a flogging), the sequence of events they describe strongly suggests it. Mark and Mathew (who have the flogging at the end of the trial) and John (who has the flogging midway through the trial) each report that immediately after the flogging Jesus was handed over to the Roman soldiers to mock him. All three present the first act of mockery as the soldiers dressing Jesus in a crown of thorns and a purple cloak (Mark 15.17), purple robe (John 19.2) or scarlet cloak (Matt. 27.28). There is no mention in Mark of needing to strip Jesus before dressing him, but stripping Jesus is explicitly stated in Matthew 27.28. Both Mark 15.20 and Matthew 27.31 also explicitly mention that after the mocking Jesus is stripped of the garb and his own clothes are put back on him for the procession to Golgotha. Brown notes that the usual custom outside Palestine was for the condemned man to be paraded naked to execution but that exceptions to this in Palestine may have been a concession to Jewish scruples on public nakedness (see Brown, *Death of the Messiah*, p. 870). It is possible that this sensitivity was especially high within the limits of the holy city.

20 This is clearest in John 19.23–24, which records that after putting Jesus on the cross the soldiers took his clothes to divide among themselves and that these included his undergarment for which they cast lots so as not to tear it. The Synoptic Gospels (Mark 15.24, Matt. 27.35 and Luke 23.34) are vaguer and simply refer to the division of his clothes by lots. In a careful assessment of the evidence Raymond Brown offers cautious support for the likelihood of full nakedness. Although Brown reports that the evangelists are not specific on the matter, and that they might not have known for sure, he offers three reasons that would support the view that Jesus was fully naked. Brown, *Death of the Messiah*, pp. 952–3.

21 On the deliberate humiliation of enemies by genital exposure, see 2 Samuel 10.4–5 which describes how David's envoys were seized by Ha'nun and sent back with their beards half shaved and their garments cut off 'in the middle at their hips'. Jewish sensitivity over insulting displays of the body is also shown in a disaster which occurred during the time that Cumanus was governor (48–52 CE). Josephus reports that a soldier on guard on the Temple colonnade during the Feast of Unleavened Bread lifted his tunic, bent over indecently and exposed himself to the crowds below while making indecent noises (*War* II. 223–7). Fearing a riot in the commotion that followed, Cumanus sent for heavy infantry but this triggered a panic, and Josephus claims that 30,000 were crushed to death as they tried to escape.

22 For Mark and Matthew this happens at the end of the trial and both mention it taking place in the praetorium. For John the mockery takes place during the trial and it appears to have been done within Pilate's headquarters (John 18.28).

23 Luke places the mocking of Jesus rather earlier in the story at a point that is unlikely to have involved Roman soldiers. According to Luke 22.63–64, the mockery takes place prior to the trial before the Jewish elders. The mocking, beating, blindfolding and challenges to prophesy (Luke makes no mention of spitting) were carried out by the men who were holding Jesus overnight before the trial before the

Council. Presumably these were members of 'the crowd' mentioned as capturing him in Luke 22.47. Mark 14.65 and Matthew 26.67–68 also report that Jesus was spat at, struck and challenged to prophesy, but they put this immediately after the Council had condemned him, rather than before, and say it was carried out by members of the Council themselves. John does not mention any parallel treatment associated with the questioning by the High Priest (John 18.19–24).

24 In addition, Matthew 27.29 also mentions placing the reed in Jesus' right hand prior to striking him. Although John makes no mention of a reed, John 19.3 records Jesus being struck.

25 This chapter is primarily concerned with how the texts present events. The picture of abuse they present is historically very plausible but further assessment of textual historicity will not be attempted here. In view of the shame and embarrassment that would have been associated with sexual abuse, it is probable that the Gospels understate it rather than exaggerate it.

26 The privacy of the praetorium (whether Pilate's palace or the Antonia fortress) means that the details of what transpired inside are inevitably circumstantial and would probably not have been known even at the time. Furthermore, even if it was believed that Jesus had been sexually assaulted in the praetorium, the absence of this in the Gospel accounts is hardly surprising. Apart from the distance of years and the desire to pass over a shameful event, the Gospels are usually seen as notably biased in excusing the Romans for Jesus' trial and death.

27 Despite the attempts of the Gospels to excuse Pilate from blame, if rape did take place in the praetorium presumably it would only have done so with Pilate's positive approval or knowing indifference. It is quite possible that Pilate deliberately handed Jesus over to be sexually assaulted by his soldiers as part of the crucifixion sentence. Such an action might have served to reinforce his own status as a triumphant lord who was able to sexually vanquish his victims through the actions of his underlings. Richard Trexler notes that a Roman master might find it more insulting to have his slaves rape his adulterous wife's young suitor rather than to rape the youth himself. Richard Trexler, *Sex and Conquest: Gendered Violence, Political Order, and the European Conquest of the Americas* (Cambridge: Polity Press, 1995), p. 22.

28 Josephus (*War*, II. 268) suggests that, at least while Felix was procurator (52–60 CE), the majority of the Roman garrison in Caesarea were raised in Syria and they readily sided with the Syrian inhabitants of Caesarea in a civil dispute against its Jewish citizens.

29 *Gorgias*, 473C, cited in Sloyan, *The Crucifixion of Jesus*, p. 16.

30 Trexler, *Sex and Conquest*, p. 20. According to Trexler, 'in the Ancient Greek world ... the premier sign of male dependence was to be anally or orally penetrated by another male without, at least fictively, being able to resist', p. 33; he continues, 'Seneca ... declared that "bad army officers and wicked tyrants are the main sources of rapes of young men"', p. 34. In this context even the widely held assumption that the soldiers forced Jesus to wear scarlet/purple clothing for solely political mockery might be reconsidered. Dressing a male victim in bright clothing might also have been a prelude to sexual assault. See also Trexler, *Sex and Conquest*, p. 34.

31 This might also have implications for the question of why Judas had profound feelings of regret and repentance for his actions (Luke 22.3–5; Matt. 27.3–5). Judas may not have anticipated the full implications of his betrayal and if the argument here is correct his despair and shame would be easy to understand.

2

Covering Up Sexual Abuse:
An Ecclesial Tendency from the Earliest
Years of the Jesus Movement?

MICHAEL TRAINOR

Australia's Royal Commission into the Sexual Abuse of Minors and Vulnerable Adults uncovered one of the consistent and shocking tendencies of leaders of religious and church communities.[1] This was the tendency to 'cover up'.[2] In order to prevent any scandal being focused on the Church, leaders sought to obfuscate the problem by moving perpetrators from one religious community to another, by blaming the one abused or by acting as though nothing was amiss and it was business as usual. This tendency was supported by an ecclesiology that regarded the Church as a 'perfect society' and its ministers as set apart through ordination, as unaccountable, and as acting in God's name without transparency.[3] Any flaws in the Church through human weakness could always be forgiven. This was applied to those who acted inappropriately and sinfully. At the heart of this ecclesiology, ministerial protectionism and cover-up, expressed through unaccountable conduct towards children, lies the culture of clericalism. The Commission summarizes this as:

> the idealization of the priesthood, and by extension, the idealization of the Catholic Church. Clericalism is linked to a sense of entitlement, superiority and exclusion, and abuse of power.[4]

The 'cover-up' tendency as a product of clericalism is not a phenomenon of recent history. This chapter will demonstrate that it occurred among members of the Jesus movement in the first century CE. What follows falls into three parts.

First, we shall see how the story of Jesus in Mark's Gospel, written around 70 CE, was a story about one who was protective of children and, like them, subject to maltreatment and abuse.[5] Mark's final story (Mark 14—16), anticipated by the disciples' attitude to children and the verbal contestation between Jesus and his opponents, as well as Jesus' own passion and death, becomes a story of sexual abuse with Jesus executed naked and ultimately shamed.[6]

Second, in Luke's Gospel we see a different portrait. Luke presents Jesus as more majestic and dignified. Its author redacts Mark's scene of the disciples' response to children coming to Jesus (Luke 18.15–17), presents him as the victor in any verbal contest, and alters – almost removing entirely – the abusive treatment of Jesus found in Mark's passion narrative. Instead of naked and shamed, the evangelist has Jesus die elegantly clothed.[7]

In the concluding section, I suggest the reasons for the alterations that Luke makes to Mark. The study will invite us – contemporary disciples concerned about the present situation that confronts our churches – to a spirit of openness, reflecting critically on the endemic that has plagued Jesus' followers from earliest years, and to act, in so far as we are able, on behalf of those who are abused as we continue to explore ways of ministerial accountability and transparency.

Mark's Gospel

Mark's Gospel offers a portrait of Jesus that would speak into a Jesus household chronologically distant and culturally different from the world of the Galilean Jesus.[8] Mark portrays Jesus as misunderstood and, as the story unfolds, someone who is gradually abandoned even by those closest to him. The ultimate moment of the sense of Jesus' abandonment comes in his death scream of dereliction, 'My God, My God, why have you abandoned me?' (Mark 15.34). This is a highpoint in Mark's Christological portrait, especially in what frames it – the lead-up to the death moment (Mark 15.21–33) and the centurion's declaration that comes immediately after Jesus' death (Mark 15.39), a point to which we shall return shortly.

Mark's Gospel begins in the wilderness with John the Baptist's teaching; from the wilderness Jesus appears calling his listeners to 'repent'. Jesus' first words in Mark are: 'The time is fulfilled and the reign of God has drawn near. Repent and believe in the Good News' (Mark 1.15).

The injunction, 'repent' (*metanoeō*), is more than a declaration to the disciples and all gospel listeners of a conviction of God's presence and moral living. It is a call to a fundamental openness of heart to what is about to unfold in Jesus' ministry. *Metanoia* is an invitation to perceive what is happening from a different point of view. As Mark shapes the narrative with a view to the final chapters, we remember the often-quoted words of Martin Kähler, who declared that the Gospels are 'passion narratives with a lengthy introduction'.[9] Mark's 'lengthy introduction' reveals Jesus alone and misunderstood as antagonism begins in Mark 3 and heightens as the narrative moves forward, reaching its crescendo in the Gospel's final chapters. All the time, the injunction *metanoeō* remains.

The Gospel auditor must listen beneath the surface of what happens to Jesus, at a second, deeper level that places the story against the backdrop of Mark's cultural and historical situation. The evangelist writes not with a desire to freeze the memory of the Galilean Jesus in time and place, but, instead, with the intention of expanding the faith insights for a later Greco-Roman Jesus movement that the Gospel addresses, shaping its Christology to address the realia of Mark's audience.

And what is that realia?

Mark's Christological portrait offers a window into the situation of the Gospel's audience. The way the evangelist portrays Jesus speaks into the situations that Mark's householders face. One of these is sexual abuse. This emerges in the passion narrative, but it is subtly anticipated in the Gospel's preceding chapters. There are, among many others, two indicators that flag or prepare the Gospel audience for the abusive treatment that Jesus will receive: the way the 'little ones' are treated by Jesus' disciples, and the verbal interchange between Jesus and his antagonists. This intensifies as the story nears the Gospel's denouement.

The 'children' in Mark's Gospel

In the beginning of the second half of the Gospel, as Jesus begins to journey towards Jerusalem with his reluctant disciples, he sets a child (*paidion*) into the midst of his posturing entourage (Mark 9.36). He encourages a change of attitude, a *metanoia*, to receive the child, the quintessential symbol of social nothingness, into their midst.[10] Their reception of the child becomes the touchstone of their openness to God (Mark 9.37). Not many verses later (Mark 9.42), Jesus reiterates his teaching about the protection of these 'little ones'. It is evident, though, that the disciples have yet to absorb this message and have a different attitude to these 'little ones'.

As some bring children (*paidion*) for Jesus to touch (Mark 10.13–16), the disciples 'rebuke them' (Mark 10.13b). Mark's language here is revealing. The 'rebuke' (*epitemaō*) is the language of exorcism.[11] The disciples see the presence of something or someone evil in a request that needs to be exorcised. They 'rebuke *them*'. To whom is the disciples' rebuke directed? Is it directed to those who bring the children to Jesus, or is it the children themselves? It seems the latter. Mark notes how Jesus reacts with indignation at the disciples' belligerent response to the request (Mark 10.14). He instructs them to let the children come to him, 'for to such belongs the kingdom of God'. The scene ends with Jesus wrapping the children in his arms and laying his hands upon them (Mark 10.16). The disciples need to undergo a radical *metanoia* if they are to receive and enter God's kingdom (Mark 10.15).

The arrogance of the disciples or, to use an anachronistic expression, their 'clericalism', permits them to see the children or their carers as demonic and therefore deserving of rejection. The disciples see themselves as 'entitled' to treat them abusively. If this is how Jesus' own disciples treat the 'little ones', what awaits the one who welcomes them with open arms? Mark prepares the auditor for this through the verbal exchange that takes place between Jesus and his adversaries. As the Gospel unfolds, the interchange directed at Jesus becomes more abusive until, finally, in the last chapters of the Gospel it reaches its expression that is more physical and sexual.[12]

The verbal interchange between Jesus and his opponents

From a cultural perspective, as the verbal disagreements and attacks on Jesus unfold, some interpret this as the classic verbal sparring of challenge and riposte.[13] The overall intent, according to this interpretation, is an agonistic engagement intending to gain greater honour. The Gospel's narrative audience to this engagement 'gossip' about Jesus, in a positive way, and speak well of him.[14] There is a cyclical pattern in the interchange with Jesus' antagonists: his honour is challenged; his critics are finally defeated; Jesus not only regains his honour but grows (through 'gossip') in the estimation of the audience who witness the contest; his antagonists are humiliated; their desire to kill Jesus only ferments more deeply.[15] This pattern repeats in the chapters leading up to Mark's passion narrative.

If we were to see a verbal contestation only in terms of a use of wit and who can outsmart the other, then we would miss an important element that anticipates Mark's passion. In the ancient world, words were intended to be affective. Words influenced deeds and people's actions.[16] Speeches by the great orators were designed to win over the crowd and move it into some action or political response.[17] Words were essential to garner support. Words of praise brought honour and glory to their addressee. Words of rejection and criticism were intended to dishonour, humiliate and spread negative gossip about the human target of the invective. Barbed words were intended to hurt, to impale their victims. Words had an impact that was both noetic *and* physical.

Mark's passion narrative

In Mark's passion narrative (Mark 14.1—16.8), the language addressed to and about Jesus by his antagonists reveals an intent to abuse him in a way that would have physical impact. His interrogators, first the religious authorities (Mark 14.53–65) and then Rome's political leader (Mark 15.1–20), complete their verbal examination of Jesus with physical violence. This violence is also sexually implicit and shameful. It leads to the ultimate act of Jesus' sexual humiliation in his death. The intent of the religious interrogation is clear: the authorities, the chief priests and the Sanhedrin, seek to discredit Jesus, to define his unholy scandal and so have reason to execute him (Mark 14.55). False testimony is called upon, but even this conflicts (Mark 14.56–60). The High Priest finally interrogates Jesus: 'Are you the Christ, the Son of the Blessed?' Jesus' affirmation to this, with the addition 'you will see the Human One seated at the right hand of Power and coming with the clouds of heaven' (Mark 14.62), results in a charge of blasphemy that leads ultimately to his condemnation and a death sentence (Mark 14.64). Likewise, it also leads to the more explicit physical enactment of his humiliation preparatory for death. 'And some began to spit on him and to cover his face, and to strike him, and say to him "Prophesy!" and the guards rained blows down on him' (Mark 14.65).

Jesus' face and head are the target of his bodily maltreatment. The ancient understanding of the human body adds further depth to the treatment that Jesus receives. Personal identity was linked to corporeality. The human body was more than a physical organ: it was a site of social identity and personhood. The body also linked the person to the wider cosmic and astral world, as borne out, for example, by Plato's micro and macro cosmology. For Plato (427–328 BCE), the human and celestial bodies that compose the cosmos were linked.[18] One influenced the other. Aristotle (384–322 BCE) had a similar regard for the human body as a social and cosmic map that mirrored the universe.[19] From their limited anthropological perspectives Plato and Aristotle affirmed the symbolic and metaphoric nature of the human body in its relationship to society and the cosmos. If anything of this Greek philosophical tradition lies behind Mark's story, then what happens to Jesus in his body has deep symbolic significance.

We know from an earlier story in Mark's passion narrative (Mark 14.3–9) that when the unnamed woman anoints Jesus she anoints his head. Gospel auditors would see this act as reaffirmation of Jesus' regal and prophetic status. The abusive treatment of Jesus' head and face in Mark 14.65 brings together the two aspects of Jesus' head and the prophecy made from the narrative's anointing story. This act has implications for the members of the wider social world symbolized by Jesus' head and, more specifically, Mark's householders who identify with him. What happens to Jesus, their prophetic head, will also happen to them, if it is not already happening. Mark's vignette shines a spotlight on the Gospel's audience for what is happening, and will possibly happen, from Rome's authorities. This is echoed in the second politically related interrogation before Rome's representative, Pilate.

Pilate's questioning of Jesus begins with the primary charge of treason or sedition: 'Are you King of the Judeans?'[20] This accusation about Jesus' kingship continues throughout the interrogation. Mark portrays Pilate as indifferent to the charge brought against Jesus by the religious authorities. To placate the crowd growing in its hostility, he scourges Jesus and then hands him over to be crucified (Mark 15.15). The violent actions perpetrated by Pilate's soldiers against Jesus add to Pilate's initiating vicious deed. They perform a mock coronation ritual that ironically underscores Jesus' regal status. The narrative's chiastic structure makes the soldiers' feigned attestation of royalty central (Figure 1).

The corporeal implications of the scene are unmistakable. Jesus is violated, maltreated, tortured, shamed and humiliated. The more demonstrable violence of this scene contrasts with the earlier humiliation from

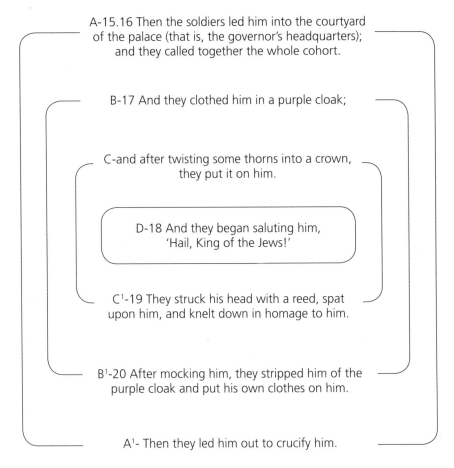

A-15.16 Then the soldiers led him into the courtyard of the palace (that is, the governor's headquarters); and they called together the whole cohort.

B-17 And they clothed him in a purple cloak;

C-and after twisting some thorns into a crown, they put it on him.

D-18 And they began saluting him, 'Hail, King of the Jews!'

C¹-19 They struck his head with a reed, spat upon him, and knelt down in homage to him.

B¹-20 After mocking him, they stripped him of the purple cloak and put his own clothes on him.

A¹- Then they led him out to crucify him.

Figure 1. The Chiastic Structure of Mark 15.16–20

the religious authorities. The sexual innuendos of the scene are heightened. He is naked – this is the implication of B¹ (Mark 15.20b) – covered only in a purple cloak. Even this is eventually 'stripped' from him. The violence in the way that the cloak is removed further underscores the intended mockery and humiliation of Jesus. The scene is one of sexual abuse. The act of humiliating Jesus' physical being has sexual implications. Sexual humiliation will become more explicit in Mark's scene of Jesus' death.

The soldiers lead Jesus away to Golgotha for execution. Mark simply notes 'they crucified him' (Mark 15.24a), leaving all the pain and anguish suffered by the crucified victim to the imagination and memory of Mark's audience. They would be well familiar with Rome's crucifixion method. It is the next part of Mark's statement that reminds Gospel auditors of the presumed nakedness of Jesus in this most humiliating moment and central story of the whole Gospel. The soldiers 'divided his garments among them, casting lots for them, to decide what each should take' (Mark 15.24b–c).

Mark presumes Jesus' nakedness, as do the Gospel auditors. It is a high point of Mark's story and a low point of humiliation and sexual shaming of the evangelist's central figure. In this context Jesus dies alone, misunderstood and experiencing a sense of divine abandonment, though retaining his faith in his God whom, despite everything, he names 'My God' (Mark 15.34). The centurion's final words sum up the scene. They question the veracity of the one declared as God's Son: 'In truth, was this man God's Son?' (Mark 15.39). Even at the moment of death, Jesus' identity remains obscured and undeclared.[21] His humiliation continues.

Much could be written about the evangelist's purpose in presenting such a Christological portrait – of a sexually abused, solitary and misunderstood figure, crying out to his God to comfort him. Perhaps it can be briefly stated, as mentioned earlier, that this speaks into the realia of Mark's audience: their own experience of abuse, maltreatment, rejection, loneliness and isolation in a Roman urban context of the 70s CE. The apparent silence of God in a time when some might have experienced violent sexual abuse warranted such a portrait.

Luke's Gospel

Living a generation after Mark and working initially with Mark's narrative, the evangelist of Luke's Gospel offers an altered Christological portrait. The purpose, similar to that of Mark, was to speak into the new realia of Luke's Greco-Roman context experienced by a culturally diverse household of Jesus followers, located in a different time and place.[22] Luke adds Jesus' birth story to Mark's beginning, redacts central narrative stories of Jesus' healing activity, and develops on his teaching, especially in a 'Sermon on the Plain' (Luke 6.20–49). Luke also expands the centre of Mark's Gospel with ten chapters of teaching (Luke 9.51—19.27) as Jesus and his disciples journey towards Jerusalem, to his passion and death. Martin Kähler's statement that the Gospels are 'passion narratives with a lengthy introduction' is as pertinent to Luke as much as to Mark.[23]

Luke's 'lengthy introduction' presents Jesus as the revealer of God's reign in word and deed. He heals, speaks and teaches in a more exalted manner than in Mark's Gospel. Luke presents an elevated or heightened Christology. Rather than Jesus' first words that recognize the closeness of God's reign and invite disciples to 'repent', as in Mark 1.5, Luke has a 12-year-old Jesus in the Temple instructing its very teachers (Luke 2.46). In response to his parents' dilemma as they search for him, Jesus speaks for the first time in Luke's Gospel: 'Did you not know that I must be in the things of my Father?' (Luke 2.49b, author's translation).

How interpreters understand the 'things' of my Father varies, from 'the house' (NRSV) to 'the affairs' (NKJV) to 'matters'.[24] Whatever 'the things' might mean, Luke portrays the young Jesus with a deep abiding relationship to his God that expresses itself early in his life. Luke's is a very mature

Jesus, even though the evangelist states later that Jesus grew in wisdom and stature (Luke 2.40, 52).

The 'infants' in Luke's Gospel

Luke's Christological portrait of Jesus as a child sheds light on the evangelist's alteration to Mark's equivalent scene in which people bring children to Jesus for him to touch (Luke 18.15–17). There are two noteworthy features to Luke's episode.

First, in Luke, those brought to Jesus are called *brephos*, a change from Mark's *paidion*. It is Luke's favoured term.[25] *Brephos* refers to an infant, even a child before birth, and therefore a creature significantly much younger and physically more immature and fragile than Mark's *paidion*.[26] The political and cultural status of the *brephos* deepens the fragility and social exclusion of the infant implied in Mark's *paidion*. Jesus' attitude to them in Luke would highlight his compassion and outreach to the most insignificant of society – a theme consistent throughout the Gospel.

The second feature in Luke's story is the response of the disciples to these infants. If there is any ambiguity in Mark, Luke retains Mark's 'rebuke' language, but it is solely directed to those bringing the *brephos* to Jesus. Jesus is not indignant at his disciples, as in Mark, but simply instructs with the same teaching found in Mark, reverting to the language of *paidion*: 'whoever does not receive the kingdom of God like a child (*paidion*) will never enter it' (Luke 18.17). Luke's Jesus has no need to repeat this teaching. His disciples get it. They do not act with the same intense aggression as in Mark. Overall, Luke presents Jesus as welcoming the more socially fragile of society and the disciples as more receptive to those coming to Jesus. In a sense, Luke's 'cover-up' of Mark begins here.

The conviction of Jesus' communion with God articulated in Jesus' earliest boyhood years is repeated in his first words expressed as an adult. In his threefold temptation (Luke 4.1–13), Jesus counters Satan's refrain ('If you are God's son') testing Jesus' fidelity to God with words drawn from Deuteronomy (Deut. 8.3; 6.13, 16; 10.20). Jesus' communion with his God is solid and unwavering.

The next words of Luke's Jesus that follow are his programmatic declaration in the Nazareth synagogue (Luke 4.16–22). This outlines for Gospel auditors how his mission will unfold in the rest of the Gospel. Drawing on Isaiah, Jesus declares that he has come to bring release, healing and empowerment to the oppressed, captives and sightless. His mission is to reveal a God of hospitality to all who experience social and economic rejection. This insight lays out the primary criterion for a disciple that follows on from Jesus' mission: disciples are invited to be witnesses of God's hospitality and to enact it.

What for Mark is *metanoia* becomes for Luke *hospitality*.[27] This expresses the nature of the God to whom Jesus witnesses as well as the foundational characteristic of the Lucan household. We have already seen something of this in Luke's scene of Jesus welcoming the *brephos*. In a Greco-Roman world structured along hierarchical lines of economic and political convenience, a hospitable household characterized by friendship transcended socially defined boundaries. To outsiders, such a household could be interpreted as subversive. Luke's agenda is to appeal to the wealthy members of the Jesus movement, a theme that suffuses the Gospel.[28] The evangelist's appeal shapes the Gospel's elevated Christology and Jesus' teaching on wealth and material asceticism. This agenda also explains the changed perspectives from Mark found in the Gospel as Luke's construction of the Gospel's portrait of Jesus emphasizes his dignity, cultural elegance and amicability. This further emerges in his interaction with his opponents.

Jesus' interchange with his opponents

Luke's Jesus is incontestably without peer. This Christology appears in episodes in Luke where Jesus contests the opposition he experiences. The evangelist draws on and reshapes Mark's equivalent scenes.[29] A closer examination of these reveals Luke's tendency to tone down the challenge–riposte cyclical strategy of agonistic contestation from the Gospel's Marcan source. Three examples illustrate this.

First, when Jesus reads and interprets Isaiah in the Nazareth synagogue to establish Luke's Christology for the rest of the Gospel (Luke 4.16–30), the reaction is initially overwhelmingly positive: 'All speak well of him and wondered at his gracious words' (Luke 4.22). Only after his reinterpretation of the biblical tradition in terms of God's hospitality and inclusivity of non-Jews does the tone of Jesus' reception change (Luke 4.28–29). In Mark's equivalent scene (Mark 6.1–6), there is no favourable disposition towards Jesus at all. It is heavily negative. His hearers take offence at him from the beginning (Mark 6.3). Mark concludes with the judgement on Jesus' audience: he 'marvelled because of their unbelief' (Mark 6.6).[30]

Second, Mark's story of Jesus' healing of a man with a withered hand (Mark 3.1–6) ends with a plan between religious and royal officials to 'destroy' (*apollumi*) Jesus. In Luke's equivalent scene (Luke 6.6–11), this authoritarian coalition is absent. Rather, his observers are filled with annoyance and 'discussed with one another what they might do to Jesus' (Luke 6.11). Mark's plot to 'destroy' Jesus is absent, replaced by a consultation about some unspecified action against him. His destruction, though available to Luke from Mark's Gospel, is played down by his detractors. Their response, though negatively intentioned, is more benign than in Mark.

Third, on the Temple Mount Jesus meets his theological opponents. They try again to test his allegiance to God and his attitude to Roman taxation. In Mark (Mark 12.13–17) an explicit alliance of religious and royal officials tries to 'entrap him in his talk' (Mark 12.13b). At the end of the attempted entrapment they are left in a state of amazement (Mark 12.17c). In Luke

(Luke 20.20–26) the coalition of officials is absent. Unwilling to confront Jesus directly, they delegate spies to record what he says. At the end of the encounter, Luke notes their inability to catch him out. Instead, their amazement is heightened, and they are reduced to silence: 'And they were not able in the presence of the people to trap him by what he said; and being amazed by his answers, they became silent' (Luke 20.26).

The verbal interchange between Jesus and his opponents is significantly reduced in Luke's Gospel. Jesus is the authoritative and unquestionable teacher and prophet. This Christological impression continues into Luke's passion narrative (Luke 22.1—24.53) as the evangelist also significantly softens, if not changes, Mark's portrait of the abused, misunderstood and abandoned Jesus.

Luke's passion narrative

The Lucan evangelist follows Mark's basic narrative of Jesus' suffering and death, but with noteworthy differences. First, Mark's story of the unnamed woman's prophetic and regal anointing of Jesus' head (Mark 14.3–9) occurs earlier in Luke's Gospel (Luke 7.36–50). Here it is a story of a sinner who anoints and washes Jesus' feet with oil and tears and becomes a lesson on forgiveness. Luke has moved it away from an action focused on Jesus that reaffirms his identity to an episode earlier in the Gospel (Luke 7.36–50) in which Jesus acts and offers moral instruction. Here, Jesus is not the subject, as in Mark, but the agent. Second, Luke adds a faction fight into the Last Supper scene (Luke 22.24–27) and converts Mark's Gethsemane scene of a struggling and soul-wrenched Jesus (Mark 14.32–38) into a prayer event in which Jesus calmly faces death comforted by God's angelic presence (Luke 22.39–46). In Mark's scene, Judas identifies Jesus to his captors with a kiss (Mark 14.45), and that act of intimacy becomes an act of betrayal. In Luke, Judas draws near to Jesus to kiss him (Luke 22.47), but there is no actual kiss. Instead, a violent act by one of Jesus' disciples that removes the ear of a high priest's slave with a sword becomes a moment of healing as Jesus touches the slave's ear and heals him (Luke 22.50–51).

Luke's alterations to Mark intensify Jesus' agency, his authority and apparent imperviousness to suffering. As Raymond Brown notes, Luke portrays Jesus as 'more reverential ... and avoids making him seem emotional, harsh or weak'.[31] Elsewhere, Brown adds, 'The resistance to portraying [Luke's] Jesus as suffering during the passion befits a Hellenistic resistance to portraying emotions.'[32] Luke's Jesus is not the target of physical violence or verbal abuse as in Mark. This is evident in the trial scenes and their aftermath. In Mark, physical and sexual violence enacted against Jesus follow his religious and political trials. In Luke, this is either toned down or absent altogether.

The violence associated with Jesus' trial by the council of Jerusalem's religious leaders occurs in both Mark (Mark 14.65) and Luke (Luke

22.63–65) (Figure 2). In Luke it comes before the council, which allows for the auditor's focus to fall on the main Christological titles of the trial. Jesus is the Christ (Luke 22.67), the Son of Man (Luke 22.69a), and the Son of God (Luke 22.70) who exercises God's authority (Luke 22.69b). With Mark, the violence perpetrated against Jesus concludes a more prolonged and dramatic trial. Noteworthy is Luke's redaction of Mark's scene in which Jesus is maltreated:

Mark 14.65	Luke 22.63–65
Some began to spit on him, to blindfold him, and to strike him, saying to him, 'Prophesy!' The guards also took him over and beat him.	Now the men who were holding Jesus began to mock him and beat him; they also blindfolded him and kept asking him, 'Prophesy! Who is it that struck you?' They kept heaping many other insults on him.

Figure 2. Jesus' mockery at his religious trial

In Mark's scene, Jesus is spat upon, struck while blindfolded and beaten a second time by the guards. Luke also has Jesus derided, but he is held, mocked and beaten only once. Though Jesus is blindfolded and beaten, Luke does not use Mark's more aggressive expression for 'striking'. Jesus is not struck – even though he is asked who struck him. With this derisory, repetitive questioning, as those holding him 'keep asking him', Luke explicates and underscores the prophetic nature of Jesus. It is a Christological theme in his Gospel.[33] In Luke the mention of Jesus' beating occurs only at the beginning of the scene. There is no other violent action. Physical violence from Mark's scene is replaced with verbal abuse in Luke, as 'they kept heaping many other insults on him' (Luke 22.65). Verbal abuse continues into the next two scenes (Luke 23.1–24), but they are otherwise devoid of physical violence.

When Luke switches to Jesus' civic trial before Pilate (Luke 23.1–5), the same emphasis from Mark – Jesus' royal status – is again the focus, though with the added accusation of his capacity to pervert the nation and refusal to pay taxes to Caesar (Luke 23.2). In other words, Jesus is a royal pretender and a threat to the Roman Empire. What is clear is Pilate's declaration of Jesus' innocence (Luke 23.4), which he twice repeats (Luke 23.14–15, 22) after the intervening trial before Herod. This second trial before Pilate (Luke 23.6–16) places Jesus in the presence of Herod, who had longed to see Jesus having heard so much about him.

Herod unsuccessfully questions Jesus as the religious leaders further accuse him 'vehemently' (Luke 24.10b). There is one final action that Herod performs after he and his soldiers mock Jesus with contempt (Luke 23.11): he places a luminescent, shining or resplendent (*lampros*) garment around Jesus.[34] For Luke's audience, its symbolism is unmistakable. Jesus reveals and reflects the radiance of God before Rome's authoritative figure.

The garment echoes Jesus' dazzlingly radiant raiment on the mountain as he becomes transfigured (Luke 9.29). His authoritative presence as God's revealer remains even in the face of mockery from Rome's emblematic authority. Moreover, this luminous garment remains on Jesus throughout the rest of Luke's passion narrative. It is never taken off and accompanies him to the cross and grave. As Jesus is handed back to Pilate (Luke 23.13–23) and finally over for crucifixion (Luke 23.24–25), Luke completely omits any ironic royal investiture and mock coronation ritual as seen in Mark. Luke's Jesus is above such physical violence and abuse. His status demands better treatment.

Luke's description of a less violent and abusive treatment of Jesus continues as the Gospel moves towards the moment of his crucifixion and death. He journeys to the place of execution accompanied by a great multitude, the women of Jerusalem and two criminals to be executed with him (Luke 24.26–33). Luke converts Mark's scene of Jesus' misunderstanding, ultimate loneliness and abandonment at the moment of death into one that displays forgiveness and prayerful communion with God. His death becomes an example of prayer: he utters the words, 'Father, into your hands I commit my spirit' as he dies (Luke 23.46). In keeping with Luke's portrait of Jesus' regal and honoured status, the luminous garment placed earlier around him by Herod is not removed. Jesus does not die naked as in Mark but covered. A synoptic comparison (Figure 3) between the two Gospels at the mention of what the guards do about Jesus' garments at the point of his crucifixion bears this out:

Mark 15.22–24	Luke 23.33–34
And they brought him to the place of Golgotha which means place of a skull, and they offered him wine mixed with myrrh, he did not take it. And they crucified him	And when they came to the place which is called 'Skull' There they crucified him, and the criminals, one on his right and one on his left.
and, dividing his clothes, they cast lots for them to decide what each should take.	And Jesus said, 'Father, forgive them, for they do not know what they are doing'. They cast lots to divide his garments.

Figure 3. The Division of Jesus' Clothing

The way that Mark describes the division of Jesus' garments and the lot-casting for them by the guards presumes that the clothing is no longer on Jesus. They are described as having divided his clothing already. He is naked, as would have been the custom in the Roman execution method.

Luke, on the other hand, has the guards cast lots *in order to* divide

Jesus' garments. There is no indication that Jesus is without them or that he is naked. At this moment of the Gospel's highpoint, Luke synthesizes a Christological portrait of Jesus forgiving his executioners, promising Paradise to a repentant thief, prayerfully offering himself into the hands of God and preserving his dignity in death. The luminous garment from Herod remains. Luke literally covers up Mark's naked Jesus.

Conclusion

Luke's Jesus is an authoritative preacher whose ultimately incontestable words place him within the Greek philosophical tradition of wisdom. The Gospel's portrait intends to appeal to those of elite social status within the Lucan household. This results in a radical modification of Mark's portrait of an abused, misunderstood and lonely figure. Luke's Jesus is a more exalted figure appealing to the gentle and refined sensibilities of the Gospel's primary – though not exclusive – audience.[35] He welcomes the most fragile creatures of human society, the *brephos*. In Luke's Gospel, the disciples' response to those who bring them to Jesus is toned down from Mark. Unlike in Mark, the disciples in Luke understand Jesus' instruction about having the attitude of the child in order to welcome the kingdom. Further, Luke moderates the verbal and physical violence done to Jesus in Mark's Gospel. Any depiction of the sexual abuse of Luke's dignified and majestic figure is inappropriate and 'covered up'.

Luke's redacted Christology has softened, if not removed, the figure of an abused, lonely and misunderstood Jesus from the contemplative gaze of the Gospel's audience. Luke clothes Mark's naked Jesus with a luminous garment given to him by Herod, Rome's representative. This accompanies him in death, in a scene that converts Mark's screaming, abandoned, naked figure into one of peaceful, serene and prayerful dignity. No mention is made of the garment's removal. It appears that it remains on Jesus as he is laid in the tomb and added to by the explicitly mentioned 'linen' cloth in which Joseph finally shrouds the body of Jesus (Luke 23.53). The Herodian garment and the linen shroud symbolizing eternity are the residual images in the Gospel's passion narrative that communicate Luke's Christology of Jesus' regal and heavenly status.

Luke's tendency to 'cover up' and dignify Jesus has mixed consequences. On the one hand, the evangelist offers a portrait of Jesus that would appeal to an elite audience far removed from the artisan and peasant world of the historical Jesus. The teachings of the Galilean Jesus offer Luke a way of socially reconstructing the Gospel household in terms of hospitality and friendship. On the other hand, Luke's 'cover-up' also pushes the issue of societal abuse and sexual oppression – dominant in Luke's world and a mechanism of control, especially within the Greco-Roman domestic scene – into the background.[36]

Whatever the reason for Luke's redactional predisposition to 'cover up'

Mark's Christological portrait, it reflects a tendency that has continued in the Jesus movement ever since. This is the inclination in ecclesial circles to conceal the truth and camouflage what is embarrassing, unpalatable and scandalous. Luke's reformulation of Mark's graphic and confronting portrait of a violated and sexually abused Jesus seeks to screen the Gospel audience from the reality of criminal execution in the Roman world. Rather, a more dignified figure emerges whose agenda is not to scandalize but affirm.

This is not to say that Mark's Christology is better or more honest than Luke's. Rather, the exercise of comparing Luke's Gospel presentation of Jesus with that of Mark highlights the human inclination to paper over what is scandalous and confronting. Whatever the reason for Luke's alteration of Mark's portrait of the suffering and dying Jesus – whether to offer a palatable Christology for Luke's more genteel audience or to reduce any possibility of scandal that Mark's portrait might produce – the evangelist's redaction of Mark does give us pause for thought, especially in the light of the present ecclesial situation in Australia. The Gospels are 'windows' and 'mirrors'.[37] They offer us a window into the social and cultural world in which they were written. They also reflect back to their readers/listeners insights and a hermeneutic pertinent for the realia of today's Gospel audience. From the context in which I write, this study invites me to reflect again on the situation which the Australian Catholic Church faces and the scandal caused through the sexual abuse of minors and vulnerable adults within my ecclesial community. It took the work of a Royal Commission over years to allow the 'mirror' to expose what had been happening in the Church and to honour the stories of those who had been abused. The bishops and other faith leaders in the Australian Catholic Church have been called to account for what has happened historically and to put in place systems of transparency and accountability. What Luke has done to Mark – again, for whatever reason – mirrors what this leadership has also done. But in the present situation, we know the reasons for the cover-up: to avoid scandal, to protect the institution, to deflect responsibility, evade accountability and reinforce clericalism. A conspiracy of silence has accompanied this tragic situation within the Church. This 'cover-up' has been exposed. Its exposure now invites a move towards a more open, humble and transparent Church that welcomes the child – the Gospel's theological metaphor for the estranged, abused and hurt.

References

Adamczewski, Bartosz, *The Gospel of Luke: A Hypertextual Commentary*, European Studies in Theology, Philosophy and History of Religions, Frankfurt: Peter Lang GmbH, 2016.

Anthony, Peter, 'What are They Saying about Luke–Acts?', *Scripture Bulletin* 40 (2010), pp. 10–21.

Aristotle, *Politics*, 1, 2; 5, 2; *De Anima* 2, 1f.

Berry, D. H., and Andrew Erskine, *Form and Function in Roman Oratory*, Cambridge: Cambridge University Press, 2010.

Briggs, Richard, *Word in Action: Speech Act Theory and Biblical Interpretation – Toward a Theory of Self-Involvement*, Edinburgh: T&T Clark, 2001.

Brown, Colin, ed., *The New International Dictionary of New Testament Theology*, vol. 1, Exeter: The Paternoster Press, 1975, pp. 280–91.

Brown, Raymond E., *An Introduction to the New Testament*, New Haven, CT: Yale University Press, 1987.

—, *An Introduction to the New Testament: The Abridged Edition*, New Haven, CT: Yale University Press, 2016.

Brown, Raymond E., and John P. Meier, *Antioch and Rome: New Testament Cradles of Catholic Christianity*, New York: Paulist Press, 1983.

Byrne, Brendan, *A Costly Freedom: A Theological Reading of Mark's Gospel*, Collegeville, MN: The Liturgical Press, 2008, pp. ix–21.

Daniels, John W. Jr, 'Gossip in the New Testament', *Biblical Theology Bulletin* 42 (2012), pp. 204–13.

Deacy, Susan, and Karen F. Pierce, eds, *Rape in Antiquity: Sexual Violence in the Greek and Roman Worlds*, London: Gerald Duckworth & Co. Ltd, 2002.

Donahue, John R., 'Windows and Mirrors: The Setting of Mark's Gospel', *The Catholic Biblical Quarterly* 57:1 (1995), pp. 1–26.

Donahue, John R., and Daniel Harrington, *The Gospel of Mark*, Collegeville, MN: Liturgical Press, 2002.

Ernst, Josef, *Das Evangelium nach Markus*, Regensburg: Pustet Verlag, 1998.

Faggioli, Massimo, 'Australia's Findings on Clerical Sexual Abuse: A Report with Ramifications', *La Croix International*, 22 December 2017, https://international.la-croix.com/news/australia-s-findings-on-clerical-sex-abuse-a-report-with-ramifications/6628.

Gadenz, Pablo T., *The Gospel of Luke*, Grand Rapids, MI: Baker Academic, 2016.

Guelich, Robert A., *Mark 1–8:26*, Dallas, TX: World Publishing, 1989.

Harrington, Daniel, *The Gospel of Matthew*, Collegeville, MN: The Liturgical Press, 1991.

Hengel, Martin, *Studies in the Gospel of Mark*, Philadelphia, PA: Fortress Press, 1985.

Hooker, Morna, 'Trials and Tribulations in Mark XIII', *Bulletin of the John Rylands University Library of Manchester* 65 (1982), pp. 78–99.

—, *Gospel According to St. Mark*, London: A & C Black, 1991.

Kähler, Martin, '[D]ie Evangelien Passionsgeschichten mit ausführlicher Einleitung nennen', in *Der sogennante historische Jesus und der geschichtliche, biblische Christus*, 2nd edn, Leipzig: A. Deichert, 1896.

Karris, Robert J., 'Windows and Mirrors: Literary Criticism and Luke's *Sitz Im Leben*', *Society of Biblical Literature 1995 Seminar Papers*, 115 (1979), pp. 47–58.

Kelber, Werner H., *Mark's Story of Jesus*, Philadelphia, PA: Fortress Press, 1979.

Levine, Amy-Jill, and Ben Witherington, *The Gospel of Luke*, New Cambridge Bible Commentary, Cambridge: Cambridge University Press, 2018.

Moloney, Francis, *The Gospel of Mark: A Commentary*, Grand Rapids, MI: Baker Academic, 2002.

Neyrey, Jerome, 'The Absence of Jesus' Emotions – the Lucan Redaction of Lk 22, 39–46', *Biblica* 61 (1980), pp. 153–71.

Oerke, Albrecht, 'λάμπω' in *Theological Dictionary of the New Testament*, eds Gerhard Kittel and Gerhard Friedrich, vol. 4, Grand Rapids, MI: Wm B. Eerdmans Publishing Co., 1964, pp. 16–28.

Plato, *Timaeus* 90 a, b.

Rohrbaugh, Richard L., 'Honor: Core Value in the Biblical World', in *Understanding the Social World of the New Testament*, eds Dietmar Neufeld and Richard E. DeMaris, New York: Routledge, 2009, pp. 125–41.

Royal Commission into Institutional Responses into Child Sexual Abuse, *Final Report*, 2017, www.childabuseroyalcommission.gov.au/.

Searle, John R., Ferenc Kiefer and Manfred Bierwisch, eds, *Speech Act Theory and Pragmatics*, Dordrecht, Holland: D. Reidel Publishing Company, 1980.

Severino Croatto, Jose, 'Jesus, Prophet Like Elijah, and Prophet-teacher Like Moses in Luke-Acts', *Journal of Biblical Literature* 124 (2005), pp. 451–65.

Struthers Malbon, Elizabeth, *Mark's Jesus: Characterization as Narrative Christology*, Waco, TX: Baylor University Press, 2009.

Trainor, Michael, *About Earth's Child: An Ecological Listening to the Gospel of Luke*, Sheffield: Sheffield Phoenix Press, 2012.

——, *The Body of Jesus and Sexual Abuse: How the Gospel Passion Narratives Inform a Pastoral Response*, Northcote: Morning Star Publications, 2014.

Whitaker, Robyn, 'Rebuke or Recall? Rethinking the Role of Peter in Mark's Gospel', *The Catholic Biblical Quarterly* 75 (2013), pp. 666–82.

Notes

1 Royal Commission into Institutional Responses into Child Sexual Abuse, *Final Report*, 2017, www.childabuseroyalcommission.gov.au/.

2 This, among other things, is summarized in vol. 16 of the Royal Commission's findings, *Final Report*, at www.childabuseroyalcommission.gov.au/religious-insti tutions.

3 For a summary of this tendency, see the analysis of the Commission's findings and its implications for the Australian Catholic Church by Massimo Faggioli, 'Australia's Findings on Clerical Sexual Abuse: A Report with Ramifications', *La Croix International*, 22 December 2017, https://international.la-croix.com/news/australia-s-findings-on-clerical-sex-abuse-a-report-with-ramifications/6628.

4 Royal Commission, *Final Report: Religious Institutions*, vol. 16, book 1, p. 43, www.childabuseroyalcommission.gov.au/sites/default/files/final_report_-_volume_16_religious_institutions_book_1.pdf.

5 For a helpful summary of the design, presumed social context and worldview behind Mark's Gospel, see Brendan Byrne, *A Costly Freedom: A Theological Reading of Mark's Gospel* (Collegeville, MN: The Liturgical Press, 2008), pp. ix–21.

6 This is explored in Michael Trainor, *The Body of Jesus and Sexual Abuse: How the Gospel Passion Narratives Inform a Pastoral Response* (Northcote: Morning Star Publications, 2014), pp. 93–124.

7 For a full study of Mark's Christology, consult Elizabeth Struthers Malbon, *Mark's Jesus: Characterization as Narrative Christology* (Waco, TX: Baylor University Press, 2009).

8 Those who received Mark's Gospel were possibly resident in one of the great urban Roman centres, perhaps even Rome itself, around the 70s CE. For those who posit Rome as the setting for Mark, see, for example, Josef Ernst, *Das Evangelium*

nach Markus (Regensburg: Pustet Verlag, 1998), pp. 112–14; Martin Hengel, *Studies in the Gospel of Mark* (Philadelphia, PA: Fortress Press, 1985), pp. 1–30; Raymond E. Brown and John P. Meier, *Antioch and Rome: New Testament Cradles of Catholic Christianity* (New York: Paulist Press, 1983), pp. 191–7; Robert A. Guelich, *Mark 1–8:26* (Dallas, TX: World Publishing, 1989), pp. xxix–xxxi; Morna Hooker, 'Trials and Tribulations in Mark XIII', *Bulletin of the John Rylands University Library of Manchester* 65 (1982), pp. 78–99. A minority posit a rural audience, not too distant from Jesus' context in ancient Palestine/Israel. Francis Moloney conjectures Mark's location as 'somewhere in southern Syria' and dates it after 70 CE but before 75 CE, in *The Gospel of Mark: A Commentary* (Grand Rapids, MI: Baker Academic, 2002), p. 11. Morna Hooker later sums up the scholarship on Mark's provenance: 'All we can say with certainty, therefore, is that the Gospel was composed somewhere in the Roman Empire – a conclusion that scarcely narrows the field at all!'; Hooker, *Gospel According to St. Mark* (London: A & C Black, 1991), p. 8. Whatever the provenance of the Gospel, the Greco-Roman cultural context shapes the Gospel narrative and the author's portrait of Jesus to enable this to speak into the realia of the Jesus movement in a context different from Galilee.

9 '[D]ie Evangelien Passionsgeschichten mit ausführlicher Einleitung nennen' in Martin Kähler, *Der sogennante historische Jesus und der geschichtliche, biblische Christus*, 2nd edn (Leipzig: A. Deichert, 1896), p. 51.

10 Daniel Harrington, *The Gospel of Matthew* (Collegeville, MN: The Liturgical Press, 1991), pp. 264–7.

11 Werner H. Kelber, *Mark's Story of Jesus* (Philadelphia, PA: Fortress Press, 1979), p. 48; Robyn Whitaker, 'Rebuke or Recall? Rethinking the Role of Peter in Mark's Gospel', *The Catholic Biblical Quarterly* 75 (2013), p. 671. This is not the only time that Mark mentions *epitemaō* (also in Mark 1.25; 3.12; 4.39; 8.30; 9.25; 10.48).

12 Examples of Mark's anticipation of the ultimate verbal–physical agonistic interchange that leads to Jesus' passion and death are seen in Mark 2.1–12, 15–19; 3.1–6; 6.1–6; 7.1–22; 8.11–13; 10.2–9; 11.27–33; 12.12–27, 35–44.

13 Richard L. Rohrbaugh, 'Honor: Core Value in the Biblical World', in *Understanding the Social World of the New Testament*, eds Dietmar Neufeld and Richard E. DeMaris (New York: Routledge, 2009), pp. 125–41.

14 On 'gossip' in the ancient world, see John W. Daniels Jr, 'Gossip in the New Testament', *Biblical Theology Bulletin* 42 (2012), pp. 204–13.

15 Mark spells out the murderous intent of Jesus' critics early in the Gospel, in Mark 3.6. This theme runs as an undercurrent through the remaining part of the Gospel narrative, reaching a climax in its final chapters.

16 On the nature of orality as speech-act, see, for example, Richard Briggs, *Word in Action: Speech Act Theory and Biblical Interpretation: Toward a Theory of Self-Involvement* (Edinburgh: T&T Clark, 2001); John R. Searle, Ferenc Kiefer and Manfred Bierwisch, eds, *Speech Act Theory and Pragmatics* (Dordrecht, Holland: D. Reidel Publishing Company, 1980).

17 D. H. Berry and Andrew Erskine, *Form and Function in Roman Oratory* (Cambridge: Cambridge University Press, 2010), pp. 7–17.

18 Plato, *Timaeus* 90 a, b.

19 Aristotle, *Politics*, 1, 2; 5, 2; *De Anima* 2, 1f.

20 My translation here seeks to render *Iudaioi* as a regional rather than national identity.

21 This interpretation flies in the face of the conventional commentary on the

centurion's words as a high point of Christological identity, and now by a representative of Rome. Contra to this and for the position I take here, see Trainor, *Body of Jesus*, pp. 114–17.

22 For a helpful summary on the current state of Lucan scholarship, see Peter Anthony, 'What are They Saying about Luke–Acts?', *Scripture Bulletin* 40 (2010), pp. 10–21. Also see Amy-Jill Levine and Ben Witherington, *The Gospel of Luke* (New Cambridge Bible Commentary, Cambridge: Cambridge University Press, 2018), pp 1–17; Byrne, *Hospitality of God*, pp. 4–22.

23 '[D]ie Evangelien Passionsgeschichten mit ausführlicher Einleitung nennen' in Kähler, *Der sogennante historische Jesus und der geschichtliche, biblische Christus*, p. 51.

24 Bartosz Adamczewski, *The Gospel of Luke: A Hypertextual Commentary*, European Studies in Theology, Philosophy and History of Religions (Frankfurt: Peter Lang GmbH, 2016), p. 65; Pablo T. Gadenz, *The Gospel of Luke* (Grand Rapids, MI: Baker Academic, 2016), p. 66.

25 *Brephós* occurs eight times in the NT, six of which are in Luke-Acts, including Luke 2.12, 16; Acts 7.19.

26 On the distinction between *paidíon* and *brephós,* see Colin Brown, ed., *The New International Dictionary of New Testament Theology*, vol. 1 (Exeter: The Paternoster Press, 1975), pp. 280–91.

27 On the theme of Lucan hospitality, see Byrne, *Hospitality of God*, pp. 8–11.

28 On Luke's appeal to the wealthy elite in the Gospel household, see Michael Trainor, *About Earth's Child: An Ecological Listening to the Gospel of Luke* (Sheffield: Sheffield Phoenix Press, 2012), pp. 7, 27–30.

29 The scenes that Luke draws on from Mark and redacts include Luke 5.17–26, 29–39; 4.16–30; 6.6–11; 20.20–40, 41–44.

30 For further on this change that Luke makes to Mark, see John Donahue and Daniel Harrington, *The Gospel of Mark* (Collegeville, MN: Liturgical Press, 2002), p. 183; Byrne, *Costly Freedom*, p. 105.

31 Raymond E. Brown, *An Introduction to the New Testament: The Abridged Edition* (New Haven, CT: Yale University Press, 2016), p. 93.

32 Raymond E. Brown, *An Introduction to the New Testament* (New Haven, CT: Yale University Press, 1987), p. 270. For further study on Jesus' absence of emotion in Luke's Christology, see Jerome Neyrey, 'The Absence of Jesus' Emotions – the Lucan Redaction of Lk 22, 39–46', *Biblica* 61 (1980), pp. 153–71.

33 Jose Severino Croatto, 'Jesus, Prophet Like Elijah, and Prophet-teacher Like Moses in Luke-Acts', *Journal of Biblical Literature* 124 (2005), pp. 451–65.

34 Albrecht Oerke, 'λάμπω' in *Theological Dictionary of the New Testament*, eds Gerhard Kittel, and Gerhard Friedrich, vol. 4 (Grand Rapids, MI: Wm B. Eerdmans Publishing Co., 1964), p. 17.

35 For a discussion on the social composition of Luke's household and the elite as the primary addressees of the Gospel see Trainor, *About Earth's Child*, pp. 26–39.

36 Susan Deacy and Karen F. Pierce, eds, *Rape in Antiquity: Sexual Violence in the Greek and Roman Worlds* (London: Gerald Duckworth & Co. Ltd, 2002).

37 The recognition of these metaphors ('windows' and 'mirrors') as descriptors for the Gospels was popular among interpreters in the late twentieth century. See, for example, Robert J. Karris, 'Windows and Mirrors: Literary Criticism and Luke's *Sitz Im Leben*', *Society of Biblical Literature 1995 Seminar Papers*, 115 (1979), pp. 47–58; John R. Donahue, 'Windows and Mirrors: The Setting of Mark's Gospel', *The Catholic Biblical Quarterly* 57:1 (1995), pp. 1–26.

3

'He Never Said a Mumbalin' Word': A Womanist Perspective of Crucifixion, Sexual Violence and Sacralized Silence

MITZI J. SMITH

Why don't we grieve for women,
For girls, the same way we do
Our men, our vanishing boys?
– 'Theodicy' by Joshua Bennett[1]

In this chapter I explore Jesus' crucifixion in the context of ancient Roman crucifixion and in comparison to the lynching of black men in the US. Particularly, I examine the relationship between crucifixion/lynching, sexual violence and sacralized silence. What are the ethical implications of viewing Jesus as a victim of sexual violence and for truth-telling in faith communities?

I am a survivor of child sexual abuse by my grandfather, a deacon in the Baptist Church.[2] The politics of church authority, family, age and gender kept me silent about the abuse for many years. I was a 12-year-old girl – or so I thought until a counsellor asked me where my younger sister was then; I answered she had not yet been born. I was actually eight – in a Christian household where rumours that my grandfather raped my mother's younger sister were dismissed as lies (their mother died when her children were all under five years old; different relatives raised them, not my grandfather). In our home, advice about sex was gendered and biased: 'Keep your dress tail down', my mother often advised. Sexual purity depended on a girl's ability to control the movement of the fabric on her body. Females carried, and still carry, the burden of male lust, loss of sexual control and sexual abuse – victim-blaming. In church we learned that the age of accountability – when things became our fault – was 12, which was the age the precocious Jesus entered the Temple and engaged in grown-up talk with the rabbis (Luke 2.41–47). Then there is the biblical mandate to 'touch not God's anointed and do them no harm'[3] imposed on the majority-female church membership. This mandate expressed itself in the following way: if a family member and/or a church leader/member sexually violates a woman/

girl/boy/man, we keep the secret lest we dismantle the family or damage the deacon or church's reputation. We are socialized to bear the shame of sexual abuse in silence and to uncritically honour religious authorities and familial relationships. We are warned to 'let sleeping/dead dogs lie'. What good could come from truth-telling after the deacon/grandfather is dead? Black women and their children (male and female) are taught that when men (most perpetrators are men but not only men) violate us, it is our fault, and the abuse is manageable. Sexual violence – including coerced and forced nudity, harassment, unwelcomed touching of bodies or genitalia, and penetration – is traumatic. The recovery – psychological, emotional, spiritual and physical – is long and torturous, even with a trained competent counsellor. The unwillingness of family, church and community to believe survivors of sexual violence compounds the trauma and increases feelings of abandonment. Many victims self-medicate, engage in risky harmful behaviours and/or commit suicide.

In black churches, but not exclusively there, it is preached, sung, prayed and taught that Jesus, God's Messiah, never spoke a mumbalin' word in his humiliation and suffering; he suffered abuse, torture and an agonizing death in silence. Christians claim the crucified Christ as the suffering servant of Trito-Isaiah 52.13—53.12 who, like a slaughtered lamb, bore the violence inflicted upon him in silence.[4] Verse 53.7 states: 'He was oppressed, and he was afflicted, yet he did not open his mouth; like a lamb that is led to the slaughter, and like a sheep that before its shearers is silent, so he did not open his mouth.' What parallels have black Americans drawn between Jesus' crucifixion and the black experience of oppression, particularly in the spiritual 'He Never Said a Mumbalin' Word', as it is performed every Easter or Resurrection Sunday in most black churches, and at other occasions? More people attend church at Easter than any other time of the year. What is the impact of the ritualized performance of silent suffering on the traumatized black women, children and men who sit in the pews? What was the content or extent of the violence inflicted upon Jesus during his crucifixion? Did it include sexual violence? Do the Gospels or other New Testament narratives depict the crucified Jesus as silent? This chapter explores these questions.

I shall first discuss black church literary and liturgical traditions that view the crucifixion of Jesus through the lens of black suffering. I particularly focus on the African American spiritual 'He Never Said a Mumbalin' Word' and ask, what is the origin of the theological and hermeneutical underpinning that depicts the crucified Jesus as the silent suffering lamb? Second, I explore the passion stories and texts about Jesus' suffering and crucifixion, primarily but not exclusively in the Gospel of Mark and Acts 8.26–40, the story of the Ethiopian eunuch. Finally, I discuss the lynching of black bodies, sexual violence and the crucifixion of Jesus. What can we know and imagine about Jesus' suffering and crucifixion in the New Testament when read in the historical context of Roman crucifixion? Crucifixion in antiquity was a gruesome public display of state-sanctioned violence, inclusive of sexual abuse, meant to instil terror that deterred other people from similar criminalized behaviours as the crucified ones. The lynching of black men and women (and some whites) are similarly described. The black theology of James H. Cone assists in comparing the lynching of black peoples with Christ's crucifixion. Cone states that 'artists and writers have made the lynching theme a dominant part of their work, and most have linked black victims with the crucified Christ as a way of finding meaning in the repeated atrocities of African American communities'.[5] The black poet Countee Cullen articulated the connection between the lynching of black people and the crucifixion of Christ in his 1922 poem 'Christ Recrucified': 'The South is crucifying Christ again ... "Lynch him! Lynch him!" O savage cry, / Why should you echo, "Crucify!"'[6] What is the significance of under-standing Jesus as a victim of sexual abuse and its implications for black women as survivors of sexual violence and the black faith community in general? For several reasons years of silence generally separate the rape or sexual violence from the survivor's truth-telling, including power dynamics between perpetrator and victim, victim-blaming, and absence of a trusted person in whom to confide. Thus I argue that traditions, including sacred texts, authoritative interpretations, and interpreters that ameliorate the traumatic and chronic impact of sexual violence on its victims and/or that promote and sacralize the silence or silencing of possible or proven victims of sexual violence, must be exposed and challenged.

Further, many victims tell their truths because they know that without truth-telling healing and justice will elude them, but they are met with dis-belief and blame. In our modern context, sexual violence response training teaches that when a child (or adult) presents or articulates that she or he has been sexually assaulted, the person being confided in has an obligation to report the possible abuse to the appropriate agency so that the matter can be investigated. Expressions of disbelief are not appropriate and will cause the abused to shut down. Why do some of us respond with disbelief to the possibility that Jesus was sexually violated during the crucifixion? Why do some take it personally and as an attack on his memory and as a shameful suggestion? Yet those same persons highlight the humiliation of the crucifixion. Jesus' humiliation is tempered by our fears and ide-ologies. In our imagination Jesus is white and male. In the imaginary of white America, he cannot have been sexually violated and still be a white male; that type of abuse is reserved for black men and might constitute a 'niggerization' of Jesus.[7] What made ancient crucifixion so humiliating and disgraceful? A violent death is brutal and evil, like the Mel Gibson cinematic spectacle, but not necessarily shameful. What or who is at stake that we feel the need to bury the very reasonable possibility that sexual abuse was a significant aspect of the shamefulness of crucifixion? Who or what do we protect by privileging silence? I propose that like the lynching of black men in America, Jesus' lynching on the cross was more likely than not accompanied by sexual violence and even castration. Like lynched black men, Jesus is not here to tell his own truth. I hope that this essay will empower victims of sexual violence, men and women, to realize that the shame and silence of sexual violence is not theirs to bear, but it has been hoisted upon their backs by people who fear certain truths above the freedom and wholeness it offers its victims.

'He Never Said a Mumbalin' Word': Silenced and silent sufferers

As noted, 'He Never Said a Mumbalin' Word', also known as 'They Hung Him on a Cross', is sung primarily, but not exclusively, on Easter or Resurrection Sunday. It dates to the antebellum days of American history and was especially well known in the southern states of Mississippi, Tennessee and Louisiana, where it was often sung along with another spiritual entitled 'Were You There [when they crucified my Lord]?' The author is unknown; perhaps it arose out of the collective experience of black worship and suffering. John White writes that

> Afro-American slave religion simultaneously provided rationalizations for a submissiveness that allowed the sufferer to embrace the divinity of the martyred Saviour ('They crucified my lord, And he never said a mumblin' word') but also the apocalyptic vision and retributive actions of a Nat Turner.[8]

Roland Hayes first recorded the song for commercial use in 1927. It was also performed by groups of Negro convicts in Louisiana State Penitentiary in Angola, Louisiana, around 1933–34. A YouTube search yields a plethora of renditions performed by people and groups that include Marian Anderson, Angela Cherry, the Sensational Nightingales, Golden Gate Quartet and Lead Belly. It is sung at large historic black churches like Alfred Street Baptist Church in Alexandria, Virginia, and TD Jakes's Potter's House. Although transcending race and denomination, it is mostly performed by black choirs, quartets and soloists. Some of the many renditions on YouTube were posted as long ago as nine years and as recently as a few months.

The spiritual is included in the United Methodist hymnal (no. 291). There the refrain 'and he never said a mumbalin' word' is repeated twice in each stanza followed by words emphasizing Jesus' silence: 'not a word, not a word, not a word'. The four verses of the spiritual are repeated twice in four stanzas:

(1) They crucified my Lord;
(2) They nailed him to a tree;
(3) They pierced him in the side; and
(4) His blood came trickling down.

Cone asserts that the spiritual 'meant that [Jesus] died on the cross for black slaves. His death was a symbol of their suffering, trial and tribulations in an unfriendly world. They knew the agony of rejection and the pain of hanging from a tree.'[9] Jeneva Wright states that the lyrics

> vividly, painfully indicate that this slave could imagine exactly how it felt to be cruelly tortured and killed – all without the ability to speak a word in their own defense. There was an empathy with the trials of Jesus that directly related to the slave experience, resonating throughout each spiritual's lyrics, rhythms, and soul.[10]

The song is representative of black pain in America.[11] That pain derived from the cruelty of enslavement, racial discrimination and the sexual violation of black women, men and children.

This popular version of 'And He Never said a Mumbalin' Word' omits much of the abuse connected with crucifixion as a public ritualized performance that culminated in the display of the tortured body on the wooden stake.[12] Crucifixion was an event, a spectacle, to which the Gospels and history attest, as discussed below. The spiritual omits other historical aspects of Roman crucifixion. When representations of events are truncated, truths are censored; a silence is imposed. The use of the third person plural pronoun 'they' in the spiritual also allows the performers and audience, primarily African American women, to further associate their own trauma with Jesus' crucifixion. 'They' therefore refers not only to Roman authorities but to their ancestors' slave masters and to America's original sin of racism and sexism and its perennial refusal to protect black people's human and civil rights and to dismantle systemic racism. The subject pronoun 'they' commits one act of violence in two strokes: they crucified him by nailing him to the cross and piercing his side. The song encourages little to the imagination for other violence associated with crucifixion, while highlighting silent suffering. By referring to Jesus using the masculine pronoun 'him' repetitively in this very emotional, ritualized oral performance, emphasis is placed on maleness and violence inflicted on black men within the community, with no acknowledgement of violence against women, girls or boys.

Contemporary black preaching tradition also links the silent lamb of Trito-Isaiah 53.7b with the crucified Jesus. For example, the dean of the chapel at Duke Divinity School, Luke Powery, an African American, wrote in a Lenten devotional entitled 'Were you there?' (also known as 'And He Never Said a Mumbalin' Word') that

> silence can be underrated ... Jesus demonstrates this at such a tragic time. He's being crucified, nailed to a tree, pierced in his side, blood tricklin' down, and he eventually died. He could have said a lot of things to his oppressors, but 'He Never Said a Mumbalin' Word'. Never. 'Like a sheep that before its shearers is silent.' ... Not a word, not a word, not a word.[13]

Powery states that Jesus said all he needed to say with his body. It is true that trauma evokes tears, harmful behaviours and depression, and renders victims unable to function, but traumatized bodies do not tell the whole truth in the absence of speech. Powery further states that if Jesus had spoken, his words would have been directed at his oppressors. But we might imagine that his words would have been (and perhaps were) *about* his oppression and his oppressors, the whole truth about the violation of his body and its impact. Powery writes that 'Sometimes, we may understate the role of silence in the spiritual life, but it can be constructive and helpful and the most appropriate response. It was for Jesus. How about you?'[14] Powery's representation of Jesus' silent suffering comes from his reading of Trito-Isaiah's suffering servant song, but the Gospels and the spectacle of ancient crucifixion do not corroborate that story. Where in the New Testament do we find this depiction of a silent crucified Jesus? And what New Testament source corroborates Powery's depiction of Jesus as the silent suffering lamb? To address this question, I turn now to the Gospels and Acts.

The suffering and crucifixion of Jesus in the Gospels and Acts 8.26–40

The Synoptic Gospels do not represent Jesus of Nazareth as the silent suffering lamb of God, and John's Gospel certainly does not present the lamb of God who takes away the sins of the world as silent (John 1.29). Mark, considered the earliest written canonical Gospel, never presents Jesus as unequivocally silent about the abuse that will be inflicted upon him or the impact of the crucifixion upon him. Jesus is prescient and prophetic and tells some of his truth prior to the events. At his last meal with his disciples, Jesus forewarns them about his imminent betrayal: as a mortal (son of a human being) his body will be violently assaulted, and one of them has conspired to betray him (Mark 8.31; 9.31; 10.33–34; 14.17–21). The existential reality of Jesus' humanness is further demonstrated when he eats bread and drinks wine with them, both of which are metaphorically, symbolically, his broken and violated body and blood. Mark 14.25 reveals that Jesus' body will not survive the assault. In our contemporary context, we know that most victims of sexual violence are assaulted by someone close to them, someone(s) they know who can overpower them. In Jesus' case, Judas colluded with certain religious leaders with the authority and power to drag Jesus before the Sanhedrin, where he is silent *and* speaks his truth (Mark 14.43–65; 15.1–5).

Jesus is not the only human being that could predict his own abuse and death. People accused of or actually practising overtly subversive behaviours could expect the wrath of the Roman Empire to be brought to bear on them. Jesus would not have been unaware of the consequences of being accused of crimes against the state or of making religio-political enemies, even among his own people, when it is in the latter's best interest to choose Rome over their own. Jesus chooses truth-telling over silence about the brutal impact of the betrayal on his own body and who would set his suffering in motion; he will die a shameful death. Not only will Judas betray Jesus, the rest of the disciples will abandon him when he is arrested. He will be both verbally and physically assaulted when his body is exposed to the public (Mark 14.26–30, 43–50; 15.16–32). Judas kisses Jesus without his permission. In our context, this would be considered uninvited physical contact, and a repeat offence might be considered sexual harassment.

As with many sexual assault victims, the authorities produced false witnesses who accused Jesus of crimes against the Temple and the state, to demonstrate that he deserved the abuse they hoped would be afflicted upon his body (Mark 14.56–59). Jesus is silent when the false witnesses speak; no one can defend him- or herself against lies (Mark 15.1–5). The crowds of people that Pilate desired to appease insisted that Jesus be crucified. Consequently, Jesus was flogged and delivered up for crucifixion. Mark does not explicitly mention that Jesus' clothes were removed, but he implies that Jesus was stripped naked: Jesus was clothed in a purple cloak; later the purple cloak is stripped off Jesus' body and his own clothes are put (back) on him. All this occurred in the presence of a Roman cohort, which is about 200–600 soldiers (Mark 15.16–17, 20). Lots are cast to determine who would take his clothing (as souvenirs of the state-sanctioned execution – Mark 15.24). François Bovon states that 'The Roman soldiers ... transformed this customary beating into a grotesque scene staged for their own amusement. No doubt imitating a carnival or circus game', thereby entertaining themselves.[15] The spectacle is what we would expect to be staged in a Roman amphitheatre during the gladiator games or at the crucifixion of a slave sentenced to die.

In Mark the crucified Jesus is also *not* silent while suspended on the cross. In agony, he cries out to God in Aramaic, '*Eloi, Eloi, lema sabachthani?*' ('My God, My God, why have you abandoned me?' Mark 15.34–37). These words are the only words that the crucified Jesus utters in both Mark and Matthew (Mark 15.34; Matt. 27.46). Matthew and Mark's Gospels, Bovon argues, 'seem to stay closer to historical truth than Luke and John'.[16] In Mark, these words contribute to Jesus' humanness: the Jesus depicted in Mark is quite human compared to the other Synoptics and John's Gospel. In Mark, Jesus has a home, he spends a lot of time in other people's homes; readers are introduced to his mother, brothers and sisters. When his behaviour appears erratic, like other humans he is accused of being possessed with a demon; his biological family must restrain him. Like human beings crucified before Jesus, he cannot save himself, as some religious leaders remind him: 'he claimed to save others but he cannot save himself' (Mark 15.31, author's translation). These words echo the sentiment of others who stopped to observe the humiliating and violent spectacle of Jesus suspended from a wooden cross (Mark 15.29–31). Like the overwhelming majority of sexual assault victims in modern times, Jesus was unable to save himself from the assaults of those with more authority or power than himself. Jesus was a grown man, and yet those in his intimate circle did not believe him. Jesus has this in common with many in our contemporary context who are not believed and so abandoned.

In John's Gospel, John the Baptist announces that Jesus is 'the lamb of God who takes away the sins of the world', but Jesus is not depicted as silent in his ministry or in his death (John 1.29–34). John the Baptist's identification of Jesus as the lamb of God is not connected with his suffering or crucifixion but with his ministry from the outset. In fact, when Pilate asks Jesus if he is a king, Jesus responds that he has come into the world to testify, not to remain silent (John 18.33–38; 19.10–11, 26–30). Yet many contemporary churches, including predominantly black churches, teach and preach that Jesus was the lamb that was silent before those who slaughtered him; he mumbled not one word. What biblical tradition connects the crucifixion of Jesus and the silent suffering lamb? As Bovon notes, when Jesus is silent during interrogation in the passion narratives, it is because of the influence of the Hebrew Bible, especially Isaiah 53.7.[17] But we find an explicit connection between Jesus and the silent slaughtered lamb in one of two extensive Gentile conversion narratives in the Acts of the Apostles, the story of the Ethiopian eunuch in Acts 8.26–40.[18]

In the ancient world and among enslaved Africans and African Americans, Ethiopia referred synecdochally to Africa, that is, Ethiopia/Cush as a country in Africa represented the whole of Africa. The Hebrew Bible oracle at Psalm 68.31 ('Let bronze be brought from Egypt; let Ethiopia hasten to stretch out its hands to God') is the most commonly quoted biblical verse in African American poetry, novels, sermons, catechisms for the enslaved, letters and other literature.[19] Allen Callahan asserts that 'African Americans took from the Bible the nomenclature of Ethiopia to speak of the magnificent future reversal of their collective fortune.'[20] But to my knowledge there are no references to the Ethiopian eunuch in African American literature that mention him together with the suffering servant passages from Isaiah. While Ethiopia symbolizes for many African and African American readers their homeland, the continent of Africa, in a positive and liberating way, I do not always find this same disposition expressed toward the Ethiopian eunuch. This is puzzling given the social status or predicament of the Ethiopian eunuch. He is the treasurer of the Kandace/Queen of Ethiopia, he is literate, and owns a scroll of Isaiah. He is royalty, but he is also physically defective as a man – emasculated.[21] Guided by the angel of the Lord, the evangelist Philip, one of the seven consecrated for table ministry in Acts 6.1–6, finds the Ethiopian eunuch on the Gaza road from Jerusalem. He finds him riding in his chariot and reading a scroll of the prophet Isaiah. Approaching the chariot, Philip asks him if he understands what he is reading. To which the eunuch replies, 'How can I, except someone guides me?' (Acts 8:31, author's translation). This is Philip's signal to enter the chariot parked alongside the road and offer hermeneutical guidance.[22] The eunuch is reading that part of the Isaiah scroll that modern scholars call the third servant song (Isaiah 52.1—53.12). More specifically, he is reading Isaiah 53.7–8: 'Like a sheep he was led to the slaughter, and like a lamb silent before its shearer, so he does not open his mouth. In his humiliation justice was denied him. Who can describe his generation? For his life is taken away from the earth.' In response to the Ethiopian eunuch's question as to whether the prophet refers to himself or to someone else, Philip takes the hermeneutical liberty to preach that the prophet is referring to Jesus of Nazareth who was crucified. The eunuch accepts Philip's interpretation and asks what hinders him from being baptized. After Philip baptizes him, they go their separate ways, the eunuch by chariot and Philip snatched away by the Spirit.

Vien Nyguyen argues that the eunuch was liberated.[23] However, I argue that unless he considers Philip's interpretation within his own context and in the light of his own experience, he has not been freed – his oppression is compounded by the burden of silent suffering. Philip's sermon could be a blues song, but whose blues? Cone argues, 'Truth is experience and experience is the Truth. If it is lived and encountered, then it is real.'[24] The blues give voice to black identity, suffering and the will to survive. Sometimes silence is a means of survival, but that does not make it liberating.[25] The Ethiopian eunuch is regarded as an example of how Christian slave masters were obligated to preach the gospel to enslaved Africans without any duty to free them.[26] Why is it that we only find this emphasis on silent suffering and 'blackness'/Africa – that part of Africa Rome could not fully conquer – in Acts? The eunuch becomes a significant example of the passive reception of the gospel by people of African descent who are robbed of the epistemological agency to determine the content of that gospel or to contextualize the gospel based on their own experiences of suffering.[27]

We must consider Acts 8.26–40 in the context of the violence by which a man was made a eunuch or was compelled to make himself a eunuch. A sexually violated man – castrated or mutilated – is told that silent suffering is a virtue. Perhaps the eunuch was contemplating his own suffering as he read Isaiah. The evangelist Philip (forced out of Jerusalem by persecution after the lynching of Stephen, a co-minister) and the Ethiopian eunuch shared the experience of violence without, perhaps, being able to tell their truths or obtain justice. They were forced to endure the violence and humiliation in silence. In the case of the Ethiopian eunuch, oppression and stigmatization based on one's physiology might to some extent be mitigated by access to power and material wealth, but in a hyper-masculinized society a castrated man is considered abnormal and feminized; his very presence is disruptive, problematic, even if it is useful to others (e.g., the Queen and her husband). If he was forcefully castrated, he might very well have wanted to see his perpetrator brought to justice. Philip might have wished the same in the case of Saul/Paul. But the eunuch's experience with suffering is not the same as Philip's.

Is it a coincidence that it was in this encounter between the marginalized Hellenist evangelist Philip – relegated to table ministry and violently forced to flee Jerusalem by persecution (Acts 6.1–6; 7.54—8.3) – and an Ethiopian eunuch that the Isaiah suffering servant song is applied to Jesus? Interestingly, when the enslaved African, Olaudah Equiano, who was kidnapped from his homeland in Benin, Africa, and enslaved in the New World, petitioned the British crown to abolish enslavement, he signed the petition using his adopted Dutch name, 'Gustavus Vassa', to which he appended 'the Oppressed Ethiopian'.[28] Olaudah's oppression was his enslavement. The Ethiopian eunuch's was the mutilation of his genitals. African American men, as sons of Ethiopia, were also castrated while being murdered during the lynching period in the US (1880–1940). Cone has compared the crucifixion of Jesus to the lynching of African American men. I now turn to explore this connection.

The crucifixion of Jesus, Roman crucifixion and lynching in the USA

The Gospels were, of course, written after Jesus' crucifixion, when his faithful followers chose to preserve his memory. What can an exploration of crucifixion in antiquity tell us that the Gospels and Acts do not? How does crucifixion in antiquity parallel the lynching of African Americans in the US? As James Cone argues, the crucifixion of Jesus can be compared to the lynching of African Americans, even though 'the cross of Jesus and the lynching tree of black victims are not literally the same – historically or theologically'.[29] Though culturally distant and distinct from the lynching of African Americans in the US, ancient crucifixion in about the first four centuries CE was, as stated, a public spectacle and a disgraceful form of state-sanctioned execution intended to instil fear in order to deter certain criminalized behaviours. Most victims of crucifixion (Latin: *cruciarii*) were already socially dishonoured and alienated (for example, enslaved persons, freeborn foreigners (*peregrini*) and prisoners of war).[30] The majority of crucifixions occurred in the amphitheatre where gladiatorial games or other spectacles were also held. Such crucifixions might include execution by wild animals, or victims could be burned alive to create a greater amusement. Roman amphitheatres were generally situated outside the city walls. The execution of persons outside the city walls constituted a forced ultimate expulsion from the community.[31]

Generally, the crucified were subject to multiple forms of torture, stripped naked, flogged, derided and suspended from the ground on a wooden stake or trident the shape of the Greek letter tau. The genitalia of some victims, including women, may have been covered with loincloths, but the majority were probably crucified nude.[32] Based on an archaeological discovery almost 50 years ago of a crucified man's remains in an ossuary in Jerusalem, a 'wooden support, placed under the buttocks, prevented the flesh from tearing and the body from thereby falling free ... the support merely prolonged the agony'.[33] This aspect also suggests that the body was nude. Early Christian art and images portrayed the crucified Christ in total (frontal) nudity without a loincloth. The only images of the crucified Christ earlier than the fifth century CE are found on 'highly unconventional engraved gems and a remarkable and enigmatic graffito from Rome'.[34] For example, archaeologists located a third-century drawing etched in plaster on a wall of the Imperial Palace on the Palatine Hill, Rome. It is a caricature of the nude crucified Christ, rear view, stretched out on a tau/T-shaped cross with a servant standing next to it worshipping the Christ. The head of the crucified figure is an ass/donkey, reflecting the pagan accusation that Jews and Christians worshipped an ass-headed deity.[35] The earliest existing image of the crucified Christ is from the late second to early third cemtury CE and is unexpectedly found on an engraved magical gemstone. The amulet/bloodstone portrays Jesus in full frontal nudity with a beard and long hair; his arms are outstretched, short strips are fastened around his wrists, and he is suspended on a T-shaped cross. Jesus' nudity is emphasized by the position of his legs that are 'bent at the knee and hanging open loosely, as though he is seated on a bar or peg'.[36] Thus, in the earliest images of the crucified Jesus, he was not wearing a loincloth. Wil Gafney asserts 'the exposure of Jesus' naked body on the cross was a particular shaming targeting a man who was not normatively, heteronormatively, coupled'.[37] Some early Christians probably wanted to minimize Jesus' shame by constructing a narrative that minimized or obscured any nudity or sexual abuse associated with crucifixion.

It is estimated that the Romans crucified well over 30,000 persons, but only 20 names of the victims survive in reliable sources.[38] During the lynching period in the US (1880–1940), over 5,000 African Americans were ritually murdered. In 2018 the National Memorial for Peace and Justice was established in Birmingham, Alabama, naming many of them. '[Q]uite consistently, "white men, women, and children would hang or burn (frequently both), shoot, and castrate the [alleged] offender, then divide the body into trophies".'[39]

We can identify differences and similarities between crucifixion in the ancient world and the lynching of African Americans. The lynching of black persons was, of course, based on racism; whites considered black people inferior to them and felt the need to consistently remind them of their non-human status. In the south, black men were primarily lynched under the guise of protecting white womanhood. Thus, to be accused of looking a white woman (or man) in the eyes, staring at her, or behaving towards her in any way that was considered threatening, was a capital offence. Often black men were lynched after white women falsely accused them of rape. Similar to crucifixion, it was a public spectacle often attended by families including children, with the intent to terrorize and control black people.[40] The ritual was predictable and standardized across the US, reflecting general consensus among white people that African Americans were not human but bestial and immoral. Mitchell notes in her book *Living with Lynching*:

> The torture of black bodies was ... invested with significance. These rituals were possible and meaningful because, in the sign-system of U.S. society, the black body was consistently presented and interpreted as a sign of evil and immorality, as a symbol of all that would destroy the nation.[41]

Lynching was an extra-state sanctioned form of punishment that primarily targeted black males accused of rape and other sexual crimes against white women.[42] Another difference that most would draw between the lynching of black men and the crucifixion of Jesus is the absence of sexual violence committed against the latter. But the evidence says otherwise.

Because of the striking similarities between the cross of Jesus' crucifixion and the lynching tree, the latter should have a prominent place in American images of Jesus' death. But instead Cone notes that 'the conspicuous absence of the lynching tree in American theological discourse and preaching is profoundly revealing, especially since the crucifixion was clearly a first-century lynching'.[43] Lynched African Americans and the crucified Jesus were subjected to public humiliation, verbal abuse, forced nudity, physical torture including beatings or flogging and unwanted touching of their bodies. Both were long, torturous deaths in front of heckling crowds. Similarly, in antiquity, crucified persons were subject to all kinds of torture.[44] In both cases, Cone argues, the intent was to terrorize and deter others like them from engaging in the same or similar behaviours of which the victims were charged.[45] Lynching or lynch law was not an American invention; first-century Roman crucifixions, including that of Jesus, were a precursor of the lynching of black bodies.[46] The lynching of African Americans took many forms, including torture, burning, shooting, dragging and mutilation, especially castration.[47]

The genital mutilation and castration of black males arguably constituted sexual violence. Niambi Carter notes that castration and the practice of lynching are generally not considered gender violence because of the absence of sexual penetration, but it should be situated as sexual violence. Carter examines the 2 September 1957 lynching of Judge Aaron by the Ku Klux Klan in Birmingham, Alabama, in which Aaron was snatched off the street, blindfolded, driven to the outskirts of town, brutally beaten, forced to remove his clothes, pinned to the ground, and his entire scrotum was excised, after which they doused his wounds with turpentine to intensify his pain. Then his white perpetrators re-dressed him, leaving him for dead. Aaron, however, survived to identify his attackers, and they were convicted. If local law enforcement had not championed Aaron's cause, he probably would not have won his case. At the trial, like other rape victims, Aaron was compelled 'to show his wounds to the all-male, white jury'.[48] Carter argues that because lynching was generally executed by white men against black men, 'we do not (want to) see the overtly sexual elements of these crimes because the bodies in these circumstances are masculinized'.[49] The White community did not widely sanction the lynching of black women in the same way it did black men, primarily because black women were viewed as occupying a weaker position, being less threatening than black men. But when black women were lynched, it usually involved some kind of sexual violence. Carter asserts that

> because of the legacy of black women's sexual violation at the hands of white men, there is a way in which we understand the lynching of black women as already sexualized ... in the case of Judge Aaron and other black men who shared a similar fate ... it becomes apparent how lynching as the apparatus of white male power is both racialized and highly sexualized.[50]

We should not be hard pressed to imagine Jesus also as the victim of sexual violence as he was led to the cross and crucified. Jesus did not remove his clothes of his own volition; the lynching-tree mob had unbridled access to his naked body, so that they touched him without his permission. It is also not impossible to imagine that the Roman officials would have wanted to further humiliate Jesus, emasculating him by castrating or otherwise sexually violating his body. Jesus was a victim of sexual violence, as part of the crucifixion ritual involving spectacular public shaming, forced nudity, blows to his body, unwanted touching, and probably castration. In Plato's fourth-century BCE *Gorgias*, Polus, a student of Gorgias, asks the following:

> How do you mean? If a man be caught criminally plotting to make himself a despot, and he be straightway put on the rack and castrated and have his eyes burnt out, and after suffering himself, and seeing inflicted on his wife and children, a number of grievous torments of every kind, he be finally crucified or burnt in a coat of pitch, will he be happier than if he escape and make himself despot, and pass his life as the ruler in his city, doing whatever he likes, and envied and congratulated by the citizens and the foreigners besides?[51]

The celebrated African American Harlem Renaissance poet Langston Hughes imagined what most Christians cannot, namely that 'Christ is a nigger'.[52]

What does it mean to deny that Jesus was treated like other criminals or enslaved persons in antiquity that the state charged with a capital crime and crucified? What does it mean to accept the probability that Jesus was sexually violated as are many women, children and men today? According to the National Organization for Women, 'on average, ... one in five women are victims of sexual assault. These numbers underscore the epidemic of sexual violence in the US, which disproportionately impacts women of color, immigrant women, LGBTQIA+ women, and disabled women.'[53] Does identifying Jesus as a victim of sexual violence feminize him? Does our denial that Jesus was sexually violated when he was crucified mean that God saved his son from the trauma of sexual violence, while electing not to spare those crucified before him, with him, and those lynched and/or sexually violated since? To accept that Jesus was sexually violated means that God, in a fleshy way, knows what it feels like when one's child is sexually violated and/or lynched. It means that Jesus had total absence of control over what was done to his body, like the woman, girl, boy or man who is sexually violated and/or raped. That the shame imposed upon Christ, especially the sexual violence, was not his own to bear but to name.[54] Are Goddess/Spirit/God the parents in denial that turn their backs on their child, pretend not to know what happened (like we do), side with the perpetrators, and project the shame that belongs to the perpetrators onto their child? Does our dismissal of the likelihood of sexual violence inflicted upon Jesus (the forced nudity, uninvited touching and genital mutilation or castration) reflect our fears and cultural taboos? Do we hide behind fourth-century creeds that allow us to temper a fully human Jesus with a fully divine son of God? Covering Jesus with a loin cloth of ignorance and fallible traditions does not eliminate the probability that Jesus too was sexually violated.

Sexual violence, black women and sacralized silence

Issues of sexual violence against African American women are 'incredibly pervasive issues that routinely go unreported and under-addressed' as '[o]ver eighteen percent of African American women will be sexually assaulted in her [their] lifetime'.[55] This percentage does not reflect the many women who do not report their abuse. Only 1 in 15 black women who are raped reports it.[56] The silence of black women is valued most when the oppressor or abuser is a black male or the black church. Her silence becomes a sign of her loyalty to the black church as the body of Christ. The strong spiritual black woman bears her abuse in silence, dissociating her body from her spirit, never naming her abuse or abusers, like Jesus supposedly did, for the sake of the black male-dominated church whose head is the male Christ and, by proxy, biological men. Often silence, sexual violence and uncritical idolatry of sacred texts intersect in the lives of black people as people of faith. At the heart of such violence we find problematic traditions and witnesses. It is well documented that slave masters raped enslaved black women, forced them to breed with enslaved black men, and coerced black women into immoral sexual relationships. Enslavers argued that it was God's sacred word that permitted them to enslave black bodies, to do with them as they pleased. In fact, Christian slave masters were considered the cruellest. When enslaved persons claimed that a slave master was kind, they were most assuredly speaking in relative terms.

In the antebellum period and well into the twentieth century, black women, children and men were sexually assaulted by both white men and black men.[57] Black women were raped by white men with impunity until the 1970s. The infamous case of Recy Taylor, a black woman gang raped by white men, was the first in which white men were convicted of their racialized sexual brutality against black women. Conversely, innocent black men were often convicted of raping white women and sentenced to death or life in prison. Black women, and the black community, felt that in order to stay alive and to prevent the escalation of violence against them and their families during the lynching period and after, the best course was to remain silent even as they continued to be brutalized by white folk and sometimes by black men. But we learned that, as Audre Lorde asserts, 'our silences had not ... [and] will not protect' us.[58]

The black church continues to practise an ethics of silence around sexuality and sexual violence within the black community and the black church. In her book *Plenty Good Room: Women Versus Male Power in the Black Church*, Marcia Riggs argues that through a combination of history, social construction and practice

> the African American church has developed a normative patriarchal institutional ethos that has transmuted the black church, a surrogate world for racially oppressed black people, into the African American church, as a 'protected space' for sexual-gender transgressions, a place where silence is kept about unethical – inappropriate and/or abusive – sexual contact or 'sexualized behavior'.[59]

This practice of an ethics of silence around sexuality and sexual violence within the Church and beyond is not, of course, unique to the black church(es). The uncritical reading and embrace of sacred texts, artifacts and traditions continues to inform our theologies, ethics and social practice. These sacred artifacts and traditions include oppressive biblical interpretations and black church hymnody and spirituals that we absorb when we gather for passive Bible studies, the weekly worship, and on special holy days like Resurrection/Easter Sunday to sing 'He Never Said a Mumbalin' Word'. In those spaces, silent suffering is often sacralized. The perennial performance of this spiritual in sacred space, based on a false and oppressive narrative and in an emotionally charged presentation, primarily but not exclusively at Easter, sacralizes an ethics and theology of silent suffering. In her analysis of lynching narratives, Angela Sims argues our 'history, and thus education, is often determined and transmitted via a predetermined sanitized curriculum as a way to silence truth',[60] or in a way that silences truth, whether that is the intention or not.

Black churches, but not only black churches, have made the policing of black women's bodies, speech and personal spiritual narratives one of its primary tasks. The black church and its dominant male leaders have usurped women's voices and often make themselves the primary truth-tellers and mouthpiece for black women's experience of sexual violence in and out of marriage; our voices and experiences have been co-opted and commodified. Black preachers like T. D. Jakes make millions telling black women how to survive sexual violence. When Jakes wrote his famous *Woman Thou Art Loose*, as a victim of sexual assault I could not digest it.[61] As a survivor, I know that we are not simply loosed from the trauma of sexual abuse, especially when it is a long and painful road to recovery. When children are abused, they cannot confront their abuse or abusers until they are older. And many are abused from childhood through to adulthood. Competent qualified counsellors for black women and men are few and far between. And being a Christian does not automatically qualify one to effectively counsel anyone. Too often the black church is a stumbling block to wholeness for black women (children and men) who have been sexually abused, since 'Black women's [and girls'] flesh and voices, concomitantly, are not to make unauthorized noise' in sacred space.[62] As Tamura Lomax argues, 'erotophobia, ignominy, and hyper-moralism' are tactics that the black church utilizes 'for social and representational control'; the sexualization of black girls and women, a 'form of dehumanization and disempowerment', is itself a source of violence.[63]

Truth-telling is the first step toward recovery from rape and other forms of sexual violence.

I am a survivor. And Jesus would say, #MeToo.

References

Bennett, Joshua, 'Theodicy', in *The Sobbing School*, New York: Penguin, 2016.

Bovon, François, *The Last Days of Jesus*, Louisville, KY: Westminster John Knox, 2006.

Callahan, Allen Dwight, *The Talking Book: African Americans and the Bible*, New Haven, CT: Yale University Press, 2006.

Carter, Niambi M., 'Intimacy without Consent: Lynching as Sexual Violence', *Politics & Gender* 8:3 (2012), pp. 414–21.

Cone, James H., *The Cross and the Lynching Tree*, Maryknoll, NY: Orbis, 2011.

Cook, John Granger, 'Crucifixion as Spectacle in Roman Campania', *Novum Testamentum* 54 (2012), pp. 68–100.

——, 'Roman Crucifixions: From the Second Punic War to Constantine', *Zeitschrift für die neutestamentliche Wissenschaft* 104:1 (2013), pp. 1–32.

Cullen, Countee, *The Black Christ and Other Poems*, New York: Harper, 1929.

Equiano, Olaudah, 'The Interesting Narrative of the Life of Olaudah Equiano, or Gustavus Vassa, the African Written by Himself (1789)', in *Slave Narratives*, William L. Andrews and Henry Louis Gates, eds, New York: Library of America, 2000, pp. 35–241.

Gafney, Wil, 'Crucifixion and Sexual Violence', *HuffPost Plus*, 28 March 2013, www.huffpost.com/entry/crucifixion-and-sexual-violence_b_2965369.

Jakes, T. D., *Woman Thou Art Loose*, Shippensburg: Treasure, 1993.

Johnson, Leónidas A., ed., 'Leviticus 17–18, "He Never Said a Mumbalin' Word"', in *Go Down, Moses!*, Valley Forge, PA: Judson, 2000.

Kay, Roy, *The Ethiopian Prophecy in Black American Letters*, Gainesville, FL: University Press of Florida, 2011.

Lomax, Tamura, 'Theorizing the Distance Between Erotophobia, Hypermoralism, and Eroticism: Toward a Black Feminist Theology of Pleasure', *Black Theology* 16.3 (2018), pp. 263–79.

—, *Jezebel Unhinged: Loosing the Black Female Body in Religion and Culture*, Durham, NC: Duke University Press, 2018.

Lorde, Audre, *Sister Outsider*, Freedom, CA: The Crossing, 1996.

McGuire, Danielle, *At the Dark End of the Street: Black Women, Rape, and Resistance – A New History of the Civil Rights Movement from Rosa Parks to the Rise of Black Power*, New York: Vintage, 2011.

Mitchell, Koritha, *Living with Lynching: African American Lynching Plays, Performance, and Citizenship, 1890–1930*, Champaign, IL: University of Illinois Press, 2011.

National Organization for Women, 'Black Women and Sexual Violence', February 2018, https://now.org/wp-content/uploads/2018/02/Black-Women-and-Sexual-Violence-6.pdf.

Nyguyen, Vien V., 'A Parallel Case of Two Conversion Stories: A Narrative Criticism of Acts 8:15–40', *Journal of Biblical Theology* 2:4 (2019), pp. 23–40.

Plato, *Gorgias*. 473c, *Plato in Twelve Volumes*, vol. 3, trans. W. R. M. Lamb, Cambridge, MA: Harvard University Press, 1967.

Powery, Luke A., *Were You There? Lenten Reflections on the Spirituals*, Louisville, KY: Westminster John Knox, 2019.

Riggs, Marcia Y., *Plenty Good Room: Women Versus Male Power in the Black Church*, Eugene, OR: Wipf and Stock, 2008.

Sims, Angela D., *Lynched: The Power of Memory in a Culture of Terror*, Waco, TX: Baylor University Press, 2016.

Smith, Abraham, '"Do You Understand What You Are Reading": A Literary Critical Reading of the Ethiopian (Kushite) Episode (Acts 8:26–40)', *The Journal of the Interdenominational Theological Center* 22:1 (1994), pp. 48–70.

Smith, Mitzi J., 'Complete silence is death and not the absence of sound', 11 June 2011, https://womanistntprof.blogspot.com/2011/06/part-2-of-coming-out-complete-silence.html.

—, *Womanist Sass and Talk Back: Social (In)Justice, Intersectionality, and Biblical Interpretation*, Eugene, OR: Cascade, 2015.

Spier, Jeffrey, et al., *Picturing the Bible: Early Christian Art*, New Haven, CT: Yale University Press, 2009.

Tombs, David, 'Crucifixion, State Terror, and Sexual Abuse', *Union Seminary Quarterly Review* 53:1–2 (1999), pp. 89–109.

West, Cornel, 'Niggerization', *The Atlantic*, November 2007, www.theatlantic.com/magazine/archive/2007/11/niggerization/306285/.

White, John, 'Veiled Testimony: Negro Spirituals and the Slave Experience', *Journal of American Studies* 17:2 (1983), pp. 251–63.

Williams, Demetrius K., 'The Acts of the Apostles', in *True to Our Native Land:*

An African American New Testament Commentary, ed. Brian K. Blount, Minneapolis, MN: Fortress, 2007, pp. 213–48.

Wilson, Brittany E., *Unmanly Men: Refigurations of Masculinity in Luke-Acts*, Oxford: Oxford University Press, 2015.

Wright, Jeneva, 'Soul Songs: Origins and Agency in African-American Spirituals', National Endowment for the Humanities: SERSAS, 2013.

Notes

1 Joshua Bennett, 'Theodicy', *The Sobbing School* (New York: Penguin, 2016), pp. 10–11. Emphasis is Bennett's.

2 I told my truth publicly for the first time on my blog in a three-part series. Part 2 of 'Coming Out' is entitled 'Complete silence is death and not the absence of sound', 11 June 2011, https://womanistntprof.blogspot.com/2011/06/part-2-of-coming-out-complete-silence.html.

3 Author's paraphrase of 1 Chronicles 16.22.

4 James H. Cone, *The Cross and the Lynching Tree* (Maryknoll, NY: Orbis, 2011), p. 123.

5 Cone, *The Cross and the Lynching Tree*, p. 97.

6 Cone, *The Cross and the Lynching Tree*, pp. 93, 99. Countee Cullen, *The Black Christ and Other Poems* (New York: Harper, 1929).

7 Cornel West, 'Niggerization', *The Atlantic*, November 2007, www.theatlantic.com/magazine/archive/2007/11/niggerization/306285/. West asserts that '[n]iggerization is neither simply the dishonoring and devaluing of black people nor solely the economic exploitation and political disenfranchisement of them. It is also the wholesale attempt to impede democratization – to turn potential citizens into intimidated, fearful, and helpless subjects.'

8 John White, 'Veiled Testimony: Negro Spirituals and the Slave Experience', *Journal of American Studies* 17:2 (1983), p. 262.

9 James H. Cone, *The Spirituals and the Blues: An Interpretation* (Maryknoll, NY: Orbis, 1972), p. 48.

10 Jeneva Wright, *Soul Songs: Origins and Agency in African-American Spirituals* (National Endowment for the Humanities: SERSAS, 2013), p. 8.

11 Leónidas A. Johnson, ed., 'Leviticus 17–18, "He Never Said a Mumbalin' Word,"' in *Go Down, Moses!* (Valley Forge: Judson, 2000), p. 107.

12 An older, not so well known and seldom sung version of the spiritual includes a verse that reads 'Oh, dey whupped him up de hill (x2), up de hill, up de hill, an' he never said a Mumbalin' word ... Oh, dey crowned him wid a thorny crown, an' he never said a Mumbalin word'. The line 'an' he never said a Mumbalin word' is connected to each verse, and the refrain is 'He jes' hung down his head an' he cried.' This version is printed in Cone, *The Spirituals and the Blues*, pp. 47–9.

13 Luke A. Powery, *Were You There? Lenten Reflections on the Spirituals* (Louisville, KY: Westminster John Knox, 2019), pp. 127–9.

14 Powery, *Were You There?*, p. 129.

15 François Bovon, *The Last Days of Jesus* (Louisville, KY: Westminster John Knox, 2006), p. 51. See also David Tombs, 'Crucifixion, State Terror, and Sexual Abuse', *Union Seminary Quarterly Review* 53:1–2 (1999), pp. 89–109.

16 Bovon, *The Last Days of Jesus*, p. 54. The other Synoptic Gospels follow Mark's lead, but they attribute more words to Jesus as he hangs from the cross.

17 Bovon, *The Last Days of Jesus*, p. 42.

18 Abraham Smith notes that both the story of the Ethiopian eunuch and that of Cornelius are conversion stories about royal officials; Smith, '"Do You Understand What You are Reading": A Literary Critical Reading of the Ethiopian (Kushite) Episode (Acts 8:26–40)', *The Journal of the Interdenominational Theological Center* 22:1 (1994), pp. 48–70.

19 Allen Dwight Callahan, *The Talking Book: African Americans and the Bible* (New Haven, CT: Yale University Press, 2006), p. 138.

20 Callahan, *The Talking Book*, p. 139.

21 See Brittany E. Wilson, *Unmanly Men: Refigurations of Masculinity in Luke-Acts* (Oxford: Oxford University Press, 2015).

22 Mitzi J. Smith, *Womanist Sass and Talk Back: Social (In)Justice, Intersectionality, and Biblical Interpretation* (Eugene, OR: Cascade, 2015), esp. Ch. 4, 'Epistemologies, Pedagogies, and the Subordinated Other: Luke's Parallel Construction of the Ethiopian Eunuch and the Alexandrian Apollos' (Acts 8:26–40; 18:24–28).

23 For example, Vien V. Nyguyen, 'A Parallel Case of Two Conversion Stories: A Narrative Criticism of Acts 8:15–40', *Journal of Biblical Theology* 2:4 (2019), pp. 23–40.

24 Cone, *The Spirituals and the Blues*, p. 106.

25 Angela D. Sims, *Lynched: The Power of Memory in a Culture of Terror* (Waco, TX: Baylor University Press, 2016), p. 22. Silence is 'sometimes a contextual response to preserve life' in a culture of terror.

26 Roy Kay, *The Ethiopian Prophecy in Black American Letters* (Gainesville, FL: University Press of Florida, 2011), esp. Ch. 2, 'Managing Blackness: Protestant Readings of Psalm 68:31 in Colonial America', p. 36.

27 Demetrius K. Williams, 'The Acts of the Apostles', in *True to Our Native Land: An African American New Testament Commentary*, Brian K. Blount, ed. (Minneapolis, MN: Fortress, 2007), pp. 213–48. Williams argues that the eunuch, the first Gentile convert in Acts, probably returned home and that 'the presumptions of the Ethiopian's ethnographic identity as "marginally significant" or "inconsequential" for the Lucan theological perspective altogether may be traced to a larger problem in Western, post-Enlightenment culture', pp. 226–7.

28 Olaudah Equiano, 'The Interesting Narrative of the Life of Olaudah Equiano, or Gustavus Vassa, the African Written by Himself (1789)', in *Slave Narratives*, William L. Andrews and Henry Louis Gates, eds (New York: Library of America, 2000), pp. 35–241.

29 Cone, *The Cross and the Lynching Tree*, p. 165. Ultimately Cone argues that 'the lynching tree is a metaphor for white America's crucifixion of black people. It is the window that best reveals the religious meaning of the cross in our land. In this sense, black people are Christ figures, not because they wanted to suffer but because they had no choice', p. 166.

30 John Granger Cook, 'Crucifixion as Spectacle in Roman Campania', *Novum Testamentum* 54 (2012), pp. 68–100.

31 John Granger Cook, 'Roman Crucifixions: From the Second Punic War to Constantine', *Zeitschrift für die neutestamentliche Wissenschaft* 104:1 (2013), p. 4.

32 Cook, 'Crucifixion as Spectacle', esp. pp. 76, 80–81. Also Cook, 'Roman Crucifixions'.

33 Bovon, *The Last Days of Jesus*, p. 52.

34 Jeffrey Spier, Herbert L. Kessler, Steven Fine et al., *Picturing the Bible: Early Christian Art* (New Haven, CT: Yale University Press, 2009), p. 227.

35 Spier et al., *Picturing the Bible*.

36 Spier, et al., *Picturing the Bible*, p. 228. 'The nudity is not used in accordance with the Greco-Roman concept of nakedness as a means to denote divinity nor is it a strictly narrative device, referring to the historical process of crucifixion.'

37 Wil Gafney, 'Crucifixion and Sexual Violence', *HuffPost Plus*, 28 March 2013, www.huffpost.com/entry/crucifixion-and-sexual-violence_b_2965369.

38 Cook, 'Roman Crucifixions'.

39 Koritha Mitchell, *Living with Lynching: African American Lynching Plays, Performance, and Citizenship, 1890–1930* (Champaign, IL: University of Illinois Press, 2011), p. 24. Mitchell is quoting Trudier Harris, *Exorcising Blackness: Historical and Literary Lynching and Burning Rituals* (Bloomington, IN: Indiana University Press, 1984), p. 6.

40 Sims, *Lynched*.

41 Mitchell, *Living with Lynching*, p. 24.

42 Some black women, as well as a few white men, were also lynched.

43 Cone, *The Cross and the Lynching Tree*, p. 30.

44 Cook, 'Roman Crucifixions', p. 27. For a comprehensive treatment of the rape of black women by white men post-emancipation, see Danielle L. McGuire, *At the Dark End of the Street: Black Women, Rape, and Resistance – A New History of the Civil Rights Movement from Rosa Parks to the Rise of Black Power* (New York: Alfred A. Knopf, 2010).

45 Cone, *The Cross and the Lynching Tree*, p. 31.

46 Cone, *The Cross and the Lynching Tree*, pp. 62–3. Cone refers to E. T. Wellford, *The Lynching of Jesus. A Review of the Legal Aspects of the Trial of Christ* (Newport News, VA: Franklin Printing Co., 1905), p. 17.

47 Cone, *The Cross and the Lynching Tree*, p. 94.

48 Niambi M. Carter, 'Intimacy without Consent: Lynching as Sexual Violence', *Politics & Gender* 8:3 (2012), p. 416.

49 Carter, 'Intimacy without Consent', p. 418.

50 Carter, 'Intimacy without Consent', pp. 418, 419.

51 Plato, *Gorgias*, 473c, *Plato in Twelve Volumes*, vol. 3, trans. W. R. M. Lamb (Cambridge, MA: Harvard University Press, 1967).

52 Cone, *The Cross and the Lynching Tree*, p. 114. From Langston Hughes' 1931 poem 'Christ in Alabama', cited in Arnold Rampersad, *The Life of Langston Hughes, Vol. 1, 1902–1941: I, Too, Sing America* (New York: Oxford University Press, 1986), pp. 224–5.

53 National Organization for Women, 'Black Women and Sexual Violence', February 2018, https://now.org/wp-content/uploads/2018/02/Black-Women-and-Sexual-Violence-6.pdf.

54 See Jayme Reaves and David Tombs, '#Me Too Jesus: Naming Jesus as a Victim of Sexual Abuse', *International Journal of Public Theology* 13 (2019), pp. 387–412.

55 National Organization for Women, 'Black Women and Sexual Violence'.

56 National Organization for Women, 'Black Women and Sexual Violence'.

57 McGuire, *At the Dark End of the Street*.

58 Audre Lorde, *Sister Outsider* (Freedom, CA: The Crossing, 1996), p. 41.

59 Marcia Y. Riggs, *Plenty Good Room: Women Versus Male Power in the Black Church* (Eugene, OR: Wipf and Stock, 2008), p. 86.

60 Sims, *Lynched*, p. 21.

61 T. D. Jakes, *Woman Thou Art Loose* (Shippensburg: Treasure, 1993). Jakes has since published a *Woman Thou Art Loose* devotional and Bible.

62 Tamura Lomax, 'Theorizing the Distance Between Erotophobia, Hyper-moralism, and Eroticism: Toward a Black Feminist Theology of Pleasure', *Black Theology* 16:3 (2018), p. 266. See also Tamura Lomax, *Jezebel Unhinged: Loosing the Black Female Body in Religion and Culture* (Durham, NC: Duke University Press, 2018).

63 Lomax, 'Theorizing', p. 266.

4

Family Resemblance:
Reading Post-Crucifixion Encounters as
Community Responses to Sexual Violence

MONICA C. POOLE

Introduction

If Jesus' crucifixion was sexual violence, then the chapters of the Gospels
that narrate the events after Jesus' crucifixion narrate various community
responses to sexual violence.[1] Today, communities continue to struggle
with the challenge of responding to sexual violence in a way that treats victims of violence with compassion, justice and honour. The crucifixion was
clearly a public act of state terror, but even acts of sexual violence that take
place 'behind closed doors' are not purely 'private matters' without community impact or political significance. In this chapter, my emphasis is not
on the harm done by the perpetrators, but rather on the harm compounded
when community responses fail victims/survivors afterwards.[2]

In this chapter, I have three principal aims: first, to interpret post-
crucifixion encounters in the Gospels to reveal how community members
responded after Jesus was victimized; second, to draw parallels between
Jesus and other victims of violence in order to spotlight some ways that
contemporary community responses do further harm to victims/survivors
of sexual violence; and third, to engage in this work as a form of praxis-
centred, liberatory, imaginative biblical interpretation dwelling outside
organized religions.

Community responses to Jesus and other victims/survivors

There is no serious argument about whether or not the Roman Empire
did the right thing when they tortured and killed Jesus. Christian or otherwise, we do not examine Jesus' behaviours in Jerusalem to try to justify
the imperial authorities' response. We do not complain that he should not
have made such a spectacle of himself with that noisy parade in the streets
(Matt. 21.1–11); indeed, Christians celebrate this as Palm Sunday. We do

not shrug and say that he should have known better than to provoke the authorities by disrupting the marketplace and destroying private property at the Temple (Matt. 21.12–13). We do not purse our lips and complain that he shouldn't have taken such an aggressive tone when calling out the scribes and Pharisees (Matt. 23). We do not say he should have made more of an effort to advocate for himself when he was accused (Matt. 26.62–66). This is normalized in the twenty-first century and has a long history of being normalized. Whatever one may think of Jesus' divinity, historicity or wisdom, there is a longstanding, widespread and unequivocal confidence that Jesus was wronged.

. This should not be a noteworthy way to regard a victim of violence. Yet it contrasts sharply with many typical responses in our contemporary communities. This includes attempting to discount the wrong done to victims by critiquing victims' supposedly 'disruptive' conduct, 'attention-seeking' behaviour, 'aggressive' tone, and/or 'inadequate' self-advocacy. Other harmful responses incorporate a false neutrality offering unearned sympathy to perpetrators, claiming to 'see both sides'. This is not to say that victims of violence are perfect innocents; only that perfect innocence on the victim's part should not be required in order for communities to respond with compassion and justice. Jesus, exceptionally among victims of violence, is exempt from the discrediting and dishonour embedded in contemporary community responses to victims of violence – sexual or otherwise.[3]

In a defining article, 'Justice from the Victim's Perspective', Judith Herman critiqued community responses that deny credibility, agency and full community participation to victims/survivors of sexual violence: not only the acts of violence but also the community responses 'dishonor[ed] and isolate[d]' them. In contrast, Herman argued that victims seek 'the restoration of their own honor and the reestablishment of their own connections with the community'.[4]

The narrative of Jesus' resurrection is a narrative of restoration of honour and re-establishment of community connections – the very thing sought by the contemporary victims in Herman's article. Jesus is a rare example of a figure whose honour is beyond reproach – again, not only among Christians, but among many readers familiar with Jesus' narrative. According Jesus the elevated status of divinity is another matter, but treating Jesus with honour is unremarkable. On the other hand, victims/survivors in our contemporary communities are dishonoured by default: as Herman described it, a 2002 slogan 'Bringing Honor to Victims' had seemed 'like a modest goal', but it remains radical: 'no honor, however well-deserved, was granted to [victims] without a fight'.[5]

In the spirit of Matthew 25.31–46, I imagine a large family of victims/survivors that includes Jesus side by side with members of our contemporary communities – our neighbours, and, sometimes, ourselves. Reading Jesus as a sibling to other victims/survivors sharpens our attention to the 'family resemblance' between community responses to Jesus narrated in the Gospels and community responses to contemporary victims/survivors.

When we are disgusted by 'Doubting Thomas's' famous demand for corporeal evidence to support Jesus' credibility, we can more acutely perceive
the analogous wrong in similar demands made to contemporary victims.
When we admire the women who cared for the dead body of Jesus post-
crucifixion, this can illuminate some ways to care for victims/survivors in
our own circles.

Interpretive approaches: reading the Bible outside Christianity

This chapter interprets texts from the Gospels with a contextual hermeneutic that does not locate itself within Christianity, nor within its close
relatives, Islam and Judaism. Praxis-driven and contextual hermeneutics of
Christian biblical texts overwhelmingly locate themselves within Christianity,
even – perhaps especially – when they are challenging traditional interpretations, including historically silenced perspectives, or reinterpreting the
Bible to reimagine social justice in the present. In parallel, non-Christian
people studying the New Testament tend to approach it as a scholarly
inquiry more than as a resource for personal or social application. However, some people who do not situate themselves in any of the religions
that traditionally engage the Bible nevertheless make biblical interpretation
part of their praxis on a personal and social level. They (we) might describe
this religious position as 'spiritual but not religious', 'unaffiliated' and/
or 'extra-religious'. In effect, I read the Bible with an emphasis on living
praxis but without an identifiable religious belonging. My approach shares
some attributes with *enfleshed*, which describes its work as a 'Christian-
adjacent' sacred praxis of 'bringing what matters back to the gospel for
justice, liberation, and delight'.[6]

A valuable point of reference is queer theorist Sara Ahmed's concept of
'dis-orientations' – ways that queer people make use of straight-coded concepts and frameworks. For example, we sometimes refer to queer kinship
networks as 'chosen families'. Ahmed uses a metaphor of familiar points on
a line encountered through a new 'oblique angle' of approach. She regards
this as rich in possibilities for making meaning, animating 'what has been
overlooked, which has been treated as furniture', in order to 'dance with
renewed life'.[7]

Beginning by understanding Jesus' crucifixion as sexual violence already
offers a new 'oblique angle' on familiar points on the line of the Gospel
narratives. A reader approaching biblical interpretation for living praxis
outside religious belonging also approaches a traditional text from a new
angle. Like queer people drawing on 'family' language to describe alternative kinships, formerly-Christian readers may engage with the Bible
for personal meaning-making in order to 'have joy in the uncanny effect
of a familiar form becoming strange', to borrow Ahmed's words. These
readings may not only have value for others who approach the Bible as
personally meaningful while being religiously unaffiliated, but also might

offer useful perspectives in a type of interreligious dialogue with religiously affiliated readers of the Bible.

I engage the Bible in some ways that resemble how other feminist writers have engaged the Greco-Roman classical tradition. Consider, for example, Christa Wolf's *Cassandra* and Judith Butler's *Antigone's Claim*, which are two works that 'think with' their respective figures from ancient Greek literature to formulate and frame their works of feminist theory. Or consider the creative retellings of classical texts by Kamila Shamsie, Ursula K. LeGuin, Madeline Miller, Nina MacLaughlin and others.[8] They draw on ancient Greek and Latin texts in subversive, liberatory, meaningful ways without belonging to a community that worships Athena or Juno. In addition, poets including Karthika Nair, Mohja Kahf and Jericho Brown engage classical texts of living religions in new, enlivening ways: Brown's poems in *The New Testament* and *The Tradition* are particularly relevant to the present chapter for many reasons, including his claiming of the Gospels as a reference point to discuss violence.[9]

My approach in this chapter is also shaped by imaginative and responsive approaches to scriptural interpretation in analytical prose. These include and are not limited to: Mitzi Smith's 'talking back' to the Bible; Elisabeth Schüssler Fiorenza's hermeneutics of creative actualization; Stephanie Buckhanon Crowder's 'ideological sandpaper' dialogue with biblical texts; Wil Gafney's womanist midrash; Jerusha Tanner Rhodes's Muslima-theology approach to the Qur'an; and Martin Nguyen's Muslim theology of the imagination.[10] Each is distinctive, but some common elements I draw on include emphasizing the reader's positionality as a part of the reader's imagination, approaching imagination as a kind of sacred practice, and tuning the imagination to listen to silences in the texts and to speak into those silences.

I approach biblical texts with reference to my own positionality and responsibility, and in a spirited dialogue – sometimes confrontation – with the text. My formation in this owes a significant debt to womanist scholars. As a white woman, I learn from womanist theology and biblical interpretation carefully, in harmony with Nyasha Junior's forecast for how 'non-African-American women biblical scholars' might draw on womanist insights, and inspired by Mitzi Smith's womanist readings that keep black women at the centre but invite white women to be included as well: Smith argues that 'we need to celebrate sass and talk-back in women of color as well as white women as a legitimate form of agency and method of truth telling', and describes her womanist readings as for 'black women (and women in general)'.[11] My reading cannot be womanist, but it is informed by womanists; I strive to locate myself in the space created by Smith's parentheticals.

Finally, the complicated significance the Bible holds for me is impossible to disentangle from the roles the Bible played in my own experiences as a victim/survivor of sexual violence. My abusers cited the Bible to try to keep me compliant, to justify their actions to themselves, and to persuade me to show affection against my will. I recited Bible passages silently in my head as a way to take my mind out of my body: the text was my safe place, my dissociative refuge. Neither cancels out the other.

Regrettably, this is not unusual. Many perpetrators weaponize Christianity and the Bible against their victims. Some survivors respond by leaving behind Christianity and the Bible altogether. Some stay and do vital critical work from the intersection of Christian and survivor, including critical biblical interpretation.[12] I have taken a third path: separating my personal faith from Christianity, while retaining – perhaps reclaiming – an imaginative engagement and ambivalent dialogue with the Bible.[13]

Three responses

> [The District Attorney] didn't believe me ... She said to me, 'Julie, I don't think you really know what happened'. That hurt more than the rape.[14]

This section explores three post-crucifixion community responses narrated in the Gospels: Thomas's demand for bodily proof; the awakening of the centurion and spectators at the cross, witnessed by the Galilean women; and the 'touch me not' encounter with Mary at the tomb. I conclude this section by assessing the broad community impact of individual community members' responses. In each case, I apply texts of the living experiences of victims/survivors in the twentieth and twenty-first centuries to enrich the meaning of the biblical text, and I apply the biblical text to sharpen understanding of the significance of comparable twentieth- and twenty-first-century community responses. This interpretive approach has many reference points, but the explicitly bidirectional relationship between biblical and living 'texts' in Stephanie Buckhanon Crowder's *When Momma Speaks: The Bible and Motherhood from a Womanist Perspective* has been especially instructive and aspirational for me.[15] Finally, while my lens as a reader focused most closely on community responses to sexual violence, many of the readings that resulted are relevant to community responses to other kinds of violent trauma.

Demanding Thomas

> But Thomas ... one of the twelve, was not with them when Jesus came. So the other disciples told him, 'We have seen the Lord.' But he said to them, 'Unless I see the mark of the nails in his hands, and put my finger in the mark of the nails and my hand in his side, I will not believe.' (John 20.24–25)

Thomas's demand to see and touch Jesus' wounds is echoed in demands for victims of sexual violence to provide physical proof to corroborate their word. This has a long history in legal requirements and cultural expectations: consider thirteenth-century English jurist Henry de Bracton's dictum that a rape victim must 'display to honest men the injury done to her, the blood and her dress stained with blood, and the tearing of her dress'.[16] In the US, the Model Penal Code (1962) indicated that homicide and burglary convictions could rest on the credible but uncorroborated testimony of one person, but not rape.[17] The corroboration requirement remains in place today; often, like Thomas, it requires corroborative evidence from the victim's body.[18]

'Rape kits' are collections of evidence obtained from a victim's body shortly after an assault. The details of the process vary, but often include plucking hairs from the victim's scalp and pubis; swabbing their mouth, rectum and (when applicable) vagina; and examining and photographing their genitals (externally and internally). It normally takes 3–5 hours. Researchers have observed that a victim's 'willingness to submit' to the rape kit was considered by the authorities in assessing the validity of the victim's case.[19] This assessment was not made based on analysis of the samples – in fact, most of the samples are never sent to a lab for testing. Rather, the authorities regarded the victim as more 'credible' if they demonstrated 'willingness to submit': in other words, if they allowed a stranger to stick swabs and speculums and scopes into their body within hours of being raped.[20]

The civil law of the ancient Roman Empire (under which Jesus was crucified) designated certain people as *infames*, including sex workers, performers and undertakers. *Infames* were effectively prevented from full legal participation: they were not allowed to hold public office, make wills, and – most significantly here – they were not recognized as legitimate witnesses in court. Instead, the testimony of *infames* was only credible if 'validated' under torture.[21] Critics of rape kits have described the process as torture upon torture for victims. One speculates: 'is it trial by ordeal – if she submits she must be telling the truth?'[22] There is ample evidence in the Anglo-American legal literature of the last 300 years that the word of rape victims is regarded as suspect until proven otherwise.[23] In light of this, are contemporary rape victims treated as *infames*?[24]

Thomas's demand could also be read figuratively: to 'touch Jesus' wounds' might also mean peering into Jesus' suffering psyche. This is another kind of credibility-by-ordeal: an advocate reflects, 'Cops will have their own idea of how the situation should be and how the survivor should be acting ... [saying] "If you were really raped you'd be crying right now".'[25] So Mayer writes, 'If you survive, you have to prove it was that bad: or else, they think *you* are ... You have to be permanently *écorchée*, heart-on-sleeve, offering up organs and body parts like a medieval female saint.'[26] Similarly, Jesus' so-called 'offer' to Thomas was reluctant consent, at best.

Despite his nickname, I would argue that the core of Thomas's wrongdoing is not his doubt, but rather his demand. But what exactly is Thomas's demand? Picture the scene in your mind if you can: what do Jesus' wounds look like? How, exactly, does Thomas demand to touch them?

Most likely, the Thomas of your imagination extends his fingertips to lightly touch a wound in the palm of Jesus' hand. Perhaps he might also gently sweep his hand over the wound in Jesus' side. This is what is depicted in much of Christian art, but it is not what was described in the Gospel of John.

Before we explore the precise body mechanics described in the biblical text, it is important to pause and acknowledge the risks and benefits of doing so. There is a persistent myth that gentleness mitigates coercion. If Thomas had demanded to delicately brush his fingertips near Jesus' wound in order to regard Jesus as a reliable witness to his own assault, the coercive element of Thomas's demand and its insult to Jesus' credibility would have remained undiminished. Nevertheless, it is also true that the physical injury of Thomas's touch is often downplayed in representations of this scene, and that in turn is used to downplay the moral injury of Thomas's demand. I hope that the opposite can also be true: that revealing the brutality of Thomas's touch will help to reveal the brutality of demands for victims to offer up their flesh to corroborate their word.

In John 20.25, Thomas describes two ways he demands to touch Jesus. First, he will put his finger into the wounds in Jesus' hands. Into – not 'on' or 'near': the Greek word, *eis*, is a preposition for purposefully entering. In the Gospels, the same expression is used when people enter a city or a boat – or when they are prevented from doing so. It is also used when a harmful spirit or demon invades an unwilling person (Mark 9.25). Most English translations of John 20.25 describe the target of Thomas's touch as the 'mark', 'scar' or 'print' of the nails. This is not inaccurate, but neither is it vivid. The word *typon* is, figuratively, a historical pattern or past precedent; literally, it is the hollow space made when a die is used to stamp a shape into a material. Thomas could have described it as a wound, connoting the raw, sensitive flesh of a living body; instead, his language connotes a prefab mechanical hollowing-out of an inanimate object. Thomas demanded: *let me use my finger to penetrate the tunnel the nails have bored through Jesus' hands*.

Thomas's second demand is similarly invasive. Once again, the touch is penetrative, *into* Jesus' side. However, this time Thomas does not intend to use his finger (*daktylos*), but instead, his hand (*cheira*) – the same word used for Jesus' body part in the previous demand. At the risk of stating the obvious, a hand is larger and clumsier than a finger. It may be that the spear-wound in Jesus' side was already so large that putting Thomas's hand inside did not enlarge it. However, it seems more likely that Thomas's insertion of his hand would have widened and deepened the pre-existing injury.

Thomas's demand is a remarkably literal illustration of how community members' intrusive demands for proof can compound and increase the scope of the harm done to victims. Far from the polite fingertip-brushing offered in much Christian art, Thomas demanded: let me stick my fingers in the hollows made by nails in your hands, let me shove my fist into your torso, offer up your flesh again to prove the truth of your word, and only then will I believe you. For Thomas, Jesus must validate his testimony by submitting his body to an ordeal, not unlike the torture required to validate the testimony of *infames* in Roman civil law. In effect, Jesus is classed as an illegitimate, dishonourable witness to his own assault.[27]

If reading this description provokes outrage on Jesus' behalf, I invite you to redirect that outrage toward supposedly reasonable demands for proof placed on contemporary victims of sexual violence. Reading Thomas's demand in the context of Jesus as a victim of sexual violence calls us to reckon with how community members respond to victims in ways that dishonour them by insisting that they must offer up their body as proof of their credibility. Recall the above-mentioned description of a rape kit as trial by ordeal, and the study that found that authorities were more likely to perceive a victim to be credible if she 'submitted' to a rape kit. Recall also So Mayer's above-mentioned reflection on the requirements for community acceptance: if you survive, you have to be forever *écorchée*, skin metaphorically peeled back in order to 'prove it was bad, or else they think you are [bad]'. When a community demands that a victim submit to painful intimate ordeals in order to be a credible witness to their own violation, the community has surely discounted their honour.

Ignorance and the centurion

> When the centurion saw what had taken place, he praised God and said, 'Certainly this man was innocent.' And when all the crowds who had gathered there for this spectacle saw what had taken place, they returned home, beating their breasts. But all his acquaintances, including the women who had followed him from Galilee, stood at a distance, watching these things. (Luke 23.47–49)

Not long ago, the Philadelphia police department openly joked that its sex crimes division was the 'lying bitch unit'.[28] Today, the language might be more polite, but similar attitudes toward rape victims remain. This section will explore ignorance and belated awakening in the centurion's realization, which appears in all three Synoptic Gospels (Matt. 27.54–56; Mark 15.39–41; Luke 23.47–49). The centurion's statement in Luke, 'this man was innocent', amounts to recognizing that Jesus was wrongfully condemned for falsehood and blasphemy. Jesus was not a 'lying bitch' after all. Too often, contemporary 'centurions' recognize the validity of complaints of sexual violence done by a usually white, powerful man only after multiple victims have come forward.

When the 'centurions' finally recognize it, the eruption of public outcry against the perpetrator – Daniel Holtzclaw, Larry Nassar, Bill Cosby,

Roger Ailes, Harvey Weinstein, or, sadly, many others – resembles the displays of grief by crucifixion spectators (Luke 23.48). The first-century crowds beat their breasts, and twenty-first-century crowds take to social media to 'process' their astonishment. Meanwhile, some are more like the Galilean women who knew all along, who had provided care all along (Matt. 27.55; Mark 15.41), who 'stood at a distance, watching' as the 'mainstream' media finally recognized some of violence in their reality.

Both the centurion and Thomas illustrate *epistemic* failures of community responses – perceiving a victim to be untrustworthy by default, maintaining wilful ignorance, and imposing frameworks for understanding that 'rig the game' against the victim. How should we respond when we, like the centurion, suddenly recognize something that we should have already known? Although the present chapter focuses on sexual violence, critical work in epistemology reveals similar patterns of ignorance in many spheres. An umbrella category that I would call 'power-based ignorance' could include white ignorance, men's ignorance, straight ignorance, cis ignorance, and many other ways that a person in a relative position of power might persist in harmful ignorance. Often this ignorance is maintained in spite of ample opportunities to learn; sometimes, a person (or institution) deliberately preserves their ignorance, perhaps to avoid accepting responsibility.

Philosopher George Yancy provides the metaphor of 'ambushed by whiteness' to describe white people's awakening to their white ignorance, with particular reference to white people committed to anti-racist behaviour who are caught off guard by recognizing yet another way that they (we) are ensnared by white supremacist patterns of thought and action. Yancy analyses this 'ambush' and possible responses by white people: if white people bring curiosity to experiences of ambush, they might have profound experiences of 'rich uncertainty', instructive about 'the insidious nature of whiteness' in a way that is 'valuable to growth, not a sign of defeat'.[29]

Power-based ignorance is sustained by discrediting or dismissing people whose knowledge would threaten the maintenance of that ignorance – especially people with less structural power. The centurion's ignorance did not persist because of a lack of 'exposure' to the possibility that Jesus was innocent; he had *heard* it, but he did not *heed* it until much too late.

In a reflective essay, Damon Young unveiled his internal monologue when listening to his wife – 'she's overreacting', 'it's not that serious' – and assessed it: 'I assume that her emotional reaction to a situation is disproportionate to my opinion of what level of emotional reaction the situation calls for. Basically, if she's on eight, I assume the situation is really a six.' Young critiqued his response, reflected on its context, and connected it to a broader social pattern of distrusting women:

> This is part of the reason why it took an entire high school football team full of women for some of us to finally just *consider* that Bill Cosby might not be Cliff Huxtable. It's how, despite hearing complaints about it from

girlfriends, homegirls, cousins, wives, and classmates, so many of us refused to believe how serious street harassment can be until we saw it with our own eyes. It's why we needed to see actual video evidence before believing the things women had been saying for *years* about R. Kelly.[30]

While people of all genders are victimized by sexual violence, it is significant that Young connects pervasive patterns of doubting women to pervasive patterns of doubting victims of sexual violence. Young acknowledges the need for structural and personal responses: larger misogynistic structures need to be dismantled, but he can still make immediate changes to his individual behaviour – such as heeding his wife's assessment of her 'level eight' situation rather than transposing it to 'level six'.

Critic Rich Smith reflected on how reading *The Incest Diary*, a recent anonymous memoir by a survivor of sexual violence, shattered his ignorance. Smith's description of how his psyche 'seized' and 'creaked' as he read recalls the earth-shaking that immediately preceded the centurion's realization. Interrogating the 'ridiculous uncertainty that surrounds reports of rape and abuse' with reference to the experiences of father–daughter incest described in the memoir, Smith speculated: 'some people simply cannot believe that one human being could be so terrible to another human being. Such acts are too uncomfortable to consider.'[31] Smith quoted Ariel Levy: 'much of society is set up specifically to assist people in ignoring the horrors of the world'.

In the early Christian writer Justin Martyr's *Dialogue with Trypho*, the sceptical interlocutor understands that Jesus had to suffer like a sacrificial lamb, but is stupefied that he would 'be crucified and die with so much shame and indecency', saying, 'we cannot even bring ourselves to think of it'.[32] This is a nearly exact parallel of Smith's language, above – the disbelief stems from their horror of human wrongdoing 'too uncomfortable to consider'.

Two centuries after Justin, Aphrahat briefly indicated that the Scriptures remain silent about some of the most disgraceful abuses Jesus suffered: 'For they added to [Jesus] many things which were not written about him: curses and abuses which not even the scripture can reveal, for their abuses were odious.'[33] Aphrahat's comment spotlights the 'silences' in the crucifixion narratives. These silences have played a significant role in previous scholarly writing on the crucifixion of Jesus as sexual violence. As David Tombs summarizes, 'a question mark needs to be put against the completeness of the Gospel narratives at this point. There is a possibility that the full details of Jesus' suffering are missing from the Gospel accounts.'[34]

No act is inherently unthinkable, unbelievable or unspeakable; there is always a would-be thinker, believer or speaker. When we reflect on Smith's assessment of *The Incest Diary*, we must ask: *for whom* is parental incest too horrible to believe? When we read Justin Martyr and Aphrahat, we must ask, *for whom* was the shame Jesus endured unthinkable? *For whom* is it better for the Scriptures to keep silent about the most odious abuses to Jesus' person? Did the Galilean women at the cross find it impossible to believe that the occupying Roman Empire was capable of torture, humiliation and violation of Judaean bodies, even before they witnessed Jesus' crucifixion? Somehow, I doubt it.

Applying recent work in epistemology illuminates the significance of the silent witness of the Galilean women. Kristie Dotson cautions her fellow philosophers to remember that a gap in 'dominant' hermeneutical resources – resources for making meaning and constructing knowledge – is not indicative of a gap in *all* hermeneutical resources.[35] In other words, just because libraries, schools, law courts or other empowered arbiters of 'truth' and 'knowledge' do not know something does not mean that it is not known. The centurion's belated, publicly acknowledged realization contrasts with the Galilean women's quiet prior knowledge. Some of the contemporary heirs of the Galilean women are the vibrant, unofficial networks that provide care for victims/survivors (often where survivors draw on expertise from lived experience to care for each other) in contrast to 'official' channels that sometimes do more harm than good.

In this section, I have called attention to additional epistemic issues in community responses. The story of the centurion illustrates power-based ignorance, considers the social structures that uphold such ignorance, and suggests some ways a person might respond ethically to belated realizations. The parallels of Aphrahat and Justin Martyr to Rich Smith and other twenty-first-century writers who comment on how acts of rape, abuse and violence are popularly imagined as 'unspeakable' and 'unthinkable' invite a question too seldom asked: *who* finds this unspeakable and unthinkable? Who is assumed to be doing this speaking and thinking? The significance of the Galilean women merits further analysis, but reading their silent, knowing witness through the lens of Kristie Dotson's theory of marginalized hermeneutical resources reminds us that power-based ignorance is never universal. Community responses that would honour survivors must include honouring survivors' knowledge, not least their hard-earned expertise through experience, distinctive frameworks for understanding and, especially, the various standards survivors have for what is 'thinkable' and 'speakable'.

'Touch me not'

> Jesus saith unto her [Mary] 'Touch me not; for I am not yet ascended to my Father: but go to my brethren, and say unto them, I ascend unto my Father, and your father, and to my God, and your God.' (John 20.17 KJV)

This section draws on Jesus' 'touch me not' to discuss navigation of touch in close relationships among survivors of sexual violence. Readers may notice that this quotation uses the King James Version. The NRSV preserves the nuances of the original Greek *haptou*, 'hold on' or 'cling'. However, as Jean-Luc Nancy writes in his analysis of the cultural significance of this moment, the vision of *noli me tangere* (Vulgate) has anchored itself into many Christian and Christian-influenced imaginations: 'touch' matters, even if it departs from the exact sense of the original text.[36]

Nancy imagines *noli me tangere* as a 'desperate' warning about a 'point of rupture' that, if touched, would 'shatter' Jesus.[37] Nancy does not discuss this in terms of trauma, but his language nevertheless recalls how touch can be a trigger for survivors of embodied trauma, including sexual violence: a friendly touch in the present day can reactivate a vivid traumatic memory. Jesus' 'touch me not' is spoken in the immediate aftermath of several kinds of traumatic body experience. These include sexual violence and torture, which are unfortunately well known as traumatic body experiences where a survivor may be triggered by touch. These also include dying, descending into hell and being resurrected – undoubtedly traumatic body experiences as well, although harder for humans to comprehend.

Mary's role in this encounter has often been connected with the Shulamite woman in the Song of Solomon, who sought out her lover and 'held him and would not let him go' (Songs 3.4). Hippolytus was among the first commentators to make this connection, writing in the early third century. However, Hippolytus went on to praise Mary for persisting to touch Jesus despite his resistance: 'O blessed woman, who did not wish to be separated from Christ!'[38] Envisioning Mary forcing her touch on Jesus is especially distressing if Jesus' 'do not touch me' is read as the self-protective boundary of a victim of traumatic touch. In a contemporary context where some Christians inflict 'corrective rape' on lesbian, gay, queer, asexual, and trans and gender non-conforming community members, praising Mary for persisting in touching Jesus when Jesus says 'do not touch me' is especially dangerous.[39]

However, the Shulamite actually promotes consent as a framework for passionate desire. In the very next verse, the Shulamite admonishes the 'daughters of Jerusalem': 'do not stir up or awaken love until it is ready!' (Songs 3.5). Concluding with this admonition is perhaps a reminder of a lover's responsibility to respect consent: yes, pursue the one you desire, sweep him off his feet – as long as he's into it. This, too, could be read in dialogue with the encounter between Mary and Jesus: Mary reaching out to embrace Jesus and then pulling back to honour Jesus' 'touch me not' would be aligned with the Shulamite's ethic of boldness-with-consent.

'Touch me not' – in more contemporary terms, 'don't touch me' – can be seen as a deficit, something to 'fix' or apologize for. Jean-Luc Nancy resists this by romanticizing a mutual non-touching love between Jesus and Mary, 'these lovers take pleasure in one another by leaving one another'.[40] While the idea of romance without touch is valuable, there are flaws in applying it here. When Jesus says 'don't touch me', Mary heeds him, but that does not mean that she 'takes pleasure' in not touching him – it simply means she is not compounding the violations to Jesus' bodily autonomy.

Yet Nancy frames it as a mutual pleasure, as if the pleasure of respecting your beloved's boundaries is equal to the pleasure of satisfying your own yearnings. Nancy's reading falls short of romance because it discounts Mary's desire.

Is there a way for 'don't touch me' to be part of a love story – a love story that neither subordinates the leading woman's desire to touch, nor constructs the leading man's 'don't touch me' as a kind of brokenness to be 'fixed'? Queer ways of touching and being touched may be useful here. 'Stone' is often associated with 'stone butch'; however, stone sexualities do not exclusively belong to butch identities. People who are stone might choose not to receive genital stimulation, might avoid being naked with a partner, and might even avoid receiving touch altogether; in effect, you can be sexually intimate while maintaining a 'don't touch me' boundary. Stone experiences are nuanced, varied, historically rooted and impossible to summarize in a two-sentence introduction. If stone sexualities are new to you, begin by pondering how 'Don't touch me' is not identical to 'I won't touch you'. Try thinking of stone sexuality as more about touching someone else than being touched.

Affirming stone sexuality does not require ignoring or hiding the ways it might be shaped by sexual trauma. It simply focuses on description, rather than etiology. This can be profoundly liberatory. As Xan West reflects:

When I first allowed myself to accept that I was stone, and have sex from a place that honoured that, it was like I was on a whole new playing field. My boundaries were clear and inviolable and that meant that I was more deeply in my body and my desire than I was able to be before. I remember my entire body feeling electric.[41]

As with any attribute, not everyone desires a stone partner – but compatibility does not define validity. Imagining Jesus as stone resists constructing 'don't touch me' as a problem to be fixed without assuming that *Mary* will be perfectly satisfied with a stone partner (or, worse, that Mary's desires are irrelevant).

What does Mary desire? In John, it remains unclear. Other Gospels offer angles on Mary that emphasize her post-crucifixion experiences of touching and being touched: in the gospel that bears Mary's name, her first act after Jesus ascends to heaven is to embrace the other disciples before giving them counsel; in Pistis Sophia, she 'springs toward' Salome to embrace her (Mary 9:12–14; Pistis Sophia 338:15–17).[42] One intriguing speculation – which merits further consideration – is that Mary was a survivor of sexual violence herself. It is far from improbable, unfortunately, and it offers another dimension to this reading. Survivors represent a tremendous diversity of attitudes toward touch: one might say 'don't touch me' while another might have a profound need to touch and be touched. When we do not erase what Mary wants and needs, we are able to approach some of the challenges and nuances that survivors navigate in intimate partnerships with each other.

While there has been limited scope for this in the present chapter, survivor/survivor relationships – intimate and otherwise – are a vital element of this conversation. At the risk of stating the obvious, communities include survivors, and so some members of a community responding to a victim/survivor *are* survivors. We who are victims/survivors can draw on the honour with which we regard Jesus as part of coming to regard *ourselves* and *each other* as worthy of honour. Locating Jesus as a victim among victims may elevate our sense of shared belonging. At the same time, the obvious differences between the Gospel narratives of Jesus and the experiences of twentieth- and twenty-first-century victims/survivors may also aid us in recognizing the particularities of each victim/survivor's experience in our own time and guard against eliding the other social identities, contexts and structures that shape their whole experiences as victims/survivors.

The topic of relationships between and among survivors requires further consideration, and the encounter between Mary and Jesus may provide further insights. For now, I hope that this reading of the encounter between Mary and Jesus offers some reference points for navigating the immense complexities of touch (and not-touch) in relationships that include at least one victim/survivor. This reading affirms an ethical commitment to consent, recognizes the power of touch, and acknowledges the realities of unsatisfied desire. Mary is not required to be pleased by Jesus' 'don't touch me' in order to honour his bodily autonomy; nor are we required to relegate Mary's desire in order to validate Jesus' boundaries.

Community responses, community impact

There may be a temptation to consider these one-on-one encounters as 'private matters', with an effect only on the victim and the few community members involved. However, just as an act of violence impacts victim and community alike, an individual community member's response to a victim of violence can impact the community as a whole. Just as Jesus' unambiguously wronged and inarguably honourable position spotlights the normalized dishonour of contemporary victims of sexual violence, Jesus' obvious importance in his community sharpens our awareness of the broader impact of one member's response.

John 20 narrates the encounter with Mary and the encounter with Thomas. In Lynne St Clair Darden's womanist-postcolonial reading of John 20, she observed that Jesus forbids Mary to touch him, but 'the same is not true for the male disciples'.[43] For Darden, Jesus' forbidding Mary to touch him, and then receiving touch from Thomas and other male disciples, signals a troubling distribution of authority. Mary's leadership is momentarily affirmed but later disregarded by the community of the disciples. As Darden's article discusses, the male disciples cite Jesus' (so-called) offer for Thomas to touch his wounds, in the presence of other male disciples, as an indication of their greater leadership and intimate access to Jesus. In parallel, Mary's non-touching of Jesus indicated she was kept at a greater distance and thus a lower level of authority. Darden considers how this continued to be used to define men's authority as greater than women's within the emerging community of disciples.

This testifies to how individual harmful responses to a victim – however understandable or well intentioned – can have far-reaching effects in a community. Yes, Thomas was allowed to touch Jesus – because Thomas demanded it. Surely it would be illegitimate for Thomas (or other men) to cite Jesus' reluctant permission as an endorsement of their leadership. Yet this is all too familiar – a Thomas gets a Jesus to give in to their demands, and then uses that to elevate their authority above a Mary. This then increases the concentration of power in people who have learned that demands yield results, and they continue the cycle. In effect, the 'blast radius' of an act of sexual violence includes not only the victim's trauma, but also how community members compound the harm; and how that may shape a community's problematic constructions of authority, relationship and honour.

Conclusion

Accountability and honour

Early in this chapter I discussed how, unlike with most victims of violence, we do not scrutinize Jesus' behaviour to discount the harm done to him. Nobody suggests that we should try to 'see both sides of the story'; Jesus was inarguably wronged and unambiguously worthy of honour. Reading Jesus as a victim among victims can inform our assessments of our own responses to victims among us – which I hope can move towards what Judith Herman described as doing honour to victims/survivors. However, Jesus' narrative does create a barrier to discussing one important aspect of honour: accountability.

Jesus is typically envisioned as sinless and blameless – and the discussion of alternatives to that is far outside the scope of the present chapter. Moreover, Jesus' narrative on earth ends with the ascension, 40 days at most after the resurrection. The Gospel narratives of the aftermath of the crucifixion are important, but ultimately brief. Jesus' narrative has no need – and no opportunity – to discuss the complex challenge of community responses that show compassion and honour to victims/survivors by holding them (us) accountable when they (we) do harm.

When we talk about contemporary victims/survivors as full participants in communities, we need to consider how a community responds in the immediate aftermath of violence, but also the long-range experience of survivors as part of a community. Jesus' story offers excellent lessons for the former and none for the latter. The rest of us do not have the narrative convenience of the end of a book, nor the extraordinary power to ascend into a cloud. Life (usually) goes on, often for a long while. Responsibility, justice and atonement are part of full participation in a community; including survivors as full members of a community means holding us accountable when we do harm. This is particularly significant if a survivor becomes a perpetrator of similar violence to what was inflicted on them, but it is relevant to all forms of harm. Although this is not possible to discuss in the present chapter, it is important to acknowledge that community responses to survivors must include holding survivors to standards of honour.

Honour to victims/honour to Jesus

Throughout this chapter, I have made use of Judith Herman's framework of community responses that honour – or dishonour – victims. Jesus is a rare figure consistently envisioned both as a victim of violence and as a person worthy of honour. Reading post-crucifixion encounters where Jesus' community dishonoured him after he was victimized spotlights the dishonour normalized in contemporary community responses to victims. This matters to everyone: an original act of violence not only harms the victim but also impacts their community, and likewise, harmful responses not only compound the harm done to a victim, but also reverberate through the whole community.

To conclude, I would return to Matthew 25.31–46. Shortly before the crucifixion narrative begins, the Gospel portrays Jesus teaching in the form of a philosophical dialogue between three parties: the discerning king of heaven, the righteous and the accursed. The king acknowledges the righteous (vv. 35–36),

> For I was hungry and you gave me food, I was thirsty and you gave me something to drink, I was a stranger and you welcomed me, I was naked and you gave me clothing, I was sick and you took care of me, I was in prison and you visited me.

When the hearers do not understand, the king explains that whatever they did to care for 'the least of these who are members of my family' – the hungry, the strangers, the sick, the incarcerated, and so on – they did for him. Similarly, the 'accursed' are those who failed to care for these vulnerable siblings.

It is sobering and instructive to consider how contemporary community responses resemble dishonourable responses from Jesus' community members. Whenever we demand physical evidence, descriptive details or emotional performances as a condition of regarding victims as credible witnesses to their own violation, we shove our hands into the wound in Jesus' torso. Whenever we try to 'see both sides' and empathize with perpetrators of state violence, we are empathizing with the Roman imperial authorities who crucified Jesus. Whenever we finally take violence seriously after dozens of victims have testified, we are the centurion who realized, too late, that Jesus was not lying after all. Whenever we say that an act of violence is 'unspeakable' or 'unthinkable', we are Aphrahat and Justin Martyr, erasing from the written record the 'odious abuses' done to Jesus' body. Whenever we reward coercion with power, we are the male disciples who elevate Thomas over Mary, multiplying the harmful effects of community responses into an unimaginably long future.

On the other hand, whenever we know the truth and care for one another as best we can, we resemble the Galilean women at the cross – grieving and unsurprised, for whom odious abuses to a Galilean body are all too speakable and thinkable. Whenever we hold our own desires in check and respect the boundaries of the people we love, we are Mary, longing to embrace Jesus and yet heeding his 'don't touch me'. Perhaps most invisibly and most importantly, whenever we resist any of the actions in the previous paragraph, we intervene in the narrative – we help to prevent Thomas, the centurion, the male disciples, from compounding the original harm. Just as we honour Jesus as a victim of violence, we can honour ourselves and each other.

References

Ahmed, Sara, 'Orientations: Toward a Queer Phenomenology', *GLQ: A Journal of Lesbian and Gay Studies* 12:4 (2006), pp. 543–74.

Akhtar, Leena, 'From Masochists to Traumatized Victims: Psychiatry, Law, and the Feminist Anti-Rape Movement of the 1970s', doctoral dissertation, Harvard University, Graduate School of Arts & Sciences, 2017, https://dash.harvard.edu/handle/1/42061501.

Anderson, Michelle J., 'The Legacy of the Prompt Complaint Requirement, Corroboration Requirement, and Cautionary Instructions on Campus Sexual Assault', *Working Paper Series: Villanova University School of Law* 20 (2004), https://digitalcommons.law.villanova.edu/wps/art20.

Aphrahat, *Demonstrations*, vol. 2., trans. Kuriakose Valavanolickal, Kerala, India: St. Ephrem Ecumenical Research Institute (SEERI), 2005.

Bernheimer, Kate, *xo Orpheus: Fifty New Myths*, New York: Penguin, 2013.

Boff, Clodovis, *Theology and Praxis: Epistemological Foundations*, trans. R. R. Barr, Maryknoll, NY: Orbis Books, 1987.

Bowman, Jeffrey A., 2003, 'Infamy and Proof in Medieval Spain', in *Fama: The Politics of Talk and Reputation in Medieval Europe*, Thelma Fenster and Daniel Lord Smail eds, Ithaca & London: Cornell University Press, 2003, pp. 95–117.

Brown, Jericho, *The New Testament*, Port Townsend, WA: Copper Canyon Press, 2014.

——, *The Tradition*, Port Townsend, WA: Copper Canyon Press, 2019.

Butler, Judith, *Antigone's Claim*, New York: Columbia University Press, 2002.

Chemaly, Soraya, 'How Police Still Fail Rape Victims', *Rolling Stone*, 16 August 2016, www.rollingstone.com/culture/culture-features/how-police-still-fail-rape-victims-97782/.

Coleman, Monica, *The Dinah Project*, Eugene, OR: Wipf & Stock, 2004.

Coyote, 'Tapping at Stone: Me and a Stone (a)sexuality', *The Ace Theist*, 28 January 2018, https://theacetheist.wordpress.com/2018/01/28/tapping-at-stone-me-a-stone-asexuality/.

Crockett, Emily, 'Rape and Sexual Assault are Common. So Why Don't We Believe Victims?' *Vox*, 17 Oct 2016, www.vox.com/2016/5/1/11538748/believe-rape-victims.

Crowder, Stephanie Buckhanon, *When Momma Speaks: The Bible and Motherhood from a Womanist Perspective*, Louisville, KY: Westminster John Knox Press, 2016.

Darden, Lynne St. Clair, 'A Womanist-Postcolonial Reading of the Samaritan Woman at the Well and Mary Magdalene at the Tomb', in *I Found God in Me: A Womanist Biblical Hermeneutics Reader*, Mitzi J. Smith ed., Eugene, OR: Wipf & Stock, 2015.

Davis, Shauna, 'Sexual Assault Detectives' Justifications for Aggressive Victim Interviewing Methods: A Qualitative Study', PhD dissertation, University of Nevada at Las Vegas, 2013, https://digitalscholarship.unlv.edu/cgi/viewcontent.cgi?article=2819&context=thesesdissertations.

Delap, Lucy, '"Disgusting Details Which Are Best Forgotten": Disclosures of Child Sexual Abuse in Twentieth-Century Britain', *Journal of British Studies* 57:1 (2018), pp. 79–107.

Doe, Jane, 'Who Benefits from the Sexual Assault Evidence Kit?', in *Sexual Assault in Canada: Law, Legal Practice and Women's Activism*, Elizabeth A. Sheehy, ed., Ottawa: University of Ottawa Press, 2012, pp. 357–88, https://books.open edition.org/uop/577?lang=en.

Dotson, Kristie, 'A Cautionary Tale: On Limiting Epistemic Oppression', *Frontiers: A Journal of Women Studies* 33:1 (2012), pp. 24–47.

—, 'Conceptualizing Epistemic Oppression', *Social Epistemology* 28:2 (2014), pp. 115–38.

Du Mont, Janice, and Deborah Parnis, 'Constructing Bodily Evidence through Sexual Assault Evidence Kits', *Griffith Law Review* 10:1 (2001), pp. 63–76.

Du Mont, Janice, D. White and Margaret McGregor, 'Investigating the Medical Forensic Examination from the Perspectives of Sexually Assaulted Women', *Social Science & Medicine* 68:4 (2009), pp. 774–80.

Edwards, Katie, and David Tombs, '#HimToo – Why Jesus Should be Recognised as a Victim of Sexual Abuse', *The Conversation*, 23 March 2018, https://theconversation.com/himtoo-why-jesus-should-be-recognised-as-a-victim-of-sexual-violence-93677.

Feinberg, Leslie, *Stone Butch Blues*, Ithaca, NY: Firebrand Books, 1993.

Feldberg, Georgina, 'Defining the Facts of Rape: The Uses of Medical Evidence in Sexual Assault Trials', *Canadian Journal of Women and the Law* 9:1 (1997), pp. 90–114.

Figueroa, Rocío and David Tombs, 'Recognising Jesus as a Victim of Sexual Abuse: Responses from Sodalicio Survivors in Peru', Project Report, Centre for Theology and Public Issues, University of Otago, 2019.

Freire, Paulo, *Pedagogy of Hope*, New York: Continuum, 2007.

Gafney, Wil, 'Crucifixion and Sexual Violence', *The Huffington Post*, 28 May 2013, www.huffpost.com/entry/crucifixion-and-sexual-violence_b_2965369.

—, *Womanist Midrash: A Reintroduction to the Women of the Torah and the Throne*, Louisville, KY: Westminster John Knox Press, 2017.

Godfrey, Chris, 'We Were Sent to Conversion Therapy for Being Gay', *Dazed*, 24

Nov 2016, www.dazeddigital.com/artsandculture/article/33814/1/gay-lgbt-con version-therapy-politics-america.

Heath, Elaine A., *We Were the Least of These: Reading the Bible with Survivors of Sexual Abuse*, Grand Rapids, MI: Brazos, 2011.

Herman, Judith, *Trauma and Recovery*, New York: Basic Books, 1997.

—, 'Justice from the Victim's Perspective', *Violence Against Women* 11:5 (2005), pp. 571–602.

Hinton, Devon E., and Byron J. Good, *Culture and PTSD: Trauma in Global and Historical Perspective*, Philadelphia, PA: University of Pennsylvania Press, 2015.

Hunter-Gault, Charlayne, 'Violated Hopes', *The New Yorker*, 28 May 2012, www. newyorker.com/magazine/2012/05/28/violated-hopes.

Inter-American Commission on Human Rights, *Violence Against Lesbian, Gay, Bisexual, Trans, and Intersex Persons in the Americas*, 2015, www.oas.org/en/ iachr/reports/pdfs/ViolenceLGBTIPersons.pdf.

Junior, Nyasha, *An Introduction to Womanist Biblical Interpretation*, Louisville, KY: Westminster John Knox Press, 2015.

Justin Martyr, *Dialogue with Trypho*, trans. Marcus Dods and George Reith, Ante-Nicene Fathers 1, reprint, Grand Rapids, MI: Eerdmans, 1986.

—, *Dialogue avec Tryphon*, Philippe Bobichon trans. and ed., 2 vols, Fribourg, Switzerland: Fribourg Academic Press, 2003.

Kahf, Mohja, *Hagar Poems*, Fayetteville, AR: University of Arkansas Press, 2016.

Lamptey, Jerusha Tanner, *Divine Words, Female Voices: Muslima Explorations in Comparative Feminist Theology*, Oxford: Oxford University Press, 2018.

LeGuin, Ursula K, *Lavinia*, New York: Houghton Mifflin Harcourt, 2008.

McGregor, Margaret, and Grace Le, 'Examination for Sexual Assault: Is the Documentation of Physical Injury Associated with the Laying of Charges? A Retrospective Cohort Study', *Canadian Medical Association Journal* 160:11 (1999), pp. 1565–9.

McGregor, Margaret, Janice Du Mont and Terri L. Myhr, 'Sexual Assault Forensic Medical Evidence: Is Evidence Related to Successful Prosecution?', *Annals of Emergency Medicine* 39:6 (2002), pp. 639–47.

MacLaughlin, Nina, *Wake, Siren: Ovid Resung*, New York: Farrar, Straus, and Giroux, 2019.

Manne, Kate, 'Brett Kavanaugh and America's "Himpathy" Reckoning', *The New York Times*, 26 September 2018, www.nytimes.com/2018/09/26/opinion/ brett-kavanaugh-hearing-himpathy.html.

Marjanen, Antti, *The Woman Jesus Loved: Mary Magdalene in the Nag Hammadi Library and Related Documents*, Leiden: Brill, 1996.

Mayer, So, 'Floccinaucinihilipilification', in *Not That Bad: Dispatches from Rape Culture*, Roxane Gay ed., London: Atlantic Books, 2018.

Mendos, Lucas Ramón, *Curbing Deception: A World Survey on Legal Regulation of So-called 'Conversion Therapies'*, Geneva: ILGA World, 2020, https://ilga.org/ downloads/ ILGA_World_Curbing_Deception_world_survey_legal_restrictions_ conversion_therapy.pdf.

Miller, Madeline, *Circe*, New York: Little, Brown & Co., 2018.

Nair, Karthika, *Until the Lions: Echoes from the Mahabharata*, Todmorden, Lancashire: Arc Publications, 2016.

Nancy, Jean-Luc, *Noli me tangere: On the Raising of the Body*, Sarah Clift, Pascale-Anne Brault and Michael Naas, trans, New York: Fordham University Press, 2008.

Nguyen, Martin, *Modern Muslim Theology: Engaging God and the World with Faith and Imagination*, Lanham, MD: Rowman & Littlefield, 2019.

Piepzna-Samarasinha and Leah Lakshmi, 'What it Feels Like When it Finally Comes: Surviving Incest in Real Life' in *Yes Means Yes: Visions of Female Sexual Power & a World Without Rape*, Jaclyn Friedman and Jessica Valenti, eds, Berkeley, CA: Seal Press, 2008.

Reaves, Jayme R., and David Tombs, '#MeToo Jesus: Naming Jesus as a Victim of Sexual Abuse', *International Journal of Public Theology* 13:4 (2019), pp. 387–412.

Schüssler Fiorenza, Elisabeth, *Bread Not Stone: The Challenge of Feminist Biblical Interpretation*, Boston, MA: Beacon Press, 1995.

——, *Empowering Memory and Movement: Thinking and Working Across Borders*, Minneapolis, MN: Fortress Press, 2014.

Shamsie, Kamila, *Home Fire*, New York: Riverhead Books, 2017.

Smith, Mitzi J., 'Fashioning our Own Souls: A Womanist Reading of the Virgin–Whore Binary in Matthew and Revelation', in *I Found God in Me: A Womanist Biblical Hermeneutics Reader*, Mitzi J. Smith ed., Eugene, OR: Wipf & Stock, 2015.

Smith, Rich, '*The Incest Diary* Afflicted Me with as Much Trauma as the Written Word Can Transfer from One Body to Another', *The Stranger*, 19 July 2017, www.thestranger.com/books/2017/07/19/25304800/the-incest-diary-afflicted-me-with-as-much-trauma-as-the-written-word-can-transfer-from-one-body-to-another.

Smith, Shanell, *The Woman Babylon and the Marks of Empire: Reading Revelation with a Postcolonial Womanist Hermeneutics of Ambivalence*, Minneapolis, MN: Fortress Press, 2014.

Smith, Yancy Warren, 'Hippolytus' Commentary on the Song of Songs in Social and Critical Context', PhD Dissertation, Texas Christian University, 2009, https://pdfs.semanticscholar.org/0087/dda6e68baf5dfe2f6f1c362490539e28a09c.pdf.

Stroop, Chrissy, and Lauren O'Neal, eds, *Empty the Pews: Stories of Leaving the Church*, Indianapolis, IN: Epiphany Publishing, 2019.

Sullivan, Shannon, and Nancy Tuana, eds, *Race and Epistemologies of Ignorance*, SUNY Press, 2007.

Tombs, David, 'Crucifixion, State Terror, and Sexual Abuse', *Union Seminary Quarterly Review* 53:1–2 (1999), pp. 89–109.

Trainor, Michael, *The Body of Jesus and Sexual Abuse: How the Gospel Passion Narrative Informs a Pastoral Approach*, Eugene, OR: Wipf & Stock, 2014.

Tuerkheimer, Deborah, 'Incredible Women: Sexual Violence and the Credibility Discount', *University of Pennsylvania Law Review* 166:1 (2017), pp. 1–58.

West, Xan, 'Stone Dynamics: Where Pleasure Resides', *Kink Praxis*, 2014, https://xanwest.wordpress.com/2014/07/05/stone-dynamics-where-pleasure-resides/.

Wolf, Christa, *Cassandra: A Novel and Four Essays*, Jan Van Heuck trans., New York: Farrar, Strauss, and Giroux, 1988.

Yancy, George, *Black Bodies, White Gazes: The Continuing Significance of Race*, Lanham: Rowman and Littlefield, 2008.

Yap, Audrey, 'Credibility Excess and the Social Imaginary in Cases of Sexual Assault', *Feminist Philosophy Quarterly* 3:4 (2017), pp. 1–24.

Young, Damon, 'Men Just Don't Trust Women. And This is a Problem', *The Root*, 16 December 2014, https://verysmartbrothas.theroot.com/men-just-dont-trust-women-and-this-is-a-problem-1822523100.

Notes

1 This chapter is built on an understanding of Jesus' crucifixion as a form of sexual violence. David Tombs proposed the essential foundations for this in a 1999 article that set the texts of the Gospels in the context of historical evidence about crucifixion in the Roman Empire and in relation to how military, police and other people with state power have used terror and torture in the twentieth and early twenty-first centuries. Many other scholars have advanced our understanding of Jesus as a victim of sexual violence in the intervening two decades; the volume that this chapter is a contribution to is yet another step in that process. I intentionally will not reiterate these arguments; instead, I simply accept this as a starting point. David Tombs, 'Crucifixion, State Terror, and Sexual Abuse', *Union Seminary Quarterly Review* 53:1–2 (1999), pp. 89–109; Jayme R. Reaves and David Tombs, '#MeToo Jesus: Naming Jesus as a Victim of Sexual Abuse', *International Journal of Public Theology* 13:4 (2019), pp. 387–412; Wil Gafney, 'Crucifixion and Sexual Violence', *The Huffington Post*, 28 March 2013, www.huffpost.com/entry/crucifixion-and-sexual-violence_b_2965369; Rocío Figueroa and David Tombs, 'Recognising Jesus as a Victim of Sexual Abuse: Responses from Sodalicio Survivors in Peru', *Religion and Gender* 10:1 (June 2020), pp. 57–75; Elaine A. Heath, *We Were the Least of These: Reading the Bible with Survivors of Sexual Abuse* (Grand Rapids, MI: Brazos, 2011); Katie Edwards and David Tombs, '#HimToo – Why Jesus Should be Recognised as a Victim of Sexual Abuse', *The Conversation*, 23 March 2018, https://theconversation.com/himtoo-why-jesus-should-be-recognised-as-a-victim-of-sexual-violence-93677; Michael Trainor, *The Body of Jesus and Sexual Abuse: How the Gospel Passion Narrative Informs a Pastoral Approach* (Eugene, OR: Wipf & Stock, 2014).

2 In this chapter, I use 'victim/survivor' as an umbrella term, and will use 'victim' and 'survivor' to accentuate different aspects of experience.

3 While this chapter focuses on sexual violence, many of the issues in this chapter are relevant to victims/survivors of violence in many forms, including but not limited to sexual violence.

4 Judith Herman, 'Justice from the Victim's Perspective', *Violence Against Women* 11:5 (2005), p. 574.

5 Herman, 'Justice from the Victim's Perspective', p. 599.

6 See www.enfleshed.com.

7 Sara Ahmed, 'Orientations: Toward a Queer Phenomenology', *GLQ: A Journal of Lesbian and Gay Studies* 12:4 (2006), p. 569.

8 Judith Butler, *Antigone's Claim* (New York: Columbia University Press, 2002); Christa Wolf, *Cassandra: A Novel and Four Essays*, trans. Jan Van Heuck (New York: Farrar, Strauss, and Giroux, 1988); Kamila Shamsie, *Home Fire* (New York: Riverhead Books, 2017); Madeline Miller, *Circe* (New York: Little, Brown & Co., 2018); Nina MacLaughlin, *Wake, Siren: Ovid Resung* (New York: Farrar, Straus, and Giroux, 2019).

9 Karthika Nair, *Until the Lions: Echoes from the Mahabharata* (Todmodern, West Yorkshire: Arc Publications, 2016); Mohja Kahf, *Hagar Poems* (Fayetteville, AR: University of Arkansas Press, 2016); Jericho Brown, *The New Testament* (Port Townsend, WA: Copper Canyon Press, 2014); Jericho Brown, *The Tradition* (Port Townsend, WA: Copper Canyon Press, 2019).

10 Mitzi J. Smith, *Womanist Sass and Talk Back: Social (In)justice, Intersectionality, and Biblical Interpretation* (Eugene, OR: Wipf & Stock, 2018). Elisabeth

Schüssler Fiorenza, *Bread Not Stone: The Challenge of Feminist Biblical Interpretation* (Boston, MA: Beacon Press, 1995); Wil Gafney, *Womanist Midrash: A Reintroduction to the Women of the Torah and the Throne* (Louisville, KY: Westminster John Knox Press, 2017); Jerusha Tanner Rhodes [published as Jerusha Tanner Lamptey], *Divine Words, Female Voices: Muslima Explorations in Comparative Feminist Theology* (New York: Oxford University Press, 2018); Martin Nguyen, *Modern Muslim Theology: Engaging God and the World with Faith and Imagination* (Lanham, MD: Rowman & Littlefield, 2019).

11 Nyasha Junior, *An Introduction to Womanist Biblical Interpretation* (Louisville, KY: Westminster John Knox Press, 2015), pp. 128–9; Mitzi J. Smith, 'Fashioning our Own Souls: A Womanist Reading of the Virgin–Whore Binary in Matthew and Revelation', in *I Found God in Me: a Womanist Biblical Hermeneutics Reader*, Mitzi J. Smith, ed. (Eugene, OR: Wipf & Stock), p. 159; Smith, *Womanist Sass and Talk Back*, p. 44.

12 Beth Crisp's chapter in the present volume explores some closely related themes.

13 The work of Shanell Smith is especially relevant here, including but not limited to her chapter in the present volume. Consider also Shanell Smith, *The Woman Babylon and the Marks of Empire: Reading Revelation with a Postcolonial Womanist Hermeneutics of Ambivalence* (Minneapolis, MN: Fortress Press, 2014).

14 Interview with Julie Cloutier in Herman, 'Justice from the Victim's Perspective', p. 582.

15 Stephanie Buckhanon Crowder, *When Momma Speaks: The Bible and Motherhood from a Womanist Perspective* (Louisville, KY: Westminster John Knox Press, 2016).

16 Michelle J. Anderson, 'The Legacy of the Prompt Complaint Requirement, Corroboration Requirement, and Cautionary Instructions on Campus Sexual Assault', *Working Paper Series: Villanova University School of Law* 20 (2004), pp. 3–4; https://digitalcommons.law.villanova.edu/wps/art20.

17 Referenced in Anderson, 'The Legacy of the Prompt Complaint Requirement', pp. 3–4.

18 Anderson, 'The Legacy of the Prompt Complaint Requirement', pp. 3–4.

19 Margaret McGregor and Grace Le, 'Examination for Sexual Assault: Is the Documentation of Physical Injury Associated with the Laying of Charges? A Retrospective Cohort Study', *Canadian Medical Association Journal* 160 (1999), pp. 1565–69; Margaret McGregor, Janice Du Mont, Terri L. Myhr, 'Sexual Assault Forensic Medical Evidence: Is Evidence Related to Successful Prosecution?', *Annals of Emergency Medicine* 39 (2002), pp. 639–47.

20 McGregor et al., in 'Sexual Assault Forensic Medical Evidence', drew this conclusion based on data from 462 women who consented to the rape kit from 1993 to 1997 in Canada, tracking their cases through the process of filing charges and other forms of response. They observed that, 'Specifically the examiner's collection of biologic samples for submission to police appears to provide some perceived scientific validation of a victim's allegations.' They underscored that this perception of 'validation' is in place after the samples are collected but before they are processed or analysed in any way; in other words, the perceived validation comes from the collection of samples (perhaps as a kind of symbolic testimony), but does not rely on any information conveyed by the samples themselves. This study has limitations – notably, the focus on women rape victims – but is still significant. Its findings align with the arguments of McGregor and Le, 'Examination for Sexual

Assault'. See also Janice Du Mont and Deborah Parnis, 'Constructing Bodily Evidence Through Sexual Assault Evidence Kits', *Griffith Law Review* 10:1 (2001), pp. 63–76; Jane Doe, 'Who Benefits From the Sexual Assault Evidence Kit?' in *Sexual Assault in Canada: Law, Legal Practice and Women's Activism*, Elizabeth A. Sheehy ed. (Ottawa: University of Ottawa Press, 2012), pp. 357–88; Georgina Feldberg, 'Defining the Facts of Rape: The Uses of Medical Evidence in Sexual Assault Trials', *Canadian Journal of Women and the Law* 9:1 (1997), pp. 90–114.

21 Jeffrey A. Bowman, 'Infamy and Proof in Medieval Spain', in *Fama: The Politics of Talk and Reputation in Medieval Europe*, Thelma Fenster and Daniel Lord Smail eds (Ithaca & London: Cornell University Press, 2003), p. 98.

22 Doe, par. 65.

23 Deborah Tuerkheimer, 'Incredible Women: Sexual Violence and the Credibility Discount', *University of Pennsylvania Law Review* 166:1 (2017), pp. 1–58.

24 This also calls us to reckon with the ways that perpetrators' credibility is wrongly inflated: see Audrey Yap, 'Credibility Excess and the Social Imaginary in Cases of Sexual Assault', *Feminist Philosophy Quarterly* 3:4 (2017), pp. 1–24.

25 Shauna Davis, 'Sexual Assault Detectives' Justifications for Aggressive Victim Interviewing Methods: A Qualitative Study' (PhD dissertation, University of Nevada at Las Vegas, 2013), p. 5; https://digitalscholarship.unlv.edu/cgi/viewcontent.cgi?article=2819&context=thesesdissertations.

26 So Mayer, 'Floccinaucinihilipilification', in *Not That Bad: Dispatches from Rape Culture*, Roxane Gay ed. (New York: Harper Perennial, 2018), p. 129.

27 In John 20.24–29, after Thomas speaks his demand to his peers, they do not reply. Instead, the narrative jumps forward to one week later. What does this say about the role of silent, complicit bystanders in harmful community responses? Thomas's demand, and the significance it was assigned by the male disciples, is discussed in this chapter, as part of assessing the 'blast radius' of a harmful community response. If some of the disciples had pushed back against Thomas's demand, would this have mitigated the long-range impact of it?

28 Soraya Chemaly, 'How Police Still Fail Rape Victims', *Rolling Stone*, 16 August 2016, www.rollingstone.com/culture/culture-features/how-police-still-fail-rape-victims-97782/.

29 George Yancy, *Black Bodies, White Gazes: The Continuing Significance of Race* (Lanham, MD: Rowman and Littlefield, 2008), p. 241.

30 Damon Young, 'Men Just Don't Trust Women. And This is a Problem', *The Root*, 16 December 2014, https://verysmartbrothas.theroot.com/men-just-dont-trust-women-and-this-is-a-problem-1822523100.

31 Rich Smith, '*The Incest Diary* Afflicted Me with as Much Trauma as the Written Word Can Transfer from One Body to Another', *The Stranger*, 19 July 2017, www.thestranger.com/books/2017/07/19/25304800/the-incest-diary-afflicted-me-with-as-much-trauma-as-the-written-word-can-transfer-from-one-body-to-another.

32 Aphrahat, *Demonstrations* 90.1. I am using the translation by Kuriakose Valavanolickal, Aphrahat, *Demonstrations I* (Kerala, India: St. Ephrem Ecumenical Research Institute (SEERI), 2005).

33 Aphrahat, *Demonstrations*, 17.10.

34 Tombs, 'Crucifixion, State Terror, and Sexual Abuse', p. 107.

35 Kristie Dotson, 'A Cautionary Tale: On Limiting Epistemic Oppression', *Frontiers: A Journal of Women Studies* 33:1 (2012), pp. 24–47. Kristie Dotson, 'Conceptualizing Epistemic Oppression', *Social Epistemology* 28:2 (2014), pp. 115–38.

36 Jean-Luc Nancy, *Noli me tangere: On the Raising of the Body*, trans. Sarah

Clift, Pascale-Anne Brault and Michael Naas (New York: Fordham University Press, 2008).

37 Nancy, *Noli me tangere*, p. 53.

38 I use the translation of the Georgian text of Hippolytus' Commentary on the Song of Songs produced by Yancy Warren Smith as a PhD dissertation: Yancy Warren Smith, 'Hippolytus' Commentary on the Song of Songs in Social and Critical Context' (PhD Dissertation, Texas Christian University, 2009), pp. 350–51; https://pdfs.semanticscholar.org/0087/dda6e68baf5dfe2f6f1c362490539e28a09c.pdf

39 Christians in the US sometimes represent corrective rape as something that happens far away. It is critical to acknowledge that corrective rape is a phenomenon in the US as well, sometimes integrated with 'conversion therapy'. One of relatively few published works describing this is Chris Godfrey, 'We Were Sent to Conversion Therapy for Being Gay', *Dazed*, 24 November 2016; www.dazeddigital.com/artsandculture/article/33814/1/gay-lgbt-conversion-therapy-politics-america. The Southern Poverty Law Center is in the midst of an ongoing project seeking to ban 'conversion therapy'; their research is another important source for discussing corrective rape in the US.

40 Nancy, *Noli me tangere*, p. 45.

41 Xan West, 'Stone Dynamics: Where Pleasure Resides', *Kink Praxis*, 5 July 2014, https://xanwest.wordpress.com/2014/07/05/stone-dynamics-where-pleasure-resides/.

42 Consider the analysis in Antti Marjanen, *The Woman Jesus Loved: Mary Magdalene in the Nag Hammadi Library and Related Documents* (Leiden: Brill, 1996), pp. 100–2.

43 Lynne St. Clair Darden, 'A Womanist-Postcolonial Reading of the Samaritan Woman at the Well and Mary Magdalene at the Tomb', in *I Found God in Me: A Womanist Biblical Hermeneutics Reader*, Mitzi J. Smith ed. (Eugene, OR: Wipf & Stock, 2015), p. 201.

5

Knowing Christ Crucified
(1 Corinthians 2.2):
Cross, Humiliation and Humility

JEREMY PUNT

Introduction: crucifying humiliation

The Pauline letters have more concern for Jesus' body than his biography, as the Corinthian correspondence shows. The corporeal slant and attention to various sexual matters has a wider berth but includes the embodied Jesus, and is underlined by Paul's claim that his primary concern is Jesus Christ crucified: *Iēsoun Christon estaurōmenon* (1 Cor. 2.2; see 1.18, 23).[1] Typically, commentators explain Paul's words in 1 Corinthians 2 as a focus on the humility of Jesus' death on the cross, given the association of crucifixion with foolishness, and that this shift allowed Paul to emphasize the humility of his own ministry in 1 Corinthians 2.3–5. However, despite Paul never explicitly claiming that Jesus was sexually violated, his strong emphasis on the shame and humiliation of Jesus' crucifixion provides a matrix within which the sexual abuse of Jesus may be implied. This brief exploration is not an attempt to (re)construct historical event(s), but rather to explore the Pauline argument in its socio-historical and rhetorical context. The ancient Mediterranean constellation of bodies, sex and gender depended on social norms and patterns such as honour, shame, hierarchy and power, and produced a discourse with various subterranean streams permeating the ancient Pauline letter yet hidden from the modern eye. Considering the socio-historical, gendered setting of crucifixion, this chapter explores the possibility of a sexually violated Christ implied in 1 Corinthians 2, as a(nother) way of making sense of Paul's insistence on the shame of the Jesus' crucifixion.

First-century crucifixion as execution and humiliation

The tendency of the modern scholarly tradition to shy away from reflections on sexuality in biblical studies has meant that sexual violation is largely neglected in work on first-century crucifixion practices.[2] So too, studies on the symbolic value of the cross[3] or the scandalous nature of Jesus' message or person[4] typically make reference to his cross but not to his sexual violation. Oftentimes, the interpretive focus on Jesus' humility turns crucifixion and its abuse into abstract notions that drown out the New Testament's emphasis on his humiliation. However, the latter was framed by prevailing first-century practices which, in turn, were informed by contemporary views of corporeality, gender and sex. Furthermore, the presentation of the crucified Christ in the first letter to the Corinthians is clothed in first-century male preoccupations and a range of gender perceptions. Although not always acknowledged, the context was overwhelmingly hierarchical, androcentric and patriarchal, while gender constructions showed a fair amount of gender fluidity with resulting ambiguities. Before exploring its gendered setting, a few brief comments on crucifixion are vital to set the scene.

Crucifixion was carried out by others in the ancient world in various different ways long before the Romans established their empire, but its practice always carried the intent of invoking maximum pain and indignity on the victims, pre- and/or post-mortem.[5] With the Romans, though, the cross soon became, more than anything else, the potent and feared symbol of their imperial power.[6] Crucifixion was the basic *supplicium servile* (slave punishment), used in the early principate against slaves, *liberti* (freed persons) and *peregrini* (non-citizens), and occasionally against citizens.[7] Crucifixion was deemed particularly effective by the Romans as an apparatus of war but also as a means for securing peace, for eroding the resistance of besieged cities, to humiliate the conquered, or to intimidate seditious soldiers or restless provinces.[8] While the general Roman sentiment saw crucifixion as 'a horrific, disgusting business',[9] few ancient authors (for example, Varro, *Sat. Men. Fr.* 24) protested against the barbarism of crucifixion, implying a general sentiment that this form of execution was a deterrent necessary to employ against the lower classes and especially slaves, in order to discourage serious crimes.[10]

Although the Romans did not concern themselves with detailed descriptions of the mechanics of crucifixion,[11] it was more than a measure of execution, it was also a calculated way of shaming and humiliating victims. As a public spectacle intended to dishonour and shame, victims were crucified in open places or along busy roads, to ensure large crowds and serving as public entertainment.[12] Lucian's fictional and humorously intended *Piscator* illustrates some common pre-crucifixion tortures, namely how men first flog someone, put out his eyes and cut off his tongue before crucifying him. So too Cicero (2 *Verr.* 5.62.161) mentioned how a victim was beaten with rods all over his body before crucifixion. Ancient authors' descriptions of pre-crucifixion torture included various forms of bodily abuse such as flogging, burning, racking, mutilation and even abuse of the victim's family (see already Plato, *Gorgias* 473bc).[13] The metaphorical use of crucifixion probably attests to its widespread use, and, although it is not a dominant aspect, an association between crucifixion and sexual actions may also be already detected early on in Latin texts. Catullus (ca 84–45 BCE) has a metaphorical use of crucifixion in a poem to his friend Iuventius, accompanied by the latter's sexual humiliation of Catullus. Killing through practices and instruments where victims were suspended, in times before hanging became prevalent,[14] meant that the distinction between crucifixion and impalement may at times have been less than explicit.[15] At times, impalement was done through the anus or vagina, which may betray sexualized undertones.

Since victims were crucified naked,[16] the public nudity of victims was an important element of crucifixion-induced shame. Hengel emphasized that 'the utter offensiveness of the "instrument for the execution of Jesus" is still to be found in the preaching of Paul' and provided a broader socio-historical framework for making sense of the offensiveness.[17] Hengel related crucifixion to the undesirable and unmanly trait of lack of self-control, since 'crucifixion satisfied the primitive lust for revenge and the sadistic cruelty of individual rulers and of the masses', and also because it usually involved other forms of torture too, most commonly flogging, which added to its allure as public spectacle. 'By the public display of a naked victim at a prominent place – at a crossroads, in the theatre, on high ground, at the place of his crime – crucifixion also represented his uttermost humiliation, which had a numinous dimension to it.'[18] Recently, David Tombs, whose work on the sexual violation of Jesus at his crucifixion has set the tone for investigating the textually inscribed events and contextually scripted discourse, similarly sees the disrobing of Jesus in the Gospel narratives as crucial for making such connections.[19] The treatment and public display of the victims' bodies, before and after death, amounted to sexually abusive humiliation and torture. Scaer concludes that although Jesus was arrested as revolutionary, mocked, beaten and crucified, Luke deliberately offered an apology for Jesus' death in terms of traditions such as Greek and Roman noble death, Socrates' unjust death, and martyrological motifs in the Jewish tradition.[20] This may explain why Jesus' sexual exploitation does not feature in Luke's passion account.

As seen in the shaming of prisoners by stripping them naked in public,[21] only to be tied up again to be flogged in public, recipients of Paul's letters would have been aware that sexual humiliation was included in Jesus' flogging and crucifixion. Like other victims, Jesus was naked and in full view of the first-century spectators to whom public nudity was a major disgrace, surpassed only by disfigurement.[22] The exact extent of the victim's nakedness is sometimes debated, whether it could have included a loincloth, but that it implied indecent bodily exposure and shame is clear.[23] Both crucifixion and accompanying actions symbolized physical violation that was at the time clearly understood in gendered and sexualized terms.[24] In first-century crucifixion practices it is thus important to acknowledge shaming together with physical violence,[25] and Paul's rhetoric in I Corinthians and elsewhere emphasizes the cross's shame and humiliation.

Contextualizing shamefulness: masculinity, and honour and shame

The shamefulness of the cross had a broad reach. The social stigma attached to crucifixion as the 'most pitiable of deaths' (Josephus, *The Life* 76) included the negative stereotype of shameful and blameworthy death,[26] since the impact of the cross went beyond the ending of life, which at any rate it accomplished effectively, if gruesomely. However, being a deterrent as much as punishment, crucifixion was a particularly effective public spectacle intent on humiliation in presenting the victim as something less than human in the eyes of society. In the first-century's gendered contexts, the humiliation, penetrability and openness to punishment and abuse was considered particularly arduous for male victims. Descriptions of how, among other punishments, executioners drove stakes through the genitals of their victims as part of crucifixion (Seneca *Dial.* 6.20.3) make the humiliation and emasculation very explicit. Therefore, since men were susceptible to being dishonoured,[27] public execution obviously posed a major threat to their masculinity.

There was no single norm of masculinity that prevailed throughout the empire, and in fact gender itself was not a given, with some people considered not even to have gender. Male slaves, defeated enemies and barbarians were seen as lacking *andreia* (Greek) or *virtus* (Latin), that is, manliness.

> Roman manliness, or the kind of manliness ancient Romans meant by the Latin word *virtus*, turns out to have little to do with the qualities and activities – sexually aggressive display and behaviour, fathering of children, support and protection of family – commonly associated with manliness in Mediterranean as well as other cultures.[28]

As noted above and to summarize a much longer discussion, the cultural setting of the time privileged masculinity and assigned gender and social roles accordingly.[29] Maleness in first-century Greek and Roman culture comprised more than biology. Biblical scholars in the past suggested that masculinity in biblical texts was defined by cross-cultural notions such as strength, violence, powerful and persuasive speech, male bonding and womanlessness.[30] But even more than those general notions, 'ancient masculinity was constituted more by the shape of one's life than by the shape of one's body'.[31] Masculinity required actions that would inscribe it,[32] or as Gleason puts it, 'Manliness was not a birthright. It was something that had to be won.'[33] Since gender often existed on a single spectrum and was therefore inherently unstable, maleness was privileged and effeminacy to be avoided. As much as masculinity has always been an indication on a broader human gender or sex spectrum, its first-century form did not allow for exhibiting what may have been perceived as femininity. Avoiding a feminine or effeminate appearance meant that discipline, self-control, military skill, good looks, modesty in dress and behaviour, intellectual growth, justified anger and being seen as 'active' were promoted among men in favour of a masculine form. 'Masculinity and femininity were located on two different poles of a spectrum, which inscribes the interrelation of masculinity or femininity as superior/inferior, societal status as more/less powerful, and sex role as penetrator/penetrated.'[34] The ambiguity and contradictions of Greek and Roman masculinity ironically ensured the efficiency of the ideological system of masculinity.[35]

In the collectivist society of the time, with its dyadic perceptions of human interrelationships, bodily integrity depended on people's ability to maintain the primary authority over their own bodies.[36] Given the pervasive androcentric and patriarchal nature of society, men's pursuit of honour was not only erotic or simply an exercise in social dominance, but patriarchal power also had to be achieved and defended in order to secure access to scarce resources.[37] The constant and pervasive jostling to secure honour was also associated with, and had, economic implications. Such considerations, determined by men and directed as men, regulated social interaction in the first-century urban landscape. Masculinity, then, was not derived but acquired, informed by biology but not determined by a body, and, accordingly, was deeply ambivalent. The shame and obstacle that crucifixion posed for any free man was, therefore, immense, being publicly and bodily at the disposal of others, losing control of one's bodily integrity. Paul's depiction of Jesus' crucifixion in 1 Corinthians reflects such sentiments of shame and the purposefulness of his emasculating denigration on the cross.

Cross and humiliation in 1 Corinthians and other Pauline letters

As much as Jesus' cross has to be understood within prevalent gender and sex-related concerns, the Corinthian letter was addressed to a community in a city renowned for its Hellenistic culture and whose conflicted history with the Roman Empire contributed to an eagerness to reflect imperial values.[38] The origins of the tensions in the community were probably less eschatological–theological and more sociological, arising from socio-economic divisions.[39] Paul's challenge to an ideology of privilege countered tensions between the more numerous but lower-status 'charter members' and the more recent converts, fewer in numbers but whose wealth, power and status may have unsettled the standards and expectations within the community.[40] Paul's first letter to the Corinthians for the largest part concerns matters related to sex and food (for example, see sexual immorality in 5.1–13; sex work in 6.12–20; marriage and sex in 7.1–16; food offered to idols in 8.1–13; and food and idols in 10.14–22) – both as markers of corporeality and as often associated in ancient discourse[41] – which in both cases concern intentions beyond their physical nature.

Paul's attention to sexual issues is understandable in the light of the city of Corinth's lingering reputation when it came to such matters, which was caused in no small way by its location and two harbours that generated a metropolitan mix of peoples, who were generally rich, prosperous and independent. The reputation of the earlier city of Corinth is typified in Strabo's remark (*Geogr.* 8.6.20) about the multitude of sex workers of Acrocorinth, but similar sentiments are found also in Aristophanes' neologism *korinthiazomai* ('act like a Corinthian', meaning 'to act sexually immoral', *Fragm.* 354), as well as Plato's use of *korinthia korē* ('a Corinthian maid', meaning 'to act like a harlot', *Rep.* 3.404d).[42] Commentators reckon that first-century Corinth, like any other metropolis, had its fair share of sex-work activities typical of harbour towns where money was easier to come by, but was probably no worse than other such towns.[43] In all likelihood, though, the lingering effects of Corinth's bad sexual reputation weighed on Paul's mind.[44] So a sexualized setting forms part of 1 Corinthians' context, but sentiments about a humiliating, shameful cross are not restricted to one Pauline letter.

Paul's use of crucifixion terminology is pervasive in his earlier letter to the Galatians, where he emphasized that Jesus was 'publicly displayed' (*proegraphē*) as 'crucified' (*estaurōmenos*, Gal. 3.1).[45] In dealing with the cross's implications (Gal. 3.13), Paul quoted from Deuteronomy 27.26 to argue that Jesus took up the curse of hanging on a wood or cross in order to push the curse of the Law aside. And in a further chapter (Gal. 5.11), Paul named the shame and humiliation associated with the cross of Jesus in a word: *to skandalon tou staurou*. Drawing out the implications of Jesus' crucifixion, Paul associates himself with it to the extent that he claims the cross as fundamental to his own identity: *Christōi sunestaurōmai* ('I was crucified with Christ', Gal. 2.19a). Paul's claim aligns with victims of crucifixion that often entered into the parodic roles assigned to them.[46] His claim forms the basis for a daring envisioning of a new existence (*kainē ktisis*, Gal. 6.12,15) derived from sharing in the humiliation and death associated with Jesus' death on the cross. Even Paul's harsh tone and strong claims in Galatians cannot hide the humiliation he experienced through his own devices (Gal. 1.11–17) as much as at the hands of others (1.18—2.10; 2.11–14). As much as Paul encouraged the Galatian community, with terminology associated with the cross, to live according to the Spirit (5.24), the shame and humiliation of the cross never disappears from his rhetoric.[47] And, what started in the earliest NT writing is carried on in the later NT documents, where the humiliation of the cross is still emphasized. Hebrews 13.13, for example, refers to the 'insult' or 'disgrace' of the cross (*ton oneidismon autou pherontes*, 'bearing its disgrace'), which may refer to the crucifixion as such or also to disgraceful actions associated with it. While *oneidismos* does not explicitly have a sexual reference, humiliation of a sexual nature should not be excluded. In Hebrews 12.2, *upemeinen stauron aischunēs kataphronēsas* ('he endured the cross despising the shame'), the author talks of Jesus' endurance of the crucifixion and again refers to shame related to the cross.

In Paul's writings, the crucified Jesus is important in the unmasking of imperial and other powers and terror, and also in the disruption of prevailing perceptions and structures, particularly in relation to the simultaneous association of Jesus with the cross and slavery. As was pointed out elsewhere,[48] Paul's portrayal of Jesus' cross is connected with other contemporary notions and symbols, and at times the relationship between cross and slavery is particularly strong.[49] Some scholars have shown the parodic element inherent to crucifixion, with regard to how the victim was vilified, denigrated and mocked. In a context beset with status concerns related to honour and shame that were often expressed in metaphors of vertical space,[50] '[c]rucifixion was intended to unmask, in a deliberately grotesque manner, the pretension and arrogance of those who had exalted themselves beyond their station'.[51] As Marcus puts it, not without some wit of his own, crucifixion was intent on 'mocking the victim's effrontery by *raising* and fixing him in a torturously *elevated* state until he expires – a form of death that drives the last nail, so to speak, into his lofty pretensions'.[52] In the remarks of 1 Corinthians 7.21–23 about slaves, Paul enigmatically stressed the importance of serving Christ regardless of one's standing.[53] The shame and humiliation induced by the cross heightened its primary connection with slavery. Since slaves were sexually available to their owners, and because of the cross's association with slavery as explained earlier, this adds another intersecting sexual dimension to the practice of crucifixion. It is understandable, then, that in 1 Corinthians Paul's consistent profiling of the shame of the cross evokes a larger web of sexually attuned humiliation associated with crucifixion in a social context with a profiled sense of sexual matters.

The crucified Christ as the sexually violated Jesus

Paul's self-presentation in 1 Corinthians 2.1–5 is often filtered through humility and linked with, or derived from, the humility of Jesus. This theological appropriation, as important a notion as it is, can, however, enfeeble the depictions and decontextualize both Jesus' fate and Paul's self-portrayal. Only once in the authentic Pauline letters does Paul explicitly link the crucifixion of Jesus and humility. In Philippians 2.1–11 he connects Jesus' life and death on the cross to humility, as evidenced in the Christ hymn following Paul's exhortation to the community: *alla tēi tapeinophrosunēi allēlous ēgoumenoi uperechontas eautōn* ('but in humility count others better than yourselves', Phil. 2.3b). But even here, Jesus' humiliation is (more) strongly emphasized, referring to his human form and (again) invoking the slave metaphor, culminating in his death on the cross: *etapeinōsen eauton genomenos upēkoos mechri thanatou, thanatou de staurou* ('he humbled himself by becoming obedient to the point of death, death on a cross', Phil. 2.8). Emphasizing humility rather than humiliation, which characterized both Jesus' death and the affliction, anguish and tears involved in Paul's Corinthian ministry (2 Cor. 2.4), can hide the cross's shamefulness and evade a more appropriate contextual reading.[54]

To make sense of Pauline terminology of the cross, the contemporary rhetorical map of the concept has to be kept in mind because the latter would have informed both the author and the recipients of the word's meaning. Words get meaning not from dictionaries but from their use in social systems and contexts, and include their connotative aspects as well as denotative aspects. The Romans deliberately and purposefully humiliated their opponents through crucifixion; ergo, shame and humiliation were not coincidental to the cross but its intended purpose. Likewise, Paul did not explicitly identify the crucified Jesus as a victim of sexual violation, but the emphasis on the shame and humiliation of the cross and literary evidence of the sexual humiliation and abuse of victims suggest that Jesus may not have been spared this indignity. Hengel suggests that Paul's emphasis on the shamefulness of the cross should take the bigger picture into consideration: 'When Paul talks of the "folly" of the message of the crucified Jesus, he is therefore not speaking in riddles or using an abstract cipher ... he deliberately wants to provoke his opponents, who are attempting to water down the offence caused by the cross.'[55] Elsewhere in the Pauline letters, it is already clear that crucifixion and bodily desires are not as far removed from each other for Paul as they probably are for modern people. In Galatians 5.24, Paul wrote '*oi de tou Christou [Iēsou] tēn sarka estaurōsan sun tois pathēmasin kai tais epithumiais*' ('those of Christ have crucified the flesh with its passions and desires'), demonstrating an association between crucifixion and sexual desire.

Furthermore, in a similar way that biblical notions and sentiments about a range of issues such as homoerotic relations, slavery, ecological concerns, gender and sexuality cannot simply be read off texts and cut and pasted into modern arguments, so too biblical texts alluding to or implying sexual violation, abuse and rape cannot simply be filtered through twenty-first-century perspectives and sensitivities.[56] The relatively sparse explicit connections between crucifixion, humiliation and sexual violation should be understood in the context where sexual violation was not determined through an individual's right to their body and personal consent. Sexual violation for the ancient would have looked different for men and women, for free and enslaved persons, for people of different levels of social status, for urban and rural folk, and for people belonging to certain social groupings, which immediately introduces another major distinction from our modern notion of sexual violation, namely our modern emphasis on the equality and dignity of all. The Pauline letters are testimony also that sexual matters were among, but not necessarily pivotal to, a number of issues related to understanding first-century social life and morality. And, of course, like most ancient literature, the Pauline letters were written from a male and a mostly literate class perspective.[57]

Considering the above elements, is the appropriation of Jesus Christ crucified today situated not so much in emulating his suffering as in taking his accomplishment as the basis for striving to eliminate such violation of human bodies? Perhaps it is not so much that, as that 'the body *as tortured, as crucified*, must be carried about, represented, embodied in the persons of his apostles, until the deadly representations of the Empire's power are brought to an end by the One to whom all powers will ultimately be subjected (1 Cor. 15.24)'.[58] In a second parodic step pertaining to Jesus' crucifixion, the powerful's mockery of the victim's aspirations are turned around again, and parody becomes reality.[59] The first turnaround established through the cross, in another ironic and parodic way, is given a further, second turn when mockery is mocked by the marginalized's appropriation of events.[60] Explicit reflection on the implications of Paul's portrayal of Jesus in relation to the sexually violated Christ forces consideration of the relation between shame and humiliation, which is a 'stumbling block', and crucifixion's inherent sexual violence. How will this reading potentially impact theologies of Christ on the cross,[61] or the ongoing Pauline legacy?[62]

Conclusion: the legacy of a sexually violated, crucified Lord

In the end, then, the question is: how do we deal with or appropriate 'texts of terror'[63] such as crucifixion in a context where the experience of sexual violation was aligned to social status and gender, and when frames of reference that differ over time meant that people's experience of reality was not equal to that of people today? This is not, of course, to deny the reality or constancy of anguish, pain and death but to acknowledge that these realities were and are appropriated differently within specific contexts. Such contexts, particularly at experiential level, were and are dependent on a range of social factors informing people's sense and intensity of being violated. Is the mixed support for the cross among the early Jesus-follower communities in contrast to the post-Constantine prevalence and even popularity of the cross as symbol, perhaps an indication of both the unsavoury, body-invasive events of the cross and the interpretive tradition's sanitizing of Jesus' crucifixion account to non-sexual torture?

Paul's explicit insistence on the crucified rather than resurrected or glorified Christ is as important for New Testament studies as for theological constructions pertaining to violence, gender, sexuality and Pauline soteriological constructions of Christology and atonement. Paul did not encourage or revere suffering, pain or death – neither his own nor that of others – and never praised suffering for its own sake. The violence of the cross does not encourage 'passion mysticism, a meditation on the wounds of Christ, or ... a spiritual absorption into the sufferings of Christ'.[64] So too, the Pauline letters' insistence on the humiliation of Jesus, which included his sexual maltreatment, cannot be read in support of sexual exploitation in the name of Jesus. On the contrary, notwithstanding its association with humiliation and violence, for Paul terminology of the cross never became the celebration of the suffering of Christ nor a celebration of human suffering, and thus may prove to be an imaginative resource for those who have suffered sexual abuse.[65] The power of symbols is evident in how the cross would become both an ultimate symbol of powerlessness during the period of colonial expansion as well as a symbol of victory and power.[66]

So, on a final note, why has the sexual violation of Jesus – not to mention his sexuality – never been a serious investigation in New Testament studies?[67] Why has the emphasis on Jesus' corporeality – or theologically, his incarnation – until recently not included references to his sexuality nor to Jesus having been a victim of sexual violation? These questions will probably be answered in different ways, because of hermeneutical, theological and other reasons. In the Pauline letters, however, the answer may lie in an apparently minor detail, the emphasis on Jesus' humility to the exclusion of considering also his humiliation on the cross and everything this could have implied.

References

Beker, J. Christiaan, *The Triumph of God: The Essence of Paul's Thought*, Minneapolis, MN: Fortress Press, 1990.

Brown, Raymond E., *The Death of the Messiah: From Gethsemane to the Grave, A Commentary on the Passion Narratives in the Four Gospels*, vol. 1, New York: Doubleday, 1994.

Chapman, David W., *Ancient Jewish and Christian Perceptions of Crucifixion*, Grand Rapids, MI: Baker Academic, 2010.

Clines, David J. A., 'Paul, the Invisible Man', in *New Testament Masculinities*, Stephen D. Moore and Janice Capel Anderson eds, vol. 45 SBL Semeia Studies, Atlanta, GA: Society of Biblical Literature, 2003, pp. 181–92.

Conway, Colleen M., *Behold the Man: Jesus and Greco-Roman Masculinity*, Oxford, New York: Oxford University Press, 2008.

Cook, John Granger, 'Crucifixion and Burial', *New Testament Studies* 57: 2 (2011), pp. 193–213.

—, *Crucifixion in the Mediterranean World*, Tübingen: Mohr Siebeck, 2014.

—, 'Envisioning Crucifixion: Light from Several Inscriptions and the Palatine Graffito', *Novum Testamentum* 50:3 (2008), pp. 262–85, https://doi.org/10.1163/156853608X262918.

Cosgrove, Charles H., *The Cross and the Spirit: A Study in the Argument and Theology of Galatians*, Macon, GA: Mercer, 1988.

Countryman, L. William, *Interpreting the Truth: Changing the Paradigm of Biblical Studies*, Harrisburg, PA: Trinity Press International, 2003.

Cousar, Charles B., *A Theology of the Cross: The Death of Jesus in the Pauline Letters*, Minneapolis, MN: Fortress, 1990.

Creangă, Ovidiu, and Peter-Ben Smit, eds, *Biblical Masculinities Foregrounded*, Hebrew Bible Monographs vol. 62, Sheffield: Sheffield Phoenix Press, 2014.

Crisp, Beth, 'Beyond Crucifixion: Remaining Christian after Sexual Abuse', *Theology & Sexuality* 15:1 (30 September 2009), pp. 65–76, https://doi.org/10.1558/tse.v15i1.65.

Edwards, Catharine, 'Unspeakable Professions: Public Performance and Prostitution in Ancient Rome' in *Roman Sexualities*, J. P. Hallett and M. B. Skinner eds, Princeton, NJ: Princeton University Press, 1997, pp. 66–95.

Elliott, Neil, *Liberating Paul: The Justice of God and the Politics of the Apostle*, Maryknoll, NY: Orbis, 1994.

——, 'The Anti-Imperial Message of the Cross', in *Paul and Empire: Religion and Power in Roman Imperial Society*, Richard A. Horsley ed., Harrisburg, PA: Trinity Press International, 1997, pp. 167–83.

——, 'The Apostle Paul's Self-Presentation as Anti-Imperial Performance', in *Paul and the Roman Imperial Order*, Richard A. Horsley ed., Harrisburg, PA: Trinity Press International, 2004, pp. 67–88.

Fiensy, David, 'Crucifixion', in *The Lexham Bible Dictionary*, John D. Barry ed., Bellingham, WA: Lexham, 2016.

Finlan, Stephen, *Sacrifice and Atonement: Psychological Motives and Biblical Patterns*, Minneapolis, MN: Fortress, 2016.

Fitzmyer, Joseph A., *First Corinthians: A New Translation with Introduction and Commentary*, vol. 32 The Anchor Yale Bible, New Haven, CT & London: Yale University Press, 2008, http://public.ebookcentral.proquest.com/choice/public fullrecord.aspx?p=3420456.

Frankemölle, Hubert, 'Peace and the Sword in the New Testament', in *The Meaning of Peace: Biblical Studies*, Perry B. Yoder and Willard M. Swartley eds, Walter Sawatsky trans., vol. 2 Studies in Peace and Scripture, Louisville, KY: Westminster John Knox, 1992, pp. 213–33.

Frederickson, David E., 'Natural and Unnatural Use in Romans 1:24–27: Paul and the Philosophic Critique of Eros', in *Homosexuality, Science and the 'Plain Sense' of Scripture*, David L. Balch ed., Grand Rapids, MI: Eerdmans, 2000, pp. 197–222.

Gilmore, David D., 'Introduction: The Shame of Dishonor', in *Honor and Shame and the Unity of the Mediterranean*, David D. Gilmore ed., vol. 22 A Special Publication of the American Anthropological Association, Washington: American Anthropological Association, 1987, pp. 1–21.

Gleason, Maud W., *Making Men: Sophists and Self-Presentation in Ancient Rome*, Princeton, NJ: Princeton University Press, 1995.

Guðmundsdóttir, Arnfríður, 'Abusive or Abused? Theology of the Cross from a Feminist Critical Perspective', *Journal of the European Society of Women in Theological Research* 15:0 (31 December 2007), pp. 37–54. https://doi.org/10.2143/ESWTR.15.0.2022767.

Hamerton-Kelly, Robert G., *Sacred Violence: Paul's Hermeneutic of the Cross*, Minneapolis, MN: Fortress Press, 1992.

Hengel, Martin, *Crucifixion: In the Ancient World and the Folly of the Message of the Cross*, London: SCM Press, 1977.

Ivarsson, Fredrik, 'Vice Lists and Deviant Masculinity: The Rhetorical Function of 1 Corinthians 5:10–11 and 6:9–10', in *Mapping Gender in Ancient Religious Discourses*, Todd Penner and Caroline Vander Stichele eds, Biblical Interpretation Series, Leiden & Boston: Brill, 2007, pp. 163–84.

Knapp, Robert, *Invisible Romans*, Cambridge, MA: Harvard University Press, 2011.

Kwok, Pui-lan, *Discovering the Bible in the Non-Biblical World*, Maryknoll, NY: Orbis, 1995.

Longenecker, Bruce W., *The Cross Before Constantine: The Early Life of a Christian Symbol*, Minneapolis, MN: Fortress, 2015.

——, 'Contradictions of Masculinity: Ascetic Inseminators and Menstruating Men in Greco-Roman Culture', in *Generation and Degeneration: Tropes of Reproduction in Literature and History from Antiquity through Early Modern Europe*, Valeria Finucci and Kevin Brownlee eds, Durham, NC and London: Duke University Press, 2001, pp. 81–108.

McCracken, David, *The Scandal of the Gospels: Jesus, Story, and Offense*, New York: Oxford University Press, 1994.

McDonnell, Myles, *Roman Manliness. Virtus and the Roman Republic*, New York: Cambridge University Press, 2006.

Marcus, Joel, 'Crucifixion as Parodic Exaltation', *Journal of Biblical Literature* 125:1 (2006): pp. 73–87.

Martin, Dale B., *The Corinthian Body*, New Haven, CT and London: Yale University Press, 1995.

Meech, John L., *Paul in Israel's Story. Self and Community at the Cross*, Oxford and New York: Oxford University Press, 2006.

Meeks, Wayne A., *The First Urban Christians: The Social World of the Apostle Paul*, New Haven. CT and London: Yale University Press, 1983.

Moore, Stephen D., *God's Gym. Divine Male Bodies of the Bible*, New York and London: Routledge, 1996.

——, '"O Man, Who Art Thou … ?": Masculinity Studies and New Testament Studies', in *New Testament Masculinities*, Stephen D. Moore and Janice Capel Anderson eds, vol. 45 Semeia Studies, Atlanta, GA: SBL, 2003, pp. 1–22.

Morris, Leon, *The Cross in the New Testament*, Exeter: Paternoster, 1979.

Murphy-O'Connor, Jerome, *Paul: His Story*, Oxford and New York: Oxford University Press, 2004, https://public.ebookcentral.proquest.com/ choice/public fullrecord.aspx?p=728727.

O'Collins, Gerald, 'Crucifixion', in *Anchor Bible Dictionary*, David Noel Freedman ed., New York: Doubleday, 1992, pp. 1207–10.

Osiek, Carolyn, and Jennifer Pouya, 'Constructions of Gender in the Roman Imperial World', in *Understanding the Social World of the New Testament*, Dietmar Neufeld and Richard E. DeMaris eds, London and New York: Routledge, 2010, pp. 44–56.

Patterson, Orlando, *Slavery and Social Death: A Comparative Study*, Cambridge, MA: Harvard University Press, 1982.

Phipps, William E., *The Sexuality of Jesus*, Cleveland, OH: Pilgrim Press, 1996.

Punt, Jeremy, 'Cross-Purposes? Violence of the Cross, Galatians, and Human Dignity', *Scriptura* 102 (2009): pp. 446–62.

———, 'Mr Paul: Masculinity and Paul's Self-Presentation (1 Cor 11–13)', *In Die Skriflig/In Luce Verbi* 50:2 (8 April 2016), pp. 1–9, https://doi.org/10.4102/ids. v50i2.2001.

Samuelsson, Gunnar, *Crucifixion in Antiquity: An Inquiry into the Background and Significance of the New Testament Terminology of Crucifixion*, Tübingen: Mohr Siebeck, 2011.

Scaer, Peter J., *The Lukan Passion Narrative and the Praiseworthy Death*, Sheffield: Sheffield Phoenix, 2005.

Schotroff, Luise, 'The Dual Concept of Peace', in *The Meaning of Peace: Biblical Studies*, Perry B. Yoder and Willard M. Swartley eds, Walter Sawatsky trans., vol. 2 Studies in Peace and Scripture, Louisville, KY: Westminster John Knox, 1992, pp. 156–63.

Smit, Peter-Ben, 'Masculinity and the Bible: Survey, Models, and Perspectives', *Brill Research Perspectives in Biblical Interpretation* 2:1 (2017): pp. 1–97.

Sugirtharajah, Rasiah S., *Postcolonial Criticism and Biblical Interpretation*, Oxford: Oxford University Press, 2002.

Swancutt, Diana M., 'Sexy Stoics and the Rereading of Romans 1.18–2:16', in *A Feminist Companion to Paul*, Amy-Jill Levine and Marianne Blickenstaff eds, vol. 6 Feminist Companion to the New Testament and Early Christian Writings, London: T&T Clark / Continuum, 2004, pp. 42–73.

Theissen, Gerd, *The Social Setting of Pauline Christianity: Essays on Corinth*, John Schütz trans., Philadelphia, PA: Fortress, 1983.

Tombs, David, 'Crucifixion, State Terror, and Sexual Abuse', *Union Seminary Quarterly Review* 53:1–2 (1999): pp. 89–109.

Trainor, Michael, *The Body of Jesus and Sexual Abuse: How the Gospel Passion Narratives Inform a Pastoral Response*, Northcote: Morning Star, 2014.

Trible, Phyllis, *Texts of Terror: Literary Feminist Readings of Biblical Narratives*, vol. 13 Overtures to Biblical Theology, Philadelphia, PA: Fortress, 1984.

Tsang, Sam, *From Slaves to Sons: A New Rhetoric Analysis on Paul's Slave Metaphors in His Letter to the Galatians*, New York: Peter Lang, 2005.

Wheeler, Everett L., 'The Army and the *Limes* in the East', in *A Companion to the Roman Army*, Paul Erdkamp ed., Malden: Blackwell, 2007, pp. 235–66.

Wright, Nicholas T., *Paul: In Fresh Perspective*, Minneapolis, MN: Fortress, 2005.

Notes

1 Although the cross is a central metaphor in Paul, the extent to which the claim is borne out in the rest of the letter is a contentious matter, as is its relationship with the resurrected body (1 Cor. 15). Scholars have pointed to the centrality of the cross in the Pauline corpus and theological constructions. See, for example, Charles H. Cosgrove, *The Cross and the Spirit: A Study in the Argument and Theology of Galatians* (Macon, GA: Mercer, 1988); Charles B. Cousar, *A Theology of the Cross: The Death of Jesus in the Pauline Letters* (Minneapolis, MN: Fortress, 1990); Robert G. Hamerton-Kelly, *Sacred Violence: Paul's Hermeneutic of the Cross* (Minneapolis, MN: Fortress Press, 1992); John L. Meech, *Paul in Israel's Story: Self and Community at the Cross* (Oxford and New York: Oxford University Press, 2006), even modelling the cross into a theological trope for atonement, applied as secondary, interpretative grid as in Leon Morris, *The Cross in the New Testament* (Exeter: Paternoster, 1979), pp. 346–419; see also Raymond E. Brown, *The Death of the Messiah: From Gethsemane to the Grave: A Commentary on the Passion Narratives in the Four Gospels*, vol. 1 (New York: Doubleday, 1994).

2 As, for example, in Martin Hengel, *Crucifixion: In the Ancient World and the Folly of the Message of the Cross* (London: SCM Press, 1977).

3 For example, Bruce W. Longenecker, *The Cross Before Constantine: The Early Life of a Christian Symbol* (Minneapolis, MN: Fortress, 2015), pp. 185.

4 For example, David McCracken, *The Scandal of the Gospels: Jesus, Story, and Offense* (New York: Oxford University Press, 1994).

5 Various verbs were used to describe such practices, such as ἀνασκολοπίζειν and ἀνασταυροῦν. 'The common factor in all these verbs is that the victim – living or dead – was either nailed or bound to a stake, σκόλοψ or σταυρός.' Hengel, *Crucifixion*, p. 24.

6 Nicholas T. Wright, *Paul: In Fresh Perspective* (Minneapolis, MN: Fortress, 2005), p. 64; also Neil Elliott, 'The Anti-Imperial Message of the Cross', in *Paul and Empire: Religion and Power in Roman Imperial Society*, Richard A. Horsley ed. (Harrisville, PA: Trinity Press International, 1997), pp. 167–83.

7 John Granger Cook, *Crucifixion in the Mediterranean World* (Tübingen: Mohr Siebeck, 2014), pp. 358–9.

8 Hubert Frankemölle, 'Peace and the Sword in the New Testament', in *The Meaning of Peace: Biblical Studies*, Perry B. Yoder and Willard M. Swartley eds, Walter Sawatsky trans., vol. 2 Studies in Peace and Scripture (Louisville, KY: Westminster John Knox, 1992), p. 217; Luise Schotroff, 'The Dual Concept of Peace', in *The Meaning of Peace: Biblical Studies*, Perry B. Yoder and Willard M. Swartley eds, Walter Sawatsky trans., vol. 2 Studies in Peace and Scripture (Louisville, KY: Westminster John Knox, 1992), pp. 156–63. Since the soldiers stationed in Palestine probably included the X Fretensis legion, and others from Syria (III Gallica; VI Ferrata; III Cyrenica or XII Fulminata), their anti-Jewish antipathies may have been all too predictable. The situation was fluid, as Everett L. Wheeler notes in 'The Army and the *Limes* in the East', in *A Companion to the Roman Army*, Paul Erdkamp ed. (Malden: Blackwell, 2007), p. 242: 'Throughout Augustus' reign (and the first century generally) legions were still mobile, dispatched as whole units when needed. *Vexillationes* (detachments from legions as expeditionary forces) became common only in the second half of the first century.' The Roman army consisted of approximately 25 legions during the early Principate. Each legion had approximately 5,000 men, further divided into ten cohorts, with each having three maniples, and with each maniple finally divided into two centuries. Auxiliary troops included infantry forces such as javelin throwers (*velites*) but also cavalry formations drawn from the equestrian order as well as from Rome's allies.

9 Hengel, *Crucifixion*, p. 37.

10 Gerald O'Collins, 'Crucifixion', in *Anchor Bible Dictionary*, David Noel Freedman ed. (New York: Doubleday, 1992), p. 1209. 'As a rule the crucified man (sic) was regarded as a criminal who was receiving just and necessary punishment' (Hengel, *Crucifixion*, p. 87). Although crucifixion was prevalent in Roman times, some authors like Tacitus appear to have purposefully avoided mentioning the innumerable Roman crucifixions in Palestine. Josephus *Hist.* 5.8–13; see O'Collins, 'Crucifixion', p. 1209.

11 John Granger Cook, 'Crucifixion and Burial', *New Testament Studies* 57:2 (2011), p. 195.

12 Philo, *Flacc* 84–85; see also Peter J. Scaer, *The Lukan Passion Narrative and the Praiseworthy Death* (Sheffield: Sheffield Phoenix, 2005), p. 2.

13 Elsewhere Plato wrote: 'The just man who is thought to be unjust will be scourged, racked, bound – will have his eyes burnt out; and, at last after suffering every kind of evil, he will be impaled [i.e., crucified]'; *Republic* 361e–362a; see Fiensy 'Crucifixion', in *The Lexham Bible Dictionary*, John D. Barry ed. (Bellingham, WA: Lexham, 2016).

14 Cook, *Crucifixion in the Mediterranean World*, p. 451.

15 Cook, *Crucifixion in the Mediterranean World*, p. 451.

16 Hengel, *Crucifixion*, pp. 21, 29, 87.

17 Hengel, *Crucifixion*, p. 18, retreated to a more generalized understanding, that the cross of Jesus 'was not a didactic, symbolic or speculative element but a very specific and highly offensive matter which imposed a burden on the earliest Christian missionary preaching. No wonder that the young community in Corinth sought to escape from the *crucified* Christ into the enthusiastic life of the spirit, the enjoyment of heavenly revelations and an assurance of salvation connected with mysteries and sacraments.'

18 Hengel, *Crucifixion*, p. 87.

19 David Tombs, 'Crucifixion, State Terror, and Sexual Abuse', *Union Seminary Quarterly Review* 53:1–2 (1999), pp. 89–109.

20 Scaer, *The Lukan Passion Narrative and the Praiseworthy Death*, pp. 1–5, 90–92.

21 Diodorus Siculus, *Bibliotheca historica* 33.151.1; see also Scaer, *The Lukan Passion Narrative and the Praiseworthy Death*, p. 2.

22 Seneca emphasized the shame of crucifixion flowing from the naked body disfigured by the machinations of the crucifixion processes; the body lost its beauty and natural dignity in the prolonged and painful process of dying. Public exposure was according to its stereotyped portrayal mostly extended with bodies left on the cross, becoming carrion for wild animals and birds, Juvenal, *Sat* 14.77–78; see Hengel, *Crucifixion*, p. 87. 'There was no shame worse than dying on the cross', Scaer, *The Lukan Passion Narrative and the Praiseworthy Death*, p. 2.

23 'The word γυμνός in itself is ambiguous and needs further semantic clarification in a text (e.g., παντελῶς or περιζώματα)', Cook, *Crucifixion in the Mediterranean World*, p. 193, n. 149. In the Palatine graffito the crucified figure wears a sleeveless short tunic (*colobium*), but literary sources note that victims were crucified naked: John Granger Cook, 'Envisioning Crucifixion: Light from Several Inscriptions and the Palatine Graffito', *Novum Testamentum* 50:3 (2008), pp. 283–85, https://doi.org/10.1163/156853608X262918. The crucified figure's tunic appears to have been pushed up to expose the buttocks and genitals. While the conceptualization of a modestly clothed Jesus on the cross is probably informed by artistic representations over centuries, exceptions do exist, such as the portrayal of Jesus and the other two crucified with him, unclothed, by Michelangelo (British Museum); see www.bmimages.com/preview.asp?image=00018259001.

24 See also Michael Trainor, *The Body of Jesus and Sexual Abuse. How the Gospel Passion Narratives Inform a Pastoral Response* (Northcote: Morning Star, 2014), pp. 17–43.

25 The double disrobing or dressing of Jesus described in Mark 15.16–20 has an interesting parallel, if recorded somewhat later and in reference to another (earlier) era and context, in Dio Chrysostom's description of the Sacian feast of the Persians (*Orat.* 4.67–70). One of the condemned prisoners is dressed in royal apparel shortly before his execution, given access to all privileges in the royal court and explicitly also to the king's concubines, only to be stripped, scourged and hanged the next day. Chrysostom's warning is that a person should not aspire to be a king before attaining wisdom. See also Joel Marcus, 'Crucifixion as Parodic Exaltation', *Journal of Biblical Literature* 125:1 (2006), p. 85.

26 Scaer, *The Lukan Passion Narrative and the Praiseworthy Death*, p. 2. Gunnar Samuelsson, *Crucifixion in Antiquity: An Inquiry into the Background and Significance of the New Testament Terminology of Crucifixion* (Tübingen: Mohr Siebeck, 2011), p. 306, concludes a lengthy study on crucifixion in the ancient Mediterranean by identifying the four elements depicting the crucifixion of Jesus Christ: executionary suspension; scourging followed by carrying a *stauros* to the place of execution; undressed and attached to a σταυρός (perhaps with nails); and a sign on the cross probably indicated the nature of his crime. Samuelsson's remark, 'Features beyond these are not to be found in the New Testament or the older literature of the Greco-Roman world' may be unnecessarily limiting.

27 Although singular cases of crucified women exist, such meagre attestation suggests that it was mostly men that were crucified. Josephus (*Jw Ant* 18.66–80) recounted that a freed woman was crucified for her involvement with the seduction of a noble woman. Tacitus (*Ann.* 14.42, 45) explicitly mentioned that slaves of both genders of the household were crucified in reprisal for Pedianus Secundus' murder. See also Cook, 'Envisioning Crucifixion', p. 278, and Fiensy, 'Crucifixion'.

28 Myles McDonnell, *Roman Manliness: Virtus and the Roman Republic* (New York: Cambridge University Press, 2006), p. xiii. See also Fredrik Ivarsson, 'Vice Lists and Deviant Masculinity: The Rhetorical Function of 1 Corinthians 5:10–11 and 6:9–10', in *Mapping Gender in Ancient Religious Discourses*, Todd Penner and Caroline Vander Stichele eds, Biblical Interpretation Series (Leiden & Boston: Brill, 2007), pp. 165–6. Slaves were without gender and its defining characteristics and expectations, and claims upon honour, status, rights and protection were ruled out. Female and child slaves were most vulnerable and at any rate slaves – male, female or child – did not have sexual privacy or control over their bodies: Carolyn Osiek and Jennifer Pouya, 'Constructions of Gender in the Roman Imperial World', in *Understanding the Social World of the New Testament*, Dietmar Neufeld and Richard E. DeMaris eds (London and New York: Routledge, 2010), pp. 47–48. Patterson described slavery as social death, since 'slavery is the permanent, violent domination of natally alienated and generally dishonoured persons' (Orlando Patterson, *Slavery and Social Death: A Comparative Study* (Cambridge, MA: Harvard University Press, 1982), p. 13). Slaves' lack of ascribed gender fits into their socially alienated status.

29 Amid recognition for both the greater social visibility of women and the commensurate bigger role in socio-economic affairs during the first century CE, the question is to what extent their communities and society at large allowed such perceptions and roles beyond masculinity. Were women allowed such roles measured by a masculine yardstick, and in word and deed judged by their ability to fulfil not only male-defined roles but roles that were inscribed in masculine perceptions?

30 For example, David J. A. Clines, 'Paul, the Invisible Man', in *New Testament Masculinities*, Stephen D. Moore and Janice Capel Anderson eds, vol. 45 SBL Semeia Studies (Atlanta, GA: SBL, 2003), pp. 181–2. Surveying the field, Moore identifies David Clines as the biblical scholar who, at the time, had published most on the intersection of Bible and masculinity studies; see Stephen D. Moore, '"O Man, Who Art Thou... ?": Masculinity Studies and New Testament Studies', in *New Testament Masculinities*, p. 7. Given a largely shared socio-historical context as well as the ubiquity of the Roman Empire and its values and a lingering, pervasive Hellenism, gender norms and values in Jewish communities did not appear vastly different. However, see more recently Peter-Ben Smit, 'Masculinity and the Bible: Survey, Models, and Perspectives', *Brill Research Perspectives in Biblical Interpretation* 2:1 (2017), pp. 1–97, for a comprehensive but nuanced overview. See also various essays in Creangă and Smit, *Biblical Masculinities Foregrounded*, vol. 62 Hebrew Bible Monographs (Sheffield: Sheffield Phoenix Press, 2014).

31 Colleen M. Conway, *Behold the Man. Jesus and Greco-Roman Masculinity* (Oxford and New York: Oxford University Press, 2008), p. 16.

32 Diana M. Swancutt, 'Sexy Stoics and the Rereading of Romans 1.18–2.16', in *A Feminist Companion to Paul*, Amy-Jill Levine and Marianne Blickenstaff eds, vol. 6 Feminist Companion to the New Testament and Early Christian Writings (London: T&T Clark / Continuum, 2004), p. 55.

33 Maud W. Gleason, *Making Men: Sophists and Self-Presentation in Ancient Rome* (Princeton, NJ: Princeton University Press, 1995), p. 159.

34 Osiek and Pouya, 'Constructions of Gender in the Roman Imperial World', p. 45.

35 So, for example, sex was 'permissible but precarious' in ancient times according to Dale B. Martin, 'Contradictions of Masculinity: Ascetic Inseminators and Menstruating Men in Greco-Roman Culture', in *Generation and Degeneration*.

Tropes of Reproduction in Literature and History from Antiquity through Early Modern Europe, Valeria Finucci and Kevin Brownlee eds (Durham and London: Duke University Press, 2001), p. 89, and compromised its ability to vet masculinity. See also Jeremy Punt, 'Mr Paul: Masculinity and Paul's Self-Presentation (1 Cor 11–13)', *In Die Skriflig/In Luce Verbi* 50:2 (8 April 2016), pp. 1–9, https://doi.org/10.4102/ids.v50i2.2001. As much as various ancient authors related the male generative function to the power of male semen as opposed to the lack of or ineffectual semen of women (see Galen, *On Semen* 1.7.5; Soranus, *Gynecology* 1.9.34), they also believed that, unlike women, males could exercise sexual control that was necessary for health reasons, either by avoiding intercourse (see Soranus, *Gynecology* 1.7.30) or moderating sexual activity (see Celsus, *De medicina* 1.10.1; 1.9.2; Galen, *On Semen* 1.16.23).

36 In the Roman era, actors, gladiators and prostitutes represented the shameful: not only were their lives characterized by *infamia*, and devoid of legal protection, '[t]heir bodies might be beaten, mutilated, or violated with impunity': Catharine Edwards, 'Unspeakable Professions: Public Performance and Prostitution in Ancient Rome', in *Roman Sexualities*, J. P. Hallett and M. B. Skinner eds (Princeton, NJ: Princeton University Press, 1997), pp. 66, 73. See also Robert Knapp, *Invisible Romans* (Cambridge, MA: Harvard University Press, 2011), pp. 203–25.

37 David D. Gilmore, 'Introduction: The Shame of Dishonor', in *Honor and Shame and the Unity of the Mediterranean*, David D. Gilmore ed., vol. 22 A Special Publication of the American Anthropological Association (Washington: American Anthropological Association, 1987), p. 4.

38 After Corinth became involved in the political issues of Sparta and Rome, the city was destroyed by the Romans in 146 BCE, but re-established in 44 BCE as a Roman colony (*Colonia Laus Julia Corinthiensis*) in honour of Julius Caesar, who was murdered in the same year.

39 For example Dale B. Martin, *The Corinthian Body* (New Haven, CT and London: Yale University Press, 1995).

40 Neil Elliott, *Liberating Paul. The Justice of God and the Politics of the Apostle* (Maryknoll, NY: Orbis, 1994), pp. 204–14. See also Wayne A. Meeks, *The First Urban Christians: The Social World of the Apostle Paul* (New Haven, CT and London: Yale University Press, 1983), pp. 117–18, and Gerd Theissen, *The Social Setting of Pauline Christianity: Essays on Corinth*, John Schütz trans. (Philadelphia, PA: Fortress, 1983), pp. 106–10.

41 Sexual desire and hunger were often associated in the Greek and Roman world, since both were to be limited by satisfaction: the pleasure of sex and a full stomach. Gluttony, like uncontrolled sexual desire, was unnatural and could lead to brutality and disorder. See David E. Frederickson, 'Natural and Unnatural Use in Romans 1:24–27: Paul and the Philosophic Critique of Eros', in *Homosexuality, Science and the 'Plain Sense' of Scripture*, David L. Balch ed. (Grand Rapids, MI: Eerdmans, 2000), p. 199; Martin, *The Corinthian Body*, pp. 344–6; Swancutt, 'Sexy Stoics and the Rereading of Romans 1.18–2.16', pp. 62, n. 101, 64–5.

42 While the epithet 'to Corinthianize' was associated with the pre-Roman city, its ill repute remained and the word is still found today in, among others, the Collins Dictionary, as even a cursory online search shows.

43 See for example Joseph A. Fitzmyer, *First Corinthians: A New Translation with Introduction and Commentary*, vol. 32 The Anchor Yale Bible (New Haven & London: Yale University Press, 2008), pp. 30–3.

44 Jerome Murphy-O'Connor, *Paul: His Story* (Oxford and New York: Oxford University Press, 2004), p. 78.

45 All scriptural quotations are author's own translation.

46 Marcus, 'Crucifixion as Parodic Exaltation', p. 82.

47 Jeremy Punt, 'Cross-Purposes? Violence of the Cross, Galatians, and Human Dignity', *Scriptura* 102 (2009), pp. 446–62.

48 Punt, 'Cross-Purposes? Violence of the Cross, Galatians, and Human Dignity', pp. 446–62.

49 Neither cross nor slave should become dead metaphors; see, for example, Sam Tsang, *From Slaves to Son: A New Rhetoric Analysis on Paul's Slave Metaphors in His Letter to the Galatians* (New York: Peter Lang, 2005), p. 14, for clichés filled with idealized, even romanticized twenty-first-century content, making them devoid of their primary purpose, namely symbolizing human life of a very real yet extremely disturbing kind. Slavery in the first century could not be disconnected from the structural social system and complex set of convictions regarding hierarchical notions of human beings, accompanied by ideas about exercising power and related expectations of submission, corporeal availability for sexual purposes, and punishment.

50 In fact, the Roman authorities often related the proportions or dimensions of the cross and location to the extent of transgression. Marcus ('Crucifixion as Parodic Exaltation', p. 79) refers to Suetonius' account (*Galba* 9.1) of Galba, who had a guardian who poisoned his ward crucified although he was a Roman citizen, and increased the prominence of the cross by white paint and added height.

51 Marcus, 'Crucifixion as Parodic Exaltation', p. 78.

52 Marcus, 'Crucifixion as Parodic Exaltation', p. 80.

53 It is a question why Paul was not as enigmatic with his instructions to various versions of married, unmarried and previously married people (1 Cor. 7), at equally great pains to qualify and nuance his argument when it came to slavery, given his concern with the avoidance of *porneia* in 1 Corinthians 5—7, his claims about the link between bodies, sex and pollution on the one hand (1 Cor. 5.16) and on the other hand sanctification (1 Cor. 7.14, 16), and the sexual availability of slaves to their owners.

54 Paul's reference to the Torah through Deuteronomy 21.23 (in Gal. 3.13), on the scourge of the cross, underlines its shamefulness among Jews in particular. Space does not allow extensive discussion of the rationale and implications of this reference here. However, Chapman traced the possible influence of ancient Jewish perceptions on Jesus' followers and early Christian views of Jesus' death on the cross. He argues that, although ancient Jewish views related to categories of shame and horror and the associations with brigandage and rebellion (especially in the Gentile world), often overlapped with those of the world around them, there were also in antiquity distinctly Jewish perceptions of the cross, which also included positive perceptions of the cross related to the death of an innocent sufferer or martyr, and also latent sacrificial images. David W. Chapman, *Ancient Jewish and Christian Perceptions of Crucifixion* (Grand Rapids, MI: Baker Academic, 2010), pp. 219, 261–2.

55 Hengel, *Crucifixion*, p. 89.

56 'Any preconception about the text, then, that makes the interpreter want to save it from embarrassment is suspect', L. William Countryman, *Interpreting the Truth: Changing the Paradigm of Biblical Studies* (Harrisburg, PA: Trinity Press International, 2003), p. 230. And, as all good archaeologists know, the absence of evidence is not evidence of absence!

57 That is, if the topic would have been broached at all. 'Crucifixion was widespread and frequent, above all in Roman times, but the cultured literary world

wanted to have nothing to do with it, and as a rule kept quiet about it.' Hengel, *Crucifixion*, p. 38. Silence on the sexual violation accompanying crucifixion is in keeping with this wider social reticence on crucifixion.

58 Neil Elliott, 'The Apostle Paul's Self-Presentation as Anti-Imperial Performance', in *Paul and the Roman Imperial Order*, Richard A. Horsley ed. (Harrisville, PA: Trinity Press International, 2004), p. 87, emphasis in original. Theological questions abound: for example, as Moore suggests in *God's Gym: Divine Male Bodies of the Bible* (New York and London: Routledge, 1996), pp. 12–13, notwithstanding the many eloquent theological answers over many centuries, the gospel narratives (Mark 14.36; Matt. 26.39; Luke 22.42) emphasize that Jesus' crucifixion is the will of God. What are the implications for the understanding of suffering today? And, by analogy, of sexual exploitation?

59 Marcus, 'Crucifixion as Parodic Exaltation'.

60 For others salvation needs to be separated from Jesus' crucifixion. 'We have gone on too long, covering the message of Jesus with a mythology about his death, a death caused by his enemies. To some degree, we have allowed his enemies – the hypocrites, the power brokers, the conductors of sacrifice – to set the agenda', Stephen Finlan, *Sacrifice and Atonement: Psychological Motives and Biblical Patterns* (Minneapolis, MN: Fortress, 2016), p. 189. To which Finlan adds, 'Not many are willing to say what I say: sacrifice was a fundamentally selfish and manipulative phase of religious development; it needs to be outgrown', Finlan, *Sacrifice and Atonement*, p. 187.

61 Of course, the perennial danger of cross theologies cannot be ignored; see, for example, Arnfríður Guðmundsdóttir, 'Abusive or Abused? Theology of the Cross from a Feminist Critical Perspective', *Journal of the European Society of Women in Theological Research* 15 (31 December 2007), pp. 37–54.

62 In his eloquent and imaginative processing of the Gospel narratives, incorporating the socio-historical circumstances accompanying ancient crucifixion practices, and with a nod to Foucault's *Discipline and Punish* (which tracks the nineteenth-century criminal justice shift from revengeful retribution with maximum suffering, to surveillance, discipline and (re)education in good citizenship), Moore, in *God's Gym: Divine Male Bodies of the Bible*, cautions that the relationship between violent punishment and internal self-policing may be symbiotic or parasitic (pp. 10–11). Moore shows how troubled theologians struggle to find the good in Paul's view of the crucifixion (deliverance from the power of sin) and to get beyond the notion of sacrificial atonement for the sins people committed (pp. 17–22).

63 Phyllis Trible, *Texts of Terror: Literary Feminist Readings of Biblical Narratives*, vol. 13 Overtures to Biblical Theology (Philadelphia, PN: Fortress, 1984).

64 J. Christiaan Beker, *The Triumph of God: The Essence of Paul's Thought* (Minneapolis, MN: Fortress Press, 1990), p. 88.

65 See, for example, Crisp, 'Beyond Crucifixion', pp. 65–76.

66 Rasiah S. Sugirtharajah, *Postcolonial Criticism and Biblical Interpretation* (Oxford: Oxford University Press, 2002), p. 85. And even earlier; on the confusing of the 'crucified' mind of Christ with the 'crusading' mind of many Christians, see also Kwok, *Discovering the Bible in the Non-Biblical World* (Maryknoll, NY: Orbis, 1995), p. 28 with reference to Koyama.

67 For an earlier but rather isolated treatment of the sexuality of Jesus, see William E. Phipps, *The Sexuality of Jesus* (Cleveland, OH: Pilgrim Press, 1996).

6

Jesus, Joseph and Tamar Stripped: Trans-textual and Intertextual Resources for Engaging Sexual Violence Against Men

GERALD O. WEST

Introduction

This chapter takes up the work of David Tombs on male sexual violence against men, including probable male sexual violence against Jesus.[1] The essay has three related strands. First, it traces 25 years of community calls for biblical resources to deal with gender-based violence, predominantly sexual violence against women and children, but also male sexual violence against men. Second, the essay traces a biblical trajectory, trans-textually and intertextually, of sexual violence, confirming the kinds of resonances Tombs analyses in his work on the stripping of Jesus. Third, community summons and intertextual and trans-textual resources combine to construct a Contextual Bible Study on the subject of male sexual violence against men (and boys).

Community cries summon the Bible

'I have surely seen the affliction of my people ... and have given heed to their cry ... for I am aware of their sufferings. So I have come down to deliver them.' (Ex. 3.7–8)[2]

This biblical text echoes across communities in their struggles for liberation. A distinctive characteristic of this God is that this God hears the cry of those struggling to survive their taskmasters. Discerning this God in the Bible is no simple task, for biblical texts are themselves sites of struggle,[3] intrinsically incorporating voices that bring death and voices that struggle for life. Remarkably, in communities of (post-colonial) Christian faith in African contexts the Bible remains a significant sacred resource. Despite the many ways in which the Bible has been used to denigrate African culture, legitimate racial, economic exploitation and hetero-patriarchy, discriminate against queer sexualities, stigmatize those living with HIV and the unemployed and affirm the idols of death, marginalized communities of faith have refused to let the Bible go until it blesses them (Gen. 32.26). They limp, having embraced an ambiguous Bible, but they continue to strive with God through their reading of the Bible.

As a response to this refusal to let go of the Bible, the Ujamaa Centre for Community Development and Research emerged. We offer our biblical-critical resources alongside the resources of interpretive resilience that local communities already use to enable eyes that are already engaged in struggles for survival and a fullness of life to discern the kin voices of the God of life in the midst of the voices of the idols of death in the Bible.

The Ujamaa Centre, previously named the Institute for the Study of the Bible, began its work within the anti-apartheid struggle, forged by the race and class resources of South African Contextual Theology and South African Black Theology. Very soon, however, we were summoned to work with women. The struggle of women for life amid the idols of death inherent in colonial-apartheid patriarchy and post-colonial neo-indigenous patriarchy refused to be silent, and we were summoned in the hope that there would be biblical voices raised alongside the voices of local communities of South African women.

Among the cries of South African women was the sustained cry from within the context of violence against women. While our community-based participatory biblical interpretation methodological model was being conceptualized, we were invited by a women's organization to construct a 'Contextual Bible Study' that engaged the reality of violence against women, including violence against women within Christian churches. Drawing on the pioneering literary-narrative work of Phyllis Trible on the story of the rape of Tamar within the household of King David, we constructed our first version of a Contextual Bible Study (CBS) on gender-based violence in 1996.[4] This CBS has gone on to be used in countless contexts of gender-based violence around the world. Part of its power then was that this biblical story was virtually an unknown text. There was amazement when the story was first read aloud in English and isiXhosa. Participants paged back and forth in their Bibles to confirm that this story was indeed in their Bibles, for none of them had ever heard of it. Yet they said, 'If this story is in the Bible, then we will not be silent/silenced.'

What had led us to this story was the clear recognition that Tamar was an articulate agent, speaking for herself amid the male voices of destruction and death that surround her story. The women we worked with were astounded that such an eloquent voice should have been ignored by their churches. Though raped by her brother Amnon and silenced by her brother Absalom, Tamar was not silent. Her resilient and resisting voice remained, despite her desolation in the house of her brother (2 Sam. 13.20) and despite the desolation of her contemporary African sisters in the house of the Church.

In almost every 'Tamar Contextual Bible Study' (as this CBS has come to be known) the concern was raised by women about how we might work with men. Summoned again by context, we began work on constructing a series of CBS on forms of 'redemptive masculinity', including a redemptive masculinity version of Tamar's story in 2 Samuel 13.[5] While less frequent, in the workshops we also heard the insistent voice of men who had been sexually abused. I remember clearly when we launched the Tamar Campaign in Kenya in 2005, a young man shared with us how he had been abused by a male relative. After he had shared his story among the many stories told by women, we had a presentation by Nairobi Women's Hospital, adding yet further contextual reality to the epidemic that is gender-based violence. The colleague from the Nairobi Women's Hospital confirmed that, while they were fewer in number, there were regular reports from men as survivors of sexual violence.

We heard the contextual summons of such men who had survived sexual violence at the hands of heterosexual men, but we were not sure how we might engage this reality. Part of the problem was the refrain from some men in our Tamar CBS work: 'What about women who are violent towards men?' We did not want what we considered to be a defensive response by men to deflect our focus on violence against women, and we also did not want our work on male sexual violence against men to be side-tracked by claims of women being violent towards men. What further complicated the summons by men who had experienced sexual violence from other men was the emerging emphasis on 'homosexuality' during this time, both because of the rise of HIV and AIDS and contestations within churches about queer sexualities.[6] Male sexual violence against men was often branded as the work of 'homosexuals'. We did not want our work on largely heterosexual male sexual violence against men to be co-opted by homophobic African churches.

CBS's work within the Ujamaa Centre is regular and ongoing, as week by week, year by year, we are summoned to work with specific local communities. Therefore, as we reflected on the summons by men who had been sexually abused by (heterosexual) men, we were doing a range of other CBS work. Unexpected resonances would often arise. In our work on issues of leadership and of land, we used the woodcut by Azariah Mbatha on the Joseph story (Gen. 37—46) as an Africa-resonant resource with which to delve into the detail of the biblical text.[7]

Among Mbatha's exegetical insights are the ways in which clothing is used within the story, often to deceive. The brothers of Joseph use the garment they have taken from him to deceive their father Jacob, inferring that Joseph has been devoured by wild animals (37.31–33, panel 3 of the woodcut). Then in panel 5 of the woodcut, the centre panel, Mbatha represents Potiphar's wife holding Joseph's garment before her husband as evidence that Joseph had tried to rape her, but which she had taken hold of in her attempt to force him to lie with her (Gen. 39.7–18). Though this panel and this part of the story would often lead men to comment on women's violence against men, we would not allow the primary focus of our work

'Joseph' (1964–65) by Azariah Mbatha. Used with permission.

on the Joseph story, and specifically matters of leadership or land expropri-
ation, to be deflected. A community summons is sacrosanct; we serve the
focus of a community-based summons. We had yet to receive a summons
by an organized group of men concerning violence against men by women.
Nevertheless, the Joseph story and Mbatha's attentiveness to clothing
remained a resource awaiting its appropriate contextual summons.

The summons came indirectly, when we were invited to work with the
Pietermaritzburg Gay and Lesbian Network in a sustained partnership that
has now spanned more than a decade. Sexual violence against gay men as
a form of sexual 'disciplining' (analogous to the more familiar 'corrective
rape' of lesbian women) is widespread. Oddly – queerly – it was our academic work among students on the queer dimensions of the story of Joseph
that prompted a textual connection with the story of Tamar, as some of the
students were also members of the Gay and Lesbian Network.

Biblical scholars have long noted the textual correspondences between
the story of Tamar and the story of Joseph,[8] among which are the only two
occurrences of the Hebrew term *'kethoneth passim'* or *'kuttoneth passim'*
to describe the garment that both Tamar (2 Sam. 13.19) and Joseph (Gen.
37.3) wear. But the significance of this for violence against women and men
has only recently been taken up in our work, for it required yet another
biblical text to activate the connection, a text from the New Testament.

The Ujamaa Centre has developed a partnership with the Centre for
Theology and Public Issues at the University of Otago, Dunedin, Aotearoa

New Zealand, working with David Tombs on gender-based violence within the Pacific region. During February to April 2018 we worked together in the Pacific region, doing joint workshops in which we used biblical and theological resources, including CBS, to engage with male violence against women and male violence against men. Over the years, Tombs has pioneered biblical and theological work in the area of male sexual violence against men, using the story of the crucifixion of Jesus as the locus of his argument. In June 2019, Tombs visited South Africa where he presented a public lecture on 'The Stripping of Jesus: Sexual Violence Hidden in Plain Sight' and then participated with the Ujamaa Centre in a workshop on 'Constructing Contextual Bible Study Resources to Engage with Sexual Violence against Men'. We invited community-based activists, university students and academic staff to participate in the workshop. After a summary of Tombs' public lecture, we divided the participants into four small groups, inviting them to work with either Mark's (15.15–20) or Matthew's (27.26–31) account of the stripping of Jesus. Each group grappled with the biblical text and did some preliminary formulations of CBS questions, focused on male sexual violence against men.

In preparation for this workshop, I had done some of my own delving into the detail of Mark's and Matthew's story of the stripping of Jesus, discovering, among other points, that both accounts use the same Greek word for the stripping of Jesus, *ekduō*, which is also used by the Septuagint to translate the Hebrew word *pashat* in the story of the stripping of Joseph (Gen. 37.23). There was now a trans-textual trace from Tamar to Joseph to Jesus.

Trans-textual summons

The CBS work of the Ujamaa Centre is shaped by both a radical hermeneutic of reception and a radical hermeneutic of production.[9] Our work has always given priority to the poor and marginalized 'reader' of the Bible. 'Readerly' agency is central to CBS processes, with each CBS having been constructed through an engagement with particular organized communities and their local contextual realities. This is the 'See' moment of the 'See-Judge-Act' CBS process.[10] The 'Judge' moment is then represented in the set of questions that constitute a particular CBS, drawing on both the details of a particular contextual reality and the details of a particular biblical text. Therefore, in this section, I will concentrate on the biblical textual detail; nevertheless, it is important to emphasize, as indicated in the previous section, that we recognize the epistemological privilege of the groups we work with. Their realities are our starting point within a radical hermeneutic of reception.

We also work with a radical hermeneutic of production, drawing on the work of Itumeleng Mosala and particularly his insistence that biblical texts are sites of inter-sectoral or class struggle. The particular sites that produced particular biblical source texts and the particular sites that redacted these source texts through collection and combination are particular socio-historical sites of socio-economic struggle. Mosala focuses on the socio-economic, but he is also attentive to the (intersecting) gender struggles that are (partially) represented within particular source texts and redacted texts.[11] CBS work uses historical-critical and sociological biblical studies resources, orientated by the gaze of the poor and marginalized sectors with whom we work, to discern source texts within the larger redacted compositions of the Bible that represent most clearly and fully the voices of poor and marginalized sectors from within the contested sites of the Bible's production. Recovered source texts, even if an 'original' sectoral source text is not completely recoverable, are then analysed using literary-narrative biblical studies resources, which provide the textual entry point for a CBS. Our work with unemployed youth, for example, attempts to recover the economically oriented parable of Jesus from Matthew's religiously oriented redaction in Matthew 20.1–16.[12]

We recognize too that there may be sectoral resonances across time and place within the particular contexts that produced the Bible. Poor and marginalized sectors within the Bible's pasts may well have re-membered and nurtured the dangerous memory of compatriot sectors from earlier times and places. Dominant sectors have almost certainly had the final word – through construction of the final redaction – but because redaction is also the process of collecting and reusing earlier sources, the voices of more marginal sectors can also be heard.[13] An intentional deployment of the resources of biblical scholarship, allied with an intentional commitment to work with contemporary poor and marginalized sectors, can and does lead to potential interpretive lines of connection between ancient sites of struggle and contemporary sites of struggle. An attentiveness to sectoral resonances across biblical texts also offers potential lines of trans-textual sectoral solidarity.

Before I move to the trans-textual detail of the story of Tamar, the story of Joseph, and the story of the stripping of Jesus, I must explain precisely what I mean by 'trans-textual' for it derives its force from our radical hermeneutic of reception. I use 'trans-textual' (with the hyphen) in a deliberate manner. Gérard Genette, for example, uses the term 'trans-textuality' as a superordinate term, including within its domain other relational forms, such as 'intertextuality'.[14] I use the term differently, following the prompting of Jione Havea, where 'trans' is understood as 'to cross over' and 'to transgress'. I include a third component, potentially constructed by these two components, 'to trans-form' or 'to trans-act'. My usage emphasizes the reader's role as agent in constructing transactions across biblical texts. However, reader-driven trans-textual resonances may lead to 'intertextual' identifications, where we might claim historical dependency.[15] The three texts discussed here are brought into dialogue because of the emancipatory potential we as socially engaged biblical scholars see in crossing over, back and forth, between them, even if this requires transgressing the boundaries that biblical scholarship constructs between them, perhaps through forging and finding unrecognized intertextual resonances.

The CBS work of the Ujamaa Centre encompasses many biblical texts across our 30 years of work, so one of the resources we as the Ujamaa Centre bring to any particular CBS workshop is the subversive memory of many other CBS workshops and their contextual concerns and associated biblical texts. Such is the case here, for as we facilitated the CBS workshop on 'Constructing Contextual Bible Study Resources to Engage with Sexual Violence against Men', my reflections moved back and forth between Jesus, Joseph and Tamar. Tamar, I recognized, was our prophet, guiding us trans-textually across these textually related stories of sexual violence.

Each of these stories is embedded within a larger narrative whose concerns are not primarily about sexual violence. Male matters tend to dominate in the same way that religious matters tend to be given precedence over economic matters by dominant redactional editions. This is why the Ujamaa Centre works with a radical hermeneutic of production. Biblical texts are sites of struggle, bearing the marks of their ideological sites of production. We look with 'eyes that are hermeneutically trained in the struggle for liberation today to observe the kin struggles of the oppressed and exploited of the biblical communities'.[16]

Trans-textual detail

Our literary-narrative work on the Tamar text in 2 Samuel 13.1–22 was shaped by four narrative features.[17] First, we identified and separated the Tamar source text (2 Sam. 13.1–22) from its larger patriarchal and monarchic frame (2 Sam. 6/7—1 Kings 2), within which it serves as a sub-plot to explain the tension between two of David's sons, Amnon and Absalom, as they contend to succeed David as king. Second, we adopted Trible's analysis of the exposition (13.1) and complication (13.2) of the narrative, identifying Amnon as a major, though flat, character. Third, we privileged, as the source narrative does, the character of Tamar, who is both a major and round character, drawing attention to her agency with respect to both her significant direct speech and her action. Finally, we identified the slow temporal and terrible spatial shifts in setting as patriarchal forces (seen in the characters of Jonadab, Amnon, David and male servants) conspire to move Tamar from safe space (her mother's compound in the royal court) to unsafe space (her brother Amnon's compound), and how patriarchy constructs 'safe' space as silent/silenced space (Absalom's house).

The impact of the Tamar CBS has been remarkable, enabling a breaking of the silence about violence against women and children.[18] Among the outcomes of this CBS, as indicated, was the call by women participants for the Ujamaa Centre to produce resources to work with men about redemptive masculinities, as well as a call to address male sexual violence against men. Because we were doing work already with the Joseph story, using Mbatha's woodcut and focusing on the intersection of economic and land issues but also attentive to other textual and artistic detail, we were aware of the significance given to clothing imagery in the narrative. The central panel of the woodcut provided a vivid depiction of Potiphar's wife holding Joseph's garment in the foreground, with Joseph semi-naked in the background. We had considered how this 'stripping' of Joseph offered potential for a CBS on how white 'madams' might use their economic power to sexually abuse black male servants, a reality of apartheid South Africa's exploitative domestic worker system. A more explicit depiction of a white madam sexually abusing her black gardener by South African artist Trevor Makhoba offered additional resources for a possible CBS.[19] But as indicated, we chose not to shift our emphasis from focusing on violence against women and on redemptive forms of masculinity. But the significance of clothing imagery in the Joseph story remained as a potential resource.

A further trans-textual narrative detail from the Tamar story proved decisive as our work with the Pietermaritzburg Gay and Lesbian Network progressed. The reality of male heterosexual sexual violence against gay men prompted us to reconsider Joseph, focusing now on his stripping by his brothers. Mbatha portrays this in his second panel. The biblical text itself is decisive, making it clear that 'they stripped him of his *kethoneth passim*' (Gen 37.23). Tamar's '*kethoneth passim*' summoned Joseph's '*kethoneth passim*'; Joseph's 'stripping' (*pashat*) in trans-textual turn summons the implied stripping of Tamar (2 Sam. 13.14, 18–19). Only now did we recognize the emphasis in the Hebrew sentence structure of verse 18 of the Tamar story: 'And/now *on her* a *kethoneth passim* ...'. What had been stripped was now 'on her'.

While other scholars have noted the trans-textual, as well as the possible intertextual,[20] connection between these two stories, and a few have reflected on the queer implications of this connection, Theodore Jennings analyses in detail the 'transgendered' and 'queer Joseph' that Jacob has produced,[21] and identifies the brothers' violence towards Joseph as canonically 'the first instance of queer bashing' in the biblical canon.[22] More importantly, while Jennings does not interrogate possible sexual violence against Joseph from his brothers or the slave-traders,[23] he does recognize that for Joseph, who the reader is explicitly told 'was handsome in form and appearance' (Gen. 39.6), sexual exploitation may well have been a factor in why he was shown favour. In both Potiphar's household and in prison, Joseph's 'survival depends upon a powerful male benefactor, who may exchange protection for sexual favours'.[24] Such queer interpretation added to our understanding of the forms that sexual violence takes.

Jennings also offers us an intriguing connection between the overt sexual violence of Potiphar's wife against Joseph and possible sexual violence from Joseph's brothers (who are clearly identified in an earlier narrative as rapists (Gen. 34.27–29)). As Jennings notes, the narrator's overt reference to Joseph's beauty is followed, immediately, by the episode in which Potiphar's wife commands (using the imperative form of *shakab*): 'Lie with me' (Gen. 39.7). Joseph, like Tamar, is 'beautiful' (*yapheh*) (Gen. 39.6; 2 Sam. 13.1), which is another trans-textual and perhaps also an intertextual resonance.[25]

Likewise, the second stripping of Joseph, by Potiphar's wife, Joseph's madam, is also trans-textually connected to the story of Tamar. Amnon 'took hold of her' and commanded her 'Come, lie (*shakab*) with me, my sister' (2 Sam. 13.11); Potiphar's wife 'caught him by his garment' and commanded Joseph, 'Lie (*shakab*) with me' (Gen. 39.12). Amnon rapes Tamar; Potiphar's wife attempts to rape Joseph.[26] Where Potiphar's wife displays Joseph's discarded garment to her husband, Jennings compares it to the earlier episode in which the brothers hold Joseph's *kethoneth passim* before their father, Jacob. 'In both cases', Jennings notes, 'what is displayed is an article of clothing that Joseph is *not* wearing.'[27] Joseph is stripped twice, once by his brothers and once by Potiphar's wife.

Narrative setting also trans-textually connects these stories of sexual violence. The reader follows the exposition of the plot to lure Tamar to Amnon's quarters, watching in trepidation and terror as Tamar becomes more and more isolated and vulnerable (2 Sam. 13.5–7). Similarly, given the tensions among the brothers presented in the exposition (Gen. 37.1–4, 5–11), the reader has a sense of foreboding as Joseph is sent (*shalach*) by his father to his brothers (as David sends (*shalach*) Tamar to Amnon (2 Sam. 13.7)). The direct speech dialogue between the brothers (Gen. 37.19–22) plays a similar narrative role to the dialogue between Tamar and Amnon (2 Sam. 13.10–16), emphasizing the vulnerability of Joseph as his brothers plot while the reader anxiously watches as he gradually 'came near to them' (Gen. 37.18). 'When Joseph came to his brothers, they stripped him of his *kethoneth passim*' (Gen. 37.23). It is here where the overt abuse of Joseph begins, continuing as he is trafficked first to Midianite traders (Gen. 37.28), then (possibly)[28] to Ishmaelite traders (Gen. 39.1), who then traffic him to Potiphar (Gen. 39.1). Likewise, Jesus is stripped four times.

Tamar leads us trans-textually to Joseph, and Joseph leads us trans-textually to Jesus. Typological interpretations of biblical texts are common to Christian biblical theological work, so it is no surprise that biblical theology scholars have analysed the typological resonances between Joseph and Jesus. James Hamilton, for example, offers a typological reading of the canonical story of Joseph, finding forms of patterning echoed, escalated and accumulated in the canonical stories of Jesus. Though Hamilton considers his form of typological interpretation a form of 'canonical exegesis' invoking notions of divine intention in the canonical form,[29] he is careful to base his typological connections on literary-narrative features of particular texts. Having noted clear linguistic and narrative sequential patterning between the story of Joseph and the story of David, he concludes that Joseph is a type of David.[30] Among the textual resonances Hamilton identifies is the *kethoneth passim* that Tamar and Joseph share, noting how in both of these Davidic stories there is a story of 'a sexually abused woman named Tamar' (Gen. 38 and 2 Sam. 13).[31]

Hamilton's next step, in a two-step hermeneutical process, is to discern if there are distinctive linguistic and narrative dimensions of the story of Joseph that are found in the stories of Jesus that are not found in the story of David. Given that David is considered a type of Jesus and that Hamilton has just established that Joseph is a type of David, distinguishing what is unique to the gospel stories and the story of Joseph is key.[32] Hamilton does find linguistic and narrative sequencing patterns between the canonical story of Jesus and the canonical texts of Luke-Acts.[33]

I have used Hamilton's analysis for two reasons. First, I want to distinguish my trans-textual interpretive process from his typological interpretive process.[34] There are of course similarities, among them Hamilton's claim that typological reading 'should shape the way we view the world'.[35] Typological readings, he argues, should be contextual readings. Here we are in agreement. Our biblical interpretation should serve (and subvert) contemporary context. But where we differ is that trans-textual interpretation views the canon as a site of struggle, with the final form of the canon predominantly the redactional ideo-theology of dominant social sectors.[36] The story of Joseph, the story of David and the story of Jesus are sites of struggle.

Second, if we are to focus on these stories as including – as well as co-opting – sources about sexual violence, then we will have to read against the ideo-theological grain of the larger narratives into which they have been collected and composed to serve dominant ideo-theological projects. In doing a trans-textual reading, driven by readerly ideo-theological agendas, we might come across textual evidence that suggests an intertextual connection between texts. Typological interpretations like Hamilton's point to textual evidence and so should be included as an argument for an inter-textual connection between the story of Joseph and the story of Jesus (in Luke, in this case). Herman Waetjen makes a similar argument with respect to an intertextual relationship between the story of Joseph and Mark's story of Jesus, identifying 'parallels' between the story of Joseph and the naked 'youth' (*neaniskos*) of Mark 14.51–52 'who mirrors the destiny of Jesus',[37] as 'a Joseph figure'.[38] Later in Mark's Gospel, this same 'youth' (*neaniskos*), it would seem, is clothed (16.5). Waetjen does not pursue the intertextual connection between Joseph and Mark's Jesus, but if he had he would have found evidence of sexual violence.

Dismissing Waetjen's 'Joseph typology' argument, finding no intertextual links, Harry Fleddermann asks, rhetorically: 'Where else do we find Joseph typology in Mark?'[39] Yet in Fleddermann's own article he hovers on the very brink of an important trans-textual, even intertextual, connection between Joseph and Mark's Jesus. Rejecting a range of interpretations of the narrative significance of the young man, he concludes:

> The young man is not a prefiguration of the risen Jesus; he is not a Joseph figure; he is not a symbol of the Christian, baptismal initiate. He is a fleeing disciple. The pericope is a dramatization and concretization of the

universal flight of the disciples. The young man is arrested and stripped; but he flees. In contrast Jesus is arrested and stripped and crucified. The unbelieving flight of the young man is opposed to Jesus' believing acceptance of the crucifixion.[40]

Mark is clear: the young man is 'seized' (*krateō*) and stripped, for when seized, 'he pulled free (*kataleipō*) of the linen cloth and fled (*pheugō*) naked' (Mark 14.52). Joseph too is 'seized (*taphas*) by his garment', and he too 'left (*azab*) his garment in her hand and fled (*nus*)' (Gen. 39.12). So clearly there are trans-textual, even intertextual, links between Joseph and the young man. More significantly, there are trans-textual, even intertextual, links between Joseph and Mark's Jesus, for Mark's Jesus is seized and stripped four times.

A trans-textual reading, with Tamar as our guide via Joseph to Jesus, discerns trans-textual and probable intertextual connections between Joseph and Jesus. In the same way that narrative setting portends the rape of Tamar and the multiple strippings of Joseph, Mark emphasizes shifts in narrative setting that make Jesus vulnerable to abuse. There is a distinct shift in setting as Pilate 'handed him over to be crucified' (Mark 15.15b). But even before this shift in narrative setting, Jesus is stripped for the first time as Pilate has him flogged (Mark 15.15b). This would almost certainly have involved Jesus being stripped fully or partially naked.[41] As with Tamar and Joseph, the reader is slowly, in narrative temporal terms, led with Jesus into vulnerable space. Jesus is led into space that is completely outside of his (narrative) experience (Mark 15.16a). The precise socio-historical reference is not clear,[42] but probably refers to a courtyard of the praetorium (see Matt. 27.27), which was Roman-controlled territory. What is clear in narrative terms is that it is empire-occupied territory.

The space is soon filled, ominously, as the soldiers summon yet more soldiers, 'the whole cohort' (Mark 15.16b), of about 500 men.[43] Mark does not dwell on the second stripping of Jesus, emphasizing ironically instead the mocking and humiliation of Jesus as 'king' (Mark 15.2). In so doing, Mark's focus is on the 'putting on' (*endiduskō*), not the stripping off that precedes *endiduskō*. But the third stripping is named as such. Like Joseph (Gen. 37.23; MT *pashat*; LXX *ekduō*), Jesus is 'stripped' (*ekduō*; Mark 15.20). The fourth stripping, like the first, is implied by crucifixion and then confirmed when the soldiers 'divided his clothes among them' (15.24). Jesus is stripped four times; and two of these times he is stripped by hundreds of soldiers who are intent on humiliating him as a man,[44] denigrating his dignity by sexually violating his masculine body.

In our preparations of a Contextual Bible Study on male sexual violence against men, the Ujamaa Centre was drawn initially to Mark's account. Mark has served our work well, with its strong emphasis on the struggle for economic justice. But in our preparatory workshop together with David Tombs we offered participants, many of whom were students in biblical studies, theology and gender, the option of using either Mark or

Matthew. Of the four groups that constructed a preliminary CBS, three chose Matthew's account and one chose Mark's. We have decided to use Matthew because it is overt, from the outset, about Jesus being stripped.

Matthew clearly uses Mark's account, but offered us potentially useful resources in the redactional innovations Matthew makes in his re-use of the Marcan account. Matthew follows Mark with respect to the first stripping, implying rather than naming it (Matt. 27.26). But with respect to both the second and third strippings, Matthew is much more overt. Matthew follows Mark with respect to the shift in setting and the summoning of 'the whole cohort' (Matt. 27.27). However, Matthew's focus is not primarily the ironic recognition of Jesus as 'king', as seen in Mark's clothing of the naked Jesus in 'purple' (Mark 15.17), which becomes in Matthew an ordinary soldier's 'scarlet robe/cloak' (Matt. 27.28). What is distinctive for Matthew is that Jesus is overtly and publicly 'stripped' (*ekduō*): 'They stripped Jesus and put a scarlet robe on him' (Matt. 27.28).

Matthew names in the second stripping what Mark implies. Mark does name the third stripping as *ekduō*: 'After they had mocked Jesus, they stripped the purple robe off him and put his garments on him' (Mark 15.20). Matthew follows Mark with reference to the third stripping: 'After they had mocked Jesus, they stripped the robe off him and put his garments on him' (Matt. 27.31). But instead of referring to the colour of the robe (purple for Mark; scarlet for Matthew), Matthew emphasizes the robe itself. The colour no longer matters; what matters for Matthew is that once again Jesus is stripped. Mark can be translated as: 'they dressed him in purple' (Mark 15.17) and they then 'stripped the purple off him' (Mark 15.20). Matthew is more overt about an actual garment: 'they put a scarlet robe/cloak on him' (Matt. 27.28) and then 'they stripped the robe/cloak off him' (Matt. 27.31). It is the robe/cloak that matters to Matthew, not its colour. Matthew emphasizes that Jesus is stripped naked. Matthew follows Mark with respect to the fourth stripping as a component of the crucifixion (Matt. 27.35). Both Mark and Matthew have a direct link between the third stripping and the fourth (Mark 15.20, 24; Matt. 27.31, 35), making it clear that Jesus is stripped a fourth time.

Matthew, it would seem, foregrounds the embodied sexual violence against Jesus. That Jesus is 'stripped' is a distinctive feature of his Gospel. This is perhaps related to how Janice Capel Anderson and Stephen Moore characterize Matthew's embodiment of 'multiple, contradictory assumptions regarding masculinity'.[45] Though Matthew regularly refers to socio-historical 'hegemonic masculine roles', including male-to-male relationships, literal socio-cultural kinship, they argue, 'regularly gives way to spiritual or fictive kinship'.[46] As Anderson and Moore go on to argue, 'Literal kinship ties are portrayed as problematic, involving discord and rejection. The spiritual kinship categories Father, brother, and son, as well as the (largely) homologous categories of master/slave, master/disciple, and king/subject, define each other through their interrelationships – and redefine "masculinity" in the process.'[47] 'The narrative identity narratively constructed for male disciples [and male readers] in Matthew', they continue, 'amounts to an *anomalous* masculinity, when measured by traditional Greco-Roman standards.'[48] Within Matthew's construction of masculinity, even eunuchs have a place (Matt. 19.12). Indeed, Jesus affirms the eunuch 'as an image for exemplary discipleship', in a narrative context about marriage and a socio-historical context where there was a 'generally negative perception of eunuchs'.[49]

Matthew portrays Jesus narratively as himself an anomalous 'man', constructing a community around anomalous forms of masculinity. While clearly an androcentric text,[50] within Matthew's recognition of masculinity as a site of struggle the stripping of Jesus is one more component of Matthew's contestation of dominant forms of masculinity. Jesus is not a 'normal' male, and so he is stripped and abused by 'hegemonic' males. Among his disciples today are those who are stripped, abused and raped because dominant forms of masculinity are intent on exerting power over anomalous men.

Accordingly, for such males who are often victims and survivors of male sexual violence against men, we offer the following Contextual Bible Study based on Matthew 27.26–31. We have chosen to delimit the narrative in this way, focusing on the two overt 'strippings', which typify forms of male sexual violence against Jesus.

The summons of CBS

The following offers a preliminary shape for a CBS on male sexual violence against men. We have drawn on the resources of our workshop participants and the resources of socially engaged biblical scholarship.

1. Listen to a 'slow' reading of Matthew 27.26–31 in a number of different translations and languages. What have you heard from this slow reading of a well-known story that disturbs you?
2. Who are the characters in this story, and what do we know about each of them?
3. How many times is Jesus stripped? Matthew makes it clear that Jesus was stripped more than once. Re-read the text carefully and identify how many times Jesus is stripped.
4. Matthew also makes it clear that Jesus was stripped in front of a whole 'cohort' of what would have been about 500 soldiers. What other forms of sexual abuse might have taken place when so many men were involved in the repeated stripping and beating of Jesus?
5. In what situations in your context are men sexually abused by other men?
6. Are there resources in your community to address male sexual violence against men?

7. What can we do to address the issue of male sexual violence against men? Devise a specific 'action plan' of an action that you can participate in.

We have worked closely with a cohort of students within Biblical Studies and Gender Studies in producing this CBS. They understand how the CBS has been constructed, both in terms of contemporary contextual realities of male sexual violence against men and in terms of CBS methodology. Tombs' work and our own analysis during the preparatory workshop provided a detailed understanding of the contexts of male sexual violence against men. The preliminary CBS clearly follows the shape of a CBS, beginning with a slow dramatic reading of the delimited biblical text. This then leads into an open-ended reception-orientated question, designed to acknowledge and affirm any and every contribution and to offer an insight into how this text is already received within the particular community doing the CBS.

Questions 2 and 3 slow down the CBS process, offering literary-narrative resources for a close and careful re-reading of the text. Question 2 enables an opportunity to notice and reflect on each of the characters. Question 3 then moves the focus deliberately to the generative theme of the CBS: male sexual violence against men.

Question 4 offers socio-historical biblical studies resources, introducing information that may not be readily accessible to most 'ordinary' readers. During Tombs' presentation it became clear both that this was significant socio-historical detail and that most of those present were not familiar with what constituted a Roman cohort. The brief socio-historical input is followed by a question that relates directly to that input. Question 4 also functions as a bridge question, slowly shifting the focus of the CBS from text to context.

Questions 5 and 6 make a decisive shift to context, as the participants bring the resources of their re-readings of the text to bear on their context. Question 5 mimics a similar question from the Tamar CBS, as does Question 6, both of which have proved useful to generations of participants.

The CBS then concludes with a summons to action through Question 7. The question is open-ended, but could be shaped quite specifically within a particular context if appropriate.

Those who have participated in and been trained by our preparatory work together will identify appropriate sites in which they will do this CBS, documenting the process, and reporting back to the group. They will be accompanied through the process by Ujamaa Centre staff and student-workers. We will reflect on the CBS and what changes might be required to make it a more useful resource for constructing sacred and safe space in which to talk about heterosexual male violence against men.[51]

Conclusion

Local African communities of women have summoned Tamar, who has in turn summoned Joseph and Jesus as victims and survivors of sexual violence. We have followed Tamar's prophetic voice and actions and they have led us, via Joseph, to Jesus as a victim of heterosexual male violence against men. The Contextual Bible Study the Ujamaa Centre has constructed using this trans-textual trajectory is offered as a potential resource for breaking the silence about heterosexual male violence against men.

References

Albright, William F., and Christopher S. Mann, *Matthew*, New York: Anchor Bible, 1971.

Allen, Graham, *Intertextuality*, 2nd edn, London and New York: Routledge, 2011.

Anderson, Janice C. and Stephen D. Moore, 2003, 'Matthew and Masculinity', in *New Testament Masculinities*, S. D. Moore and J. C. Anderson eds, Semeia Studies, Atlanta, GA: Society of Biblical Literature, pp. 67–91.

Buisch, Pauline P., *Situating Tamar: The Relationship between Genesis 37–39 and 2 Samuel 13*, University of Notre Dame, undated.

Draper, Jonathan A., 'African Contextual Hermeneutics: Readers, Reading Communities, and their Options between Text and Context', *Religion & Theology* 22 (2015), pp. 3–22.

Fleddermann, Harry T., 'The Flight of a Naked Young Man (Mark 14:51–52)', *The Catholic Biblical Quarterly* 41:3 (1979), pp. 412–18.

Fontaine, Carole R. '"Here comes this dreamer": Reading Joseph the Slave in Multicultural and Interfaith Contexts', in *Genesis*, Athalya Brenner-Idan, Archie Chi Chung Lee and Gale A. Yee eds, Minneapolis, MN: Fortress Press, 2010, pp. 131–45.

Gates, Jennifer D., 'Reading the Joseph of Genesis as Transgender: Joseph in Drag', PhD Thesis, Eden Theological Seminary, St Louis, MO, 2014.

Genette, Gérard, *The Architext: An Introduction*, Berkeley, CA: University of California Press, 1992.

Hamilton, James M., 'Was Joseph a Type of the Messiah? Tracing the Typological Identification between Joseph, David, and Jesus', *Southern Baptist Journal of Theology* 12 (2008), pp. 52–7.

Jennings, Theodore W., *Jacob's Wound: Homoerotic Narrative in the Literature of Ancient Israel*, London: A&C Black, 2005.

Mosala, Itumeleng J., 'The Use of the Bible in Black Theology', in *The Unquestionable Right to be Free: Essays in Black Theology*, Itumeleng J. Mosala and Buti Tlhagale eds, Johannesburg: Skotaville, 1986, pp. 175–99.

—, *Biblical Hermeneutics and Black Theology in South Africa*, Grand Rapids, MI: Eerdmans, 1989.

—, 'Race, Class, and Gender as Hermeneutical Factors in the African Independent Churches' Appropriation of the Bible', *Semeia* 73 (1996), pp. 43–57.

Quiñones-Román, Luis, 'Rape Culture: Males and Females Sexual Assault in the Biblical Accounts of Joseph and Tamar: Genesis 39 & 2 Samuel 13:1–22', Final Paper, Princeton Theological Seminary, 2015.

Schwartz, Baruch. J., 'How the Compiler of the Pentateuch Worked: The Composition of Genesis 37', in *The Book of Genesis: Composition, Reception, and Interpretation*, Craig A. Evans, Joel N. Lohr and David L. Petersen eds, Leiden: Brill, 2012, pp. 263–78.

Skinner, John, *A Critical and Exegetical Commentary on Genesis*, 2nd edn, Edinburgh: T&T Clark, 1930.

Taylor, Vincent, *The Gospel According to St. Mark*, 2nd edn, London: MacMillan, 1966.

Tombs, David, 'Crucifixion, State Terror, and Sexual Abuse', *Union Seminary Quarterly Review* 53:1–2 (1999), pp. 89–109.

——. 'Silent No More: Sexual Violence in Conflict as a Challenge to the Worldwide Church', *Acta Theologica* 34:2 (2014), pp. 142–60.

——, 'Hidden in Plain Sight: Seeing the Stripping of Jesus as Sexual Violence', *Journal for Interdisciplinary Biblical Studies* 2:1 (2020), pp. 224–47, https://jibs.group.shef.ac.uk/volume-2/.

Waetjen, Herman C., 'The Ending of Mark and the Gospel's Shift in Eschatology', *Annual of the Swedish Theological Institute* 4 (1965), pp. 117–20.

——, *A Reordering of Power: A Socio-Political Reading of Mark's Gospel*, Minneapolis, MN: Fortress, 1989.

Waters, Julie, 'The Intersection of Law, Theology, and Human Trafficking in the Narrative of Joseph: Linking the Past to the Present', Second Annual Interdisciplinary Conference on Human Trafficking, University of Nebraska-Lincoln, 2010.

West, Gerald O., 'Deploying the Literary Detail of a Biblical Text (2 Samuel 13:1–22) in Search of Redemptive Masculinities', in *Interested Readers: Essays on the Hebrew Bible in Honor of David J. A. Clines*, James K. Aitken, Jeremy M. S. Clines and Christl M. Maier eds, Atlanta, GA: Society of Biblical Literature, 2013, pp. 297–312.

——, 'Reading the Bible with the Marginalised: The Value/s of Contextual Bible Reading', *Stellenbosch Theological Journal* 1:2 (2015), pp. 235–61.

——, Reconfiguring a Biblical Story (Genesis 19) in the Context of South African Discussions about Homosexuality', in *Christianity and Controversies over Homosexuality in Contemporary Africa*, Ezra Chitando and Adriaan van Klinken eds, Oxford: Routledge, 2016, pp. 184–98.

——, *The Stolen Bible: From Tool of Imperialism to African Icon*, Leiden and Pietermaritzburg: Brill and Cluster Publications, 2016.

——, 'Redaction Criticism as a Resource for the Bible as "A Site of Struggle"', *Old Testament Essays* 30:2 (2017), pp. 525–45.

——, 'African Biblical Scholarship as Tri-polar, Post-colonial, and a Site-of-struggle', in *Present and Future of Biblical Studies: Celebrating 25 Years of Brill's Biblical Interpretation*, Tat-siong Benny Liew ed., Leiden: Brill, 2018.

——, 'The Bible and/as the Lynching Tree: A South African Tribute to James H. Cone', *Missionalia* 46:2 (2019), pp. 236–54.

West, Gerald O., and Phumzile Zondi-Mabizela, 'The Bible Story that Became a Campaign: The Tamar Campaign in South Africa (and Beyond)', *Ministerial Formation* 103 (2004), pp. 4–12.

West, Gerald O., and Silindokuhle Zwane, '"Why Are You Sitting There?" Reading Matthew 20:1–16 in the Context of Casual Workers in Pietermaritzburg, South Africa', in *Matthew: Texts @ contexts*, Nicole Duran Wilkinson and James Grimshaw eds, Minneapolis, MN: Fortress Press, 2013.

West, Gerald O., Phumzile Zondi-Mabizela, Martin Maluleke, Happiness Khumalo, P. Smadz Matsepe and Mirolyn Naidoo, 'Rape in the House of David: The Biblical Story of Tamar as a Resource for Transformation', *Agenda* 61 (2004), pp. 36–41.

Notes

1 David Tombs, 'Crucifixion, State Terror, and Sexual Abuse', *Union Seminary Quarterly Review* 53:1–2 (1999), pp. 89–109; David Tombs, 'Silent no More: Sexual Violence in Conflict as a Challenge to the Worldwide Church', *Acta Theologica* 34:2 (2014), pp. 142–60; David Tombs, 'Abandonment, Rape, and Second Abandonment: Hannah Baker in *13 Reasons Why* and the Royal Concubines in 2 Samuel 15–20', in *Rape Culture, Gender Violence, and Religion*, Caroline Blyth, Emily Colgan and Katie B. Edwards eds (Cham, Switzerland: Palgrave Macmillan, 2018), pp. 117–41.

2 All Scripture quotations are from the New American Standard Bible (1995), or are author's own translation.

3 Itumeleng J. Mosala, *Biblical Hermeneutics and Black Theology in South Africa* (Grand Rapids, MI: Eerdmans, 1989), p. 185.

4 Gerald O. West and Phumzile Zondi-Mabizela, 'The Bible Story that Became a Campaign: The Tamar Campaign in South Africa (and beyond)', *Ministerial Formation* 103 (2004), pp. 4–12.

5 Gerald O. West, 'Deploying the Literary Detail of a Biblical Text (2 Samuel 13:1–22) in Search of Redemptive Masculinities', in *Interested Readers: Essays on the Hebrew Bible in Honor of David J. A. Clines*, James K. Aitken, Jeremy M. S. Clines and Christl M. Maier eds (Atlanta, GA: Society of Biblical Literature, 2013), pp. 297–312.

6 Gerald O. West, 'Reconfiguring a Biblical Story (Genesis 19) in the Context of South African Discussions about Homosexuality', in *Christianity and Controversies over Homosexuality in Contemporary Africa*, Ezra Chitando and Adriaan van Klinken eds (Oxford: Routledge, 2016), pp. 184–98.

7 Gerald O. West, *The Stolen Bible: From Tool of Imperialism to African Icon* (Leiden and Pietermaritzburg: Brill and Cluster Publications, 2016), pp. 410–20.

8 John Skinner, *A Critical and Exegetical Commentary on Genesis*, 2nd edn (Edinburgh: T&T Clark, 1930), p. 444.

9 Gerald O. West, 'The Bible and/as the Lynching Tree: A South African Tribute to James H. Cone', *Missionalia* 46:2 (2019), pp. 236–54.

10 Gerald O. West, 'Reading the Bible with the Marginalised: The Value/s of Contextual Bible Reading', *Stellenbosch Theological Journal* 1:2 (2015), pp. 235–61.

11 Mosala, *Biblical Hermeneutics and Black Theology in South Africa*, pp. 154–89; Itumeleng J. Mosala, 'Race, Class, and Gender as Hermeneutical Factors in the African Independent Churches' Appropriation of the Bible', *Semeia* 73 (1996), pp. 43–57.

12 Gerald West and Silindokuhle Zwane, '"Why Are You Sitting There?" Reading Matthew 20:1–16 in the Context of Casual Workers in Pietermaritzburg, South Africa', in *Matthew: Texts @ contexts*, Nicole Duran Wilkinson and James Grimshaw eds (Minneapolis, MN: Fortress Press, 2013), pp. 175–88.

13 Gerald O. West, 'Redaction Criticism as a Resource for the Bible as "a Site of Struggle"', *Old Testament Essays* 30:2 (2017), pp. 525–45.

14 Gérard Genette, *The Architext: An Introduction* (Berkeley, CA: University of California Press, 1992), pp. 83–4.

15 For a fuller discussion of notions of 'intertextuality', see Graham Allen, *Intertextuality*, 2nd edn (London and New York: Routledge, 2011).

16 Itumeleng J. Mosala, 'The Use of the Bible in Black Theology', in *The Unquestionable Right to Be Free: Essays in Black Theology*, Itumeleng Mosala and Buti Tlhagale eds (Johannesburg: Skotaville, 1986), p. 196.

17 West, 'Deploying the Literary Detail of a Biblical Text', pp. 302–11.

18 Gerald O. West, Phumzile Zondi-Mabizela, Martin Maluleke, Happiness Khumalo, Phidian Smadz Matsepe and Mirolyn Naidoo, 'Rape in the House of David: The Biblical Story of Tamar as a Resource for Transformation', *Agenda* 61 (2004), pp. 36–41.

19 West, *The Stolen Bible*, p. 415.

20 Baruch J. Schwartz, 'How the Compiler of the Pentateuch Worked: The Composition of Genesis 37', in *The Book of Genesis: Composition, Reception, and Interpretation*, Craig A. Evans, Joel N. Lohr and David L. Petersen eds (Leiden: Brill, 2012), pp. 263–78; Pauline Buisch, *Situating Tamar: The Relationship between Genesis 37–39 and 2 Samuel 13* (University of Notre Dame, undated).

21 Theodore W. Jennings, *Jacob's Wound: Homoerotic Narrative in the Literature of Ancient Israel* (London: A&C Black, 2005), pp. 177–96; see also Jennifer D. Gates, 'Reading the Joseph of Genesis as Transgender: Joseph in Drag' (PhD, Eden Theological Seminary, St Louis, MI, 2014); G. O. West and C. Van der Walt, 'A Queer (Beginning to the) Bible', *Concilium* 5 (2019), pp. 109–18.

22 Jennings, *Jacob's Wound*, p. 182.

23 Julie Waters, 'The Intersection of Law, Theology, and Human Trafficking in the Narrative of Joseph: Linking the Past to the Present', *Second Annual Interdisciplinary Conference on Human Trafficking*, University of Nebraska-Lincoln, 2010.

24 Jennings, *Jacob's Wound*, p. 183.

25 Buisch, *Situating Tamar*.

26 Luis Quiñones-Román, 'Rape Culture: Males and Females Sexual Assault in the Biblical Accounts of Joseph and Tamar: Genesis 39 & 2 Samuel 13:1–22', Final Paper, Princeton Theological Seminary, 2015; Buisch, *Situating Tamar*.

27 Jennings, *Jacob's Wound*, p. 186.

28 The reference in Genesis 37.28 to 'Midianites' and then in 39.1 to 'Ishmaelites' may signify text-critical confusion around the intrusion of the story of Judah and Tamar (Gen. 38) in the Joseph story, or may reflect another step in the trafficking of Joseph to Egypt. There is a growing body of both scholarly and popular literature reflecting on Joseph as (sexually) trafficked. See for example Waters, 'The Intersection of Law, Theology, and Human Trafficking in the Narrative of Joseph'; Carole R. Fontaine, '"Here Comes This Dreamer": Reading Joseph the Slave in Multicultural and Interfaith Contexts', in *Genesis*, Athalya Brenner-Idan, Archie Chi Chung Lee and Gale A. Yee eds (Minneapolis, MN: Fortress Press, 2010), pp. 131–45.

29 James M. Hamilton, 'Was Joseph a Type of the Messiah? Tracing the Typological Identification between Joseph, David, and Jesus', *Southern Baptist Journal of Theology* 12 (2008), p. 53.

30 Hamilton, 'Was Joseph a Type of the Messiah?', pp. 54–61.

31 Hamilton, 'Was Joseph a Type of the Messiah?', p. 56.

32 Hamilton, 'Was Joseph a Type of the Messiah?', p. 62.

33 Hamilton, 'Was Joseph a Type of the Messiah?, p. 69.

34 I want to thank my colleague M. Sam Tshehla for prompting me to explain the difference between a trans-textual reading and typological readings.

35 Hamilton, 'Was Joseph a Type of the Messiah?', p. 69.

36 African biblical hermeneutics operates within a tripolar metatheoretical framework, in which African context (as the subject of interpretation) is brought into dialogue with biblical text through an ideo-theologically mediated process. We use the notion of 'ideo-theological' to acknowledge that all biblical interpretation is always shaped by ideological and theological orientations (hence, ideo-theological); see for example Jonathan A. Draper, 'African Contextual Hermeneutics: Readers, Reading Communities, and their Options between Text and Context', *Religion & Theology* 22 (2015), pp. 3–22; Gerald O. West, 'African Biblical Scholarship as Tri-polar, Post-colonial, and a Site-of-struggle' in *Present and Future of Biblical Studies: Celebrating 25 Years of Brill's Biblical Interpretation*, Tat-siong Benny Liew ed. (Leiden: Brill, 2018), pp. 240–73.

37 Herman C. Waetjen, *A Reordering of Power: A Socio-Political Reading of Mark's Gospel* (Minneapolis, MN: Fortress, 1989), p. 195 n. 161.

38 Herman C. Waetjen, 'The Ending of Mark and the Gospel's Shift in Eschatology', *Annual of the Swedish Theological Institute* 4 (1965), p. 120.

39 Harry T. Fleddermann, 'The Flight of a Naked Young Man (Mark 14:51–52)', *The Catholic Biblical Quarterly* 41:3 (1979), pp. 415.

40 Fleddermann, 'The Flight of a Naked Young Man (Mark 14:51–52)', p. 417.

41 William F. Albright and Christopher S. Mann, *Matthew* (New York: Anchor Bible, 1971), p. 346.

42 Vincent Taylor, *The Gospel According to St. Mark*, 2nd edn (London: MacMillan, 1966), p. 585.

43 Vincent, *The Gospel According to St. Mark*, p. 585. See further, David Tombs, 'Hidden in Plain Sight: Seeing the Stripping of Jesus as Sexual Violence', *Journal for Interdisciplinary Biblical Studies* 2:1 (2020), pp. 238.

44 Tombs, 'Crucifixion, State Terror, and Sexual Abuse', pp. 92–6, 100–7.

45 Janice C. Anderson and Stephen D. Moore, 'Matthew and Masculinity' in *New Testament Masculinities*, Stephen D. Moore and Janice Capel Anderson eds (Semeia Studies; Atlanta, GA: Society of Biblical Literature, 2003), pp. 71.

46 Anderson and Moore, 'Matthew and Masculinity', p. 75.

47 Anderson and Moore, 'Matthew and Masculinity', pp. 75–6.

48 Anderson and Moore, 'Matthew and Masculinity', p. 76.

49 Anderson and Moore, 'Matthew and Masculinity', p. 90.

50 Anderson and Moore, 'Matthew and Masculinity', p. 71.

51 As indicated above, Contextual Bible Study is a component of the See-Judge-Act praxis cycle. Not only is lived reality analysed, judged, and then acted on for change, so too is the CBS. A revised version of this CBS has already been generated from feedback from workshops. Some reflection on the revision process and the revised CBS itself can be found in the collaborative work of Tombs, 'Hidden in Plain Sight, pp. 224–47. The revised CBS is available both from the Ujamaa Centre and from the Centre of Theology and Public Issues, University of Otago, http://hdl.handle.net/10523/10236 and a resource card at http://hdl.handle.net/10523/10233. The Ujamaa Centre will offer further analysis and reflection on the praxis cycle of this CBS in a forthcoming article.

PART 2

Stations of the Cross

7

This is ~~My~~ A Body

PÁDRAIG Ó TUAMA

The Stations of the Cross is a devotion where a person walks around a church, stopping in front of 14 images, each depicting some scene along the way of torture. Beginning with 'Jesus Stands Before Pilate' and ending with 'Jesus' Body is Laid in the Tomb'. Along the way, a man is stripped, a man falls down, a man's circumcised penis is made a mockery of by soldiers with foreskins and weapons, a woman offers help, a stranger's body is made use of, a woman grieves, people speak.

To stare at these images long enough is to question and query the reason behind these images. I did the Stations every day for ten years, and by the end I knew less about what I thought of them than I did at the beginning. Why is a body's torture something to turn to? Would a fleeing have been a failure?

Living through my own small tortures – and, let me be clear, being a torturer too, and not just of myself – I have begun to imagine new stations of the cross. A person survives a rape and wonders who to text. A person picks up a phone to phone a stranger for the help they know they need. A person tries out languages and stories to make meaning.

Along with imagining new stations, I also began to pick the cross apart. Maybe it could be used to make a fire, something to warm a body. In a religious culture saturated by the idolization of sacrifice, perhaps the most radical thing to do is to empty the notion of sacrifice. What if *that* was the hell that was harrowed?

What if a body is a sacrament, not a sacrifice?

Here are new stations for old stories, repeated round and round and round, defying the imagination that a body's torture brings anything good. Instead of a crown of thorns, a crown of poems, sonnets, little songs. Nothing is new. Under the sun or moon. My god, my god, I wish that I were wrong. But this is true for anybody who has lived through torture. And the dying too. This is a body.

Jesus Is Hung

Edging empires,
a man's laid bare for everyone to see.
Don't cross me, he said,
but nobody believed him
capable of such blasphemy,
they'd rather see him as a pleasing offering
to some god, than a harrower of hellish stories they had
authored. And anyway, Rome knew how to treat a man
provided he was adequately hung.
Some cop was watching,
waiting for the climax as
blood barbed up hard places.
And also, asphyxiation's excruciating,
depending on your tastes.

Jesus Can't Believe Himself

In the beginning, you didn't
believe it could happen.
Then it happened
and you began believing.

Somebody said stand up,
and you stood up; they demanded
you raise your hands and you did.

You worried about small things:
how to get the dirt out from your
clothes; if that tear could be mended;
how you'd be late and you hated being late.

You held your breath until
the end, barely noticing when
it was finished.

Jesus In The Hands Of Men

To you, oh Lord, I lift up my
shame. Open your eyes and look,
you who locked them shut for
many generations.

If I say my body is a temple,
they burn it down. If I say my body is a river,
they dam it.
If I say my body is a flame, they piss on it.

This is my body, now, broken for
nobody but me. Broken by all these
men whose gazes make me
less than I could ever have imagined.

Glory be to the Hammer and the
Nail. Glory be to the Body and the Blood.

Jesus Fills In A Questionnaire

You know your spirituality is abusive if:

Places of worship are torture for you.
You find sanctuaries unsafe.
Your trauma is covered over.
People tell your story without asking you your story.

Your authorities are not open to questions.
Your shame has been denied.
You were threatened when you spoke about leaving.
You entered based on misinformation.

You were asked to tolerate intolerable things.
Your privacies were discussed in public.
You are dissuaded from changing your mind.
Your body is discussed as if you do not own it.

If you answered at all, you should seek help.

Jesus Is Not Believed

when
believers
hear
things
they
don't
want
to
believe,
often
they
simply
won't
believe.

Jesus In Abu Ghraib

The way to be a man is
not to be a girl, so the
way to break a man is to
make him be a girl, or
some other kind of animal.
Dress him up, or down, or
turn him round and bend him
over. Make him show her
what he doesn't want to show
her. Make him beg
for what she will not give.
Bag his head, but not his body
yet. Wait. Shame him. And again.
Take a picture. Smile.

Jesus Texts

You text your friend.
They don't reply.
Never mind. You're not sure
what you'd say anyway.

You scroll through feeds,
hoping something might
make anything make sense.

Oh Lord, my grief is like a
river inside me; filled
with dead things I didn't
kill.

You lock the door. You
check it. Check again.

Oh Lord.   Dead Things.   Kill.

Jesus Comes Out

You open your mouth.
Nothing comes out but air
& hesitation.

Worlds unmade by words.
So you hold your breath
a little longer.

I need to tell you something,
you begin, something
that you need to know.

As watchmen keep watch,
you watch them as they
watch you.

Waiting for the dawn,
or a never ending night.

Jesus Phones The Samaritans

Samaritans, how can I help?
Of course I'm happy to talk.
What name can I call you?

You don't need to say anything.
That's quite alright. I'm in no rush.
I'm just a set of ears for you.

It might help if you tell me what is happening.
But even if you don't, that's okay.

You're welcome to tell me more.

What will you do after you hang up?
I'm not here to tell you what to do.
Are you feeling suicidal?

You can call us any time. Night or day.

Yes, I'm still here.

Jesus Considers Pronouns

The way He has never worked for you.
She neither. The way They sounds
plural and that's just how you like it.
The way Them makes you feel
like you belong. The way Their
can be possessed and you've never
felt like anything you owned would
fit. The way you like conjugating
your selves in the first, and the second
and the many. The way We Are Legion
makes sense in a way that nothing else
makes sense. The way you breathe now
that your plurals are made personal.
The way you are the singular and the slew.

Jesus Dresses

Not that one, you decide,
replacing the top that suits you beautifully
with one they won't deride,
or at least, won't use to justify
your firing.

You lay out an outfit on the bed
– like the clothing for a corpse –
and text your friend a shot
to check it's not
too gay.

Texting me your costume of the day
is very gay, your friend replies.
You set everything you wear.
on fire. Plus: fuck them.

Jesus Fears

It's hard being frightened
all the time. You see a tree
and imagine it spells death.
You select a leader, totally
expecting he'll reject you.
You spot a guard and know
the only way he'd touch you
is to torture you.

Even friends; even ones you
wrapped your arms round; even
ones you did your best to love; them too.

What do you do when you're abandoned?
You return to songs you sang at school.

There is a green hill far away.

Jesus Refuses

I know I'm here for the
same reasons others do
and the doubts that plague me
plague them too.

I know I barely understand
anything of what makes me me –
but lack of understanding
never bothered me.

I know some people who face fear
by making other people fear.
It's not great, I know; but I know it
makes their lives seem easier.

Here is a body. Broken. But
not for you. This won't help you.

Jesus Fantasizes

It's the desexing that bothers me –
as if I never had a boner or some lust,
as if I had so much of God's business
to consider that I never wanted kisses
or a nail run down my back. I woke
every morning the way men wake
every morning. I sought some comfort in
some touch and thought that much

could be achieved if people made more
love more often. I think I'd have made a
pretty average father, by which I mean
okay, by which I mean I wish. I would
like to age and watch my children grow.

I would like to hold on to my body.

Jesus Speaks

When I was young, I read
stories of a god and imagined
I'd always love the meanings.

These days, bloodied and defiant
I write my own. What's a limp
or a broken bone? Just a reminder

of a body. Somebody told me I'd
survive; they didn't tell me how.
Somebody told me I'd inspire. #same.

I've always woken early. I walk and
swing my arms. I pray, demand,
conspire, and I plan.

It hurts, but so does everything
worth doing. It works.

PART 3

Parsing Culture, Context and Perspectives

8

Conceal to Reveal: Reflections on Sexual Violence and Theological Discourses in the African Caribbean

CARLTON TURNER

The premise of this book opens up a space for understanding the kinds of Christianity that legitimize the most intimate and pervasive kinds of violence, particularly sexual violence. As contributors point out, the very act of 'not' recognizing nor acknowledging the sexual violence and abuse that Jesus suffered perpetuates such forms of Christian discourses and practices. This is particularly evident in the African Caribbean where, because of its deep experience of plantation slavery and colonial Christianity, non-recognition perpetuates complex and ambivalent attitudes, discourses and practices regarding sexual abuse and violence. While being predominantly Christian, it also has one of the highest rates of sexual assault against women in the world, according to United Nations statistics in 2015.[1] I suggest that concomitant with slavery and its consumerist and materialist attitudes towards the body – particularly the black body – was, and continually is, a dualistic and ambivalent colonial theological hermeneutic that legitimizes and normalizes sexual abuse and violence, often through silence and taboo.

Since very little is written on this area from a theological point of view within the region, this chapter offers an interdisciplinary, contextual theological exploration.[2] I want to suggest that within the context of the very explicit and pervasive trauma of sexual violence and assault meted out to black life in the African Caribbean, there exists within ancestral religious and cultural traditions a counter-hermeneutic and a counter-process that constantly seek to both criticize the sexual violence of plantation slavery and its legacies, but also heal the clear trauma of this generational sexual abuse and violence. The title, 'conceal to reveal', signals that through subversion, the deeper critique given by dancehall artists, women in particular, as well as Junkanoo and other African Caribbean traditional religious heritages, is that the abusive hermeneutics hidden within colonial Christianity are very sexual. In multiple ways they permit and perpetuate sexual violence and assault against women (and men) as they exist in the aftermath of slavery and colonialism. Such colonial Christian discourses continually function to hide or reframe sexual abuse, but also to blame and shame victims of such sexual abuse. Ultimately, this chapter, like the book, aims to expose and name the deep histories and narratives of sexual abuse and violence at the heart of the Christian story itself.

Preliminary considerations

Reflecting on David Tombs' article 'Crucifixion, State Terror, and Sexual Abuse', a number of hermeneutical vistas open up for considering the African Caribbean context.[3] First, acts of state terror and oppression have consistently had sexual aspects. At a micro-level, sexual humiliation and sexual assault of individual victims serve to spread fear and terror and ensure continued domination of the oppressed. At a macro-level, oppressive regimes, such as the first-century Roman Empire and Latin American military regimes of the twentieth century, are in themselves sexualized invasions of the deepest boundaries held by oppressed peoples. In other words, looking at state terror and oppression requires us to theorize beyond the individual and into the collective. Sexual abuse is not simply something that happens to individuals; it is an act that transgresses and traumatizes the community to which that person belongs and those who will become part of it.

Second, there is a particular method of balancing private sexual humiliation and assault and public sexual violence that heightens this sense of fear and submission. Part of the pathology of state terror is its trauma bonding: what is seen is played off against what is not, in order to spread the myth of the oppressor's might. Tombs suggests that in the light of the very sexualized nature of state oppression, the Gospels themselves fail to disclose what might have happened to Jesus in the secrecy of the praetorium. Tombs writes:

> Although it is vital to acknowledge the sexual humiliation that is revealed in the text, however, what the texts might conceal may also be significant. There may have been a level of sexual abuse in the *praetorium* that none of the Gospels immediately discloses.[4]

Furthermore, there was also the perpetuation of sexual abuse and violence rife within the *Pax Romana*. Sexual dominance and its consequences were part of the Roman military chain of command. The very structure of Roman control and power was maintained by how its own military personnel were managed. They were managed through domination, oppression and humiliation, without recourse for revenge on those up the ladder. This kind of resentment and hostility was naturally passed on to other victims, often in sexualized ways.[5]

Third, and more importantly, the kind of hermeneutics that glosses over the very sexualized nature of Jesus' trial, crucifixion and death is also deeply problematic. This pattern seems consistent with biblical accounts in the way that such accounts are written. They are also evident in how disrupting the suggestion is that Jesus might have been both sexually humiliated and assaulted as part of the passion narrative. For Tombs, humiliation is defined as 'enforced nudity, sexual mockery, and sexual insults', and assault as 'forced sexual contact that ranges from molestation to penetration, injury, or mutilation'.[6] Such insights are instructive and allow for a cogent way of reading the African Caribbean context. These dynamics become very clear when taking the experience of slavery and colonialism in the African Caribbean seriously, but particularly in how they have shaped hermeneutics and attitudes towards sexual abuse and violence, particularly by the Church.

The nature of plantation slavery

We cannot overemphasize the formative power of institutionalized plantation slavery as it was exercised within the New World generally and the African Caribbean in particular. We also cannot overemphasize the pervasive sexualized nature of its violence meted out to black people, both male and female. Scholarship suggests that not only was sexual abuse and violence commonplace, but that every possible aspect of black sexuality and existence was policed and, when decided, punished and assaulted. To begin with, Anthony B. Pinn traces the complex interconnection between race and sexuality and the shaping of North American society and church (and no doubt the African Caribbean as well).[7] Pinn explains that black bodies were both epistemologically and ontologically framed as less than human within a social structure that kept this status firmly and violently in place. While race and class distinctions included sexual relations, it was in fact sexual relations that reinforced such rigid racial and class distinctions. Pinn puts it this way:

> While understood as irrational and of lesser value, Africans in North America were sufficient fodder for slaveholder's erotic pathologies and the general sexual release of any white person who desired black flesh. Enslaved Africans in this sense, both men and women, became acceptable repositories for sexual desire and repulsions because subduing the racial other in the New World implied the ability to sexually have them.[8]

Long before Pinn, Frantz Fanon, the noted French Caribbean radical intellectual and revolutionary, became one of the earliest persons to theorize the colonial context and the manner of imperial domination. For Fanon, the colonial context is always shaped by dichotomizing and polarizing mechanisms meant to distinguish between the 'native' and the 'colonizer' or 'settler'. These processes are inherently violent and relegate the indigenous 'other' to the status of non-being. He states:

As if to show the totalitarian character of colonial exploitation the settler paints the native as a sort of quintessence of evil. Native society is not simply described as a society lacking in values. It is not enough for the colonist to affirm that those values have disappeared from, or still better never existed in, the colonial world. The native is declared insensible to ethics; he represents not only the absence of values, but also the negation of values. He is, let us dare to admit, the enemy of values, and in this sense he is the absolute evil.[9]

Such a characterization of the 'other' necessarily leads to punitive measures. Fanon also outlines the sexual nature of such measures. Sexual relations between colonizer and colonized, between black and white, were rarely without violence, or without violent consequences. Commenting on his French colonial context, Fanon wrote:

We know historically that the Negro guilty of lying with a white woman is castrated. The Negro who has had a white woman makes himself taboo to his fellows. It is easy for the mind to formulate this drama of sexual preoccupation.[10]

Pinn reflects on Fanon's work, demonstrating how totally and sexually absorbed the context of plantation slavery was with its violence: 'In a sense, discourse of sex(uality) became ritualized annihilation – a controlling of bodies – that provided whites (and some blacks) with psychological and physical pleasure that was orgasmic (i.e., gratifying on the level of the individual and the social).'[11]

When surveying the work of womanist scholars, we begin to see more deeply into the sexualized nature of plantation slavery. To begin with, Angela Davis argued quite early on that, as a method, the raping of female slaves was institutional. It was targeted state terrorism.[12] In line with Tombs' study, she states: 'In the same way that rape was an institutionalized ingredient of the aggression carried out against the Vietnamese people, designed to intimidate and terrorize the women, slave owners encouraged the terroristic use of rape in order to put Black women in their place.'[13] Also, like Tombs, she problematizes what is clearly a reframing of the sexualized nature of plantation slavery:

Despite the testimony of slaves about the high incidence of rape and sexual coercion, the issue of sexual abuse has been all but glossed over in the traditional literature on slavery. It is sometimes even assumed that slave women welcomed and encouraged the sexual attentions of white men.[14]

Similarly, bell hooks considers the process of enslavement, from the middle passage to integration into the plantation machinery, as underpinned by a violence meant to break and bring slaves to submission in every possible way, especially sexually.[15] After being stripped of their clothing, the naked female slave signalled sexual vulnerability within such a society. Hence, rape was the preferred form of punishment for women who were seen as defiant. Furthermore, 'the threat of rape or other physical brutalization inspired terror in the psyches of displaced African females'.[16] In addition, hooks notes how sexual violence shaped the experience of females who, in the mind of the slaver, required 'breaking in' and 'taming' since they were more likely to work intimately with the slave master's family. She writes: 'Since the slaver regarded the black woman as a marketable cook, wet nurse, housekeeper, it was crucial that she be so thoroughly terrorized that she would submit passively to the will of the white master, mistress, and their children.'[17] In the world of plantation slavery, females were heavily brutalized and terrorized, and rape, especially of young girls, was pervasive. Katie Cannon puts it this way:

> Slavocracy was the rude transformation of African people into market-able objects. Slaves were rightless and lacking in responsibility. Slave women were answerable with their bodies to the sexual casualness of 'stock breeding' with Black men and to the sexual whims and advances of white men. Being both a slave and a female, the Black woman survived wanton misuse and abuse.[18]

But men did not escape the sexual abuse and assault. Kelly Brown Douglas reminds us that men, as well as women, were the objects of sexual violence and terror. With regard to castration, she states: 'Black male bodies were attacked and dismembered with impunity. Castration, though objected to by some Englishmen and abolitionists, became a punishment meted out to Black men.'[19] And, while acknowledging the plight of women, she further states, 'Yet slave masters often castrated those enslaved males whom they believed to be barriers to their own vile desires to ravish a particular black woman.'[20] With regard to lynching, Douglas explains:

> Even as lynching was clearly a sexually directed and motivated attack against Black male bodies, it was a primary weapon employed to control Black men and women socially, economically, and politically. Lynching is thus a classic example of the tools used to enforce and uphold White patriarchal hegemony. Lynching rose in popularity after emancipation.[21]

Returning to Tombs' assessment of the sexualized nature of state violence and terror, and how they might inform our reading of Jesus' very public state execution, the following becomes clear when considering the African Caribbean context. Plantation slavery as it manifested in the African Caribbean was the most brutal experience of that institution. Sexual violence was pervasive. Acts of sexual abuse and terror were not isolated and individual events but were legally and culturally part of the plantation society. Sex was a weapon used to maintain a white European power structure that permitted atrocious acts towards black and brown people collectively.

Within the African Caribbean, control over the sexual lives of slaves was so acute and severe that it was the intention to introduce 'breeding farms' into Caribbean plantation life. Margaret Tweeny explored this specific popular myth about African Caribbean slavery. She concluded that while historical evidence is sparse about the actual practice of slave breeding farms, what is certain is that Barbuda, not least in the mind of absentee slave plantation owner Christopher (Bethell) Codrington, was deemed a good site for breeding profitable slaves in the late 1700s in what he referred to as a 'nursery for negroes'.[22]

Furthermore, there is something dissonant and pathological about the levels of sexual abuse and violence, apart from the genocidal nature of colonial oppression. This dissonance and pathology is seen in the very public, but also very private, nature of these abuses. When considering the work of persons like Fanon, the strict machine-like abuse of plantation society bred, like sexual abuse and assault generally, other maladies – hostility, self-hatred, anger, depression, anxieties, toxic relationships, toxic community secrecies that ignored, or even further permitted ongoing sexual violence and assault.[23] What must be understood, as Orlando Patterson has shown, is that slave societies were never meant to be 'societies' in the usual sense of the word.[24] They were meant solely for producing capital and furthering the agenda of the plantocracy. The idea of sexual freedom and dignity for slaves, male or female, parents or children, was inconsequential. Slaves were non-persons and non-persons could not claim to be sexually abused or assaulted.

Before looking at the contemporary Caribbean scene regarding sexual abuse and violence, more must be said about the kinds of hermeneutics involved in perpetuating this systemic sexual violence and abuse. The kinds of sexual violence informing African Caribbean plantations were justified and perpetuated by colonial Christian hermeneutics that were ambivalent about spirituality, the body and purity. Those hermeneutics were also very clear about the Africans not being equal human beings before God.

Colonial hermeneutics and ambivalent theologies

As we reflect on the contemporary African Caribbean context, we come to see an ambivalence. While the region is very religious – in fact, particularly Christian – there still exist high levels of sexual abuse and violence within ordinary life. But this ambivalence traces back to slavery and colonialism where the hermeneutics of missionary Christianity were designed to serve colonial expansion and oppression while silencing all forms of alterity: non-Western cultures, philosophies and theologies. The indigenous had to be silenced and undergo a process of Europeanization. In the African Caribbean, church preaching and teaching not only supported the idea that slave cultures, philosophies, bodies and sexual expressions were heathen and idolatrous, but also that they needed integration into the mercantilist machinery of slavery. Caribbean theologians have insisted on this as crucial to doing any kind of theological reflection in the region.[25] In tracing the plight of the region back to what he terms missionary culture and colonial Christianity, Lewin Williams explains that the process of making Christianity indigenous to the region has never quite been successful since the indigenous themselves rejected the method by which it came. Christianity came through foreign imposition of the culture of the colonizer. He states, 'the colonizing culture cannot avoid presenting itself as superior to the host culture. Colonization is the presumption of superiority.'[26]

Noting the dualistic nature of missionary Christianity and its legacy on the black Church, particularly in the areas of sexuality, Douglas explains that the Western Christian tradition made use of the sexual act, and sexuality in general, as a way of perpetuating their othering of non-Western groups.[27] She explains that this was done in a number of ways:

> First, it tended to make genital sexual activity the defining feature of sexuality. Therefore, maligning the sexual ethics of a particular people became sufficient in a Christian society for challenging their entire personhood. Second, by associating sexual activity with passionate, irrational, and even satanic behavior, the Christian tradition provided persons with a means for placing a sacred canopy over their acts of domination and oppression.[28]

For Douglas such an outlook finds its roots in a Graeco-Roman dualistic philosophical world, whose legacy of the Enlightenment framed a particularly anti-black undercurrent. And, in matters of sexuality, those undercurrents were violent. She explains that such historic dualism was misogynistic and sexist:

> Women have been consistently associated with the body, passion, and the irrational, while men have been associated with the soul, reason, and rationality. While pre-Christian Hebrew thought may not have contributed to the denigration of human flesh, it certainly laid the foundation for the demonizing of women's sexuality.[29]

In such an imagination, therefore, sex and sexuality were not to be positive experiences for black people, but rather, experiences inherently intertwined with violence and shame. Sex was not to be an experience of love, wholeness, pleasure and communion. In such a colonial missionary worldview, sex was to be kept secret, and even if black people, male or female, were sexually abused or assaulted in some way, there was no recourse since such trauma was permissible. After all, in such a worldview, black was equated with non-being.

In the contemporary African Caribbean context, churches have always had ambivalent attitudes to sexuality in general, and to sexual abuse and violence in particular. Conversations about sex are relegated to the realm of the secular – for the attention of the police, or the doctor, or the privacy of the home, but not for the Church. With a Neoplatonic theological outlook that insists on absolutes and dogma while avoiding involvement in the complexities of everyday brokenness, cultures of sexual abuse and violence, a consistent taboo topic in churches, remain unaddressed. We will now have a closer look at the contemporary African Caribbean scene.

The contemporary scene

A number of research reports have highlighted sexual abuse and violence as particularly high within the Latin American and Caribbean region. In gathering data from disparate research reports, the desk review entitled 'Sexual Violence in Latin America and the Caribbean' makes general conclusions about the contemporary state of affairs.[30] It links the pervasive practices of sexual violence and abuse to colonial conquests, civil wars, military dictatorships and United States military interventions. With particular reference to the Caribbean, the review has the following:

> A population-based survey among adolescents and young adults conducted in Barbados, Jamaica and Trinidad and Tobago found that between 52% and 73% of women reported experiences of sexual violence by a partner, defined as a partner forcing or attempting to force the respondent into any sexual activity she did not want by threatening, holding down or hurting the respondent in some way. Again, this is an example of a study that included attempted – not just completed acts of force.[31]

With regard to male experiences of sexual abuse and violence, the same report further states:

> Several studies from the Caribbean have found relatively high rates of sexual violence and coercion against males. For example, one study from Barbados, Jamaica and Trinidad and Tobago found that 40–54% of male respondents aged 19–30 reported experiencing sexual abuse at some point in their life.[32]

There was further report that almost 10 per cent of adolescent males experienced inappropriate and forced touching by close members of the family. One third of adolescent males who were sexually active reported that their first sexual experience was through force, with most of these incidents taking place before age 11.

Caribbean female scholars and activists have not remained quiet in exposing the problem of sexual abuse and violence and the Church's lack of response, or the general silence and permissiveness around sexual abuse and violence – especially when such activities involve the clergy themselves. To begin with, Anna Kasafi Perkins directly problematizes the high instances of Intimate Male Partner Violence (IMPV or IPV) in Jamaica and women's reluctance to find intervention. In fact, part of the problem is a pervasive silence around such experiences taking place in the Church itself. After researching this phenomenon, Perkins reports that part of the silence has to do with fear over losing membership or tarnishing the image of individual members of the Church, particularly church leaders. The other reason, unfortunately, has to do with an anti-divorce hermeneutic that states that the Bible is against divorce, seeing it as dangerous to family life and the role of the male in the home.[33] She further protests:

> Clearly, sacred texts like the Bible and pastors and ministers, who are the elite interpreters of this text, play an important role in how the issues surrounding IMPV are framed and directly impacts how a woman perceives violence against women, the appropriateness of seeking intervention and other services as well as gender roles in the family.[34]

It is not surprising that Perkins identifies church hermeneutics as problematic, and therefore a change in hermeneutics as vital for any kind of deep address of sexual violence within the African Caribbean context.

Nicole Ashwood reflects more broadly on the Caribbean, interrogating particular incidences of clergy sexual misconduct hitting the media and their traumatic aftermath. Ashwood states: 'Clergy sexual misconduct continues to be a troubling issue in the Caribbean region and in Jamaica in particular. There have been at least three cases of ministerial sexual abuse which have made the headlines in the Jamaican papers.'[35] She further explains, as Perkins does, that public responses to the cases, while varied, become overshadowed by other topics. In other words, it seems all too easy for cases that draw national attention to sexual abuse and violence to become silent or hidden, but also unaddressed, conversations. Ashwood particularly focuses on the silence around sexual misconduct within churches, naming the chief reason for this as fear. There is significant fear in dealing with sexuality in general, let alone clergy sexual misconduct. She, like Perkins, argues that the kinds of hermeneutics around sexuality inevitably lead to victim shaming, which is quite acute given the history and cruelty of slavery in which victims of slave sexual abuse and oppression were deemed non-human and beasts of burden. In fact, in her professional capacity as a clergywoman Ashwood has found it difficult to find help within the biblical text for counselling victims of clergy sexual abuse. In her estimation, 'In many parts of the biblical canon, females are categorized as either harlots or princesses, and once her virtue is taken, she has no recourse from moral society.'[36]

I now turn to this motif of silence that has undergirded much of the discussion thus far. My contention is that the ambivalence towards black bodies and towards sexuality, concomitant with the quest for an absolute and neutral Christianity, creates a culture that denies and casts a blind eye on the real lives of ordinary people within the region, particularly those who have been sexually abused and exploited. But even more than this, it allows for an institution that will not confront its own complicity in perpetuating and legitimizing sexual assault and abuse. However, as we shall see, there has always been a counter hermeneutic within the African Caribbean.

African Caribbean religious and cultural heritages: a counter-hermeneutic

The ambivalence and play on what is concealed and what is revealed is deeply characteristic of legacies of trauma within colonized contexts. In line with Tombs' 'Crucifixion, State Terror, and Sexual Abuse', scholars such as Joy Degruy and Christina Sharpe have theorized post-slavery contexts as post-traumatic, whose legacies are perpetuated into contemporary life.[37] While Degruy speaks of post-traumatic slave syndrome as the reality that explains the pervasive incarceration, mental and emotional health concerns, poverty and debt among black people, Sharpe describes the notion of a 'wake', a trail of early death that haunts generation after generation of black people. What is interesting is that such legacies are very silent and play out subconsciously within black communities. This seems to be adequate for the African Caribbean as it exists within multiple spheres of trauma. But this notion of silence is key. Yael Danieli explains that trauma works through a 'conspiracy of silence'. It often goes unaddressed and impacts the lives of generations, not only those of survivors and perpetrators; it also manifests in the lives of their children, precisely because it remains unaddressed. He further explains that these silent reactions to trauma are often societal, and for survivors 'have a significant negative effect on their post-trauma adaptation and their ability to integrate their traumatic experiences'.[38]

However, we must not forget a crucial fact about the context of plantation slavery. Trauma is not the only story. William E. Cross Jr explains that within the 400 or so years of plantation slavery, Africans and their descendants learned to survive using their ancestral religiosity. What we see as post-traumatic syndrome must be countered with a sense of post-traumatic growth. While plantation society was managed through violence and oppression in every possible way, slaves had to survive through secrecy, subversion and cunning. African cultural heritages such as carnival, voodoo, reggae and dancehall music, to name but a few, were ways in which the descendants of slaves navigated power structures and preserved deep ancestral philosophies and theologies. To begin with, Junkanoo, a carnival-like Christmastime street festival in the anglophone African Caribbean, has consistently been designated as a secular space for vulgarity and sexual lewdness, particularly by Christian ministers from historic denominations. My own research into the contemporary Junkanoo scene suggests that what actually takes place in Junkanoo is a celebration of the goodness and sanctity of the body, and of African traditional ways of worship.[39]

In fact, what is evidenced is a re-appropriation of a non-dualistic African pneumatology within a colonial context that seeks always to separate the sacred and the secular. In Junkanoo, as in carnival, African Caribbean people contest and then reframe the colonial idea that censorship, shame and violence should always be linked to African bodies and sexuality. What looks to the outsider as frolic, play and vulgarity is secretly a revelation of the dancers' true identity as people made in the image and likeness of God, deserving simply to be as they are.

Taking this notion of secrecy a bit further, Dwight Hopkins explains that slaves used secrecy as a means to reconstitute and heal themselves in the context of the trauma of the plantation. In his exploration of slave religion and its importance for Black Theology, Hopkins argues two important points. First, slave secret meetings were for the purpose of reinterpreting Christianity and the kind of hermeneutics that denied their personhood. He writes: 'Stealin' the meetin', what enslaved religious blacks called the secret (reinterpreted) Christian gatherings – commonly termed the Invisible Institution – were the institutional location out of which the future black theology of liberation emerged.'[40] Second, part of their theological strategy of re-imagining freedom was by seizing the domain of pleasure. Hopkins also writes:

> As part of their theological strategy of re-imaging and living as free creations of the divine in a comprehensive holy environment, enslaved Africans and African Americans stole and claimed the sacred domain of pleasure, either as fun times or during corn-shucking episodes or other labors initially organized by the plantation master. Even in pleasure, black workers knew who they were and how to nourish themselves.[41]

Similarly, Bahamian theologian Kirkley Sands suggests that the slaves were reconstructing Christianity and affirming their own dignity and right to freedom through their festivals.[42]

Another example of this is the literature on Jamaican dancehall. Roman Catholic theologian Anna Kasafi Perkins sees the female dancehall artist as consistently critiquing and responding to the misogyny and violent anti-female lyrics usually associated with dancehall music. Looking at the work of female dancehall artist Tanya Stephens, Perkins argues that Stephens' music directly confronts the misogyny within dancehall cultures by disrupting its imagery: 'Her in-your-face-no-holds-barred feistyness makes both men and women uncomfortable, particularly when she is explicit about female sexual desire and sexual needs and performance.'[43]

It becomes evident that the dancehall is an ambivalent space in which complex issues are addressed, sexuality being one of them. One such clear commentary is that women's bodies are sacred, and that sexuality and violence need to be uncoupled. In fact, the right to freedom and pleasure for the African person is asserted, even in the face of church and cultural censorship.

While Perkins reflects theologically on dancehall hermeneutics, Carolyn Cooper comes to similar conclusions as a literary and cultural theorist. Cooper reveals the counter-hermeneutic within the dancehall that works to reshape sexuality and sexual politics away from violence and oppression and towards pleasure and freedom, particularly the freedom of identity. Cooper notes:

> Arguing transgressively for the freedom of women to claim a self-pleasuring sexual identity that may even be explicitly homoerotic, I propose that Jamaican dancehall culture at home and in the diaspora is best understood as a potentially liberating space in which working-class women and their more timid middle-class sisters assert the freedom to play out eroticised roles that may not ordinarily be available to them in the rigid social conventions of the everyday. The dancehall becomes an erogenous zone in which the celebration of female sexuality and fertility is ritualised as men pay homage to the female principle.[44]

Cooper further explains that the African Caribbean carnivalesque tradition, of role-play and reversal is also found within the dancehall aesthetic and works specifically to address the deep wounds inflicted by slavery and colonial oppression and their attendant theologies of domination and power. She states:

> There are, it is all too true, profound psycho-sociological underpinnings of this desire to be/play the other that cannot be simply written off as mere entertainment. Role-play both conceals and reveals deep-seated anxieties about the body that has been incised with the scarifications of history.[45]

The lyrics of Lady Saw, whose words and images at first glance seem to reify the misogynistic sexual attitudes towards women, are actually double talk or word play, reminding the hearer that violence, objectification and abuse, particularly of the female, are not the only legacies of sexuality within the region. Pleasure, and the right to be free and to choose freely within the sexual act, is the dominant theme. This serves as a critique of the hidden hermeneutics of colonial missionary Christianity and its influences within the region: that sex, generally, and the bodies of women in particular, ought to be controlled, regulated and censored according to quite duplicitous, anachronistic and oppressive value systems. As Douglas and others have already asserted, the legacy of missionary Christianity on the existence of black cultures, particularly church cultures, is to deny the materiality and lived existence of the colonized.[46] In other words, violence against the body, be that sexual or otherwise, is permissible because this world is temporary and only that which is spiritual is worthy of consideration and reflection. Of course, within African Caribbean cosmology, this is nonsense. The material and the spiritual co-exist and cannot be separated. The immanent and the transcended are co-eternally bound together.

Conclusion

Tombs' observations about the sexualized nature of state violence and our tendency to gloss over this reality are fruitful points of reflection for the African Caribbean.[47] In this chapter I have argued that the African Caribbean has been shaped by this kind of state violence and have tried to tease out the multiple and complex ways in which such sexual violence and oppression have become culturally and theologically ingrained in the everyday lives of African Caribbean people. However, we need to be reminded that the descendants of slaves were always providing a counter-hermeneutic, contesting the dangerous hermeneutics of colonial missionary Christianity: that sexuality for the black person would/should always be imbued with violence, censorship and trauma. It seems that, ultimately, the very places where sexual violence, oppression, hypocrisy and abuse have been laid bare for discussion, and structures of power laid bare for critique, have also been the spaces most stigmatized within the African Caribbean and relegated to the ecclesiastical fringe.

References

Ashwood, Nicqui, 'Self-questioning from the Caribbean', in *When Pastors Prey: Overcoming Clergy Sexual Abuse of Women*, Geneva: World Council of Churches, 2013, pp. 117–20.

Cannon, Katie G., *Black Womanist Ethics*, Atlanta, GA: Scholars Press, 1988.

Contreras, J. M., S. Bott, A. Guedes and E. Dartnall, *Sexual Violence in Latin America and the Caribbean: A Desk Review*, Sexual Violence Research Initiative, 2010.

Cooper, Carolyn, 'Sweet & Sour Sauce: Sexual Politics in Jamaican Dancehall Culture'; The Sixth Jagan Lecture, York University, ON, Canada (CERLAC, 2005).

Danieli, Yael, 'Introduction: History and Conceptual Foundations', in *International Handbook of Multigenerational Legacies of Trauma*, Yael Danieli ed., New York: Plenum Press, 2010, pp. 1–17.

Davis, Angela Y., *Women, Race and Class*, London: The Women's Press, 1981.

Davis, Kortright, *Emancipation Still Comin': Explorations in Caribbean Emancipatory Theology*, Maryknoll, NY: Orbis, 1990.

Degruy, Joy L., *Post Traumatic Slave Syndrome: America's Legacy of Enduring Injury and Healing*, Milwaukie, OR: Uptone Press, 2005.

Douglas, Kelly Brown, *Sexuality and the Black Church: A Womanist Perspective*, Maryknoll, NY: Orbis, 1999.

Erskine, Noel L., *Decolonizing Theology: A Caribbean Perspective*, Trenton, NJ: Africa World Press, 1998.

Fanon, Frantz, *Black Skin, White Masks*, New York: Grove Press, 1967.

——, *The Wretched of the Earth*, Harmondsworth: Penguin, 1967.

Halcón, Linda, Trisha Beuhring and Robert Wm Blum, *A Portrait of Adolescent Health in the Caribbean*, Minneapolis, MN: World Health Organization Collaborating Centre on Adolescent Health, University of Minnesota, 2000.

Halcón, Linda, Trisha Beuhring, Robert Wm Blum, Ernest Pate, Sheila Campbell-Forrester and Anneke Venema, 'Adolescent Health in the Caribbean: A Regional Portrait', *American Journal of Public Health* 93:11 (2011), pp. 1851–7.

hooks, bell, *Ain't I a Woman: Black Women and Feminism*, London: Pluto Press, 1981.

Hopkins, Dwight N., *Down, Up, and Over: Slave Religion and Black Theology*, Minneapolis, MN: Fortress Press, 2000.

LeFranc, Elsie, Maureen Samms-Vaughan, Ian Hambleton, Kristin Fox and Dennis Brown, 'Interpersonal Violence in Three Caribbean Countries: Barbados, Jamaica, and Trinidad and Tobago', *Revista Panamericana de Salud Pública* 24:6 (2009), pp. 409–21.

Patterson, Orlando, *The Sociology of Slavery: An Analysis of the Origins, Development and Structure of Negro Slave Society in Jamaica*, Studies in Society, London: MacGibbon & Kee, 1967.

Perkins, Anna Kasafi, 'Christian Norms and Intimate Male Partner Violence: Lessons from a Jamaica Women's Health Survey', in *The Holy Spirit and Social Justice: Interdisciplinary Global Perspectives*, Antipas L. Harris and Michael D. Palmer eds, Lanham, MD: Seymour Press, 2019.

—, '"Tasting Tears and [Not] Admitting Defeat": Promoting Values and Attitudes through the Music of Tanya Stephens?', Inaugural Lecture of the Centre for Social Ethics, St. Michael's Theological College, Kingston, Jamaica, 2008.

Pinn, Anthony B., *Embodiment and the New Shape of Black Theological Thought*, New York: New York University Press, 2010.

Sands, Kirkley C., *Early Bahamian Slave Spirituality: The Genesis of Bahamian Cultural Identity*, Nassau, Bahamas: The Nassau Guardian Ltd, 2008.

Sharpe, Christina Elizabeth, *In the Wake: On Blackness and Being*, Durham, NC: Duke University Press, 2016.

Tombs, David, 'Crucifixion, State Terror, and Sexual Abuse', *Union Seminary Quarterly Review* 53:1–2 (1999), pp. 89–109.

Turner, Carlton J., 'Overcoming Self-Negation: An Examination of the Relationship between Junkanoo and the Church in Contemporary Bahamian Society', Unpublished PhD Thesis, University of Gloucestershire, 2015.

Tweedy, Margaret T., 'A History of Barbuda under the Codringtons, 1738–1833', M.Litt. Thesis, University of Birmingham, 1981.

United Nations, 'The World's Women 2015: Trends and Statistics', New York: United Nations, Department of Economic and Social Affairs, Statistics Division, 2015.

Williams, Lewin L., *Caribbean Theology*, New York: Peter Lang, 1994.

Notes

1 United Nations, 'The World's Women 2015: Trends and Statistics' (New York: United Nations, Department of Economic and Social Affairs, Statistics Division, 2015).

2 It is helpful to note here that I'm writing as a contextual and practical theologian and, as such, interdisciplinarity is important, as well as a deep dive into the complexities of the African Caribbean context. It is usual to draw on insights from historians, sociologists, psychologists, etc., as well as theologians.

3 David Tombs, 'Crucifixion, State Terror, and Sexual Abuse', *Union Seminary Quarterly Review* 53:1–2 (1999), pp. 89–109.

4 Tombs, 'Crucifixion, State Terror, and Sexual Abuse', p. 104.

5 Tombs, 'Crucifixion, State Terror, and Sexual Abuse', pp. 105–6.

6 Tombs, 'Crucifixion, State Terror, and Sexual Abuse', p. 100.

7 Antony B. Pinn, *Embodiment and the New Shape of Black Theological Thought* (New York: New York University Press, 2010).

8 Pinn, *Embodiment and the New Shape of Black Theological Thought*, p. 81.

9 Frantz Fanon, *The Wretched of the Earth* (Harmondsworth: Penguin, 1967), p. 32.

10 Frantz Fanon, *Black Skin, White Masks* (New York: Grove Press, 1967), p. 52.

11 Pinn, *Embodiment and the New Shape of Black Theological Thought*, p. 83.

12 Angela Davis, *Women, Race and Class* (London: The Women's Press, 1981).

13 Davis, *Women, Race and Class*, p. 24.

14 Davis, *Women, Race and Class*, p. 25.

15 bell hooks, *Ain't I a Woman: Black Women and Feminism* (London: Pluto Press, 1981).

16 hooks, *Ain't I a Woman*, p. 18.

17 hooks, *Ain't I a Woman*, p. 20.

18 Katie Cannon, *Black Womanist Ethics* (Atlanta, GA: Scholars Press, 1988), p. 36.

19 Kelly Brown Douglas, *Sexuality and the Black Church: A Womanist Perspective* (Maryknoll, NY: Orbis, 1999), p. 47.

20 Douglas, *Sexuality and the Black Church*, p. 47.

21 Douglas, *Sexuality and the Black Church*, p. 48.

22 Margaret T. Tweedy, 'A History of Barbuda under the Codringtons, 1738–1833' (M.Litt. Thesis, University of Birmingham, 1981), p. 245.

23 Fanon, *Black Skin, White Masks*; Fanon, *Wretched of the Earth*.

24 Orlando Patterson, *The Sociology of Slavery: An Analysis of the Origins, Development and Structure of Negro Slave Society in Jamaica*, Studies in Society (London: MacGibbon & Kee, 1967).

25 Lewin Williams, *Caribbean Theology* (New York: Peter Lang, 1994); Kortright Davis, *Emancipation Still Comin': Explorations in Caribbean Emancipatory Theology* (Maryknoll, NY: Orbis, 1990); Noel Erskine, *Decolonizing Theology: A Caribbean Perspective* (Trenton, NJ: Africa World Press, 1998).

26 Williams, *Caribbean Theology*, pp. 18–19.

27 Douglas, *Sexuality and the Black Church*.

28 Douglas, *Sexuality and the Black Church*, p. 29.

29 Douglas, *Sexuality and the Black Church*, p. 27.

30 Juan M. Contreras et al., *Sexual Violence in Latin America and the Caribbean: A Desk Review* (Sexual Violence Research Initiative, 2010).

31 Contreras et al., *Sexual Violence in Latin America and the Caribbean*, p. 24; Elsie LeFranc et al., 'Interpersonal Violence in Three Caribbean Countries: Barbados, Jamaica, and Trinidad and Tobago', *Revista Panamericana de Salud Pública* 24:6 (2009), pp. 409–21.

32 Contreras et al., *Sexual Violence in Latin America and the Caribbean*, p. 35; Linda Halcón, Trisha Beuhring and Robert Blum, *A Portrait of Adolescent Health in the Caribbean* (Minneapolis, MN: World Health Organization Collaborating Centre on Adolescent Health, University of Minnesota, 2000); Linda Halcón et al.,

'Adolescent Health in the Caribbean: A Regional Portrait', *American Journal of Public Health* 93:11 (2003), pp. 1851–7.

33 Anna K. Perkins, 'Christian Norms and Intimate Male Partner Violence: Lessons from a Jamaica Women's Health Survey', in *The Holy Spirit and Social Justice: Interdisciplinary Global Perspectives, History, Race and Culture*, Antipas Harris and Michael Palmer eds (Lanham, MD: Seymour Press, 2019), pp. 242–3.

34 Perkins, 'Christian Norms and Intimate Male Partner Violence', p. 243.

35 Ashwood, 'Self-Questioning from the Caribbean', in *When Pastors Prey: Overcoming Clergy Sexual Abuse of Women*, Valli Boobal Batchelor ed. (Geneva, Switzerland: World Council of Churches, 2013), p. 117.

36 Ashwood, 'Self-Questioning from the Caribbean', p. 117.

37 Joy Degruy, *Post Traumatic Slave Syndrome: America's Legacy of Enduring Injury and Healing* (Milwaukie, OR: Uptone Press, 2005); Christina Sharpe, *In the Wake: On Blackness and Being* (Durham, NC: Duke University Press, 2016).

38 Yael Danieli, 'Introduction: History and Conceptual Foundations', in *International Handbook of Multigenerational Legacies of Trauma*, Yael Danieli ed. (New York: Plenum Press, 2010), p. 4.

39 Carlton Turner, 'Overcoming Self-Negation: An Examination of the Relationship between Junkanoo and the Church in Contemporary Bahamian Society' (Unpublished PhD Thesis, University of Gloucestershire, 2015).

40 Dwight Hopkins, *Down, Up, and Over: Slave Religion and Black Theology* (Minneapolis, MN: Fortress Press, 2000), p. 135.

41 Hopkins, *Down, Up, and Over*, p. 116.

42 Kirkley Sands, *Early Bahamian Slave Spirituality: The Genesis of Bahamian Cultural Identity* (Nassau, Bahamas: The Nassau Guardian Ltd, 2008).

43 Perkins, '"Tasting Tears and [Not] Admitting Defeat": Promoting Values and Attitudes through the Music of Tanya Stephens?', in *Inaugural Lecture of the Centre for Social Ethics* (St Michael's Theological College, 2008), p. 11.

44 Carolyn Cooper, 'Sweet & Sour Sauce: Sexual Politics in Jamaican Dancehall Culture'; The Sixth Jagan Lecture, York University, ON, Canada (CERLAC, 2005), p. 2.

45 Cooper, 'Sweet & Sour Sauce', p. 3.

46 Douglas, *Sexuality and the Black Church*.

47 Tombs, 'Crucifixion, State Terror, and Sexual Abuse'.

9

'Not pictured': What *Veronica Mars* Can Teach Us about the Crucifixion

RACHEL STARR

The second season finale of *Veronica Mars* begins with teen detective Veronica returning to a neighbourhood diner to take another look at a team photo on display there, in the hope that she will see something she missed.[1] But it is what is 'not pictured' that helps her solve the mystery of multiple murders and, as it turns out, her own rape.

Veronica Mars ran from 2004 to 2007 on the United Paramount Network and The CW, with a film in 2014 and revival in 2019, following cancellation of the original series. Widely compared to *Buffy the Vampire Slayer*, a show which also employed a sunny California setting to explore conflict, trauma and female-led resistance, *Veronica Mars* draws stylistically from the Raymond Chandler tradition of the isolated detective, working cases in the shadows of the law.[2] Veronica's high school experience is fractured by violence, a violence which is both assumed and denied. It is not so much her identity as a victim of violence that results in her social exclusion, but rather her determination to speak the truth of it and to seek the justice required.

I first encountered *Veronica Mars* in Argentina. It was there that I completed my doctoral studies and learned about doing theology in a context of historic and ongoing state and political violence, in which bearing witness was expected but costly for people of faith. While Veronica lives in the fictional town of Neptune, which is clearly distinct from Argentina, there are shared themes of structural violence, abuse of power and the demands of truth-telling, as this chapter will explore.

Like David Tombs, whose 1999 research on the sexual violence of the crucifixion arose from his research related to torture practices in Guatemala and El Salvador, my own lived experience of Latin America was transformative and continues to shape my theological work.[3] A lasting influence has been the Brazilian theologian Ivone Gebara, whose work makes visible the impact of inequality and violence on women's everyday lives, and the necessary work of solidarity and resistance. Beginning with ordinary lives and vulnerable bodies, Gebara's theology is messy and fluid, disrupting the neat answers offered by dominant forms of Christianity.

Feminist research could be understood as a form of investigative journalism, undertaken with dogged determination to discover the causes of violence and confront them.[4] Such investigatory work requires close observation of what are often complex and traumatic situations, a willingness to use overlooked sources, and the courage to draw new conclusions. Perhaps, then, alongside theologians such as David Tombs and Ivone Gebara, it might also be helpful to consider how a (fictional) detective[5] could help readers of the Bible to construct a new narrative from shared facts[6] and, in the process, reveal what is 'not pictured' in the crucifixion narratives. Out of her own experience of sexual violence, and from her marginal perspective, we might imagine that Veronica would approach the crucifixion narratives with a hermeneutic of suspicion,[7] willing to read from the gaps in the text and its reception and in so doing name both violence and complicity as well as seek social transformation.

Using the motif of what is 'not pictured', this chapter will first explore the portrayal of male sexual victimization and violence in the aforementioned episode of *Veronica Mars*. It will place this account in conversation with contemporary studies of male sexual victimization, before summarizing Tombs' work on making visible sexual violence as an intrinsic part of Roman crucifixion practices. Making use of Gina Hens-Piazza's method of reading violent texts, it will build on Tombs' work to see how portraying Jesus as a victim of sexual violence might challenge dominant interpretations of the crucifixion which seek to explain or claim the violence of the cross. The final section recognizes the fractured nature of the crucifixion narrative and asks whether resisting 'cleaning up' the mess of a bloody and traumatic death may be more liberative in allowing the violence of the cross to be more clearly pictured and, thus, resisted.

'Not pictured': what Veronica struggled to see

In the Season 2 finale of *Veronica Mars*,[8] Veronica identifies the killer of her fellow students by noticing the boy 'not pictured' in a photograph of a youth baseball team that was coached by a known sex offender. Fearful of being exposed as a survivor of sexual violence, the boy, Cassidy Casablancas, is revealed to have killed other survivors in order to silence them.[9]

Sexual violence is a consistent feature in all three of the original series of *Veronica Mars*. It is pervasive, impacting directly on Veronica's well-being and that of those around her. While Veronica is well aware of the corrupting influence of power and wealth, and how strongly they are sought and defended, the programme falls short of exploring the wider socio-cultural reasons or risk factors[10] that make sexual violence more likely to occur, or that identify certain groups (children, women, and men who are temporarily or permanently marginalized) as appropriate victims.[11] In part, this is consistent with wider social dynamics that seek to hide how social inequality uses the threat and enactment of violence, including sexual violence, to maintain control. Thus, in *Veronica Mars*, male perpetrators of sexual violence are portrayed as wounded, vulnerable or deviant, rather than fulfilling roles made normative within many patriarchal societies.[12]

Even though *Veronica Mars* falls short of attending fully to the social and cultural causes of sexual violence, the portrayal of Cassidy Casablancas, especially how he responds to his own victimization, is consistent, in part, with wider studies of the potential impact of sexual violence against men, as outlined in the following section. Cassidy, or 'Beaver', is presented as a subordinate male, consistently humiliated and shamed by his older, more visibly dominant brother 'Dick', who in turn is subordinated to his father, 'Big Dick'.[13] To be the victim of sexual violence is understood as shaming by Cassidy, and he is therefore preoccupied with preventing information about his own sexual abuse coming out. Fearful that the news of his abuse will be received by his brother and peers as a reason for further humiliation,[14] he uses violence to silence others – that is, his fellow victims and the perpetrator, as well as bystanders. He also uses violence to seek to assert his masculinity, for example, by raping Veronica in a previous episode.[15] In a final act of silencing, he kills himself.

Not pictured: sexual violence against men

In England and Wales, women are four times more likely than men to be victims of sexual violence.[16] Because sexual violence has tended to be framed as a crime against women, there has been long-term resistance to seeing men as its victims. Yet in recent decades, male sexual victimization has become more widely acknowledged. In part, this is due to changes to the legal definition of rape[17] to include non-consensual anal, vagina or oral penile penetration, and of sexual assault to include non-consensual penetration by any object, as well as non-penetrative sexual acts.[18] Nevertheless, the underreporting of sexual violence is widely recognized,[19] and for men there are additional barriers to reporting experiences of sexual violence. These include 'a fear of being disbelieved, blamed, exposed to other forms of negative treatment and/or concern that such disclosure might interfere with one's masculine self-identity'.[20]

Although men are more likely to be victims of violent crimes,[21] dominant models of masculinity, which portray men as physically strong and heterosexually active, serve to suggest that men cannot be sexually assaulted because they do not 'encourage' sexual interest from other men,[22] and are physically able to prevent an attack.[23] Thus, according to dominant gender narratives, if a man is not 'man enough' to prevent sexual assault, such an attack serves to feminize him. This is especially true if a man is raped, since, in the dominant framing of sexual activity, rape places him in the position of the receptive partner.[24] Research suggests that men who have been raped often seek to re-establish their sense of masculinity through engaging in stereotypical masculine activity such as having heterosexual sex; risk-taking and violent behaviour; and self-reliance, including failing to seek support.[25] That male sexual assault is understood as shaming and therefore less likely to be acknowledged by survivors or by wider society is evident. How such an acknowledgement is even more difficult when it occurs within an act seen by many as salvific will be explored in the next section.

Not pictured: sexual violence in the Gospel Accounts of the crucifixion of Jesus

Readers of the Bible are trained to respond to violence in the text in a variety of ways. They may seek to sanctify such violence as directly or indirectly revelatory of God's justice and righteousness, God's freedom to act, or perhaps God's ability to work through even the most unlikely of characters. Behind such an interpretative approach is often a desire to affirm the Bible as the incontestable, inspired word of God. Yet such readings risk legitimating violent acts not only within the text, but also within the interpretative context. A different strategy is to, sometimes literally, 'bracket out' the violence of the text (for example, the bracketing out of violent or otherwise problematic verses of the psalms in some liturgical texts).[26] Here, violence is framed as 'un-Christian', following a long and problematic move within the Christian tradition of distancing itself from the supposedly violent God of the Hebrew Bible. While sometimes appropriate for pastoral or liturgical reasons, such an approach prevents violence being recognized, explored and challenged by faith communities.

In naming Jesus as a victim of sexual abuse and a possible victim of sexual assault, Tombs rejects both of these strategies. Tombs' approach fits well with the suggestion made by biblical scholar Gina Hens-Piazza, who argues that violence in the Bible must be named in order for it to be resisted. Hens-Piazza offers the following strategy for reading violent texts:

1. Make use of social-scientific research to gain an accurate understanding of the context from which the text emerged and which it reflects.
2. Read stories of violence in memory of the victims within the text and beyond it.
3. Resist the promptings of the narrator or one's own instincts when they lead the reader to justify the violence of the text or identify with the characters who are painted in the most positive light.
4. Search out counter-texts that offer alternative ways of responding to violence.[27]

Reviewing Tombs' work in the light of Hens-Piazza's approach, what is noticeable at first is how Tombs is willing to reframe the crucifixion narratives to make clear the presence of sexual humiliation,[28] as well as the likelihood of some form of sexual assault, when read alongside other accounts of Roman crucifixion.[29] He therefore takes due account of the social dynamics reflected in the Gospel Accounts. Second, Tombs' work disrupts the silence around crucifixion established first in Roman society[30] and later by the Church, in as far as the sexual aspects of this violent death were covered over and forgotten.[31] In reading the crucifixion narratives alongside accounts of Latin American state-sponsored torture and abuse, Tombs makes visible the continuing impact of the violence recorded within these texts. The remainder of this chapter continues Tombs' work by considering the third and fourth elements of Hens-Piazza's approach: resisting justification of the violence of the cross; and, in the closing section of the chapter, seeking out texts that counter violence.

Not pictured: saving heroes, blameless victims and perfect sacrifices

According to dominant Christian theories of the atonement,[32] Jesus saves humanity from sin through his death and, although often awarded less attention, his resurrection. In some accounts, Jesus' death forms part of a cosmic battle against the forces of death and chaos, in which Jesus emerges victorious as the all-conquering hero.[33] In other accounts, Jesus' death as a blameless victim is received as the perfect sacrifice that restores God to the world and the world to God. The suggestion that Jesus was a victim of sexual violence disrupts both these readings.

Under Roman imperial rule, the sexual violence inflicted during the process of crucifixion served to dissuade further rebellion by emasculating the victim, dishonouring their memory,[34] and thus preventing their death from becoming a rallying point for resistance.[35] To be a victim of sexual violence was incompatible with hero status. Thus, by framing Jesus as a hero, dominant Christian traditions have prevented discussion of the possibility that Jesus was a victim of sexual violence, since the feminization of men through sexual violence is seen as incompatible with accounts of male heroism. In order to overcome the shame of death on a cross, the early Church sought to locate Jesus' death within the wider tradition of the hero-martyr and in so doing re-establish his honour. But this re-establishment was only possible if Jesus was understood as actively entering into a chosen arena of conflict and ultimately emerging victorious from it. As a victim of sexual violence, Jesus would have been understood, instead, as not active but passive – not manly but feminine – lacking control over his body and its integrity.[36]

The possibility of sexual violence further problematizes Jesus' identity as the blameless victim. In secular society, to be a victim is associated with weakness.[37] It is not surprising, therefore, that although men are more likely to be victims of violent crime, men tend to reject a victim identity, perceiving it to put their established masculine identity at risk.[38] In contrast, dominant Christian traditions have romanticized victimhood and in so doing prevented challenge of the structures and hierarchies that create victims and oppressors. Indeed, it is notable, as Christine Gudorf observes, that women, children and other marginalized groups are those who are encouraged to model Jesus' victimhood.[39] In this way, dominant Christian discourse reinforces the notion that to be a victim is a role most suited to female disciples, despite claims that Jesus' victimhood is celebrated.

It may be that through his victimhood Jesus is positioned as a passive female figure in contrast to God the Father. While this dynamic is present in some atonement theories, and in much Christian art and hymnody, it exists as subtext since to name it would undoubtedly be problematic. By identifying Jesus as a victim of sexual violence, such a feminization of Jesus is made explicit and therefore becomes disruptive.

Where dominant Christian traditions have managed to hold together Jesus' masculinity and his victimhood, they have done so via a narrative of Jesus as blameless.[40] Yet in accounts of sexual violence there is strong tendency for the victim to be blamed for the attack, suggesting that they made themselves vulnerable and thus, in some way, deserved what happened. Thus, as Jayme Reaves and David Tombs note, a further tension exists between seeing Jesus as blameless and as a victim of sexual violence.[41]

To recognize Jesus as a victim of sexual violence further disrupts his ability to save if such violence is seen to endanger Jesus' bodily integrity and the purity of his blood. For Jesus' blood to be considered salvific – if dominant Christian models of atonement are to be taken into account – he must bleed as a hero or sacrifice, not as a victim of sexual violence. Sexual violence not only works to feminize Jesus; it also risks making his bleeding on the cross similar to forms of bleeding associated with women, an association that would probably be problematic for dominant patriarchal Christian traditions.[42]

In contrast to menstrual bleeding or bleeding as a result of anal or vagina penetration, appropriate male bleeding, according to patriarchal constructs, is associated with external wounds. When men are portrayed as bleeding, it tends to be as a result of violence inflicted publicly by other men, in what are understood to be appropriate ways and for honourable purposes. Jesus' crucifixion is presented as a spectacular act of violence. Jesus bleeds from lashes and spears, thorns and nails. Christ the warrior-hero bears his battle scars with pride. While Jesus' surface wounds are the marks of a saviour, there is little space within the dominant tradition to consider the possibility of internal bleeding caused by sexual violence. Such bleeding would frame Jesus as a passive recipient of forms of violence associated with female victims. His wounds would no longer identify him as a hero.

Moreover, bleeding like a woman[43] risks incurring social stigma.[44] From their first period, women are placed under social pressure to hide their bleeding and are taught not to speak of it directly, if at all.[45] Although there are lasting spiritual traditions that associate Jesus' bleeding with menstrual blood,[46] within dominant Christian thinking blood flowing from a woman has tended to be associated with shame and decay.[47] Thus Gebara observes that, within the dominant Christian tradition, '[m]ale sacrifice is the only kind that redeems and restores life; male blood is the only blood of any value ... Women's bleeding is filthy, impure, dangerous.'[48]

Women's bleeding often works to place them at a distance from men and, in many religious traditions, from the sacred. That the body leaks of its own accord is particularly problematic since it indicates a fluidity and lack of bodily boundaries. According to the priestly law as set out in Leviticus, any genital emissions, normal or abnormal, male or female, place the person, and those who come into contact with them, in an impure state.[49] To bleed as a result of sexual assault, due to anal fissures for example,[50] would presumably have rendered Jesus ritually impure. Priestly sacrificial traditions recorded in the Hebrew Bible required that the animals offered for sacrifice were to be male and without blemish.[51] Thus, to consider Jesus to have suffered from sexual violence further disrupts Jesus' saving identity. No longer in possession of a perfect male body, Jesus is unable to be offered as a sacrifice according to the sacrificial traditions.[52]

Dominant Christian theories of atonement seek to claim and justify the violence of the cross by presenting Jesus as a saving hero, a blameless victim, or a perfect sacrifice. Yet, as this section considers, all three of these interpretations are disrupted if Jesus is understood as a victim of sexual violence. No longer a hero of his own making and no longer without stain or shame, we see Jesus once again as a man who dies on a cross: a death that holds no purpose or power. Such a reading of the crucifixion is in agreement with wider feminist and womanist rejection of the violence of the cross as in any way salvific.

Not pictured: a fractured and fragmented tale

Employing Hens-Piazza's method of engaging with violent texts enables the crucifixion narrative to bear witness to the possibility of sexual violence within the text and the lives of its readers, and the need to resist such violence. By investigating the social and cultural realities of the first-century Roman Empire, Tombs enables the reader to see the crucifixion of Jesus as an act of sexual violence. In the same way as Veronica Mars rearranges widely known facts to form a new narrative, such an approach enables the Gospel Accounts to be read as accounts of sexual humiliation and likely assault. Hens-Piazza's encouragement to resist justification of violence is further helpful in interrogating the framing of Jesus as hero and sacrifice. As for her encouragement to seek out counter-texts, rather than suggesting the resurrection as the answer, perhaps a counter-narrative to the crucifixion accounts would be readings of the Gospels that resist violent accounts of God's saving work.

The claim that violence is in contrast to salvation is at the heart of much Latin American feminist theology. Rather than seeking salvation through death, the invitation is to work with God in 'the establishment of spaces of peace, the meeting of bodily needs and loving desires, and the development of just and right relationships'.[53] For Veronica, healing and redemption do not come about through further violence, but instead through truth-telling, friendship, solidarity and, where possible, the return to everyday life. Similarly, Gebara suggests communities of faith must work together for salvation, and that the work is ongoing:

> In practice we must always begin again every day the search for salvation just as every day we have to begin again the actions of eating and drinking … this salvation is not a state one attains once and for all. It is there like a glass of water that quenches thirst for the moment, but thirst comes again, sometimes stronger than before … The moment of the hoped-for salvation comes, sometimes seen, sometimes unforeseen. No sooner it comes than it is gone: it escapes, flying away to prepare another and another. This fragile redemption is what we find in the everyday life of every person.[54]

Hens-Piazza's method also calls for the reading of violent texts in memory of those who suffer in and through them. Veronica's memory and the witnesses of others concerning the night in which she was raped are fragmented and conflicting.[55] Perhaps the same might be said of Christian readings of the crucifixion of the man Jesus. Through millennia of retelling and reframing, what happened to Jesus and what it might mean for Christian faith becomes muddled and messy, with unanswered questions and elements that don't quite fit into a coherent narrative.[56] Yet perhaps this is a truer, and ultimately more liberating, way of telling the story.[57]

References

'A Trip to the Dentist', *Veronica Mars*, Season 1, Episode 21, United Paramount Network, 3 May 2005.
'Not Pictured', *Veronica Mars*, Season 2, Episode 22, United Paramount Network, 9 May 2006.
Berridge, Susan, 'Teen Heroine TV: Narrative Complexity and Sexual Violence in Female-fronted Teen Drama Series', *New Review of Film and Television Studies* 11:4 (2013), pp. 477–96.
Bineham, Jeffery L., 'Theological Hegemony and Oppositional Interpretive Codes: The Case of Evangelical Christian Feminism', *Western Journal of Communication* 57:4 (1993), pp. 515–29.
Braithwaite, Andrea, 'It's the Beast Thing: Victimization, Violence, and Popular Masculine Crises', *Feminist Media Studies* 11:4 (2011), pp. 417–32.
Criminal Justice and Public Order Act 1994, www.legislation.gov.uk/ukpga/1994/33/contents.

Fedele, Anna, 'Reversing Eve's Curse: Mary Magdalene, Mother Earth and the Creative Ritualization of Menstruation', *Journal of Ritual Studies* 28:2 (2014), pp. 23–36.

Gebara, Ivone, *Out of the Depths: Women's Experience of Evil and Salvation*, Minneapolis, MN: Fortress Press, 2002.

Gillingham, Susan E., *Psalms Through the Centuries: volume 1. Blackwell Bible Commentaries*, Oxford: Blackwell, 2008.

Graybill, Rhiannon, 'Fuzzy, Messy, Icky: The Edges of Consent in Biblical Rape Narratives and Rape Culture', presented at The Shiloh Project, *Religion and Rape Culture Conference*, University of Sheffield, 6 July 2018, https://shiloh-project. group.shef.ac.uk/fuzzy-messy-icky-the-edges-of-consent-in-biblical-rape-narratives-and-rape-culture/.

Gudorf, Christine, *Victimization: Examining Christian Complicity*, Philadelphia, PA: Trinity Press International, 1992.

Hall, Amy Laura, 'Heroism', *Word and World: Masculinity* 36:1 (Winter 2016), pp. 53–63.

Heise, Lori L., 'Violence Against Women: An Integrated, Ecological Framework', *Violence Against Women* 4:3 (1998), pp. 262–90.

—, *What Works to Prevent Partner Violence: An Evidence Overview*, London: STRIVE, 2011, http://strive.lshtm.ac.uk/resources/what-works-preventpartner-violence-evidence-overview.

Hens-Piazza, Gina, *Nameless, Blameless and Without Shame: Two Cannibal Mothers Before a King*, Collegeville, MN: Liturgical Press, 2003.

Javaid, Aliraza, 'The Dark Side of Men: The Nature of Masculinity and Its Uneasy Relationship with Male Rape', *Journal of Men's Studies* 23:3 (2015), pp. 271–92.

Johnson, Judith Ann, 'Shedding Blood: The Sanctifying Rite of Heroes', in *Wholly Woman, Holy Blood: A Feminist Critique of Purity and Impurity*, Kristin De Troyer, Judith A. Herbert, Judith Ann Johnson and Anne-Marie Korte eds, Harrisburg, PA: Trinity Press International, 2003, pp. 189–222.

Johnston-Robledo, Ingrid, and Joan C. Chrisler, 'The Menstrual Mark: Menstruation as Social Stigma', *Sex Roles* 68 (2013), pp. 9–18.

Johnston-Robledo, Ingrid and Margaret L. Stubbs, 'Positioning Periods: Menstruation in Social Context: An Introduction to a Special Issue', *Sex Roles* 68 (2013), pp. 1–8.

Kamionkowski, S. Tamar, *Leviticus: Wisdom Commentary Volume 3*, Collegeville, MN: Liturgical Press, 2018.

Korte, Anne-Marie, 'Female Blood Rituals: Cultural-Anthropological Findings and Feminist-Theological Reflections', in *Wholly Woman, Holy Blood: A Feminist Critique of Purity and Impurity*, Kristin De Troyer, Judith A. Herbert, Judith Ann Johnson and Anne-Marie Korte eds, Harrisburg, PA: Trinity Press International, 2003, pp. 165–88.

Lowe, Michelle, and Paul Rogers, 'The Scope of Male Rape: A Selective Review of Research, Policy and Practice', *Aggression and Violent Behavior* 35 (2017), pp. 38–43.

Mayordomo Marín, Moisés, 'Construction of Masculinity in Antiquity and Early Christianity', *Lectio difficilior-europäische elektronische Zeitschrift für feministische Exegese* 2 (2006), pp. 1–33.

O'Collins, Gerald, *Christology: A Biblical, Historical, and Systematic Study of Jesus*, Oxford: Oxford University Press, 2009.

Office for National Statistics, *Sexual offences in England and Wales: Year Ending March 2017*, 8 February 2018, www.ons.gov.uk/peoplepopulationand community/crimeandjustice/articles/sexualoffencesinenglandandwales/yearend ingmarch2017.

—, *The Nature of Violent Crime in England and Wales: Year Ending March 2018*, 7 February 2019, www.ons.gov.uk/peoplepopulationandcommunity/ crimeandjustice/articles/thenatureofviolentcrimeinenglandandwales/yearending march2018#which-groups-of-people-are-most-likely-to-be-victims-of-violent-crime.

Reaves, Jayme, and Tombs, David, 'Acknowledging the Sexual Abuse of Crucifixion: #MeToo as an Invitation to a New Conversation', Research Seminar, Queen's Theological Foundation, Birmingham, 17 January 2018.

Schüssler Fiorenza, Elisabeth, *Bread Not Stone: The Challenge of Feminist Biblical Interpretation*, Boston, MA: Beacon Press, 1984.

Sexual Offences Act 2003, www.legislation.gov.uk/ukpga/2003/42/contents.

Slee, Nicola, *Seeking the Risen Christa*, London: SPCK, 2011.

Starr, Rachel, 'Research as Resistance: Survival Strategies for Researching Violence', presented at The Shiloh Project, *Religion and Rape Culture Conference*, University of Sheffield, 6 July 2018, http://shiloh-project.group.shef.ac.uk/research-as-resistance-survival-strategies-for-researching-violence/.

Starr, Rachel, *Reimagining Theologies of Marriage in Contexts of Domestic Violence: When Salvation Is Survival*, Explorations in Practical, Pastoral and Empirical Theology, London: Routledge, 2018.

Thomas, Rob, with Leah Wilson, *Neptune Noir: Unauthorized Investigations into Veronica Mars*, Dallas, TX: BenBella Books, 2006.

Tombs, David, 'Crucifixion, State Terror, and Sexual Abuse', *Union Seminary Quarterly Review* 53:1–2 (1999), pp. 89–109.

—, 'Lived Religion and the Intolerance of the Cross', in *Lived Religion and the Politics of (In)tolerance*, Ruard Ganzevoort and Srdjan Sremac eds, Cham, Switzerland: Palgrave Macmillan, 2017, pp. 63–83.

—, *Crucifixion, State Terror, and Sexual Abuse: Text and Context*, Centre for Theology and Public Issues Series, Otago: Centre for Theology and Public Issues, University of Otago, 2018, http://hdl.handle.net/10523/8558.

Turchik, Jessica A. and Katie M. Edwards, 'Myths about Male Rape: A Literature Review', *Psychology of Men & Masculinity* 13:2 (2012), pp. 211–26.

Veronica Mars, 2004–2007, United Paramount Network and The CW.

Wilkenfeld, Daniel A., 'Not Pictured: What Veronica Knew but Didn't See', in *Veronica Mars and Philosophy: Investigating the Mysteries of Life (Which is a Bitch Until You Die)*, George A. Dunn and William Irwin eds, Chichester: John Wiley & Sons, 2014, pp. 184–97.

Notes

1 'Not Pictured', *Veronica Mars*, Season 2, Episode 22, United Paramount Network (9 May 2006).

2 Rob Thomas (with Leah Wilson), *Neptune Noir: Unauthorized Investigations into Veronica Mars* (Dallas, TX: BenBella Books, 2006).

3 Rachel Starr, *Reimagining Theologies of Marriage in Contexts of Domestic*

Violence: When Salvation Is Survival, Explorations in Practical, Pastoral and Empirical Theology (London: Routledge, 2018).

4 Rachel Starr, 'Research as Resistance: Survival Strategies for Researching Violence', presented at The Shiloh Project, *Religion and Rape Culture Conference*, University of Sheffield, 6 July 2018, http://shiloh-project.group.shef.ac.uk/research-as-resistance-survival-strategies-for-researching-violence/.

5 The character Veronica Mars is both a journalist, for the school paper, and assists her father in his work as a private investigator.

6 Daniel A. Wilkenfeld, 'Not Pictured: What Veronica Knew but Didn't See', in *Veronica Mars and Philosophy: Investigating the Mysteries of Life (Which is a Bitch Until You Die)*, George A. Dunn and William Irwin eds (Chichester: John Wiley & Sons, 2014), pp. 186.

7 Elisabeth Schüssler Fiorenza, *Bread Not Stone: The Challenge of Feminist Biblical Interpretation* (Boston, MA: Beacon Press 1984), pp. 15–18.

8 Wilkenfeld, 'Not Pictured'.

9 Andrea Braithwaite, 'It's the Beast Thing: Victimization, Violence, and Popular Masculine Crises', *Feminist Media Studies* 11:4 (2011), pp. 422.

10 Lori L. Heise, 'Violence Against Women: An Integrated, Ecological Framework', *Violence Against Women* 4:3 (1998), pp. 262–90; Lori L. Heise, *What Works to Prevent Partner Violence: An Evidence Overview* (London: STRIVE, 2011), http://strive.lshtm.ac.uk/resources/what-works-preventpartner-violence-evidence-overview.

11 Susan Berridge, 'Teen Heroine TV: Narrative Complexity and Sexual Violence in Female-fronted Teen Drama Series', *New Review of Film and Television Studies* 11:4 (2013), pp. 483; Braithwaite, 'It's the Beast Thing', p. 419.

12 Berridge, 'Teen Heroine TV', pp. 489–90; Braithwaite, 'It's the Beast Thing', pp. 422–3.

13 Such nicknames function to reinforce gender hierarchies, here placing the younger brother in a subordinate sexual position through his identification with a slang term for female genitalia. Aware of this, Cassidy repeatedly rejects his nickname.

14 Braithwaite, 'It's the Beast Thing', p. 423.

15 'A Trip to the Dentist', *Veronica Mars*, Season 1, Episode 21, United Paramount Network (3 May 2005).

16 Office for National Statistics, *Sexual Offences in England and Wales: Year Ending March 2017* (8 February 2018), www.ons.gov.uk/peoplepopulationandcommunity/crimeandjustice/articles/sexualoffencesinenglandandwales/yearendingmarch2017.

17 Michelle Lowe and Paul Rogers, 'The Scope of Male Rape: A Selective Review of Research, Policy and Practice', *Aggression and Violent Behavior* 35 (2017), pp. 39.

18 *Criminal Justice and Public Order Act* (1994) and *Sexual Offences Act* (2003).

19 Lowe and Rogers, 'The Scope of Male Rape', p. 39.

20 Lowe and Rogers, 'The Scope of Male Rape', p. 40.

21 Office for National Statistics, *The Nature of Violent Crime in England and Wales: Year Ending March 2018* (7 February 2019), www.ons.gov.uk/peoplepopulationandcommunity/crimeandjustice/articles/thenatureofviolentcrimeinengland andwales/yearendingmarch2018#which-groups-of-people-are-most-likely-to-be-victims-of-violent-crime.

22 A persistent myth about male-on-male rape is that both perpetrator and victim are more likely to be homosexual.

23 Jessica A. Turchik and Katie M. Edwards, 'Myths about Male Rape: A Literature Review', *Psychology of Men & Masculinity* 13:2 (2012), pp. 211–13.

24 Aliraza Javaid, 'The Dark Side of Men: The Nature of Masculinity and Its Uneasy Relationship with Male Rape', *Journal of Men's Studies* 23:3 (2015), pp. 275–6.

25 Javaid, 'The Dark Side of Men', pp. 276–7.

26 Susan E. Gillingham, *Psalms Through the Centuries: Volume 1. Blackwell Bible Commentaries* (Oxford: Blackwell, 2008), p. 258.

27 Gina Hens-Piazza, *Nameless, Blameless and Without Shame: Two Cannibal Mothers Before a King* (Collegeville, MN: Liturgical Press, 2003), pp. 119–22.

28 David Tombs, 'Crucifixion, State Terror, and Sexual Abuse', *Union Seminary Quarterly Review* 53:1–2 (1999), pp. 102–4.

29 Tombs, 'Crucifixion, State Terror, and Sexual Abuse', pp. 104–7.

30 David Tombs, 'Lived Religion and the Intolerance of the Cross', in *Lived Religion and the Politics of (In)tolerance*, Ruard R. Ganzevoort and Srdjan Sremac eds (Cham, Switzerland: Palgrave Macmillan, 2017), p. 68.

31 Tombs, 'Lived Religion and the Intolerance of the Cross', pp. 70, 76.

32 Dominant Christian theological traditions may be defined as those that occur most consistently within authorized creeds, confessional statements of belief, authorized liturgy, iconography, popular hymnody and homiletics. Such interpretations of Christian belief are assumed as normative. Other theologies, rightly or wrongly, are considered an interruption of dominant traditions. On this last point, see: Jeffrey L. Bineham, 'Theological Hegemony and Oppositional Interpretive Codes: The Case of Evangelical Christian Feminism', *Western Journal of Communication* 57:4 (1993), pp. 515–29.

33 Amy Laura Hall, 'Heroism', *Word and World: Masculinity* 36:1 (Winter 2016), pp. 53–63.

34 Tombs, 'Crucifixion, State Terror, and Sexual Abuse', pp. 95, 101.

35 Tombs, 'Lived Religion and the Intolerance of the Cross', p. 76.

36 Moisés Mayordomo Marín, 'Construction of Masculinity in Antiquity and Early Christianity', *Lectio difficilior-europäische elektronische Zeitschrift für feministische Exegese* 2 (2006), p. 7.

37 Javaid, 'The Dark Side of Men', p. 273.

38 Javaid, 'The Dark Side of Men', p. 272.

39 Christine Gudorf, *Victimization: Examining Christian Complicity* (Philadelphia, PA: Trinity Press International, 1992), pp. 2, 60, 91.

40 On Christ being without sin, see, for example, Hebrews 4.14–15; Definition of the Council of Chalcedon. For further references, see Gerald O'Collins, *Christology: A Biblical, Historical, and Systematic Study of Jesus* (Oxford: Oxford University Press, 2009), p. 280–1.

41 Jayme R. Reaves and David Tombs, 'Acknowledging the Sexual Abuse of Crucifixion: #MeToo as an Invitation to a New Conversation', Research Seminar, Queen's Theological Foundation, Birmingham, 17 January 2018.

42 Nicola Slee, *Seeking the Risen Christa* (London: SPCK, 2011), p. 79.

43 Slee, *Seeking the Risen Christa*, p. 148.

44 Ingrid Johnston-Robledo and Margaret L. Stubbs, 'Positioning Periods: Menstruation in Social Context: An Introduction to a Special Issue', *Sex Roles* 68 (2013), p. 2.

45 Ingrid Johnston-Robledo and Joan C. Chrisler, 'The Menstrual Mark: Menstruation as Social Stigma', *Sex Roles* 68 (2013), pp. 11–12.

46 Anna Fedele, 'Reversing Eve's Curse: Mary Magdalene, Mother Earth and the Creative Ritualization of Menstruation', *Journal of Ritual Studies* 28:2 (2014), pp. 23–36; Anne-Marie Korte, 'Female Blood Rituals: Cultural-Anthropological Findings and Feminist-Theological Reflections', in *Wholly Woman, Holy Blood: A Feminist Critique of Purity and Impurity*, Kristin De Troyer, Judith A. Herbert, Judith Ann Johnson and Anne-Marie Korte eds (Harrisburg, PA: Trinity Press International, 2003), p. 166.

47 Judith Ann Johnson, 'Shedding Blood: The Sanctifying Rite of Heroes', in *Wholly Woman, Holy Blood*, pp. 189–90.

48 Ivone Gebara, *Out of the Depths: Women's Experience of Evil and Salvation* (Minneapolis, MN: Fortress Press, 2002), p. 7.

49 Leviticus 15.

50 Lowe and Rogers, 'The Scope of Male Rape', p. 40.

51 Leviticus 1.3. The sacrifice of a female animal is sometimes stipulated, for example, Leviticus 4.35.

52 Leviticus 22.22–24; S. Tamar Kamionkowski, *Leviticus: Wisdom Commentary Volume 3* (Collegeville, MN: Liturgical Press, 2018), pp. 8–10. The early Church's application of sacrificial traditions to the death of Jesus is at odds with descriptions of child sacrifice as abhorrent (Deut. 12.31).

53 Starr, *Reimagining Theologies of Marriage in Contexts of Domestic Violence*, p. 176.

54 Gebara, *Out of the Depths*, p. 123.

55 'A Trip to the Dentist'; Berridge, 'Teen Heroine TV', p. 489.

56 Acknowledging that sexual violence and its impact are messy opens up space for survivors of sexual violence to tell their own story, without it needing to fit within an agreed framework. On this point, see Rhiannon Graybill, 'Fuzzy, Messy, Icky: The Edges of Consent in Biblical Rape Narratives and Rape Culture', presented at The Shiloh Project, *Religion and Rape Culture Conference*, University of Sheffield, 6 July 2018, https://shiloh-project.group.shef.ac.uk/fuzzy-messy-icky-the-edges-of-consent-in-biblical-rape-narratives-and-rape-culture/. To recognize that death, grief and memory are muddled and messy allows space for complex and changing responses to the death of Jesus, and to the suffering, violence and death within all lives. To allow for a messy and muddled account of salvation encourages ongoing questioning and openness to dialogue.

57 Hens-Piazza, *Nameless, Blameless and Without Shame*, p. 72.

10

Jesus is a Survivor: Sexual Violence and Stigma within Faith Communities

ELISABET LE ROUX

Introduction

For me, I do not think I can consider a woman who has been sexually violated. For me, she is no longer a perfect woman, because she has now been violated, she just lost her value. From my point of view I can no longer even go to her family, to look for a wife, because I know that family is already cursed, she is no longer valuable once sexually violated. I know she can be treated, but that is just in terms of letting her forget what happened to her, but she is no longer valuable in the society.[1]

These words, spoken by a male church member in Sake in the Democratic Republic of Congo (DRC), are a typical example of the stigma and discrimination that sexual violence survivors often face. Seen as devalued because of what happened to them, their partners, family members, faith community and society generally, both indirectly and directly, view them as lesser human beings. Many survivors across the world have described the stigma they are confronted with, which is often experienced as more traumatic than the actual event of sexual violence. The way others treat them inhibits them from processing and moving on from what happened to them, as was illustrated by these words of a survivor from South Africa: 'there is no-one who wants to listen to me, so I just go with this that I experienced. I just live in it. There is no solution or help, it seems to me.'[2]

Faith communities are not exempt from this stigmatizing treatment. As the research studies included in this chapter will illustrate, many survivors who belong to faith communities experience harsh stigma at the hands of their families and faith communities. They also tend to stigmatize themselves, buying into religious narratives that view survivors as (at least partly) to blame for what happened to them and less worthy of God's love and care.

This chapter will explore sexual violence stigma within Christian faith communities, offering theological engagement with the concept of Jesus as a sexual violence survivor as a potentially effective intervention to address stigma within Christian faith communities. I will first draw on several studies I conducted with Christian survivors, exploring their experiences of stigma and their faith communities. This is followed by a section on stigma theory, exploring how and why stigma happens. This is used to unpack how the concept of Jesus as a sexual violence survivor can be used to address the different forms of stigma as they occur within faith communities. The chapter concludes with a discussion about the potential challenges of such an approach.

Survivors' experiences of stigma

Over the past decade I have been involved in several research projects that engaged directly with sexual violence survivors to talk about their experiences of stigma and support at the hands of their churches, church leaders and church members. In this chapter I draw on the empirical data collected during four different studies of churches and sexual violence, done in six different countries (the DRC, Rwanda, Burundi, Liberia, South Africa and Colombia). I use these very different settings to illustrate the pervasiveness of the stigmatization of survivors and how it impacts their life projects.[3] What is important to note is that the studies were conducted in vastly different settings: different countries, different continents, different fragile settings (for example, internally displaced, refugee, active conflict, post-conflict, post-genocide, no conflict) and different ethnic groups. Despite all these differences, these Christian survivors' experiences of stigma are starkly similar. Also similar is the fact that they experience it at the hands of different members of society: at the hands of their immediate family, including intimate partners; from community members; from members of their faith community, including the leaders; and they stigmatize themselves. The overview of experiences of trauma will be organized around these categories.

The stigmatizing behaviours of close family members, especially intimate partners, were for many the most traumatic. In the DRC, Liberia, Burundi and Rwanda, all of the survivors interviewed feared that their husbands would find out what happened, for then they would be divorced and rejected. In Burundi, survivors told heart-breaking stories of trying to hide it from their husbands, knowing that they would be rejected from the home if he found out. Some told stories of husbands who did find out and immediately ended the marriage and forced them to leave the family home.[4] In a focus group with survivors in Colombia, they explained their most traumatic experience as being the stigma and rejection they experienced at the hands of their own mothers, who refused to believe them and even evicted them from the family home.[5] In Rwanda, some of the survivors from sexual violence during the genocide told of their family marginalizing them and their children born from rape, while in the DRC survivors told of how they are mocked and mistreated by their family. These are not just psychological wounds. Many survivors experienced beatings, had their personal effects taken, and/or lost their homes and their husband's financial support. Families-in-law have been known to set the survivor's house and personal effects on fire.[6]

A clear theme that emerged from all of the studies is that a survivor is judged for what happened to her. For example, if she was well behaved prior to the rape (dressing modestly, not drinking alcohol, and so on), she will not be treated much differently afterwards. However, if she was perceived as engaging in immodest behaviours, she was usually blamed for what happened to her. As two leaders from Rwanda explained:

> It depends how someone was raped. When you have been badly behaved, then they [family and community members] don't care, they can think you are the one who caused you to be raped ... But when you are really good in your behaviours, really they try to care for you.[7]

In many communities, the stigma attached to someone who experiences sexual violence extends to her family, especially if she is seen as in some way inviting or causing the sexual violence. Families are then angry at the survivor for bringing this shame and judgement on the whole family. A mother from Liberia, talking about her 13-year-old daughter who was gang-raped after being given a date-rape drug, expressed fury:

> I am so angry with her. How could she do this to us? How could she behave so? Kids her age should do better things, like sing in the choir. Why did she go out, why did she be with such boys, why did she let herself be drugged?[8]

Survivors experience their communities as vilifying and excluding them for being sexually violated, seeing them as having less value because of it. A DRC survivor explained that her community does not see a sexually violated woman as having any value, while a South African survivor felt that the community actually enjoys stigmatizing survivors and seeing how hard their lives are:

> what I hate about neighbours [is that] your neighbours want you to look the way you do. They enjoy it. Instead of seeing how they can help, they enjoy it. They stand in their doorways, they look at you and you feel embarrassed.[9]

Condemned for what another did to them, survivors are seen as useless and excluded from community activities. For example, a Burundi schoolgirl who was raped by the headmaster could no longer attend school as her classmates refused to attend school with a pregnant girl.[10] A Rwandan survivor of genocide rape spoke wistfully of how she wished she could be accepted and included by the community, yet knows that they will never accept her: 'If really it is possible, I would want to live in harmony with other people, loving each other, working together, caring [for] each other.'[11]

Many survivors explained that their faith communities and leaders refuse to speak about sexual violence at all, seeing it as a taboo topic. This increases the stigma attached to it and to those experiencing it. Churches do not see sexual violence as appropriate or important enough to talk about in churches, which contributes to survivors' feelings of stigma and isolation from their faith communities. They also experience very direct stigma and discrimination, aimed at them because they experienced sexual violence; many shared stories of the painful stigmatizing treatment they experienced at the hands of church leaders and members. In South Africa one survivor explained how she disclosed to her pastor, needing his help and support, but that he avoided her from that day onwards. Another told the story of a church leader offering support after hearing what had happened to her, just to phone her late at night making suggestions of a sexual nature. A third survivor, already the mother of six children, was ostracized by her church after word got out that she had undergone an abortion for a pregnancy that was a result of rape.[12] In one community in Rwanda none of the survivors interviewed actually disclosed to anyone in their respective churches, as they did not trust them to keep it confidential and did not think there would be any support forthcoming. They thus saw no benefit in risking disclosure. Some Rwandan churches also force survivors to forgive perpetrators, citing Jesus' call to forgive others, and condemn survivors who testify in court against their perpetrators.[13]

In addition, survivors themselves also add to the burden they carry. In all of the studies, survivors spoke about the shame they feel for what had happened to them. They feel too ashamed to disclose to others and seek help. A survivor in South Africa explained it poignantly, stating that she chooses to 'die silently' rather than tell anyone about what happened to her.[14] A survivor from Liberia explained that she does not want to talk about it as it brings too much shame: 'I have not told anyone at my church. I do not like to talk about it, to talk about what happened. It brings shame.'[15] This shame is debilitating, with one stating that a survivor feels like she is 'dead, you are nothing, you are, you are useless, you have been used and then discarded'.[16] Furthermore, many survivors explained that they feel there is something wrong with them, or that the sexual violence (or subsequent happenings) are due to something being wrong with them. For example, a Colombian survivor explained that she understood her young daughter's attempted suicide as a punishment.[17] Likewise, a survivor in South Africa felt that she must have some form of label that identifies her as a target:

I was five years old, then he started to sexually molest me. Even the gardener did it ... Everyone just did it ... But there was that scar, it is as if the boys ... they took their chances and tried, so it feels as if the scar was there, everyone could see it ... you get that label, I call it a label, because you feel like you have the label, because all men try it with you, you know, it is as if it is written on your head.[18]

This brief reflection on the findings from four different studies, done in very different settings, serves as an illustration of the comprehensiveness of the stigma that survivors experience. Irrespective of where and when they experienced sexual violence, at what age or during what circumstances, survivors echo the same narrative: judged and condemned for what happened to them, by others and themselves, they do not (often) seek or receive the help they need. This is true also of Christian survivors and their faith communities. Often the stigma and discrimination they experience from fellow church members and religious leaders are the most hurtful.

If this is the reality of stigma, how does one address it? Responding to the comprehensiveness of these experiences of stigma requires an understanding of what it is, as well as how and why it happens. This is what the next section will explore.

Understanding stigma

Erving Goffman's 1963 work *Stigma: Notes on the Management of Spoiled Identity* heralded a new wave of interest in the phenomenon of stigma. Goffman defined it as 'the situation of the individual who is disqualified from full social acceptance'.[19] While there are many definitions of stigma, related to the fact that it is studied within various disciplines, most definitions of stigma identified two core components: namely the recognition of difference and devaluation. Most definitions also emphasize that stigma happens within social contexts. In other words, stigma is not inherently part of a person, but is the result of a particular situation. Thus what is considered stigmatizing in one social context may not be considered stigmatizing in another social context.[20]

Pryor and Reeder's more recent stigma model (2011) explains it as manifested in four different but interrelated ways.[21] These manifestations are: public stigma, self-stigma, stigma by association, and institutional stigma. All four of these can be identified in our earlier reflection of survivors' experiences of stigma. *Public stigma* is at the core of the model, present and a prerequisite to the other three manifestations. Public stigma is defined as 'people's social and psychological reactions to someone they perceive to have a stigmatized condition'.[22] *Self-stigma* refers to the social and psychological impact of possessing a stigma. This is both the fear of being stigmatized (also called 'anticipated stigma') and the potential internalization of the negative beliefs connected to the stigma (or 'stigma internalization').[23] It is important to realize that anticipated stigma or stigma internalization cannot happen without the existence of public stigma: '(T)his internalizing of stigma by individuals could not occur without prior exposure to victim-blaming messages from the broader society.'[24] *Stigma by association* refers not only to the social and psychological reactions of people who are associated with the stigmatized, but also people's reactions to being associated with the stigmatized. Last, *institutional stigma* (or 'structural stigma') refers to the 'legitimatization and perpetuation of a stigmatized status by society's institutions and ideological systems'.[25] This form of stigma is the result of, for example, official policies that call for different treatment of certain groups, or laws that directly or indirectly legitimize discrimination against such groups.

These four different, but interrelated, ways of defining stigma help to understand it as a process with different components or steps. These steps are comprised of labelling, negative stereotyping, separation, emotional responses, status loss, discrimination, and responses related to power. Distinguishing and labelling differences are important components of stigma because certain characteristics are then selected to identify difference and labels created for these differences. The labelled difference is then linked to negative stereotypes. These social labels are used to clearly distinguish between 'us' and 'them'. The stigmatizer readily experiences emotions (for example, fear, anger, disgust) in reaction to stigma and the stigmatized, and these emotional responses can influence the stigmatizer's subsequent behaviour towards the stigmatized. At the same time, the stigmatized also experiences emotions (for example, shame, embarrassment) in response to stigma and the stigmatizer's emotional responses. Through labelling, stereotyping and separating, justification is created for devaluing and rejecting the stigmatized, resulting in the stigmatized losing status and experiencing discrimination.[26]

The critical feature of all these components is power. Stigma only happens when elements of labelling, stereotyping, separation, and discrimination happen within a context of social, economic and political power.[27] While those with less power can label, stereotype and separate, they do not have the social, economic or political power to link it with serious discriminatory consequences.[28] It should be noted, however, that theorists approach this issue differently. Some define stigma as inherently including discrimination. In other words, stigma cannot happen if the stigmatizer does not have the power to enforce discriminatory consequences. Other theorists differentiate between stigma and enacted stigma (or discrimination). With this understanding, persons may stigmatize others without it necessarily leading to the negative treatment of those possessing the stigmatized condition.[29]

What both these understandings of the relationship between stigma and discrimination emphasize is that power plays a crucial role. Those with power can choose to deploy stigma and its negative consequences. Stigma is thus 'frequently the power mechanism of choice',[30] a resource used by those in power to dominate or exploit others, to enforce social norms, or to avoid those that deviate from the norm. Therefore, 'while the exercise of stigma power can be brutishly obvious, it is more generally hidden in processes that are just as potent, but less obviously linked to the interests of stigmatizers'.[31] Stigmatizing someone or something can be a highly effective strategy to get what you want. Yet, by reflecting further on why people stigmatize, it is important to realize that stigma is also an effective response to what is feared or seen as threatening: It is 'a highly pragmatic, even tactical response to perceived threats, real dangers, and fear of the unknown. This is what makes stigma so dangerous, durable, and difficult to curb.'[32]

Thus three key functions of stigma have been identified. The first is exploitation and dominance, where those with power stigmatize those without power in order to ensure the continuation of power inequalities. Second, stigma can be an effective way of enforcing social norms, as the threat of stigma encourages people to adhere to in-group norms. Stigma both creates and reinforces in-group power.[33] Research has shown that group-oriented cultures have a stronger tendency to stigmatize than individual-oriented cultures, and stigma is used to create and maintain social cohesion around traditional values.[34] The third function of stigma is disease avoidance. This refers to the way stigma is used to exclude those that deviate from whatever is considered normal.[35] The blaming model of stigma[36] is particularly relevant to explaining how stigma is used in avoiding what is feared, describing stigma as an emotional response to danger. Stigmatizing thus makes people feel safer: '[It] helps people feel safer by projecting controllable risk, and therefore blame, onto outgroups. Stigmatisation thus helps to create a sense of control and immunity from danger at an individual and a group level.'[37] This response is a result of the human defence mechanism of splitting and projection. Splitting is the process of identifying everything (including experiences, beliefs, ideas, etc.) as either good or bad. What has been identified as bad is then projected onto the other, as a way of reducing anxiety and stress.[38]

The previous section gave poignant examples of the stigma that survivors experience in the different facets of their lives. The aim of this section was to give an overview of what stigma is and how and why it happens. Now, taking into account the lived experiences of survivors as well as this theoretical overview of stigma and how it functions, the next section reflects on possible ways of addressing survivor stigma within faith communities.

Responding to stigma within faith communities: Jesus as a survivor

David Tombs first introduced the idea of Jesus as a sexual violence survivor in a 1998 conference paper entitled 'Bible Interpretation in Latin America: Crucifixion, State Terror, and Sexual Abuse'.[39] The following year, his work was published as 'Crucifixion, State Terror, and Sexual Abuse'.[40] Since then he has developed the concept further in successive publications.[41] Drawing on the Bible as well as Seneca, Josephus and other historical texts, Tombs explains what crucifixion represented in Roman times and highlights the sexual humiliation Jesus experienced in the stripping, mockery and naked exposure of crucifixion. Tombs also raises the possibility that there may have been additional sexual assault beyond the stripping and exposure. While the crucifixion passages are silent on this, and the answer may never be known with certainty, Tombs argues that the way the Romans mistreated other prisoners makes this a genuine possibility.

Tombs acknowledges that these ideas are initially disturbing but suggests that there is value in taking them seriously. He argues from a Christian point of view that God identifies with those who experience sexual abuse, and calls for theological engagement on sexual violence and the imperative need for churches to respond to this issue. Understanding Jesus as a survivor can also influence churches' pastoral response to survivors, sensitizing people to sexual violence.[42] To explore this reading of crucifixion, Tombs, Gerald West, Charlene van der Walt and colleagues at the Ujamaa Centre at the University of KwaZulu-Natal in South Africa have developed a contextual Bible study on Matthew 27.26–31.[43] At the same time, Figueroa and Tombs are also interviewing survivors to learn more about survivor responses to the idea of Jesus as a survivor of sexual abuse, as discussed in their chapter in this volume.[44]

As illustrated in this chapter's earlier discussion of survivors' experiences of stigma at the hands of their faith communities, religious leaders and communities often harbour very harmful beliefs about sexual violence and those that experience it. For two reasons, the concept of Jesus as a survivor can potentially be very effective in countering these stigmatizing beliefs and practices within Christian faith communities, especially if it is introduced through contextual Bible studies or similar discussion groups engaging with the Bible. First, this is a scriptural/theological approach which has been shown to be effective in engaging with religious leaders and communities on various sensitive issues, including sexual violence, female genital mutilation/cutting, and child marriage.[45] With such an approach, interventions include (or are based on) engaging with sacred texts on the chosen topic. For example, in an intervention focused on sexual violence in a Christian community, the biblical story of the rape of Tamar will be read and discussed. With religions that hold a central sacred text as absolutely authoritative, such engagement carries much weight. Relevant scriptures are read, discussed and re/interpreted as motivation for a new way of understanding and/or responding to a chosen issue. This approach has been effective because it introduces new ideas through a medium (the sacred text) that is seen as relevant and authoritative, and with which people (especially religious leaders) are comfortable. These new ideas are then not as easily viewed as controversial or threatening, seeing that it is shown to be in agreement with existing religious beliefs. The need to change existing ideas and practices then becomes easier to accept. For example, if the Bible is understood as opposing child marriage, then religious leaders and communities are much more easily convinced to also oppose child marriage. Of course, such engagement with sacred texts is a highly sensitive, contentious process. A rereading and reinterpretation of sacred text is often much needed as it is often interpreted in ways that justify gender inequality, violence and stigma.[46] A number of faith-based organizations (FBOs) have designed their interventions with religious leaders and/or communities around this scriptural/theological approach on a number of different contentious forms of gender-based violence.[47]

Second, scriptural engagement with the concept of Jesus as a survivor of sexual abuse is an effective intervention because it has the ability to serve both the stigmatizer (in as far as it responds to public stigma, institutional stigma and stigma by association) and the stigmatized (in as far as it responds to self-stigma). In working with religious leaders and communities, the concept of Jesus as a survivor can debunk beliefs in the sinfulness of survivors, that they have lesser value, are not to be trusted, and are deserving of what happened. Jesus as a survivor explains how a person can experience sexual violence through no fault of their own, and that such a person remains a valuable, good, worthwhile human being. In introducing the concept of Jesus as a survivor through a scriptural approach, institutional stigma is addressed. The institutional culture within the faith community can be transformed to be supportive, accepting and non-judgemental of survivors. If Jesus is a survivor, how can the Church refuse survivors entry into the Church? If Jesus, the Christian figure representing all that is good and faithful, was also a survivor, how can people of faith stigmatize survivors? This can serve as a direct counter-narrative to the process of splitting and projection, where having experienced sexual violence immediately designates a person as being a bad person. For how can a Christian say that Jesus is bad? With churches often holding and enforcing rigid social norms that ostracize survivors (for example, that involvement in any form of sex outside of marriage is the ultimate sin), this form of engagement can counter institutional stigma that is the result of the need to enforce in-group norms, by revisiting these norms and how they are understood. Intervention at this level can also serve to respond to public stigma, not only as common within the faith community, but also in the community more broadly. Faith communities are key spaces where harmful or helpful understandings of sexual violence and survivors are promulgated.[48] Especially in the Global South, where the vast majority of society is religious, this influence can be considerable. This is arguably even more so within fragile settings, such as those explored earlier in the reflection on the empirical research. Within fragile communities, religious institutions are often the only ones that continue functioning and they can have a very influential role in forming the norms, beliefs and perceptions that are held by the entire community.[49] Working with faith communities on stigma therefore potentially not only impacts how the faith community responds to survivors (and those associated with them), but also how the broader community does.

The concept of Jesus as a survivor can serve as a point of intervention with the stigmatized as well, by addressing tendencies towards self-stigmatization. The concept has the potential to assist Christian survivors in resisting the process of internalized stigma, through helping them re-envision what having experienced sexual violence means to their sense of self and self-identity. If Jesus, the Son of God, experienced sexual violence and *still* remains loved, good, God's Son and the Christian Saviour, what does this mean for them? If the central figure within the Christian faith tradition is also a survivor, this is a strong counter-narrative to the tendency of many Christian survivors to see themselves as sinful, spoiled and un-Christian for having been violated. Working with survivors to re-envision the way they see themselves, based on the idea of Christ as a survivor, can therefore be an important way of responding to the lived experienced of self-stigma by survivors. For survivors of faith this response may be a crucial step in helping them reconnect with their faith in the aftermath of the traumatic event, as it engages at the level where stigma threatens 'what makes life matter'.[50] When experiences of sexual violence threaten a person of faith's ability to see themselves as faithful and worthy of God's love, anti-stigma interventions that target such harmful internalized stigma are very important.

Reflecting on stigma interventions within faith communities

I have introduced the idea of Jesus as a survivor with a number of FBOs that I work with. These organizations have sexual violence interventions in various countries across the globe, working with Christian communities. All of them also use a scriptural approach as the core, or at least a key dimension, of many of their interventions. Using Tombs' academic work to explain the rationale behind Jesus as a survivor, I have also presented the contextual Bible studies on Mark 15.16–24 and Matthew 27.26–31, suggesting these as a component to their sexual violence interventions that can be used to directly work on the issue of stigma. I have experienced some resistance to this suggestion for sexual violence stigma intervention, and it is important to reflect on why this is the case.

While these FBO representatives were convinced by Tombs' argument, and found the Bible studies clear and user-friendly, they were hesitant to introduce the concept during their interventions, for they felt that the idea of Jesus as a survivor is *too* controversial. Working in communities where people are usually already resistant to ideas of gender equality and non-violence, often branding these as Western and not culturally appropriate, the FBO representatives believed that talking about Jesus as a survivor would have a backlash effect. Repulsed by the idea that Jesus could be a survivor, communities could reject *all* their programming, seeing the FBO as harbouring dangerously outrageous and un-Christian beliefs. This perception (that communities would react negatively to the concept) affirms the tenacious hold (or, at least, the perception of the existence of such a hold) that sexual violence stigma has in many communities. Sexual violence and survivors are vilified to such an extent that seeing Jesus as a survivor can be perceived as the ultimate blasphemy. The very real fear of such a negative reaction actually confirms the need for this kind of intervention. If survivors are stigmatized to such an extent that the concept of Jesus as a survivor is seen as profane and sacrilegious, then it is desperately important to engage with the stigmatizing beliefs and perceptions in these faith communities, especially in a way (scriptural/theological engagement) that has been shown to be effective in transforming the way religious leaders and communities understand and respond to sensitive issues.

However, I believe that it is also important to take heed of what these FBO representatives believe will be the result of introducing the concept of Jesus as a survivor. Insensitive or inappropriate stigma interventions run the risk of a backlash that strengthens and reinforces existing stigma. It appears that a faith community has to be ready for the idea of Jesus as a survivor. This kind of intervention may thus require longer engagement that only later on introduces the concept of Jesus as a survivor. It thus is advisable to first critically and honestly assess whether the faith community is ready to engage with the concept, or whether some groundwork must first be done.

Conclusion

Stigma is one of the most debilitating consequences that survivors may face. They are judged, marginalized and rejected for an act that they did not choose to be part of. Aside from the immense mental health challenge of dealing with the event, they have to deal with the often daily trauma of psychological and material mistreatment by others. While the Christian faith is understood to be a religion calling for unconditional love and acceptance, Christian faith communities are unfortunately also hotbeds of stigmatizing beliefs and behaviours, where survivors are in various ways projected as lesser human beings and Christians. Yet faith is potentially a very important component of a religious survivor's journey to healing. Religious and spiritual experiences can have a strong influence on the health and wellness of survivors.[51] This potential as a source of aid and coping is unfortunately not only underutilized, but often has the opposite effect. Negative religious and spiritual experiences can hamper survivors' healing – as was illustrated in the empirical studies explored in this chapter. Recognizing this influence of religion and religious communities, this chapter has argued that it is important to intentionally engage with religion and religious communities when addressing stigma. These spaces are key spaces, either in promoting stigma or in countering it.

The concept of Jesus as a survivor, introduced and explored through a theological/scriptural approach, has been suggested as a potentially effective way of working within faith communities to address the stigma attached to sexual violence and survivors. Such an intervention can work with both the stigmatizer and the stigmatized, thus enabling engagement with all forms of stigma. Yet it is important to remember that such a response to stigma is *a component* of a holistic response to stigma. People's stigmatizing beliefs and behaviours are not formed under the sole influence of their religion and religious communities. To comprehensively respond to stigma will always also require engagement with other sectors, for example working with government to ensure adequate legislation and its implementation, and working with health care providers to ensure adequate health response and care (physical and psychological). Working with faith communities by introducing the concept of Jesus as a survivor through a scriptural approach is therefore only one dimension of the needed response. Nevertheless, as argued in this chapter, I believe it can be an effective one in working with faith communities, potentially also influencing the broader community.

References

Bos, Arjan E. R., John B. Pryor, Glenn. D. Reeder and Sarah E. Stutterheim, 'Stigma: Advances in Theory and Research', *Basic and Applied Social Psychology* 35 (2013), pp. 1–9.

Bowland, Sharon, Bipasha Biswas, Stavroula Kyriakakis and Tonya Edmond, 'Transcending the Negative: Spiritual Struggles and Resilience in Older Female Trauma Survivors', *Journal of Religion, Spirituality & Aging* 23:4 (2011), pp. 318–37.

Bridger, Emma, and Jo Sadgrove, *Keeping Faith in Faith Leaders*, London: United Society Partners in the Gospel, 2019, www.uspg.org.uk/docstore/223.pdf.

Crawford, Robert, 'The Boundaries of the Self and the Unhealthy Other: Reflections on Health, Culture and AIDS', *Social Science & Medicine* 38:10 (1994), pp. 1347–65.

Deacon, Harriet, Inez Stephney and Sandra Prosalendis, *Understanding HIV/AIDS: A Theoretical and Methodological Analysis*, Cape Town: HSRC Press, 2005.

De la Rosa, Ivan A., Timothy Barnett-Queen, Madeline Messick and Maria Gurrola, 'Spirituality and Resilience among Mexican American IPV Survivors', *Journal of Interpersonal Violence* 31:20 (2015), pp. 3332–51.

Figueroa, Rocío, and David Tombs, 'Recognising Jesus as a Victim of Sexual Abuse: Responses from Sodalicio Survivors in Peru', *Religion and Gender* 10:1 (2020), pp. 57–75.

Goffman, Erving, *Stigma: Notes on the Management of Spoiled Identity*, London: Penguin Books, 1963.

Joffe, Helene, *Risk and 'the Other'*, Cambridge: Cambridge University Press, 1999.

Johnston, Jo, *Breaking the Silence: The Role of the Church in Addressing Sexual Violence in South Africa*, Durban: Tearfund, 2013, http://learn.tearfund.org/~/media/Files/TILZ/HIV/Breaking_the_silenceweb_FINAL.pdf?la=en.

Kaviti, L. K., 'Impact of the Tamar Communication Strategy on Sexual Gender-based Violence in Eastern Africa', *International Journal of Humanities and Cultural Studies* 2:3 (2015), pp. 492–514.

Kennedy, Angie C., and Kirsten A. Prock, '"I still feel like I am not normal": A Review of the Role of Stigma and Stigmatization among Female Survivors of Child Sexual Abuse, Sexual Assault, and Intimate Partner Violence', *Trauma, Violence & Abuse* 19:5 (2013), pp. 512–27.

Le Roux, Elisabet, *An Explorative Baseline: The Role of the Church in Sexual Violence in Countries that Are/were in Armed Conflict, in a Preventative Sense and as a Caring Institution*, London: Tearfund, 2010.

—, *Sexual Violence in South Africa and the Role of the Church*, Stellenbosch: University of Stellenbosch Unit for Religion and Development Research/Tearfund, 2013, http://blogs.sun.ac.za/urdr/files/2019/07/TF-Report_SV-in-SArole-of-church_Aug2013_pict.pdf.

—, 'The Role of African Christian Churches in Dealing with Sexual Violence against Women: The Case of the Democratic Republic of Congo, Rwanda and Liberia', Doctoral dissertation, University of Stellenbosch, Stellenbosch, 2014.

—, *Religion, Development, and GBV: Suggestions for a Strategic Research Agenda*, Stellenbosch: University of Stellenbosch Unit for Religion and Development Research/Joint Learning Initiative on Faith and Local Communities, 2019, https://gender-based-violence.jliflc.com/2019/06/religion-development-and-gbv-agenda-setting-report-published/.

Le Roux, Elisabet, and Brenda Bartelink, 2017, *No More 'harmful traditional practices': Working Effectively with Faith Leaders*, https://jliflc.com/wp/wp-content/uploads/2017/11/HTP-report-final-draft.pdf.

Le Roux, Elisabet, and Nadine Bowers-Du Toit, 'Men and Women in Partnership: Mobilizing Faith Communities to Address Gender-based Violence', *Diaconia* 8 (2017), pp. 23–37.

Le Roux, Elisabet, and Denise Niyonizigiye, *A View on the Current Situation Regarding Sexual Violence in Burundi: The Role of the Church and Possible Avenues for Intervention*, Stellenbosch: University of Stellenbosch Unit for Religion and Development Research/Tearfund, 2011, www.wewillspeakout.org/wp-content/uploads/2011/10/Burundi-Report-FINAL-English.pdf.

Le Roux, Elisabet, and Selina Palm, *What Lies Beneath? Tackling the Roots of Religious Resistance to Ending Child Marriage*, Girls Not Brides, 2018, www.girlsnotbrides.org/wp-content/uploads/2018/11/FINAL-Religious-leaders-report-High-Res.pdf

Le Roux, Elisabet, and Laura Cadavid Valencia, '"There's no-one you can trust to talk to here": Churches and Internally Displaced Survivors of Sexual Violence in Medellín, Colombia', *HTS Teologiese Studies/ Theological Studies* 75:4 (2019), a5491.

Link, Bruce, and Jo C. Phelan, 'Conceptualizing Stigma', *Annual Review of Sociology* 27 (2001), pp. 363–85.

—, 'Labeling and Stigma', in *A Handbook for the Study of Mental Health: Social Contexts, Theories, and Systems*, Teresa I. Scheid and Tony N. Brown eds, Cambridge: Cambridge University Press, 2010, pp. 571–88.

—, 'Stigma Power', *Social Science & Medicine* 103 (2014), pp. 24–32.

Murray-Swank, Nichole A., and Kenneth Pargament, 'God, Where Are You? Evaluating a Spiritually-integrated Intervention for Sexual Abuse', *Mental Health, Religion & Culture* 8:3 (2005), pp. 191–203.

Overstreet, N. M., and D. M. Quinn, 'The Intimate Partner Violence Stigmatization Model and Barriers to Help Seeking', *Basic and Applied Social Psychology* 35 (2013), pp. 109–22.

Parker, Richard, and Peter Aggleton, 'HIV and AIDS-related Stigma and Discrimination: A Conceptual Framework and Implications for Action', *Social Science & Medicine* 57 (2003), pp. 13–24.

Pryor, John B., and Glen D. Reeder, 'HIV-related Stigma', in *HIV/AIDS in the Post-HAART Era: Manifestations, Treatment, and Epidemiology*, John C. Hall, Brian J. Hall and Clay J. Cockerell eds, Shelton, CT: People's Medical Publishing House, 2011, pp. 790–806.

Reaves, Jayme R., and David Tombs, '#MeToo Jesus: Naming Jesus as a Victim of Sexual Abuse', *International Journal for Public Theology* 13:4 (2019), pp. 387–412.

Sadiq, Adina, 'The Paradigm of Violence against Women in Pakistan: A Conflict Between Law, Culture and Religion', *European Journal of Social Sciences Studies* 2:1 (2017), pp. 65–73.

Shin, Hyeyoung, John F. Dovidio and Jaime L. Napier, 'Cultural Differences in Targets of Stigmatization between Individual- and Group-oriented Cultures', *Basic and Applied Social Psychology* 35 (2013), pp. 98–108.

Tombs, David, 'Crucifixion, State Terror, and Sexual Abuse', *Union Seminary Quarterly Review* 53:1–2 (1999), pp. 89–108. Republished in David Tombs, *Crucifixion, State Terror, and Sexual Abuse: Text and Context*, Dunedin: Centre for Theology and Public Issues, University of Otago, 2018.

——, 'Prisoner Abuse: From Abu Ghraib to The Passion of The Christ' in *Religions and the Politics of Peace and Conflict*, Linda Hogan and Dylan Lehrke eds, Princeton, NJ: Princeton Theological Monograph Series, 2009, pp. 179–205.

——, 'Silent No More: Sexual Violence in Conflict as a Challenge to the Worldwide Church', *Acta Theologica* 34:2 (2014), 142–60.

——, 'Confronting the Stigma of Naming Jesus as a Victim of Sexual Violence', in *Enacting a Public Theology*, Clive Pearson ed., Stellenbosch: SUNMedia, 2019, pp. 71–86.

Ujamaa Centre, 'A Contextual Bible Study on the Crucifixion of Jesus', Pietermaritzburg: Ujamaa Centre, 2019.

Yang, Lawrence H., Arthur Kleinman, Bruce G. Link, Jo C. Phelan, Sing Lee and Byron Good, 'Culture and Stigma: Adding Moral Experience to Stigma Theory', *Social Science & Medicine* 64 (2007), pp. 1524–35.

Notes

1 Elisabet le Roux, 'The Role of African Christian Churches in Dealing with Sexual Violence against Women: The Case of the Democratic Republic of Congo, Rwanda and Liberia', Doctoral dissertation (Stellenbosch: University of Stellenbosch, 2014), p. 106.

2 Elisabet le Roux, *Sexual Violence in South Africa and the Role of the Church* (Stellenbosch: University of Stellenbosch Unit for Religion and Development Research/Tearfund, 2013), http://blogs.sun.ac.za/urdr/files/2019/07/TF-Report_SV-in-SArole-of-church_Aug2013_pict.pdf, p. 12.

3 Research in two communities each in the DRC, Rwanda and Liberia was conducted in 2010 and commissioned by Tearfund. The research project focused on African Christian churches' response to sexual violence against women; Elisabet le Roux, *An Explorative Baseline: The Role of the Church in Sexual Violence in Countries that Are/were in Armed Conflict, in a Preventative Sense and as a Caring Institution* (London: Tearfund, 2010). Similar research in Burundi was commissioned by Tearfund and conducted in two communities in 2011 on the current role

of churches in sexual violence in Burundi; Elisabet le Roux and Denise Niyonizigiye, *A View on the Current Situation Regarding Sexual Violence in Burundi: The Role of the Church and Possible Avenues for Intervention* (Stellenbosch: University of Stellenbosch Unit for Religion and Development Research/Tearfund, 2011), www. wewillspeakout.org/wp-content/uploads/2011/10/Burundi-Report-FINAL-English. pdf. Research in South Africa was conducted in four communities in 2013, also commissioned by Tearfund, on sexual violence in South Africa and the role of the church: Le Roux, *Sexual Violence in South Africa and the Role of the Church*; Johnston, *Breaking the Silence: The Role of the Church in Addressing Sexual Violence in South Africa* (Durban: Tearfund South Africa, 2013), http://learn.tearfund.org/~/media/Files/TILZ/HIV/Breaking_the_silenceweb_FINAL.pdf?la=en). Research in Colombia was conducted as part of a grant from the Templeton World Charity Foundation that was awarded to researchers at the Fundación Universitaria Seminario Bíblico de Colombia (FUSBC) in Medellín, Colombia, for a study entitled 'Integral missiology and the human flourishing of internally displaced persons in Colombia'. Drawing on an international team of researchers, empirical research was conducted within six IDP communities in Colombia. As part of the broader project, faith leaders from each community were asked questions on sexual violence and churches' response to it. However, a more focused investigation of the issue was included through an in-depth case study conducted in one IDP community in Medellín. This chapter draws on this case study in Elisabet le Roux and Laura Cadavid Valencia, '"There's no-one you can trust to talk to here": Churches and Internally Displaced Survivors of Sexual Violence in Medellín, Colombia', *HTS Teologiese Studies/ Theological Studies* 75:4 (2019), a5491.

4 Le Roux and Niyonizigiye, *A View on the Current Situation*, p. 4.

5 Le Roux and Valencia, '"There's no-one you can trust to talk to here"', pp. 5–6.

6 Le Roux, *The Role of African Christian Churches*, p. 107.

7 Le Roux, *The Role of African Christian Churches*, p. 143.

8 Le Roux, *The Role of African Christian Churches*, p. 176.

9 Le Roux, *Sexual Violence in South Africa*, p. 12.

10 Le Roux and Niyonizigiye, *A View on the Current Situation*, p. 8.

11 Le Roux, *The Role of African Christian Churches*, p. 143.

12 Le Roux, *Sexual Violence in South Africa*, pp. 11–14.

13 Le Roux, *The Role of African Christian Churches*, p. 154.

14 Le Roux, *Sexual Violence in South Africa*, p. 38.

15 Le Roux, *The Role of African Christian Churches*, p. 185.

16 Le Roux, *Sexual Violence in South Africa*, p. 24.

17 Le Roux and Valencia, '"There's no-one you can trust to talk to here"', p. 6.

18 Le Roux, *Sexual Violence in South Africa*, p. 13.

19 Erving Goffman, *Stigma: Notes on the Management of Spoiled Identity* (London: Penguin Books, 1963), p. 9.

20 Bos, Arjan E. R., John B. Pryor, Glenn. D. Reeder and Sarah E. Stutterheim, 'Stigma: Advances in Theory and Research', *Basic and Applied Social Psychology* 35 (2013), p. 1.

21 John B. Pryor and Glenn D. Reeder, 'HIV-related Stigma', in *HIV/AIDS in the post-HAART era: Manifestations, Treatment, and Epidemiology*, John C. Hall, Brian J. Hall and Clay J. Cockerell eds (Shelton, CT: People's Medical Publishing House, 2011), pp. 790–806.

22 Bos et al., 'Stigma', p. 2.

23 Bos et al., 'Stigma', p. 2; Nicole M. Overstreet and Diane M. Quinn, 'The

Intimate Partner Violence Stigmatization Model and Barriers to Help Seeking', *Basic and Applied Social Psychology* 35 (2013), p. 111.

24 Angie C. Kennedy and Kirsten A. Prock, '"I still feel like I am not normal": A Review of the Role of Stigma and Stigmatization among Female Survivors of Child Sexual Abuse, Sexual Assault, and Intimate Partner Violence', *Trauma, Violence & Abuse* 19:5 (2013), p. 513.

25 Pryor and Reeder, 'HIV-related Stigma', p. 793.

26 Bruce G. Link and Jo C. Phelan, 'Conceptualizing Stigma', *Annual Review of Sociology* 27 (2001), pp. 363–85; Bruce G. Link and Jo C. Phelan, 'Labeling and Stigma', in *A Handbook for the Study of Mental Health: Social Contexts, Theories, and Systems*, Teresa I. Scheid and Tony N. Brown eds (Cambridge: Cambridge University Press, 2010), pp. 571–88.

27 Link and Phelan, 'Conceptualizing Stigma', p. 367.

28 Link and Phelan, 'Labeling and Stigma', p. 579.

29 Bos et al., 'Stigma', p. 3.

30 Bruce G. Link and Jo C. Phelan, 'Stigma Power', *Social Science & Medicine* 103 (2014), pp. 24–32.

31 Link and Phelan, 'Stigma Power', p. 30.

32 Lawrence H. Yang, Arthur Kleinman, Bruce G. Link, Jo C. Phelan, Sing Lee and Byron Good, 'Culture and Stigma: Adding Moral Experience to Stigma Theory', *Social Science & Medicine* 64 (2007), p. 1528.

33 Link and Phelan, 'Conceptualizing Stigma', p. 375; Richard Parker and Peter Aggleton, 'HIV and AIDS-related Stigma and Discrimination: A Conceptual Framework and Implications for Action', *Social Science & Medicine* 57 (2003), p. 16.

34 Hyeyoung Shin, John F. Dovidio and Jaime L. Napier, 'Cultural Differences in Targets of Stigmatization between Individual- and Group-oriented Cultures', *Basic and Applied Social Psychology* 35 (2013), pp. 98–108.

35 Bos et al., 'Stigma', p. 2.

36 Harriet Deacon, Inez Stephney and Sandra Prosalendis, *Understanding HIV/ AIDS: A Theoretical and Methodological Analysis* (Cape Town: HSRC Press, 2005); Helene Joffe, *Risk and 'the Other'* (Cambridge: Cambridge University Press, 1999); Robert Crawford, 'The Boundaries of the Self and the Unhealthy Other: Reflections on Health, Culture and AIDS', *Social Science & Medicine* 38:10 (1994), pp. 1347–65.

37 Deacon et al., *Understanding HIV/AIDS*, p. 18.

38 Joffe, *Risk and 'the Other'*, pp. 734–7.

39 The term 'survivor' is mine and is used intentionally rather than the term 'victim'. Working with those that experienced sexual violence, this is an important difference in terminology. The term 'survivor' is used in order to recognize that those who experience sexual violence retain their sense of agency and are not defined by their positioning during a sexually violent act. For the purpose of designing interventions, it is important that Jesus is defined as a survivor and not simply a victim.

40 David Tombs, 'Crucifixion, State Terror, and Sexual Abuse', *Union Seminary Quarterly Review* 53:1–2 (1999), pp. 89–109. Republished in David Tombs, *Crucifixion, State Terror, and Sexual Abuse: Text and Context* (Dunedin: University of Otago, Centre for Theology and Public Issues, 2018).

41 David Tombs, 'Prisoner Abuse: From Abu Ghraib to The Passion of The Christ', in *Religions and the Politics of Peace and Conflict*, Linda Hogan and Dylan Lehrke eds (Princeton, NJ: Princeton Theological Monograph Series, 2009),

pp. 179–205; David Tombs, 'Silent No More: Sexual Violence in Conflict as a Challenge to the Worldwide Church', *Acta Theologica* 34:2 (2014), pp. 142–60; David Tombs, 'Confronting the Stigma of Naming Jesus as a Victim of Sexual Violence' in *Enacting a Public Theology*, Clive Pearson ed. (Stellenbosch: SUNMedia, 2019), pp. 71–86; Jayme R. Reaves and David Tombs, '#MeToo Jesus: Naming Jesus as a Victim of Sexual Abuse', *International Journal for Public Theology* 13:4 (2019), pp. 1–26.

42 Tombs, 'Confronting the Stigma', pp. 84–6.

43 Ujamaa Centre, 'A Contextual Bible Study on the Crucifixion of Jesus' (Pietermaritzburg: Ujamaa Centre, 2019); see the chapter by Gerald West, 'Jesus, Joseph, and Tamar Stripped: Trans-Textual and Intertextual Resources for Engaging Sexual Violence Against Men', in this volume.

44 See also Rocío Figueroa and David Tombs, 'Recognising Jesus as a Victim of Sexual Abuse: Responses from Sodalicio Survivors in Peru', *Religion and Gender* 10:1 (2020), pp. 57–75.

45 Elisabet le Roux and Brenda Bartelink, *No More 'harmful traditional practices': Working Effectively with Faith Leaders* (London: Tearfund, 2017), https://jliflc.com/wp/wp-content/uploads/2017/11/HTP-report-final-draft.pdf; Elisabet le Roux and Selina Palm, *What Lies Beneath? Tackling the Roots of Religious Resistance to Ending Child Marriage* (Girls Not Brides, 2018), www.girlsnotbrides.org/wp-content/uploads/2018/11/FINAL-Religious-leaders-report-High-Res.pdf.

46 Emma Bridger and Jo Sadgrove, *Keeping Faith in Faith Leaders* (United Society Partners in the Gospel, 2019); www.uspg.org.uk/docstore/223.pdf; L. K. Kaviti, 'Impact of the Tamar Communication Strategy on Sexual Gender-based Violence in Eastern Africa', *International Journal of Humanities and Cultural Studies* 2:3 (2015), pp. 492–514; Adina Sadiq, 'The Paradigm of Violence Against Women in Pakistan: A Conflict Between Law, Culture and Religion', *European Journal of Social Sciences Studies* 2:1 (2017), pp. 65–73.

47 Elisabet le Roux, *Religion, Development, and GBV: Suggestions for a Strategic Research Agenda* (London: Tearfund, 2017), p. 14, https://gender-based-violence.jliflc.com/2019/06/religion-development-and-gbv-agenda-setting-report-published/.

48 Elisabet le Roux, Neil Kramm, Nigel Scott, Maggie Sandilands, Lizle Loots, Jill Olivier, Diana Arango and Veena O'Sullivan, 'Getting Dirty: Working with Faith Leaders to Prevent and Respond to Gender-Based Violence', *The Review of Faith & International Affairs* 14:3 (2016), pp. 22–35.

49 Elisabet le Roux and Nadine Bowers-Du Toit, 'Men and Women in Partnership: Mobilizing Faith Communities to Address Gender-based Violence', *Diaconia* 8 (2017), pp. 23–37.

50 Yang et al., 'Culture and Stigma', p. 1533.

51 Sharon Bowland, Bipasha Biswas, Stavroula Kyriakakis and Tonya Edmond, 'Transcending the Negative: Spiritual Struggles and Resilience in Older Female Trauma Survivors', *Journal of Religion, Spirituality & Aging* 23:4 (2011), pp. 318–37; Ivan A. De la Rosa, Timothy Barnett-Queen, Madeline Messick and Maria Gurrola, 'Spirituality and Resilience among Mexican American IPV Survivors', *Journal of Interpersonal Violence* 31:20 (2015), pp. 3332–51; Nichole A. Murray-Swank and Kenneth I. Pargament, 'God, Where Are You? Evaluating a Spiritually-integrated Intervention for Sexual Abuse', *Mental Health, Religion & Culture* 8:3 (2005), pp. 191–203.

11

Why Do We See Him Naked?
Politicized, Spiritualized and Sexualized
Gazes at Violence

R. RUARD GANZEVOORT, SRDJAN SREMAC
AND TEGUH WIJAYA MULYA[1]

> Evil resides in the gaze which sees evil everywhere.
> *Friedrich Hegel*

Introduction

Nails went through his hands and feet. A spear pierced his side. A crown of thorns pushed onto his head. Sharp objects on the lead-tipped whip dug deep into his skin. The torturous attacks penetrated Jesus' physical body during the crucifixion. Some claim that Jesus could have suffered penetrative sex too as part of the humiliation and torture. Among them is David Tombs, who has convincingly demonstrated how Jesus suffered forms of sexual humiliation when he was stripped naked, but the possibility that Jesus was raped – he argues – can never be textually and historically confirmed due to the privacy of the Roman praetorium. Since prisoner rape was a standard torture practice in the first-century Roman Empire as well as in modern-day oppressive regimes, Tombs suggests that we cannot simply dismiss such likelihood, particularly considering its significant theological and pastoral implications for present-day survivors of sexual violence.[2] We argue that, while historical accuracy of the rape of Jesus may never be claimed, there might be an interpretive community who, through their particular interpretive lens, give meaning to and subjectively experience Jesus' crucifixion as penetratively sexual. While this entire volume builds on the work by Tombs and others who have proposed to construe the crucifixion of Jesus as an act of torture with dimensions of sexualized violence,[3] this chapter will focus specifically on the viewers of those torturous acts. Seeing, touching and penetrating are considered in many criminal codes to be three levels of sexual transgression. Visual (and auditory) exposure includes being forced to watch pornography of exhibitionism, being forced to undress and show oneself, or unwillingly being exposed to sexualized language or imagery. The second level of transgression, through touch, refers to one's body being approached without consent for bodily contact, including stroking and masturbation. Penetration of the body, usually oral, vaginal or anal, is the third level. This three-level categorization shows that viewing is intrinsically connected to the other levels of sexual transgression. Put more clearly, viewing is the first level of transgression of sexual boundaries.

If it is indeed meaningful to read the crucifixion narrative as a story of sexualized violence, which is a matter of grave pastoral and ethical importance, what then does it mean that Christians over the centuries have gazed at Jesus' tortured body and meditated on his dying process? Rambuss, for example, critically examined seventeenth-century poems contemplating the ways in which Jesus' body was penetrable and penetrated.[4] The opening of the body in these devotional lyrics becomes a locus for the believer engaging most intimately and erotically with Christ. An example from our own times could be Mel Gibson's graphically violent movie *The Passion of the Christ*, drawing hundreds of millions of viewers to their local cinemas and garnering massive support and special viewings from churches for their youth and not-yet-believing visitors, as if this revelling in torture, blood and body mutilation was the best way to convey a message of love and grace. In another form of spiritualized gaze on sexualized violence in our contemporary postmodern world, certain Christian BDSM (Bondage-Discipline, Dominance-Submission, Sadism-Masochism) subcultures deploy spiritual and sexual readings of violent biblical narratives, including the crucifixion of Jesus.[5] To claim that there is an intrinsic connection between religion, sexuality and violence is not new. Whereas Freud stressed the importance of the sexual dimension and interpreted religion as a symbolization (and sublimation) of sexuality, Girard saw violence as the more primary impulse and interpreted religion as a response to it. This implies that when we study sexual violence and religion, we should expect these three dimensions to overlap, interact and even amalgamate.

Therefore, how does this blurring of spirituality, power/violence, and sexuality make sense in our contemplation of the crucifixion? The focus of this chapter will be on these intersections from the perspective of the viewer and it will reflect on the intimate connection between contemplation and complicity, between veneration and perversion, and between violence, sexuality, testimony and the sacred. What do our politicized, spiritualized or sexualized gazes at violence imply? Obviously, we do not claim to know what individual persons believe or experience when they are spiritually moved by the crucifixion narratives or their visual representations. Our intention is to critically highlight possible meanings of the fact that this grotesque story of (sexualized) violence has become such an important source for spiritual contemplation. We do so by exploring three dimensions of gazing at the crucified body: the politicized gaze of sexualized violence, the spiritualized gaze of the political violence, and the sexualized gaze of spiritual violence.

Politicizing the gaze

Visual technologies not only represent traumatic events that are in many ways unrepresentable and unimaginable in their brutality and terror. The representation itself also has potentially traumatizing effects on its viewers. This effect also means that viewing violence can change the viewer by transcending the ordinary experiences and conventions.[6] Many religious traditions play into this through their violent images and narratives. Violence can indeed be understood as a dimension of the sacred in its life-giving and destructive shapes.[7] Žižek even argues that the fundamental value of Christianity lies precisely in this 'perverse core' of violence.[8]

Watching violence is never merely symbolic or entertaining. Research on visual media violence has shown that exposure to violence on movies, media or video games increases the risk of violent behaviour on the viewer's part, although it is never the only factor to explain violence.[9] Seeing is always in a certain sense affective. The media frames of horror that become more graphic and realistic can increase violent behaviour.

Similarly, violence – and even more watching violence – is culturally and socially embedded. In our previous research on wartime male-to-male sexual torture, we showed how sexual violence is not simply the act of one individual against another but is embedded in group-based performances aiming at the visible evidentiary.[10] Similarly, Eichert argues, from an audience-focused perspective in the context of wartime male sexual violence, that 'the audience of violence is the perpetrator's fellow soldiers, and violence becomes a way for the perpetrator to impress or bond his peers'.[11] This spectatorship of pain and its iconography of torture always requires visual confirmation, as Sontag would put it: if there is no evidence, there is no atrocity.[12] Being exposed to the ritualistic violation of sexual brutality undermines the self-evident boundary between the self and the other. With these intersections of violence, spectatorship, atrocity images and religion in mind, how are we to understand the gazing at the spectacle of Jesus' brutalized body? Are the viewers of Caravaggio's *Flagellation of Christ* or Gibson's *The Passion of the Christ* looking for spiritual redemption or inspiration? Is this visuality of violence what Sontag calls the ultimate horror of revelation, 'a negative epiphany'?[13] How do these visual tropes of horror and its modes of representation become part of an intrinsic socio-political and even spiritual routine of being witness?

Jennifer Glancy argues that 'Jesus' tortured body is a truth-telling corpus'.[14] An important question for us here is: how do religious practitioners understand it in order to bear witness to an aesthetic pursuit of this 'tortured truth'?[15] Or more precisely, is bearing witness to the images of the tortured truth/body what Ricoeur calls the 'total engagement not only of words but of acts and, in the extreme, in the sacrifice of a life' that belongs to 'the tragic destiny of truth'.[16] In a somewhat similar vein, Dutch philosopher of religion Stoker argues that the testimonial character of faith refers on the one hand to a manifestation and proclamation of the sacred and on the other to the individual witness of what he or she has seen.[17]

Kyo Maclear argues similarly in her research of 'testimonial art', wherein 'the art of witness ... bids us to consider how a remembered image might gain new hold on our lives and actions'.[18] In this sense, the visual testimonial representation of the crucifixion might be seen as a kind of existential act that sets up special ethical, spiritual and epistemological demands.

Therefore testifying is an ethical (and spiritual) action, and visual *testimonio* is its result, an intelligible act of re-creating the real. Within the context of bearing witness, the attitude of trust is ultimate, but not blind. We do not claim here that the material image of Jesus' tortured body has some sort of sublime or intrinsic 'ontological weight'; it is, rather, grounded in the performative function of bearing witness.[19] In line with this, Guerin and Hallas remark that the visual role in religious mediation in the process of witnessing 'can be seen to rely not upon faith in the image's technological ability to furnish empirical evidence of the event, but upon faith in the image's phenomenological capacity to bring the event into iconic presence and to mediate the intersubjective relations that ground the act of bearing witness'.[20] In this sense, the central aspect of visual *testimonio* is confession; a mechanism of reinforcement and spiritual commitment.

The testifying gaze thus makes a connection between the brutality of the (political) violence and the commitment of the viewer. This can turn into a political statement, as in Metz's notion of the 'dangerous memories', linking the suffering of Christ with the suffering of others. These are, to borrow Moltmann's coining, very specific memorial testimonies of 'vicious circles of death', situated in various dimensions of life.[21] All of them together – the vicious circle of *poverty* situated in the economic dimension of life; the vicious circle of *power* situated in the political dimension of life; the vicious circle of *racial*, *cultural* and *sexual* violence situated in the cultural dimension of life; the vicious circle of industrial *pollution* situated in the environmental dimension of life – culminate in a testimonial vicious circle of meaninglessness and God-forsakenness, situated in the sphere of lived religion.

These testimonies may also imply a cry for justice, as when they are brought to judicial hearings.[22] Viewing the sexualized humiliation and violence of the crucifixion through the lens of testimony, the viewer is invited to take seriously the inhuman brutality exerted against Jesus, just as it has been and is exerted against the millions of victims of political violence. By testifying about and against this brutality, the viewer takes up the 'ethical memory'[23] and responsibility to act in the service of restoring human dignity.

Spiritualizing the gaze

The second dimension we want to explore is one of spiritualizing the violent gaze as exemplified in Mel Gibson's *The Passion of the Christ*. This highly controversial 2004 film was described by Gibson himself as

> my own personal meditation. I focused on that because I found it healing for me because, like most of us, you get to a point in your life where you're pretty wounded by everything that goes on around you ... by your own transgressions ... by other people's. Life is kind of a scarring thing. So I used the passion as a meditation of healing myself.[24]

While Gibson himself is known to be committed to a very traditional – and even sectarian – strand of Roman Catholicism, his movie was widely acclaimed, especially by evangelical churches and televangelists. According to Abbott, Gibson's choice in directing films has clearly moral overtones connected to his faith. Nevertheless, it is equally possible to read his filmography from *Mad Max* (1977) through *Lethal Weapon* (1987–1998), *Braveheart* (1994) and *Hacksaw Ridge* (2016) as displaying a consistent interest in violence, perhaps even 'redemptive violence', as Walter Wink called it.[25] Gibson himself stated that 'the audience has to suffer in order to understand it more'.[26]

Although Gibson claims that his movie was an effort to offer an authentic interpretation of the suffering of Jesus, as opposed to other depictions being 'inaccurate and influenced by the politics of the time',[27] Gibson's version fits perfectly in the post 9/11 experience of a tremendously violent world. It is worth noting that the infamous violent abuse by American soldiers of prisoners in the Abu Ghraib prison in Baghdad became headline news in the same year that *The Passion of the Christ* was released. Regardless, the explicit way in which the movie suggests that it provides an authentic rendering of the passion narrative is most probably the reason why many Christian organizations and news outlets were so positive about it even though they would usually speak out against similarly violent movies without explicit Christian content.[28] *The Passion of the Christ* focuses almost entirely on the final 12 hours of Jesus' life. Apart from some flashbacks, the whole movie is devoted to the portrayal of the extreme suffering of Jesus, essentially following the 14 classic Stations of the Cross.[29] However, the movie is much more graphic and explicit about the violence than the biblical texts it purports to depict.[30] Moreover, the (androgynous) demonic figure that appears throughout the movie can be seen by some as a strange addition that undermines the authenticity that the film claims, whereas others see it as a strong reminder of the cosmic battle between good and evil that offers the background to the story.[31]

All of this leads us to this question: what happens when we spiritualize the gaze at violent torture in the way that Gibson suggests? Obviously, within the framework of the classic theology of the cross, this dramatized rendering of the passion narrative can indeed serve as a source for meditation, not unlike medieval paintings and statues. The grotesque violence then serves to impress the viewers with the sacrificial willingness of Jesus to surrender his life for humankind. The role of God remains mostly invisible but becomes apparent in the scene where a tear falling from God's eye falls to the earth and causes an earthquake upon its impact. This ambiguous image – is it love, sorrow or revenge? – follows immediately after a scene in which a large dark bird pecks out the eyes of the rebel who mocked Jesus.[32] Again, the question could be raised whether God desires, requires or abhors the violence the viewer is witnessing.

This ambiguity is directly linked to a fundamental ambiguity about the position of the viewer per se. According to Karpman's drama triangle, the three positions of perpetrator, victim and bystander are constantly in motion, so that who is in the role of the bystander at one point may be in the role of victim or perpetrator at the next moment.[33] Especially is the bystander – the viewer in this chapter – continuously challenged to move to one of the other positions. The theological question then is whether the viewer is invited to see themselves as victim or as perpetrator. Gibson's quote about his meditation on the passion actually refers to both when he speaks of his own transgressions and those of others, thereby not distinguishing between the victim and the perpetrator. Because it is unclear whether one should identify with the suffering Jesus or with the evil humans causing that suffering, a fundamental ambiguity remains at the centre of interpretation. One might argue that this is commonly the case in theological reflections on the cross, but the ensuing ambivalence may be problematic for contemporary victims of violence, as their confusion between the two roles is not resolved but exacerbated. As victims of sexualized violence may be particularly prone to this kind of confusion, the ambivalence becomes all the more pertinent.

The spiritualized gaze at violence may thus reinforce and inspire those with specific theological assumptions, but it may also blur the fundamental distinctions between victims and perpetrators. Moreover, the spiritual gaze may obfuscate the ethical discernment that is directly linked to this fundamental distinction.

Sexualizing the gaze

To explore the meaning of the sexualizing gaze, we need to ask first how some Christians indulge in worshipping the suffering so much – including different cinematic treatments of the crucifixion. This simple question involves many others. How does visual violence affect us? Does this pleasure-in-pain add something to our spiritual experience? What is the visual and spiritual pleasure (*jouissance* in Lacanian terms) of watching the pain and suffering of others? This enjoyment can best be grasped via the question: what are we aiming and striving for when we look at a sexually tortured body? This goes, of course, beyond a simple phenomenological account of the symbolic and fictional narrative of the extreme (sexual) violence of the cross. Referring to Sade's victim characters – and the ambivalent 'aesthetics' of crucifixion – where the 'sufferers' endure all manner of horrific torturous practices but retain their primeval beauty nevertheless, Lacan claims that in this *jouissance* and its radical objectivization of the 'suffering other' 'the sadist himself occupies the place of the object, but without knowing it, to the benefit of another, for whose *jouissance* he exercises his action as sadistic pervert'.[34] Or in the words of Žižek, what eludes our gaze in violence is precisely 'an endeavour to strike a blow at this unbearable surplus-enjoyment contained in the Other'.[35] How does this iconography of (sexual) torturous practices and aestheticization of suffering negotiate the relation between the individual and the sacred, the symbolic and the lived, the political and the cultural, and the spiritual and the sexual? Are we still aware of the brutality of images of sexually tortured bodies or have we become desensitized or, even more, sadistically enjoy this idea of 'beauty' obscuring the horror? In what way does this iconography of extreme violence contribute to the production and construction of the lived religious realities and imaginaries, the spiritual contemplative practices of the cross, the sacred texts, rituals, and ultimately the truth and the sublime – all as mediums of transcendental material/aesthetic world-making?

In this section we therefore seek to explore the possibility of reading the passion narrative as penetrative sexual violence and how such reading might potentially generate an alternative sense of spirituality for some Christian readers. The final part of this chapter then discusses not only that the passion narrative may involve sexual violence, as eloquently argued by Tombs, but also the possibility that the gaze on the crucifixion scene and its grotesque violence might generate a form of sexualized engagement.[36] Specifically, we ask: in what ways can the visuality of the torturous practices of the cross be experienced as both sexual and spiritual by Christian audiences? To explore this question, we have built on and sought to extend contemporary academic conversations between sadomasochism and Christian theology[37] to elucidate what happens when we *sexualize* the gaze at violent torture in the way that, for example, Mel Gibson suggests in *The Passion of the Christ*.

Both BDSM practitioners and scholars have identified how pain, torture and humiliation can be and have been connected to Christian traditions, including the passion narrative, in sadomasochistically sexualized ways. The queer theologian Robert Shore-Goss – who is also a chaplain for a premier gay BDSM club in Los Angeles – has narrated how he had a plenitude of sadomasochistic inspirations from the Church, from looking at the barely clothed body of Jesus on the cross every Sunday, meditating on torturous stories of the martyrs and saints, self-flagellating himself, and even wearing the *catenulae*, a chain-like device with barbs and spikes turned inward, when he started Jesuit novitiate.[38] In *Indecent Theology*, Marcella Althaus-Reid has also criticized theologies at that time, such as liberation theology and even sexual theologies, for being still too decent and reluctant to include sadomasochistic fetishisms in their analyses.[39] She gave an example of how Jesus dressed as a Peruvian peasant was rendered comprehensible and even invited empathy; but Jesus depicted as Xena the warrior princess, dressed in sexy leather clothes and crucified with her lesbian lover, was deemed outrageous and perverse. She proposed that such fetishism might be an obscene trace of Christianity, in the way that this closeted world of perversion might just be a new form of the centuries-old praxis of pain and worship. Indeed, there has been a rather poor joke among contemporary Christian BDSM practitioners about Jesus forgetting the safe word and dying on the cross. While such fatal abandonment is precisely what BDSM practices avoid,[40] it is evident that Shore-Goss, Althaus-Reid and contemporary BDSM practitioners put the crucifixion scene at centre stage in connecting sadomasochism and Christian traditions.

In line with the focus of this chapter on the gaze of the audience of the crucifixion, we draw attention to how sadomasochistic eroticism might not only be experienced in a 'real' BDSM practice but also through the act of watching, reading or imagining. The global success of the *Fifty Shades* novels and films, for example, demonstrates how such fictions and visual representations may offer a way for non-practitioners to virtually experience forms of sadomasochistic pleasure. It might not be very surprising, then, that a contemporary Christian audience with a slight sadomasochistic taste might find eroticism in contemplating the torturous practices in the passion narrative as depicted by Mel Gibson, such as the naked Jesus moaning and groaning when flogged. Whether identifying with the sacrificial willingness of the bottom, the top who hardened his heart for the atonement of humankind, or bystanders who were intensely watching in fear, the crucifixion provides a culminating moment of pain, trust, surrender and resurrection for a contemporary Christian audience. In what ways, then, can this sadomasochistic resonance be experienced as spiritual?

In the last two decades, scholars and authors have documented how BDSM practitioners reported a sense of spirituality in sadomasochistic engagements; there were also workshops specifically offered to teach how to reach spiritual goals through BDSM. One of the earliest works in this area is Geoff Mains' book *Urban Aboriginals: A Celebration of Leathersexuality* published in 1984, which has often been considered the first to connect sadomasochism and spirituality.[41] Some contemporary examples include Lee Harrington's *Sacred Kink: The Eightfold Paths of BDSM and Beyond* and Raven Kaldera's *Dark Moon Rising: Pagan BDSM and the Ordeal Path*.[42] In Christian traditions, Shore-Goss proposed that the key concept linking sadomasochism and Christian spirituality is the notion of transcendence through voluntary pain. In the modern world, we medicate ourselves immediately to escape pain; sacred pain has very little religious significance, although traces of it can still be found, such as the practice of fasting, barefoot pilgrimage, sensory deprivation, social isolation and, in some other religious traditions, body piercing. In this sense, sadomasochism and Christianity have a spiritual compatibility: 'Both ... use pain to transcend the self and create a new self.'[43] This notion of transcendence through voluntary pain resonates with other theologians and social researchers who have studied sadomasochism and spirituality.[44] We identify at least three recurring themes within this scholarship that explain the ways transcendence were experienced through sadomasochism. The first is ascetical spirituality. As in monastic traditions, BDSM positions the body as a site of discipline in order to grow, transform and perfect oneself. Ordeal and suffering of the body become one of the paths into spiritual awakening or communion with the Divine.[45] The second is a sense of freedom in radical submission. The notions of surrender and obedience have long been associated with religions and religious practices. It is unsurprising that studies have documented how BDSM communities report a sense of spirituality and transcendence in being the submissive bottom.[46] A bondage practitioner in Greenough's study, for instance, feels very 'freeing from the inside' while being severely constricted on the outside.[47] Correspondingly, the tops often reported a sense of being a caregiver, ritual facilitator, spiritual guide and therapist or healer in supporting the bottom's growth as a person.[48] The third theme is ecstatic experience through an intensified sense of the here and now. The experience of intense pain and intense pleasure heightens our awareness of the here and now, creating an altered state of consciousness as compared to our usual self.[49] As Stein describes it: '(BDSM) banish(es) all mundane distractions ... you spin away free into no place and no time, the universe and eternity.'[50] As a result, it is common to have a very peaceful feeling after a BDSM scene.[51]

Nevertheless, the context of these studies is real-life BDSM practice and practitioners; little is known about how virtual or imagined sadomasochistic eroticism could have spiritual potential for a non-practising audience. To our best knowledge, only Wijaya Mulya has discussed this potential in his examination of a specific Japanese-originated subculture of sadomasochism (*otaku*),[52] in which a sense of spirituality is found in the coming together of ostensibly incommensurable desires, such as pain and pleasure, real and unreal, the material and the spiritual, violence and ethics. However, further explorations are needed, particularly to respond to the pressing question of ethics: if what makes BDSM practice ethical is its consensuality (careful negotiations of pain and pleasure to avoid injury and promote care), what are the ethics of sexual *jouissance* in watching the suffering of others in a non-simulated, and perhaps non-consensual, context such as the passion narrative? Can Jesus' willing sacrifice be considered a form of consent to his suffering? Or, as feminist theologians have argued, is a Father making his son willingly sacrifice his life not consent but 'divine child abuse'?[53] Is Jesus' crucifixion 'an evil, unnecessary, violent, unjust act done by humans which should not be glorified, and cannot be justified' as a religion?[54] Even depictions of simulated and 'consensual' sexual violence as in pornography and extreme films have generated an amplitude of academic debates hitherto unresolved on the question of ethics.[55] While these thorny issues may indeed require deep and careful examination, it is beyond the scope of this chapter, which modestly seeks to argue that gazing on Jesus' crucifixion sexually, namely through a BDSM interpretive lens, is a possibility; and that such ways of seeing might also have potential for the spiritual – although this is not completely unproblematic.

Conclusion

Taking clues from Tombs and others about the (possibly) sexualized nature of the crucifixion, this chapter has aimed to offer some reflections on the role of the viewer. Looking at very distinct cases, the chapter distinguished three dimensions of the viewer's gaze. The politicizing gaze leads to a socio-political stance, the spiritualizing gaze may inspire but also obfuscate the ethical requirements by intentionally leaving open ambiguity between the role of victim and perpetrator, the sexualizing gaze may appropriate a new connection with the sacred. Whether these three dimensions are the most significant or indeed relevant for viewers should be assessed in more empirical studies.

References

Abbott, James, 'Following His True Passion: Mel Gibson and *The Passion of the Christ*', in *Through a Catholic Lens: Religious Perspectives of 19 Film Directors from Around the World*, Peter Malone ed., Plymouth: Rowman & Littlefield, 2007, pp. 225–38.

Althaus-Reid, Marcella, *Indecent Theology: Theological Perversions in Sex, Gender and Politics*, London: Routledge, 2000.

Baker, Alexandria C., 'Sacred Kink: Finding Psychological Meaning at the Intersection of BDSM and Spiritual Experience', *Sexual and Relationship Therapy* 33 (2018), pp. 440–53.

Bartchy, S. Scott, 'Reflections on Mel Gibson's *The Passion of the Christ*', in *Mel Gibson's The Passion: The Film, the Controversy, and its Implications*, Zef Garber ed., West Lafayette, IN: Purdue University Press, 2006, pp. 76–92.

Brown, Joanne Carlson, and Rebecca Ann Parker, 'For God so loved the world?', in *Christianity, Patriarchy, and Abuse: A Feminist Critique*, Joanne Carlson Brown and Carole R. Bohn eds, Cleveland, OH: Pilgrim Press, 1989, pp. 1–30.

Butler, Judith, *Frames of War: When is Life Grievable?*, London: Verso Books, 2009.

Cahana, Jonathan, 'Dismantling Gender: Between Ancient Gnostic Ritual and Modern Queer BDSM', *Theology & Sexuality* 18 (2012), pp. 60–75.

Crisp, Beth, 'Beyond Crucifixion: Remaining Christian after Sexual Abuse', *Theology & Sexuality* 15 (2009), pp. 65–76.

Downing, Lisa, '*Baise-moi* or the Ethics of the Desiring Gaze', *Nottingham French Studies* 45 (2006), pp. 52–65.

Eichert, David, '"Homosexualization" Revisited: An Audience-focused Theorization of Wartime Male Sexual Violence', *International Feminist Journal of Politics* 21 (2019), pp. 409–33.

Figueroa, Rocío, and David Tombs, 'Lived Religion and the Traumatic Impact of Sexual Abuse: The Sodalicio Case in Peru', in *Trauma and Lived Religion: Transcending the Ordinary*, Ruard Ganzevoort and Srdjan Sremac eds, London: Palgrave Macmillan, 2019, pp. 155–76.

Ganzevoort, Ruard, 'Violence, Trauma and Religion', paper presented at the International Association for the Psychology of Religion Conference, Leuven, Belgium, 28–31 August 2006.

——, 'The Drama Triangle of Religion and Violence', in *Religion and Violence: Muslim and Christian Theological and Pedagogical Reflections*, Ednan Aslan and Marcia Hermansen eds, Vienna: Springer, 2017, pp. 17–30.

Ganzevoort, Ruard, and Srdjan Sremac, 'Masculinity, Spirituality, and Male Wartime Sexual Trauma', in *Interdisciplinary Handbook of Trauma and Culture*, Yochai Ataria, David Gurevitz, David Pedaya and Yuval Neria eds, New York: Springer, 2016, pp. 339–51.

Glancy, Jennifer, 'Torture: Flesh, Truth, and the Fourth Gospel', *Biblical Interpretation* 13 (2005), pp. 107–36.

Greenough, Chris, *Undoing Theology: Life Stories from Non-Normative Christians*, London: SCM Press, 2018.

Guerin, Frances, and Roger Hallas eds, *The Image and the Witness: Trauma, Memory, and Visual Culture*, New York: Wallflower Press, 2007.

Harrington, Lee, *Sacred Kink: The Eightfold Paths of BDSM and Beyond*, 2nd edn, Anchorage, AK: Mystic Production Press, 2016.

House, Kathryn, 'Torture and Lived Religion: Practices of Resistance', in *Trauma and Lived Religion: Transcending the Ordinary*, Ruard Ganzevoort and Srdjan Sremac eds, London: Palgrave Macmillan, 2019, pp. 15–44.

Huesmann, L. Rowell, 'The Impact of Electronic Media Violence: Scientific Theory and Research', *Journal of Adolescent Health* 41:6, Supplement 1 (2007), pp. S6–S13.

Johnston, Robert K., '*The Passion* as Dramatic Icon: A Theological Reflection', in *Re-Viewing The Passion: Mel Gibson's Film and its Critics*, Brent S. Plate ed., New York: Palgrave Macmillan, 2004, pp. 55–70.

Kaldera, Raven, *Dark Moon Rising: Pagan BDSM and the Ordeal Path*, Hubbardston, MA: Asphodel Press, 2006.

Koopman, Eva M., 'Reading Rape: Toward an Ethics of Responding to Literary Depictions of Suffering and Violence', Master Thesis, Utrecht University, 2010.

King, Neal, 'Truth at Last: Evangelical Communities Embrace *The Passion of The Christ*', in *Re-Viewing The Passion: Mel Gibson's Film and its Critics*, Brent S. Plate ed., New York: Palgrave Macmillan, 2004, pp. 151–62.

Lacan, Jacques, *The Seminar of Jacques Lacan XI: The Four Fundamental Concepts of Psychoanalysis, 1964*, Jacques-Alain Miller ed., Alan Sheridan trans., New York: W. W. Norton, 1977.

Latour, Bruno, *Reassembling the Social: An Introduction to Actor-Network-Theory*, Oxford: Oxford University Press, 2007.

LeFranc, Kate Moore, 'Kinky Hermeneutics: Resisting Homonormativity in Queer Theology', *Feminist Theology* 26 (2018), pp. 241–54.

Luckhurst, Roger, *The Trauma Question*, New York: Routledge, 2008.

McGrath, Alistair E., *Christian Theology: An Introduction*, Malden, MA: Blackwell Publishing, 2017.

Maclear, Kyo, *Beclouded Visions: Hiroshima-Nagasaki and the Art of Witness*, Albany, NY: State University of New York Press, 1999.

Mains, Geoff, *Urban Aboriginals: A Celebration of Leathersexuality*, Los Angeles, CA: Daedalus Publishing, 1984.

Moltmann, Jürgen, *The Crucified God: The Cross of Christ as the Foundation and Criticism of Christian Theology*, Minneapolis, MN: Fortress Press, 1993.

Morgan, David, 'Catholic Visual Piety and *The Passion of The Christ*', in *Re-Viewing The Passion: Mel Gibson's Film and its Critics*, Brent Plate ed., New York: Palgrave MacMillan, 2004, pp. 85–96.

Mueller, Michelle, 'If All Acts of Love and Pleasure are Her Rituals, What about BDSM?: Feminist Culture Wars in Contemporary Paganism', *Theology & Sexuality* 24 (2018), pp. 39–52.

Rambuss, Richard, 'Pleasure and Devotion: The Body of Jesus and Seventeenth-Century Religious Lyric', in *Queering the Renaissance*, J. Goldberg ed., Durham, NC: Duke University Press, 1994, pp. 252–79.

Reaves, Jayme R., and David Tombs, '#MeToo Jesus: Naming Jesus as a Victim of Sexual Abuse', *International Journal of Public Theology* 13:4 (2019), pp. 387–412.

Ricoeur, Paul, 'The Hermeneutics of Testimony', in *Essays on Biblical Interpretation*, Lewis Mudge ed., Philadelphia, PA: Fortress Press, 1979, pp. 119–53.

—, *Memory, History, Forgetting*, Kathleen Blamey and David Pellauer trans., Chicago, IL: The University of Chicago Press, 2004.

Rowlett, Lori, 'Violent Femmes and S/M: Queering Samson and Delilah' in *Queer Commentary and the Hebrew Bible*, Ken Stone ed., New York: Sheffield Academic Press, 2001, pp. 106–15.

Shore-Goss, Robert E., 'Queer Incarnational Bedfellows: Christian Theology and BDSM Practices', in *Contemporary Theological Approaches to Sexuality*, Lisa Isherwood and Dirk von der Horst eds, New York: Routledge, 2018, pp. 222–44.

Smit, Peter-Ben, 'Sadomasochism and the Apocalypse of John: Exegesis, Sense-making and Pain', *Biblical Interpretation* 26 (2018), pp. 90–112.

Sontag, Susan, *Illness as a Metaphor*, New York: Farrar, Straus and Giroux, 1978.

—, *Regarding the Pain of Others*, New York: Farrar, Straus and Giroux, 2003.

Sremac, Srdjan, and Ruard Ganzevoort, 'Trauma and Lived Religion: Embodiment and Emplotment', in *Trauma and Lived Religion: Transcending the Ordinary*, Ruard Ganzevoort and Srdjan Sremac eds, Cham, Switzerland: Palgrave Macmillan, 2019, pp. 1–14.

Stein, David, *Boots, Bondage, and Beatings: Leathersex Stories*, New York: Perfectbound, 2009.

Stoker, Wessel, *Is Faith Rational: A Hermeneutical-Phenomenological Account for Faith*, Leuven: Peeters, 2006.

Tombs, David, 'Crucifixion, State Terror, and Sexual Abuse', *Union Seminary Quarterly Review* 53:1–2 (1999), pp. 89–109.

Wink, Walter, *The Powers That Be: Theology for a New Millennium*, New York: Doubleday, 1999.

Wijaya Mulya, Teguh, 'Fifty Shades of the Bible: Sadomasochism, Otaku Sexuality, and Christian Spirituality', paper presented at the Changing Minds and Hearts: Towards Acceptance of Queer Identities within Religions and Cultures Conference, Jakarta Theological Seminary, 21–24 November 2019, http://doi.org/10.13140/RG.2.2.31371.64803/1.

Žižek, Slavoj, *The Fragile Absolute, or Why is the Christian Legacy Worth Fighting For?*, London: Verso, 2000.
——, *Interrogatiing the Real*, London: Continuum, 2006.

Notes

1 Some parts of the section 'Sexualizing the gaze' have been presented by Teguh Wijaya Mulya in the conference 'Changing Minds and Hearts: Towards Acceptance of Queer Identities within Religions and Cultures' at the Jakarta Theological Seminary, 21–24 November 2019, in a paper entitled 'Fifty Shades of the Bible: Sadomasochism, Otaku Sexuality, and Christian Spirituality', https://doi.org/10.13140/RG.2.2.31371.64803/1.

2 See also Beth Crisp, 'Beyond Crucifixion: Remaining Christian after Sexual Abuse', *Theology & Sexuality* 15 (2009), pp. 65–76; Rocío Figueroa and David Tombs, 'Lived Religion and the Traumatic Impact of Sexual Abuse: The Sodalicio Case in Peru', in *Trauma and Lived Religion: Transcending the Ordinary*, Ruard Ganzevoort and Srdjan Sremac eds (London: Palgrave McMillan, 2019), pp. 155–76.

3 For an overview, see Jayme R. Reaves and David Tombs, '#MeToo Jesus: Naming Jesus as a Victim of Sexual Abuse', *International Journal of Public Theology* 13:4 (2019), pp. 387–412.

4 Richard Rambuss, 'Pleasure and Devotion: The Body of Jesus and Seventeenth-Century Religious Lyric', in *Queering the Renaissance*, J. Goldberg ed. (Durham, NC: Duke University Press, 1994), pp. 252–79.

5 Wijaya Mulya, 'Fifty Shades of the Bible'.

6 Srdjan Sremac and Ruard Ganzevoort, 'Trauma and Lived Religion: Embodiment and Emplotment', in *Trauma and Lived Religion: Transcending the Ordinary*, Ruard Ganzevoort and Srdjan Sremac eds (Cham, Switzerland: Palgrave Macmillan, 2019), pp. 1–14.

7 Ruard Ganzevoort, 'Violence, Trauma and Religion', paper presented at the 2006 conference of the International Association for the Psychology of Religion, Leuven, Belgium, 28–31 August 2006.

8 Slavoj Žižek, *The Fragile Absolute, or Why is the Christian Legacy Worth Fighting For?* (London: Verso, 2000).

9 L. Rowell Huesmann, 'The Impact of Electronic Media Violence: Scientific Theory and Research', *Journal of Adolescent Health* 41 (2007), pp. 6–13.

10 Ruard Ganzevoort and Srdjan Sremac, 'Masculinity, Spirituality, and Male Wartime Sexual Trauma', in *Interdisciplinary Handbook of Trauma and Culture*, Yochai Ataria. David Gurevitz, David Pedaya, Yuval Neria eds (New York: Springer, 2016), pp. 339–51.

11 David Eichert, '"Homosexualization" Revisited: An Audience-Focused Theorization of Wartime Male Sexual Violence', *International Feminist Journal of Politics* 21 (2019), p. 41.

12 Susan Sontag, *Regarding the Pain of Others* (New York: Farrar, Straus and Giroux, 2003); see also Judith Butler, *Frames of War: When is Life Grievable?* (London: Verso Books, 2009), p. 69.

13 Susan Sontag, *Illness as a Metaphor* (New York: Farrar, Straus and Giroux, 1978), cited in Roger Luckhurst, *The Trauma Question* (New York: Routledge, 2008), p. 162.

14 Jennifer Glancy, 'Torture: Flesh, Truth, and the Fourth Gospel', *Biblical Interpretation* 13 (2005), pp. 107–36 (108).

15 See Kathryn House, 'Torture and Lived Religion: Practices of Resistance', in *Trauma and Lived Religion: Transcending the Ordinary*, Ruard Ganzevoort and Srdjan Sremac eds (London: Palgrave Macmillan 2019), pp. 31.

16 Paul Ricoeur, 'The Hermeneutics of Testimony', in *Essays on Biblical Interpretation*, Lewis Mudge ed. (Philadelphia, PA: Fortress Press, 1979), pp. 130–1.

17 Wessel Stoker, *Is Faith Rational: A Hermeneutical-Phenomenological Account for Faith* (Leuven: Peeters, 2006), p. 102.

18 Kyo Maclear, *Beclouded Visions: Hiroshima-Nagasaki and the Art of Witness* (Albany, NY: State University of New York Press, 1999), p. 23.

19 Bruno Latour, *Reassembling the Social: An Introduction to Actor-Network-Theory* (Oxford: Oxford University Press, 2005).

20 Frances Guerin and Roger Hallas eds, *The Image and the Witness: Trauma, Memory, and Visual Culture* (New York: Wallflower Press, 2007), p. 12.

21 Jürgen Moltmann, *The Crucified God: The Cross of Christ as the Foundation and Criticism of Christian Theology* (Minneapolis, MN: Fortress Press, 1993), pp. 329–32.

22 Ganzevoort and Sremac, 'Masculinity, Spirituality, and Male Wartime Sexual Trauma'.

23 Ricouer, Paul, *Memory, History, Forgetting*, Kathleen Blamey and David Pellauer trans. (Chicago, IL: The University of Chicago Press, 2004), p. 86.

24 James Abbott, 'Following His True Passion: Mel Gibson and *The Passion of the Christ*', in *Through a Catholic Lens: Religious Perspectives of 19 Film Directors from Around the World*, Peter Malone ed. (Plymouth: Rowman & Littlefield, 2007), pp. 236.

25 Walter Wink, *The Powers That Be: Theology for a New Millennium* (New York: Doubleday, 1999).

26 Abbott, 'Following His True Passion', p. 232.

27 Abbott, 'Following His True Passion', p. 233.

28 Neal King, 'Truth at Last: Evangelical Communities Embrace *The Passion of the Christ*', in *Re-Viewing The Passion: Mel Gibson's Film and its Critics*, Brent Plate ed. (New York: Palgrave MacMillan, 2004), pp. 151–62.

29 Editorial note: see Pádraig Ó Tuama's chapter in this volume on the 14 Stations of the Cross.

30 David Morgan, 'Catholic Visual Piety and The Passion of The Christ', in *Re-Viewing The Passion*, pp. 85–96.

31 Robert K. Johnston, '*The Passion* as Dramatic Icon: A Theological Reflection', in *Re-Viewing the Passion*, pp. 55–70.

32 S. Scott Bartchy, 'Reflections on Mel Gibson's *The Passion of the Christ*', in *Mel Gibson's The Passion: The Film, the Controversy, and its Implications*, Zef Garber ed. (West Lafayette, IN: Purdue University Press, 2006), pp. 76–92.

33 Ruard Ganzevoort, 'The Drama Triangle of Religion and Violence', in *Religion and Violence: Muslim and Christian Theological and Pedagogical Reflections*, Ednan Aslan and Marcia Hermansen eds (Vienna: Springer, 2017), pp. 17–30.

34 Jacques Lacan, *The Seminar of Jacques Lacan XI: The Four Fundamental Concepts of Psychoanalysis, 1964*, Jacques-Alain Miller ed., Alan Sheridan trans. (New York: W.W. Norton, 1977), p. 185.

35 Slavoj Žižek, *Interrogating the Real* (London: Continuum, 2006), p. 268.

36 David Tombs, 'Crucifixion, State Terror, and Sexual Abuse', *Union Seminary Quarterly Review* 53:1–2 (1999), pp. 89–109.

37 For example, Kate Moore LeFranc, 'Kinky Hermeneutics: Resisting Homonormativity in Queer Theology', *Feminist Theology* 26 (2018), pp. 241–54; Lori Rowlett, 'Violent Femmes and S/M: Queering Samson and Delilah', in *Queer Commentary and the Hebrew Bible*, Ken Stone ed. (New York: Sheffield Academic Press, 2001), pp. 106–15; Robert E. Shore-Goss, 'Queer Incarnational Bedfellows: Christian Theology and BDSM Practices', in *Contemporary Theological Approaches to Sexuality*, Lisa Isherwood and Dirk von der Horst eds (New York: Routledge, 2018), pp. 222–44; Peter-Ben Smit, 'Sadomasochism and the Apocalypse of John: Exegesis, Sensemaking and Pain', *Biblical Interpretation* 26 (2018), pp. 90–112.

38 Shore-Goss, 'Queer Incarnational Bedfellows'.

39 Marcella Althaus-Reid, *Indecent Theology: Theological Perversions in Sex, Gender and Politics* (London: Routledge, 2000).

40 Smit, 'Sadomasochism and the Apocalypse of John'.

41 Geoff Mains, *Urban Aboriginals: A Celebration of Leathersexuality* (Los Angeles, CA: Daedalus Publishing, 1984).

42 Lee Harrington, *Sacred Kink: The Eightfold Paths of BDSM and Beyond*, 2nd edn (Anchorage, AK: Mystic Production Press, 2016); Raven Kaldera, *Dark Moon Rising: Pagan BDSM and the Ordeal Path* (Hubbardston, MA: Asphodel Press, 2006).

43 Shore-Goss, 'Queer Incarnational Bedfellows', p. 224.

44 For example, Alexzandria C. Baker, 'Sacred Kink: Finding Psychological Meaning at the Intersection of BDSM and Spiritual Experience', *Sexual and Relationship Therapy* 33 (2018), pp. 440–53; Jonathan Cahana, 'Dismantling Gender: Between Ancient Gnostic Ritual and Modern Queer BDSM', *Theology & Sexuality* 18 (2012), pp. 60–75; Smit, 'Sadomasochism and the Apocalypse of John'.

45 Smit, 'Sadomasochism and the Apocalypse of John'.

46 Baker, 'Sacred Kink'; Chris Greenough, *Undoing Theology: Life Stories from Non-Normative Christians* (London: SCM Press, 2018).

47 Greenough, *Undoing Theology*, p. 145.

48 Michelle Mueller, 'If All Acts of Love and Pleasure are Her Rituals, What about BDSM? Feminist Culture Wars in Contemporary Paganism', *Theology & Sexuality* 24 (2018), pp. 39–52.

49 Baker, 'Sacred Kink'; Shore-Goss, 'Queer Incarnational Bedfellows'.

50 Stein, *Boots, Bondage, and Beatings: Leathersex Stories* (New York: Perfectbound, 2009), p. 23.

51 Greenough, *Undoing Theology*, p. 145.

52 Wijaya Mulya, 'Fifty Shades of the Bible'.

53 Joanne Carlson Brown and Rebecca Parker, 'For God so loved the world?', in *Christianity, Patriarchy, and Abuse: A Feminist Critique*, Joanne Carlson Brown and Carole R. Bohn eds (Cleveland, OH: Pilgrim Press, 1989), pp. 1–30.

54 Alister E. McGrath, *Christian Theology: An Introduction* (Malden, MA: Blackwell Publishing 2017), p. 269.

55 Lisa Downing, '*Baise-moi* or the Ethics of the Desiring Gaze', *Nottingham French Studies* 45 (2006), pp. 52–65; Eva M. Koopman, 'Reading Rape: Toward an Ethics of Responding to Literary Depictions of Suffering and Violence', Master Thesis, Utrecht University, 2010.

12

The Crucified Christa: A Re-evaluation[1]

NICOLA SLEE

Introduction

There is a compelling body of evidence to suggest that the historical Jesus was sexually assaulted and very possibly raped as part of the state machinery of crucifixion.[2] That the idea of Jesus being a victim of sexual abuse remains scandalous and abhorrent to the majority of Christian believers is due, in large part, to the falsification of visual representations of the death of Jesus in Christian art which, as Jayme Reaves and David Tombs argue, 'misrepresent the historical scene and suppress the disturbing truth' and by covering up Jesus' nakedness among other things, Christian art tends 'to suppress the sense of violence and threat in the scene'.[3]

One place where the nakedness, sexual humiliation and abuse of Jesus do come together in public view – albeit in an unexpected, re-gendered form that is not well known by the majority of Christian believers or even theologians – is in the so-called Christa, or female Christ figure.[4] In multiple images of the Christa, found in a wide variety of media by a wide range of artists, she is fully naked on a cross or in cruciform shape, suggestive of the sexual humiliation, abuse and victimization of women, and associating sexual violence against women with the Christ event. In their recent article, Reaves and Tombs note the possible significance of the Christa in passing, referring to the work of Elaine Heath who, in her book, *We Were the Least of These*, calls attention to Edwina Sandys' sculpture, *Christa*, as a shocking and controversial image that 'links Jesus's crucifixion with the sexual abuse of women'.[5] Yet neither Reaves and Tombs nor Heath pursue the topic or consider the ambivalence of a suffering and crucified naked woman as a religious symbol. This is the remit I set myself in this chapter, drawing upon and extending my earlier work on the Christa[6] in order to consider how the image of the Christa might express and reflect the sexual abuse of the historical Jesus as well as that of countless women, children and men throughout history and in our own time. I want to critically interrogate images of the crucified Christa in order to explore the ambivalence of this symbol, particularly in relation to the key features of nakedness and sexual abuse which are prominent features of most (but not all) such images.[7]

I shall argue that, while images (and associated theologies) of the Christa are important in exposing and bringing to judgement sexual abuse in all its various historic and contemporary forms (including that of Jesus of Nazareth), such representations may also be problematic and as a genre are therefore ambivalent. As others, including myself, have previously argued, notions of the Christa that fuse the violent suffering, abuse and death of women into a central image of a crucified woman may reinforce cultural tropes of woman as helpless suffering victim, as object of male sexual voyeurism, and as responsible for (sexual) sin, rather than challenging and reworking patriarchal representations of the female body. Replacing the idealized, youthful and covered body of a European male Jesus in visual representations of Christ with that of a young, thin, white naked female form may also mask the racism and ableism of much cultural and theological thought, as well as the necrophiliac obsession with suffering and death that feminists such as Mary Daly and Grace Jantzen have critiqued.[8] At the same time, the symbol of a naked, crucified female Christ figure may deflect attention away from the historical reality of Jesus' sexual abuse and make it more difficult for contemporary believers to confront the scandal of Jesus' passion and death. It may thereby unwittingly deny and protect male nakedness from being incorporated into a contemporary religious imaginary. The figure of the Christa, while an important and necessary corrective to the Christolatry that has reified masculinity in Christian thought and practice and denied the feminine divine, will only be a potent religious symbol if it finds a wide range of forms beyond that of a suffering and/or dying Christa *and* if the male Christ symbol is also reworked in significant ways that embrace male sexual vulnerability and that show forth the ethnic as well as sexual diversity of contemporary masculinities.[9]

My argument will proceed in a number of stages. First, I will review visual representations of the Christa to demonstrate both the wide range of such images and their tendency to reinforce certain dominant tropes such as passive suffering, sexual victimization, nakedness, white privilege, youthfulness and idealized versions of the (white) feminine form. Next, I will consider ways in which nakedness has been gendered in Christian thinking, culture and representation, in order to investigate different meanings of a male and female naked Christ figure. I will propose that a naked male Christ does not carry similar or parallel meanings to that of a naked female Christa; they function very differently in the cultural and religious imaginary in ways that challenge any equivalence of forms. This will bring the discussion back to some specific images of the Christa, in order to consider different renderings of female subjectivity, sexuality and agency. I will suggest that, while some images and readings of the Christa may contribute positively towards a reworked feminist imaginary, others have no useful place in contemporary religious thought or practice. I will conclude with a sequence of statements or hypotheses that attempt to summarize the wide-ranging argument.

The crucified Christa in feminist art and theology

The figure of the female Christ or the Christa has been a recurring motif in Christian feminist theological writings[10] since the 1970s (although the idea and image of a female Christ figure have a much older history[11]), provoked by the creation of a sculpture of that name by Edwina Sandys in 1974 for the United Nations Decade for Women: Equality, Development and Peace (1976–1985).[12] The sculpture – a nude woman wearing a crown of thorns with arms outstretched in the form of a crucified figure – was originally displayed in the Cathedral of St John the Divine, New York, during Holy Week 1984, but was quickly removed by the Dean of the Cathedral in response to the strongly divided reactions from those who viewed it. Only recently, in 2017, has the sculpture been reinstated in the cathedral, in the Chapel of St Saviour, forming the focal point of a large exhibition entitled 'The Christa Project' and now on permanent display over the altar in one of the side chapels. In the catalogue for the exhibition, there is a short statement by Edwina Sandys about the sculpture, in which she states: '*Christa* means many things to many people. To me, Christ on the cross symbolizes sacrifice – *Christa* symbolizes the sacrifice of woman.' She describes the making of the sculpture as a 'largely subconscious act' which was 'not a conscious feminist statement' although she 'wanted to make it as womanly as possible'.[13]

Edwina Sandys' Christa, *detail. Photo credit: Nicola Slee.*

At around the same time as Sandys' creation of *Christa*, a second sculpture, *Crucified Woman*, was made by Almuth Lutkenhaus-Lackey in 1974, and displayed in the chancel of Bloor St United Church, Toronto, during Lent, Holy Week and Eastertide 1979.[14] Lutkenhaus-Lackey was initially hesitant about lending the sculpture to a church, 'arguing that my message was merely a portrayal of human suffering'. Yet 'being asked, "Can you see Christ in a Chinese man? Can you see Christ in a black man? Can you see Christ – in a woman?" made [her] change [her] view'. The artist comments: 'I was deeply touched by the many women who told me that for the first time they had felt close to Christ, seeing suffering expressed in a female body.'[15] She subsequently offered the work as a gift to Emmanuel College, Toronto, and the sculpture was installed in the grounds in 1986.

A third graphic sculpture, *Christine on the Cross*, by James M. Murphy, was exhibited in the James Memorial Chapel at Union Theological Seminary in New York at Easter 1984, at the same time as Sandys' *Christa* was on display in the cathedral (Union is only a few blocks away from the Cathedral of St John the Divine).[16] Murphy's sculpture shows a woman pinned to an inverted cross, with her legs spread-eagled and her feet nailed to the arms of the cross, such that her whole body is more exposed than in the other two sculptures. Stephen Moore describes it as a 'highly unsettling sculpture of a cruelly tortured woman symbolically spread-eagled on a cruciform bed of pain'.[17] Murphy himself has described the sculpture as:

> a vehicle for acknowledging the world's crucifixion of women by denigrating them, dehumanizing them, and placing them in the state of being an animal or a sex object ... 'Christine' is a symbol of the world's abuse of women. She is humiliated, demeaned, tortured, raped, and murdered. She is spread apart and mounted on the cross. She is slaughtered sacrificially. She is the object of the patriarchal world's morbid sadomasochistic sexuality. She is the bearer of the world's contempt and disgust toward lower-realm beings.[18]

While these three works are some of the best known of the so-called Christa figures, there are multiple forms of the crucified or cruciform woman in art, literature and film, as well as in feminist theology. I have found dozens of images, well over 100, in my quest for images of a *risen* Christa.[19] Mary Grey offers literary as well as visual examples of the Christa from early Christian martyr narratives, from Asian and African iconography and in Chaim Potok's novel, *My Name is Asher Lev*, in which Asher Lev paints an image of his mother on a cross.[20] Julie Clague has reviewed representations of the Christa, highlighting in particular *Crucifixion, Shoalhaven* by Arthur Boyd (1979–80) and *Bosnian Christa* by Margaret Argyll (1993), alongside the works by Sandys and Lutkenhaus-Lackey.[21] Kittredge Cherry brings together a range of images of the female Christ, alongside those of a gay Jesus, by Jill Ansell, Robert Lentz, Janet McKenzie, William McHart Nichols and Sandra Yagi, in her book *Art that Dares: Gay Jesus, Woman*

Christ, and More.[22] Kim Power discusses various images of the crucified Christa, including *Crucifixion* by Eric Drooker and *Woman Crucified (On Her Own Reproductive System)* by Maggi Thickston, which, as Thickston's title indicates, depicts a crucified woman hanging from a cross that is her own fallopian tubes, uterus and ovaries.[23] As well as paintings and sculptures, a number of photographic images of the Christa figure have appeared recently, including reworkings of the Last Supper depicting a female Christ and female disciples[24] and more examples of the crucified female Christ,[25] as well as film and video versions.[26]

The vast majority of the images of the Christa depict a suffering if not crucified woman, almost always naked, sometimes nailed or impaled on a cross; at other times in cruciform shape, suggestive of the cross even when there is no cross as such (as in Sandys' *Christa* and Lutkenhaus-Lackey's *Crucified Woman*). There are a few images of a risen Christa: for example Jill Ansell's *Missa solemnis*, depicting a naked Christa surrounded by animals and other aspects of creation,[27] Robert Lentz's icon of Christ Sophia,[28] and Emmanuel Garibay's various female versions of the Emmaus Christ,[29] but these are the exception rather than the rule. Interestingly, where almost all images of the crucified Christa show her naked, the risen Christa is generally clothed.

The figure of a crucified woman – and, occasionally, of a child – continues to emerge in new contexts and situations, as a powerful and shocking symbol of violence against women but also as protest against other forms of injustice against a variety of dispossessed and marginalized individuals and groups. For example, Stephen Burns draws attention to a powerful art work entitled *Deterrence* by Uniting Church in Australia deacon, John Tansey.[30] This installation of three crosses, exhibited outside St Paul's Anglican Cathedral in Bendigo, rural Victoria, in Passiontide 2017, places three figures, twined from barbed wire, on the crosses – that of a man, a child and a pregnant woman. Each cross bears a sign, showing the names of off-shore Australian detention centres – Christmas Island, Manus, Naura.

Tansey has spoken of the sculptures being intended 'to explore the questions and links between the crucifixion, the way the Romans used crucifixion as a deterrent and how the Australian Government has become obsessed with the harsh treatment of asylum seekers'.[31] Burns contextualizes Tansey's piece within wider instances of the Christa, as well as within the reality of 'crucified children' in our contemporary world, citing the deaths of children at sea (such as that of Aylan Kurdi, 'whose limp body washed up on a beach near Bodrum, Turkey, on September 2, 2015, stir[red] up international attention'), the sexual abuse of children by clergy and other authority figures, and the beheading and burning alive of children by ISIS/Islamic State/Daesh. Burns compares Tansey's sculpture of a crucified child to Erik Ravelo's 'difficult images, *Untouchables* (2013)', a series of six photographs showing children and adolescents slung against the backs, in turn, of a Catholic priest, a sex tourist, a soldier, a medic, a young man bearing guns, and a fast-food worker, variously symbolizing

John Tansey's Deterrence *sculptures. Photo credit: John Tansey.*

paedophilia in the church, child sex tourism in Asia, the death of children in the Syrian war, the trafficking of children's organs on the black market, the death of children in gang violence and via obesity fuelled by fast-food companies.[32] If the image of a crucified woman on the cross is shocking, images of crucified children are probably even more disturbing to viewers for whom childhood most acutely represents powerlessness, dependence and vulnerability in any society.

Images of the female Christ figure (and images of a crucified child) are produced by a wide variety of artists and cultural commentators; some may have an overt theological agenda or linkage to religious practice but many, perhaps the vast majority, know nothing of feminist theological debates about Christ and the cross and appear to be motivated (so far as one can tell) by broader socio-political trends and debates. While feminist theologians have taken up the suggestive notion of the Christa and developed it in a range of ways, the visual images of the Christa appear to both reflect and speak into a wider, more popular cultural milieu created by and within film, music videos, pop culture, street art and so on.[33] They are examples of contemporary artists and cultural commentators employing the historic symbol of Christ on the cross in shocking, subversive and/or paradoxical ways, variously parodying, critiquing and re-imagining the central Christian symbol of the cross to represent female and child suffering, sexuality and victimhood in patriarchal religion and society. As Rachel Anderson suggests:

> images of crucified women are necessarily potent; they combine two of the most intensely evocative motifs of Western culture, the image of the Crucified Christ and the image of the alluring Female Body [capitals in the original]. The result of their combination yields an extraordinarily freighted image.[34]

Anderson suggests that the image of a crucified woman, per se, is likely to cause a 'complicated and confusing morass of emotions' in the viewer because of the inherently paradoxical, contradictory frisson of bringing together the holy and the erotic in one symbol.[35]

This leads into the question of how to assess the meaning and value of images of the Christa (in particular, those of a crucified female figure). We might ask, in Kim Power's words, 'are the Christa images proliferating in contemporary fine arts an obscene modern fad or a new leading of the Spirit, challenging old certainties that assert a false obscenity against her?'[36] Or, more tersely, 'Does the Christa perpetuate the abuse of women?'[37] Or, to turn the question around, and given the largely negative reactions to many images of the Christa, we might ask, with Ivone Gebera, 'Why should the naked body of a crucified man be an object of veneration while that of a woman be judged pornographic?'[38]

Nakedness, gender and representation: what does a naked Christa signify?

In order to assess the various meanings of a naked crucified Christa – especially, but not exclusively, in visual representations and three-dimensional form – we need first to consider female nakedness and religious meaning more widely, in Western culture and religious tradition. Margaret Miles' authoritative study, *Carnal Knowing: Female Nakedness and Religious Meaning in the Christian West*, shows how nakedness has been a significant feature of Christian practice, theology and representation from the earliest times onwards.[39] In early Christian practice, naked baptism was the norm and held a range of rich religious meanings, from imitation of Christ in his nakedness on the cross (as acknowledged by Cyril of Jerusalem and others), through various associations with death and rebirth, the stripping off of the world or the old life, to a form of quasi-martyrdom and so on.[40] Baptism was also a gendered ritual; one which, for women, was both empowering and, at the same time, confirmed their confinement to supportive roles in Christian churches and communities. In a rite which could not be conferred by women but in which naked women were anointed by male clergy and baptized last, after children and men, the symbolic enactment of secondary status is clear.[41]

What was begun in the practice of naked baptism was amplified and extended in subsequent theology and in visual representations of male and female nakedness. In ascetic practice and martyrdom, the tension already noted between gender equality and female subservience continued in the meanings ascribed to the naked female body. Female nakedness could be used as a symbol of a religious self characterized by 'courage, conscious choice, and self-possession' in narrative accounts such as *The Acts of Paul and Thecla* and *The Martyrdom of Ss. Perpetua and Felicitas* and, at the same time, as an object of the male gaze in which women's appearance and its effects upon men become the primary concern. As Miles asserts, 'Female beauty created temptation for male Christians'; and therefore 'women were to obscure their beauty to protect men's salvation'.[42] The female body both was, and was not, a site of female subjectivity and agency and herein lay a contradiction that has continued throughout Christian history and arguably continues still.

This contradiction becomes most evident in readings and representations of Adam and Eve, in which the naked body of Eve became seen 'as symbol of sin, sexual lust, and dangerous evil',[43] while the naked body of Adam, although sharing in the fruits of Eve's fall into sin and therefore partaking of shame, was generally read in a more positive light as signifying superior and heroic strength, enlightened reason and a 'glory and prestige' far beyond female beauty.[44] Such meanings were discussed and elaborated in theological texts but, above all, they were disseminated in religious images. Alongside the dominant image of Eve as the symbol of 'every woman', images of other naked or semi-naked biblical women such as Susanna and Mary Magdalene reinforced the range of meanings of the female form for the male voyeur as representing 'simultaneously threat, danger, and delight'.[45] Figures of the ideal woman, pre-eminently the Virgin Mary, helped to solidify such readings by offering a binary of female good and female evil.[46] By contrast, figures such as Michelangelo's David, as well as many representations of Adam and Christ (the Second Adam), demonstrate how 'male nakedness represented spiritual discipline and physical control and order – the body as perfect vehicle and expression of the difficult and committed work of the creation and cultivation of religious subjectivity'.[47] In Renaissance painting and imagery, Leo Steinberg argues that there is a new emphasis on the naked genitals of Christ, displayed by the Virgin in scenes of mother and child or on display in images of the crucified and dead Christ.[48] Drawing on Steinberg's scholarship, Miles argues that 'the heroic male nakedness of athletic asceticism adds visual associations to Christ's nakedness, constructing a richly complex visual symbol in which strength and weakness, triumph and vulnerability are resolved'.[49] Thus, in the naked female form, frailty and strength, sexuality and holiness are in unresolved tension, while in the naked male form the tensions are held together and resolved.

Having surveyed female nakedness throughout Christian art and tradition, Miles concludes that 'female bodies, in the societies of the Christian West, have not represented women's subjectivity or sexuality but have, rather, been seen as a blank page on which multiple social meanings could be projected'.[50] 'Men have figured "woman" as a frightening and fascinating creature whose anger and rejection could deprive them of gratification, delight, and, ultimately, of life and salvation.'[51]

In the final chapter of *Carnal Knowing*, Miles turns to the question of whether 'more equitable' public images of women can be produced in our own time, in light of the problematic inheritance of Christian theology and symbolism. She queries whether 'the female body [can] be a usable symbol for women's articulation of themselves as subjects?' Miles is sceptical about the possibilities of 'turning the symbols', to use Janet Martin Soskice's evocative phrase.[52] She considers, briefly, Edwina Sandys' *Christa*, regarding it as an image that 'makes vivid the perennial suffering of women' and which, 'as a private devotional image … may have great healing potential for women who have themselves been battered or raped'.[53] Yet she considers the sculpture problematic as a public image, because of the way in which, according to her, it 'fetishizes suffering women'. 'The *Christa*, by its visual association with the crucified Christ, glorifies the suffering of women in a society in which violence against women has reached epidemic proportions.'[54]

While Miles is right to recognize the enormous challenge of undoing and revising existing patriarchal representations of the female body and the inherent difficulties of 'turning the symbols' and making new religious meaning out of female nakedness, I suggest that the figure of the Christa *may* be one place where meanings of female suffering, nakedness, sexuality and subjectivity can be revised and represented. I do not claim that any or all versions of the Christa are useful or liberating; some (perhaps many?) of them reinscribe a voyeuristic male gaze and thus undermine female subjectivity and agency, employing an authoritative religious symbol to endorse and baptize familiar tropes of the naked female body as a site of the male gaze, heteronormative sexual desire and masochistic voyeurism. In such cases, the symbol of a naked female Christ figure may be superficially novel, but in every other way is only too familiar as a pornographic image. The most obvious instances of such Christas are the multiple photographic and filmic versions created by Ramon Martinez.[55] Although there are multiple versions, his Christa is in essence the same image repeated from different angles and in different postures, all of which assume the voyeuristic male gaze and reduce the naked female form to an object of male arousal, pleasure and violence. The fact that the exposed female body is superimposed on a cross only heightens the frisson of dangerous pleasure, giving religious legitimacy to sadomasochistic fantasies and practices. Such images merely reproduce and reinforce a tired, jaded but still potent pornographic rendering of the female body.

In light of such representations of the female Christ figure, we do right to be cautious about the significance of the Christa. Yet the crucified Christa cannot be reduced to such pornographic readings. Other symbolic renderings are possible, ones in which women represent themselves in ways that claim female subjectivity and agency even as they demonstrate and protest against the sexual violation of women. Thus I would offer an alternative reading of Edwina Sandys' *Christa*, particularly in its replaced positioning above the altar in the Chapel of St Saviour in the Cathedral of St John the Divine. Positioned in the place where Christian celebration of the Eucharist is publicly and regularly enacted, highlighted against the rainbow colours of the enormous stained-glass window in the chapel, Sandys' *Christa* is capable of evoking a wide range of reactions and readings: not only ones that affirm Christ's identification with the suffering and abuse of women, but also those that read women's bodies and blood – in birth, as well as in life and death – as a primary symbol of the divine feminine. There is an ambivalence about the female form, too, that resists conventional readings; whatever Sandys intended by her endeavour to create an image that is 'as womanly as possible', this is not a conventionally beautiful female form. It is muscular in ways that may confuse gender expectations. Its naked form hides sexuality as much as it reveals it. The bowed face cannot easily be gazed into, resisting occupation or colonization.

Edwina Sandys' Christa. *Photo credit: Nicola Slee.*

Tansey's barbed-wire figures that form his *Deterrence* installation, in different ways also resist conventional or voyeuristic responses. The fact that the bodies are composed of barbed wire is a potent symbol of imprisonment and allows many readings, but also disallows literalistic interpretations of the bodies. Faceless and lacking detailed features, the bodies take on a wider symbolic meaning and do not permit a voyeuristic gaze.

In the same way, images of the Christa that are more suggestive or abstract in outline, such as Arnulf Rainer's *Wine Crucifix* – where the outline of a pregnant body can be seen within the explosion of dripping colour on the canvas – refuse to allow the viewer to reduce the female body to sexual function or availability.[56] Despite its explicit sexual morphology, Margaret Argyll's *Bosnian Christa* – a textile work, showing the faint outline of a female form on a cross within the opening of a vulva, worked in blood red – refuses pornographic appropriation by being both explicitly representational of women's sexual organs and, at the same time, lacking detail.[57] As in Rainer's *Wine Crucifix*, colour and shape represent women's sexualized suffering (in Argyll's case, the multiple rape of Bosnian women in the Bosnian war) yet this is clearly not a realistic portrayal of a woman's sexual organs.

John Tansey's Deterrence *sculptures, detail.*
Photo credit: John Tansey.

The attempt to represent the crucifixion as a symbol of female healing and empowerment is a risky undertaking, and every Christa – particularly every naked, crucified or cruciform Christa – walks a dangerous tightrope between reinscribing patriarchal renderings of the female form and forging new, liberationist, readings. Each representation must be considered on its own terms, and viewers will differ in their judgements according to their own contexts, interests and agendas. Kim Power proposes that 'principles of justice, inclusiveness and respect for women's bodies be the touchstone of discernment for the legitimacy of the Christa', although she does not spell out how these might be applied.[58] While open to wide application, such criteria may be helpful in assessing the variety of renderings of the Christa.

Alongside a wide range of images and theologies of the Christa, including renderings that move away from a fixation on the cross, more is needed. However various and rich, the image and concept of Christa cannot do all the work that Christian theology and representation needs to do around understandings of human sexuality, violence and salvation. We need renewed attention to the male body of Jesus and to theologies and images of the man Jesus on the cross (and off it!) that reveal his nakedness and his wounded, abused sexuality. As Clague argues,

> Jesus has been systematically stripped of his sexuality throughout art history. A lifetime of seeing his male form on the cross has inoculated us against its sexual impact. The male Jesus on the cross is gendered but not sexual, because the viewer has unwittingly castrated the Christ.[59]

A number of male theologians have explored and sought to reclaim the nakedness and the sexuality of Jesus for new theologies of masculinity. For example, in his 1996 article, 'Does Jesus Have a Penis?', Robert Beckford appeals for 'the production of images of Jesus that symbolize the quest for a black socio-political sexual wholeness' (such as Robert Lentz's portrayal of Jesus as a squatting Maasai warrior with visible testicles).[60] In his fascinating study of nakedness and clothing in the Bible and early Christianity, Dan Lé develops an atonement theology based on the nakedness of Christ on the cross, what he calls the *Christus nudus* model.[61] These are two instances of a much wider project of reconfiguring masculinity in the light of a rereading of Jesus' own sexuality and masculinity.

Only by reclaiming the naked body of the man Jesus as a central symbol within Christianity can the reality of Jesus' own suffering of sexual abuse be grasped and reflected upon by theologians and ordinary believers alike, while at the same time the objectification and sexualization of women's bodies in the male gaze is challenged and corrected. Only such a reclamation of the sexed, male body of Jesus can offer a potent symbol to men seeking new forms of masculinity, *and* convey to women the solidarity of men with their sexual victimization and abuse.

Conclusion

My discussion of the Christa has ranged round a number of interconnected themes concerning female embodiment, representation and subjectivity: sexual and other forms of violence against women; readings and renderings of the cross of Christ/a and whether the Christa has a place within a renewed feminist religious imaginary. I will now try to bring together the various themes and restate my argument in a series of statements or hypotheses.

Images of the Christa are multiple, and have an ancient pedigree; scholars continue to unearth previously neglected ones, as artists continue to create new ones. The image of a crucified woman continues to be potent in our time. The vast majority of images of the Christa are of a suffering, crucified or cruciform woman on a cross or something suggestive of a cross. Nevertheless, there are other images of a female Christ figure and I have argued elsewhere that these may be particularly significant for women seeking their own subjective agency and 'risenness'.[62]

Insofar as they function on the symbolic plane, ideas and visual representations of the Christa *qua* symbol are multivalent, capable of more or less endless interpretation, and cannot be reduced to one reading or meaning. By bringing together the central symbol of Christianity, the cross of Christ, with the image of a suffering and naked female body, the Christa functions as a highly charged symbol which tends to elicit strong, visceral and emotive reactions, tapping into deep human experiences of sexuality, suffering and subjectivity and uncovering unconscious attitudes towards gender, sexuality, holiness, nakedness, sin and shame. It is in this sense that Althaus-Reid speaks of the Christa as an 'obscene' image, in its capacity to uncover or undress the obscenities of sexism, racism and other unconscious prejudice in the viewer.[63]

While readings of the Christa are multiple and cannot be reduced to any particular meaning, certain interpretations appear to be common or recurring. Thus for many the Christa is a symbol of the physical and sexual abuse of women, both historically and in our own time, including and focusing particularly the abuse of women perpetuated by the Church in the name of Christ. The Christa brings to light violence against women in a potent way, drawing on the authority of the cross of Christ to do so. This is clear in the statements from Edwina Sandys, Almuth Lutkenhaus-Lackey and, most obviously, James M. Murphy, quoted above, in discussion of their representations of the Christa. As such, the image of a crucified woman may be therapeutic, liberating and healing for women, most particularly women who have suffered physical and sexual abuse at the hands of men, especially where this has been perpetuated or endorsed by male religious authorities. There is a good deal of anecdotal and pastoral evidence that women viewers do, indeed, find the Christa such a potent therapeutic symbol, capable of expressing and conveying the theological claim that God is present to redeem and save all those victimized by oppressive structures and all victims of sexual violence.

The Christa, as a re-gendering of the cross of Christ, may also shock viewers into recognizing the historic violence perpetuated against Jesus, including sexual violence, in ways that more familiar images of the male Christ on the cross generally fail to do, viewers having become habituated to such imagery. The Christa is one of the few symbols that makes visible the sexual abuse of Jesus on the cross, even as it hides it by placing the reality of sexual violence in the naked bodies of women. It is thus a paradoxical symbol, which may generate both disruption and confusion of both traditional understandings of the cross of Christ and of meanings associated with the naked bodies of women.[64]

By associating sexual violence against women with the suffering of Jesus on the cross, the Christa is an ambivalent symbol that can be read both as a protest against sexual and other kinds of violence against women *and* as a reinforcement of female victimization and suffering. Theologians, art critics and cultural commentators alike are divided in their reading of the symbol of the Christa. Where some see the image as a powerful symbol of the feminine divine, claiming and reworking a traditional patriarchal symbol to invoke new religious meaning and sacralizing female bodily experience, others regard it as reinscribing patriarchal readings of the female body as symbolic of sin, suffering, sexuality and shame. Feminist theologians who have critiqued the dominance of theologies of death and violence in Christian tradition are particularly concerned that the figure of a suffering, dying Christa may reinforce, rather than challenge, the centrality of death, suffering and violence at the heart of Christian theology and iconography. Thus Mary Grey asks pointedly: 'If the central symbol of Christianity contains with it a message which keeps women impaled on that cross, with societal approval, what message of resurrected hope and redemption can it bring?'[65]

For these and other reasons, a number of theologians and artists have developed theologies and images of the Christa that do not focus on the cross or on the suffering of women/Jesus. My own search for a theology of the risen Christa is one such example;[66] Kim Power's reworking of theologies of Eucharist via the Christa in order to relocate suffering as part of the painful labour of birth,[67] and Karen O'Donnell's reconfiguring of Eucharist through the lens of incarnation, Marian theology and maternal experience,[68] are two others that each seek to shift the balance of Christian theology away from death and violence towards natality and fecundity. Within these theologies, as Power asserts, the Christa 'can be considered the Easter dawning of a divine horizon for women through the sacrality of the female body, embraced in all its fluidity and fecundity'.[69]

The symbol and notion of a crucified woman, however multivalent, is not capable of bearing or expressing the whole range of theological, political and ethical terms necessary for a renewed theology of human sexuality, suffering and redemption in our time. We also need new imaginings and new theologies of the male Christ that affirm his naked vulnerability and sexuality. By stating the need for new masculine and feminine images of Christ on the cross, I do not wish to reinscribe a gender binary that reinforces tired notions of biological essentialism. Gender-ambivalent and gender-queer images of Christ/a are also needed, and indeed already exist.

In conclusion, I suggest that neither the image of a naked female body on the cross, nor the reclaimed sexual body of a male Jesus on the cross, however potent and liberating these may be, can do all the work required for a 'turning of the symbols' and a renewed religious imaginary. Nevertheless, to develop such new (or reclaimed) iconographies in parallel and dialogue with each other – as well as in conversation with alternative images of a risen Christ/a – may go some way towards reconfiguring the relationships between nakedness, gender, sexuality, subjectivity, redemption and holiness, endorsing new forms of practice, thought and action.

References

Althaus-Reid, Marcella, *Indecent Theology*, London: Routledge, 2000.

Anderson, Rachel, 'The Crucified Woman: A Paradox of Prurience and Piety', research paper, Introduction only, 21 May 2007, https://digital.lib.washington.edu/researchworks/handle/1773/3101.

Beckford, Robert, 'Does Jesus have a Penis? Black Male Sexual Representation and Christology', *Theology and Sexuality* 5 (1996), pp. 10–21.

Burns, Stephen, 'Deterrence', in *Feminist Fractures and Intersections*, Carolyn Alsen ed., Lanham, MD: Lexington, 2021.

Cherry, Kittredge, *Art that Dares: Gay Jesus, Woman Christ, and More*, Berkeley, CA: AndroGyne Press, 2007.

Clague, Julie, 'The Christa: Symbolizing My Humanity and My Pain', *Feminist Theology* 14:1 (2005), pp. 83–108.

Cornwall, Susannah, 'Ambiguous Bodies, Ambiguous Readings: Reflections on James M. Murphy's "Christine on the Cross"', in *Bound and Unbound: Interdisciplinary Approaches to Gender and Sexualities*, Zowie Davy, Julia Downes, Lena Eckert, Natalia Gerodetti, Dario Llinares and Ana Christine Santos eds, Newcastle: Cambridge Scholars Publishing, 2008.

Crawford, Bobbie, 'A Female Crucifix?', *Daughters of Sarah* 14:6 (1988), pp. 24–7.

Daly, Mary, *Gyn/Ecology: The Metaethics of Radical Feminism*, London: Women's Press, 1979.

——, *Beyond God the Father: Towards a Philosophy of Women's Liberation*, London: Women's Press, 1986.

Figueroa, Rocío and David Tombs, 'Recognising Jesus as a Victim of Sexual Abuse: Responses from Sodalicio Survivors in Peru', *Religion and Gender* 10:1 (2020), pp. 57–75.

Gebara, Ivone, *Out of the Depths: Women's Experience of Evil and Salvation*, Minneapolis, MN: Fortress Press, 2002.

Grey, Mary, 'Who do you say that I am? Images of Christ in Feminist Liberation Theology', in *Images of Christ: Ancient and Modern*, Stanley E. Porter, Michael A. Hayes and David Tombs eds, Sheffield: Sheffield Academic Press, 1997, pp. 189–203.

Heath, Elaine A., *We Were the Least of These: Reading the Bible with Survivors of Sexual Abuse*, Grand Rapids, MI: Brazos Press, 2011. Republished as *Healing the Wounds of Sexual Abuse: Reading the Bible with Survivors*, Grand Rapids, MI: Brazos Press, 2019.

Jantzen, Grace, *Becoming Divine: Towards a Feminist Philosophy of Religion*, Manchester: Manchester University Press, 1988.

Lé, Dan, *The Naked Christ: An Atonement Model for a Body-Obsessed Culture*, Eugene, OR: Pickwick Publications, 2012.

Lentz, Robert, and Edwina Gateley, *Christ in the Margins*, Maryknoll, NY: Orbis, 2009.

Mercadatne, Linda, 'Bess the Christ Figure? Theological Interpretations of *Breaking the Waves*', *Journal of Religion and Film* 5:1 (2001), pp. 1–14.

Miles, Margaret R., *Carnal Knowing: Female Nakedness and Religious Meaning in the Christian West*, Tunbridge Wells: Burns & Oates, 1992.

Moore, Stephen, *God's Beauty Parlor: And Other Queer Spaces in and around the Bible*, Stanford, CA: Stanford University Press, 2001.

Murphy, James M., 'A Female Christ for Men and Women', unpublished manuscript, 1990.

O'Donnell, Karen, *Broken Bodies: The Eucharist, Mary, and the Body in Trauma Theology*, London: SCM Press, 2018.

Power, Kim, 'Embodying the Eucharist', in *Reinterpreting the Eucharist: Explorations in Feminist Theology and Ethics*, Anne Elvey, Carol Hogan, Kim Power and Claire Renkin eds, Sheffield: Equinox, 2013, pp. 152–85.

Reaves, Jayme R., and David Tombs, '#MeToo Jesus: Naming Jesus as a Victim of Sexual Abuse', *International Journal of Public Theology* 13:4 (2019), pp. 387–412.

Sandys, Edwina, 'Christa: A Statement from the Artist', in *The Christa Project: Manifesting Divine Bodies*, New York: The Cathedral of St John the Divine, 2016.

Senn, Frank C., *Embodied Liturgy: Lessons in Christian Ritual*, Minneapolis, MN: Fortress, 2016.

Slee, Nicola, *Seeking the Risen Christa*, London: SPCK, 2011.

——, 'Visualizing, Conceptualizing, Imagining and Praying the Christa: In Search of Her Risen Forms', *Feminist Theology* 21:1 (2012), pp. 71–90.

——, 'Reimaging Christ as a girl: An Advent experiment', in *Future Present: Embodying a Future World Now*, Jonny Baker, Steve Collins and Cathy Ross eds, Proost, 2018, pp. 45–60.

Soskice, Janet Martin, 'Turning the Symbols', in *Swallowing a Fishbone? Feminist Theologians Debate Christianity*, Daphne Hampson ed., London: SPCK, 1996, pp. 17–32.

Steinberg, Leo, *The Sexuality of Christ in Renaissance Painting and Modern Oblivion*, New York: Pantheon, 1984.

Tombs, David, 'Crucifixion, State Terror, and Sexual Abuse', *Union Seminary Quarterly Review* 53:1–2 (1999), pp. 89–109.

United Society for Propagation of the Gospel [USPG], *The Christ We Share*, 2nd edn, London: USPG, 2000.

Notes

1 I am grateful to Stephen Burns for his helpful comments on an earlier draft of this article, and for putting me in touch with John Tansey, to whom I am also grateful for permission to include photos of his *Deterrence* sculptures.

2 For a summary of the evidence, see David Tombs, 'Crucifixion, State Terror, and Sexual Abuse', *Union Seminary Quarterly Review* 53:1–2 (1999), pp. 89–109; and Rocío Figueroa and David Tombs, 'Recognising Jesus as a Victim of Sexual Abuse: Responses from Sodalicio Survivors in Peru', *Religion and Gender* 10:1 (2020), pp. 57–75.

3 Jayme R. Reaves and David Tombs, '#MeToo Jesus: Naming Jesus as a Victim of Sexual Abuse', *International Journal of Public Theology* 13:4 (2019), pp. 387–412.

4 For a summary and discussion of the emergence and development of the idea and image of the Christa, see Mary Grey, 'Who do you say that I am? Images of Christ in Feminist Liberation Theology', in *Images of Christ: Ancient and Modern*, Stanley E. Porter, Michael A. Hayes and David Tombs eds (Sheffield: Sheffield Academic Press, 1997), pp. 189–203; Julie Clague, 'The Christa: Symbolizing My Humanity and My Pain', *Feminist Theology* 14:1 (2005), pp. 83–108; Nicola Slee, *Seeking the Risen Christa* (London: SPCK, 2011), Ch. 1; and Kim Power, 'Embodying the Eucharist', in *Reinterpreting the Eucharist: Explorations in Feminist Theology and Ethics*, Anne Elvey, Carol Hogan, Kim Power and Claire Renkin eds (Sheffield: Equinox, 2013), pp. 152–85.

5 Reaves and Tombs, '#MeToo Jesus', p. 402; Elaine A. Heath, *We Were the Least of These: Reading the Bible with Survivors of Sexual Abuse* (Grand Rapids, MI: Brazos Press, 2011), p. 124. Heath's book is republished as *Healing the Wounds of Sexual Abuse: Reading the Bible with Survivors* (Grand Rapids, MI: Brazos Press, 2019).

6 See Slee, *Seeking the Risen Christa*; Nicola Slee, 'Visualizing, Conceptualizing, Imagining and Praying the Christa: In Search of Her Risen Forms', *Feminist Theology* 21:1 (2012), pp. 71–90; Nicola Slee, 'Reimaging Christ as a Girl: An Advent Experiment', in *Future Present: Embodying a Future World Now*, Jonny Baker, Steve Collins and Cathy Ross eds (Sheffield: Proost, 2018), pp. 45–60.

7 I am by no means the first to interrogate images of the Christa theologically. See, in particular, Grey, 'Who do you say that I am?'; Clague, 'The Christa'; Susannah Cornwall, 'Ambiguous Bodies, Ambiguous Readings: Reflections on James M. Murphy's "Christine on the Cross"', in *Bound and Unbound: Interdisciplinary Approaches to Gender and Sexualities*, Zowie Davy, Julia Downes, Lena Eckert, Natalia Gerodetti, Dario Llinares and Ana Christine Santos eds (Newcastle: Cambridge Scholars Publishing, 2008); and Stephen Burns, 'Deterrence', in *Feminist Fractures and Intersections*, Carolyn Alsen ed. (Lanham, MD: Lexington, 2021).

8 Mary Daly, *Beyond God the Father: Towards a Philosophy of Women's Liberation* (London: Women's Press, 1986); Mary Daly, *Gyn/Ecology: The Metaethics of Radical Feminism* (London: Women's Press, 1979); Grace Jantzen, *Becoming Divine: Towards a Feminist Philosophy of Religion* (Manchester: Manchester University Press, 1988).

9 As Robert Beckford argues in 'Does Jesus have a Penis? Black Male Sexual Representation and Christology', *Theology and Sexuality* 5 (1996), pp. 10–21, to which I shall return.

10 In this article I am focusing primarily on visual representations of the Christa,

rather than the theologies that have developed in dialogue with Edwina Sandys' original *Christa* sculpture.

11 See Grey, 'Who do you say that I am?' and Slee, *Seeking the Risen Christa*, for ancient examples of the idea and image of a female Christ.

12 The image is included in the study pack, United Society for Propagation of the Gospel, *The Christ We Share*, 2nd edn (London: USPG, 2000).

13 Edwina Sandys, 'Christa: A Statement from the Artist', in *The Christa Project: Manifesting Divine Bodies* (New York: The Cathedral of St John the Divine, 2016).

14 At www.dittwald.com/torontosculpture/image.php?Artist=Lutkenhaus&Title =Crucified%20Woman.

15 Cited in Bobbie Crawford, 'A Female Crucifix?', *Daughters of Sarah* 14:6 (1988), pp. 24–7.

16 Images of *Christine on the Cross* can be found in Clague, 'The Christa', p. 92 and Cornwall, 'Ambiguous Bodies', pp. 101, 104. I have not been able to find out if the exhibition of Murphy's sculpture was planned to coincide with that of Sandys' *Christa*.

17 Stephen Moore, *God's Beauty Parlor: And Other Queer Spaces in and around the Bible* (Stanford, CA: Stanford University Press, 2001), p. 158.

18 James M. Murphy, 'A Female Christ for Men and Women', unpublished manuscript, 1990, pp. 67–8; quoted in Clague, 'The Christa', p. 94.

19 See Slee, *Seeking the Risen Christa*.

20 Grey, 'Who do you say that I am?'

21 Clague, 'The Christa'.

22 Kittredge Cherry, *Art that Dares: Gay Jesus, Woman Christ, and More* (Berkeley, CA: AndroGyne Press, 2007). See also her website, 'Gallery', https:// jesusinlove.org/.

23 Power, 'Embodying the Eucharist', pp. 175, 177.

24 For example, Renée Cox's *Yo Mama's Last Supper*, a 5-panel colour portrayal with Cox herself as a naked Christ figure surrounded by 12 black apostles – at www.reneecox.org/yo-mamas-last-supper; and Francois Girbauld's portrayal of the Last Supper with female Christ and eleven female disciples, one male, at www.theguardian.com/world/2005/feb/04/media.arts.

25 For example, a whole sequence of stylized photographs of a female crucified Christ by Ramon Martinez, can be found at his website: https://ramon-martinez. pixels.com. Warning: some of these may be considered pornographic in content and approach.

26 Linda Mercadatne proposes Bess, in Lars von Trier's 1996 *Breaking the Waves* film as a female Christ figure, in 'Bess the Christ Figure? Theological Interpretations of *Breaking the Waves*', *Journal of Religion and Film* 5:1 (2001), pp. 1–14; https://digitalcommons.unomaha.edu/cgi/viewcontent.cgi?article=1795&context= jrf. Arnfríður Gudmundsdóttir considers Beth, alongside Sister Helen Prejean in Tim Robbins' *Dead Man Walking* (1995), as female Christ-figures; see 'Female Christ-figures in Films: A Feminist Critical Analysis of *Breaking the Waves* and *Dead Man Walking*', *Studia Theologica* 56 (2002), pp. 27–43.

27 At https://jesusinlove.org/artthatdares/atd1-ansell-z.html.

28 At www.pinterest.co.uk/pin/346003183845537302/. Also in Robert Lentz and Edwina Gateley, *Christ in the Margins* (Maryknoll, NY: Orbis, 2009), p. 112.

29 Garibay's *Emmaus* exists in a number of versions, one of which can be found

at https://imagejournal.org/article/recognizing-the-stranger/, and forms the cover image of my *Seeking the Risen Christa*. Other versions can be found online.

30 Burns, 'Deterrence', p. 1.

31 Burns, 'Deterrence', p. 3.

32 http://themicrogiant.com/the-untouchables-erik-ravelo/.

33 See Slee, *Seeking the Risen Christa*, Ch. 1 for a survey of theological discussions of the Christa.

34 Rachel Anderson, 'The Crucified Woman: A Paradox of Prurience and Piety', research paper, 21 May 2007, p. 2; https://digital.lib.washington.edu/research-works/handle/1773/3101, accessed 26.05.2020.

35 Anderson, 'Crucified Woman', p. 2. Note the assumption that the naked female body is an erotically charged image in Western culture, in ways which are not commonly suggested of the representation of the naked male.

36 Power, 'Embodying the Eucharist', p. 159.

37 Power, 'Embodying the Eucharist', p. 160.

38 Ivone Gebara, *Out of the Depths: Women's Experience of Evil and Salvation* (Minneapolis, MN: Fortress Press, 2002), p. 117.

39 Margaret R. Miles, *Carnal Knowing: Female Nakedness and Religious Meaning in the Christian West* (Tunbridge Wells: Burns & Oates, 1992).

40 Miles, *Carnal Knowing*, p. 35. For further consideration of the significance of nakedness in baptism, see Frank C. Senn, *Embodied Liturgy: Lessons in Christian Ritual* (Minneapolis, MN: Fortress, 2016), pp. 53–89.

41 Miles, *Carnal Knowing*, p. 45.

42 Miles, *Carnal Knowing*, p. 70.

43 Miles, *Carnal Knowing*, p. 81.

44 As in Luther's account. Miles, *Carnal Knowing*, p. 107.

45 Miles, *Carnal Knowing*, p. 124.

46 Miles, *Carnal Knowing*, p. 139.

47 Miles, *Carnal Knowing*, p. 142.

48 Leo Steinberg, *The Sexuality of Christ in Renaissance Painting and Modern Oblivion* (New York: Pantheon, 1984).

49 Miles, *Carnal Knowing*, p. 143.

50 Miles, *Carnal Knowing*, p. 169.

51 Miles, *Carnal Knowing*, pp. 169–70.

52 Janet Martin Soskice, 'Turning the Symbols', in *Swallowing a Fishbone? Feminist Theologians Debate Christianity*, Daphne Hampson ed. (London: SPCK, 1996), pp. 17–32.

53 Miles, *Carnal Knowing*, p. 177.

54 Miles, *Carnal Knowing*, p. 177.

55 See https://ramon-martinez.pixels.com/.

56 For Rainer's *Wine Crucifix*, see www.tate.org.uk/art/artworks/rainer-wine-crucifix-t03671.

57 An image of Argyll's *Bosnian Christa* can be found at https://efecwomen.com/2017/12/13/date-announced-lecture-in-partnership-with-luther-king-house-12-february-2018/.

58 Power, 'Embodying the Eucharist', pp. 164–5.

59 Clague, 'The Christa', p. 103.

60 Beckford, 'Does Jesus have a Penis?'.

61 Dan Lé, *The Naked Christ: An Atonement Model for a Body-Obsessed Culture* (Eugene, OR: Pickwick Publications, 2012).

62 Slee, *Seeking the Risen Christa*.

63 Marcella Althaus-Reid, *Indecent Theology* (London: Routledge, 2000), pp. 110ff.

64 Clague, 'The Christa', pp. 99–100.

65 Grey, 'Who do you say that I am?', p. 193.

66 Slee, *Seeking the Risen Christa*.

67 Power, 'Embodying the Eucharist'.

68 Karen O'Donnell, *Broken Bodies: The Eucharist, Mary, and the Body in Trauma Theology* (London: SCM Press, 2018).

69 Power, 'Embodying the Eucharist', p. 179.

13

Jesus as a Victim of Sexual Abuse: A Womanist Critical Discourse Analysis of the Crucifixion

MMAPULA DIANA KEBANEILWE

Introduction

Sexual violence is a global concern. As observed by Reaves and Tombs, abusive sexual behaviour is widespread and happens across many sectors of life, including homes and workplaces.[1] Sadder still, sexual violence also happens in church, a situation which has offered additional context from which to see Jesus as a victim of sexual abuse.[2] Nonetheless, naming Jesus as a victim of sexual violence might seem hideous given the sacredness associated with Jesus' death on the cross. Many Christians highly regard the crucifixion as a necessary act of God's love for the lost. Thus the cross and the crucifixion of Jesus are at the heart of the Christian faith.[3] Notably central to the interpretation of New Testament texts for many is that the crucifixion was the decisive saving event.[4] Brintnall, in reference to Jesus' crucifixion, maintains that 'the mystery of physical brutality, and its possible redemptive power, has been in the air, ready to be scripted, interrogated, displayed and deployed time and again'.[5]

Following on that, I intend to interrogate the crucifixion in the light of sexual violence. Moreover, is there not an imperative to explore the subject from the perspectives of those who are no strangers to sexual abuse, harassment and assault? Biblical texts can be legitimately read with the social and political situations of contemporary cultures of oppression.[6] Thus naming Jesus as a victim of sexual abuse may not only raise our awareness of the brutality surrounding the crucifixion, but also it may help us to rethink our own stories and those of others who have been stripped naked in public, those who are less powerful, and those who, like Jesus, have been sexually humiliated and even murdered.

In this chapter, I maintain that the crucifixion entails much more than eyes can see. I will employ a Womanist Critical Discourse Analysis (WCDA) as a theoretical framework. Through this framework, I hope to explore the crucifixion in the light of the multiple sexual abuses suffered especially by women and girls, with special focus on my own context of Botswana. This framework allows me to stand back momentarily, to gain a different perspective on the crucifixion not only as an act of salvation but also an outrageous act of sexual humiliation and abuse. This is a subversive reading that problematizes the crucifixion.

In Botswana, there have been cases of women being stripped naked and accused of dressing in ways that contravened Botswana traditions and cultures. The situation led to the creation of the #IWEARWHATIWANT movement – a gender activist group against gender-based violence.[7] Ultimately, my reading aims to explore what lessons could be learnt by both the survivors and perpetrators of sexual violence by seeing Jesus too as a victim of sexual abuse. The exercise is a fitting one given that Botswana is a Christian context. Previous studies indicate that more than 70 per cent of the population of Botswana subscribe to Christianity.[8]

We infer, therefore, that Christian discourse dominates the religious landscape of the country and Jesus is a familiar figure in our context. Although speaking of Jesus as a victim of sexual violence may not be a widely known or accepted practice among Christians in Botswana, it may prove relevant given the rampancy of sexual violence in the country. My conviction is that if read from different perspectives and with particular contexts in mind, the crucifixion ordeal has the potential to reveal more than is commonly known or accepted. By engaging in a Womanist Critical Discourse Analysis (WCDA), it is recognized that this narrative has the potential to unsettle, re-settle, undo and re-do hegemonic and conservative readings and interpretations of the crucifixion. Importantly, this particular means of analysing the subject may yield a fresh understanding of the sexual violence that stems from the practice of publicly stripping naked (without their consent) those deemed less powerful.

The chapter will start with an explanation of the theoretical framework, namely describing what is entailed in using the WCDA method. This will be followed by an overview of the Botswana context of gender-based violence, which will set the backdrop against which our reading and interpretation happens. The exercise seeks to explore the complex layers of gender inequality and culture and how the two intersect in issues of sexual violence. The analysis section will investigate the crucifixion narrative of Matthew 27.32–56 in the light especially of sexual violence experienced by women and girls (hence gender-based violence) in Botswana. The aim of this section is to see to what extent the experiences of sexual violence by contemporary Botswana women and girls might be likened to those of Jesus during the crucifixion. I will ask the question: what insights can contemporary victims of sexual violence get from seeing Jesus as having suffered the crime, and what lessons can perpetrators learn by approaching the crucifixion from the perspective of sexual violence? This will be followed by the conclusion, which will highlight lessons learnt for the empowerment of both the victims and perpetrators of sexual violence.

Womanist Critical Discourse Analysis

The theoretical framework here proposed is a combination of two separate methodological approaches to texts: namely, womanist theory and critical discourse analysis. The two approaches have been combined for the purpose of exploring Jesus' crucifixion ordeal as an act of sexual violence. The approaches will be discussed separately in order to illustrate how they complement each other and how they will be used for the purpose of this chapter.

Womanist approach

According to Linda Hogan, the term 'womanist' represents a 'feminist of color'.[9] Womanism or womanist theory was born out of dissatisfaction with feminism and feminist theory. As asserted by Margaret Kamitsuka, white, middle-class feminists who pioneered feminist theory tended to overlook issues of race and sexualities outside of the dominant white, heterosexual paradigm in their efforts to debunk patriarchy.[10] In their efforts to redefine male definitions of women and the female experience, they did so from their specific contexts which eventually excluded African/black women and other women of colour.[11] Thus womanist theory seeks to close the gap by exploring the interplay and intersections of gender, race, ethnicity, sexual orientation and class.[12] Womanist theory seeks to assert the voices of black women and women of colour in an empowering way and underscores their identity as a reader as important to their situational context. It is especially done with the experiences and stories of those who have suffered gender-based violence at one time or other in their life. Consequently, my use of the term womanist aims at an inclusive, ideological and contextual reading and interpretation of the crucifixion. Womanist theory gives authentication to my own voice and perspective so that I can speak of the passion narratives and the crucifixion from my own contextual standpoint. By employing a womanist lens to read the crucifixion, I can boldly speak about how it resonates, at varying levels, with the lived, complex experiences of those in my context. And by combining womanist theory with critical discourse analysis I can explore those complexities at some length. I will now, therefore, explain critical discourse analysis.

Critical discourse analysis

Critical discourse analysis (CDA) is a theory and method of text analysis that focuses on the intersection of discourse and social experience.[13] The core principle of CDA is that many aspects of our lived experience are socially constructed and mediated through language, to which they are dialectically related.[14] CDA is concerned with 'analyzing opaque as well as transparent structural relationships of dominance, discrimination, power and control as manifested in language'.[15] The analysis helps us to make sense of the cultural ideologies that were at work at the time of the crucifixion and how to read the passion narratives creatively in order to reveal the deeper issues at play. In the words of Jørgensen and Phillips, language (or discourse) is 'a machine that generates and ... constitutes the social world'.[16] Thus CDA is interested in the interface between the structures of the discourse as well as the structures of society.[17]

In this chapter, I intend to explore the crucifixion and the entire discourse of the passion narrative of Matthew 27.32–56 from the standpoint of the sexually abused and those who have suffered the brunt of gender-based violence, with special interest in Batswana women and girls. It is worth noting that I am writing as a biblical scholar and a Motswana woman whose own life (and those of others in my social and family circles) has been scarred by violence and, more specifically, gender-based violence.[18] As such, my reading and interpretation of the crucifixion is inevitably marked by these experiences. I believe that acknowledging such a subjective and ideological position will act as a filter in the meaning-creating process. Before venturing into the analysis, the next section will provide an overview of the contextual background against which this particular interpretive exercise is done. This is the context of gender-based violence in Botswana.

Gender-based violence in Botswana: an overview

The Inter-Agency Working Group on Reproductive Health in Crises defines gender-based violence as 'an umbrella term used to describe any harmful act that is perpetrated against a person's will and is based on socially ascribed (gender) differences between males and females'.[19] Gender-based violence takes many forms including rape, sexual exploitation, sexual assault and abuse, forced sex and other types of sexual violence, domestic violence, trafficking of women and girls, forced prostitution, sexual harassment and discrimination, and denial of rights.[20]

In Botswana, many women and girls have suffered and continue to suffer the brunt of many of the above forms of violence.[21] As noted by Mookodi, male violence against women is widespread in Botswana and it is reinforced by patriarchal beliefs and practices.[22] Mookodi further maintains that men in Botswana act out their dominance over women through acts of violence that constitute gender-based violence.[23] According to *The Gender Based Violence (GBV) Indicator Study: Botswana*, almost 70 per cent of women in the country experience gender-based violence in their lifetime.[24] The same study asserts that patriarchal attitudes rooted in the Botswana culture are a significant factor in incidences of gender-based violence in the country.[25] Because the patriarchal culture affords men dominance over women, it has perfidious effects because it makes men think women and children, and especially girls, are subordinate to them.[26] Consequently, gender inequity norms in Botswana are tied to male sexual dominance, perpetration of rape and sexual violence.[27] Yet another devastating form of gender-based violence is the notorious 'passion-killings' – the phrase used to refer to the murder of a person by their intimate partner.[28] Sadly, 'passion killings' in Botswana are a gendered epidemic in which women and girls are disproportionately victims while men are almost always perpetrators.[29] In 2020, with the outbreak of the novel Coronavirus disease (Covid-19), which forced countries around the world to impose extreme social distancing measures or lockdowns, cases of gender-based violence in Botswana increased. The country went on Covid-19 lockdown from 2 April 2020 to 21 May 2020. In an interview with a representative of a women's shelter, it was revealed that they had recorded so many cases that the shelter overflowed, forcing them to seek further housing for the victims, who are women.[30] Yet another report indicates that cases of child rape were also on the increase during the lockdown.[31] Worse still, cases of 'passion killings' were also reported during this time.[32]

Notably, 'passion killings' occur when a woman who has suffered abuse by her partner decides to end the relationship.[33] Under such circumstances, the male partner feels disrespected as his power is challenged and his ego bruised by the woman's assertiveness, and so he kills her. As noted by Mookodi, conflicts that often result in gender-based violence against women are due to a perceived threat to male power by the women's increased assertiveness.[34]

Jesus' crucifixion and gender-based violence in Botswana: a WCDA analysis

> As they went out, they met a man named Simon, and they forced him to carry the cross. They went to a place called Golgotha and there they offered Jesus wine mixed with gall to drink. Jesus tasted it but refused to drink it. They crucified him and afterwards divided his clothes among themselves. Above his head they placed a placard with charges they laid against him: 'THIS IS THE KING OF THE JEWS'. Two rebels were crucified with him. Those who passed by hurled insults at him saying 'you were going to destroy the temple and build it three days, save yourself ...' Likewise those crucified with him heaped insults at him. The chief priests, teachers of the law and the elders also mocked him. Many women were there, watching from a distance.[35]

The above is my summary of the crucifixion narrative of Matthew 27.32–56. The summary is intended to bring attention to crucial issues in the narrative, as far as this chapter is concerned. Before carrying out a detailed analysis of the narrative, I will share a story of one incident (out of the many) in Botswana that I intend to juxtapose with the crucifixion story in an attempt to contextualize Jesus' ordeal with the ordeals of gender-based violence. Consider the following newspaper report:

> One Sunday, a young woman was stripped naked at the Gaborone Bus Rank by what appeared to be a crazed group of adult men old enough to be her father. She was insulted and mocked. Not a single member of the mob tried to protect the young woman. Not even the women who were clearly in the midst. They too laughed and apparently encouraged others to abuse the girl. The video went viral on social media, triggering an uncomfortable national debate on patriarchy, gender abuse as well as rape culture in the country.[36] Notably, some of the mockers were heard on the video urging the men, yelling 'give it to her', 'she is not dressed'.[37]

It is important to highlight that in this case women also took part in the abuse of the woman stripped naked at the bus rank. One may wonder: why? The participation of women in the incident should be understood against the culturally encoded structures of patriarchy. Women, in this situation, risk dangerous and even lethal consequences if they dare to challenge men's actions of oppression. We have already seen how cases of passion killing occasion death for women. Moreover, because of the systemic power of patriarchy in Botswana and how women are socialized, many have accepted their inferior status and subordination to men.[38]

Reading the above narratives simultaneously using a WCDA method, several themes can be identified: hidden as well as visible structural issues of dominance, power and control; the use of force to dominate and intimidate the victim; wrong accusations against the victim; victim blaming; physical abuse; stripping naked; hurling insults; and humiliating and demeaning the victim. These themes will be explored in what follows.

The use of force on victims: domination and intimidation

What is of major concern here is how sexual violence may be associated with the perpetrators' use of force on their victims. As observed by Alao and Molojwane, sexual violence is an attempt to exert power and control over the other, to humiliate, or to satisfy the sexual urges of the perpetrator.[39] Whatever reasons may be advanced, sexual violence is wrong. The use of force on victims, whether physical or otherwise, is involved throughout instances of sexual violence.

A WCDA approach reveals that in both the case of Jesus and that of the Motswana woman at the bus rank, the victims were subjected to domination and force by the perpetrators. In the case of Jesus, the Roman soldiers flogged and scourged him, forcing him to his place of trial and crucifixion. It is also reported that they forced a certain man, named Simon, to carry the cross (Matt. 27.32). As argued by Fleming Rutledge, a person who is crucified inevitably suffers violence, and yet the New Testament pays little or no attention to the physical aspects of the crucifixion.[40] The overarching idea here is that violence and brutality pervade the entire crucifixion, and it is not surprising that force is used at every opportunity. Thus, as noted by Neufeld, the crucifixion is suffused with violence, where violence involves the use of force, coercion, abuse, aggression, hostility, vehemence and the like.[41]

The narrative of the events of the crucifixion of Jesus resonates with what happened in the case of the young Motswana woman who was forcefully and aggressively stripped naked at the bus rank. Insofar as violence is the exercise of physical force, both the crucifixion and the bus rank stripping ordeals were wrought with violence. Reports of beating and stripping women naked in public have a long history in Botswana, when women in mini-skirts have been brutally attacked.[42] The incidents demonstrate the cultural value of patriarchy, where women, their choices and their bodies are dominated and controlled by men. Both cases, the crucifixion of Jesus and the Motswana woman stripped naked at the bus rank, are full of sexual violence overtures, showing that the use of force is a characteristic of all forms of violence including sexual violence, if not an actual strategy.

Wrong accusations against the victim: self-justification by the perpetrator

The Motswana woman in the Mmegi story was first accused of indecent dressing, or dressing in a way not approved by males according to prevailing Botswana culture. In reference to the crucifixion ordeal in the New Testament, Jesus too was unjustly accused and condemned.[43] He was alleged to have claimed to be king of the Jews and he was charged as stated in Matthew 27.37. It is interesting that as readers we already know that the accusation laid against him was false, for Judas confessed earlier, in Matthew 27.4, but the accusing authorities dismissed the truth in favour of the false accusations. Jesus' accusers claimed that they had found a man (Jesus) who was trying to incite an insurgency, and though Pilate found no evidence to that effect, he decided to have Jesus flogged anyway.[44] The issue of power is also apparent in the questions that Pilate asked Jesus: 'Do you refuse to speak to me? Do you not know that I have power to release you and power to crucify you?' (John 19.10). As noted by Agamben, there is resentment in Pilate's questions to Jesus and this is due to the supposed threat to his power.[45] Therefore false accusations serve to validate not just the perpetrators' horrendous acts but, even more, their power over their victim. They want to show the vulnerability and defeat of their victim, and, as Tombs further argues, crucifixion in the Roman Empire was more about public shame.[46] By using physical force, victims were terrorized into fatalistic submission.

When going beyond the transparent to the opaque structures of dominance involved in the crucifixion, we uncover the fear of those in power at play in the ordeal. By examining with suspicion the charge laid upon him, 'This is Jesus, the King of the Jews' (Matt. 27.37), it appears that the Roman Empire felt threatened and clung to their power, perceiving themselves to be under siege. Cassidy maintains that Jesus' accusers claimed that he was perverting the nation, stirring insurrection and claiming to be 'Christ a king'.[47] The claim made here suggests that a perceived threat to political power was stirred by Jesus' autonomy in calling for radically new social patterns.[48] He had been criticizing existing patterns and those who maintained them, but had not done anything to resist Roman rule by force.[49]

The lurking fear of those in power can also be seen in the Motswana woman's stripping ordeal and in many others who have suffered abuse. To demonstrate autonomy of mind and body by wearing what one likes is translated as a power challenge for the men at the taxi rank, and they wanted to force her into submission by stripping her naked in public. This echoes other instances throughout the Bible and in Botswana where power has been wrongly used to humiliate less-powerful others. We have noted already that in the case of 'passion killings' in Botswana, women are victimized for their assertiveness and ability to say 'no' to oppression. Such a stance is translated by Batswana men as a challenge to their power and, hence, is highly resented and can be lethal. Thus, as observed by Weatherall, violence against women is the most devastating consequence of gender inequality, which in its extreme form is a lethal act.[50]

Beating, stripping naked and humiliation of the victim: sexual violence as power display

Batswana women are beaten and stripped naked. Jesus too was beaten (flogged), stripped naked and mocked by not just his crucifiers but also by a mob of passers-by and everyone at the scene (vv. 38–44). The language used to mock him indicates that his accusers were power hungry and longed to dominate and subjugate him because of their fear of his challenge to their authority. The powerful others, whether leaders or not, can choose to display their dominance over those they deem vulnerable. In the book of Esther, the case of Vashti reveals just such a state of affairs.[51] Her refusal to act as a striptease for the gaze of male dignitaries, including the king and his council of men (eunuchs), led her to be banished for ever from the palace.[52] It is notable that Vashti's ordeal too is loaded with overtones of sexual violence, especially as she was summoned by her husband King Xerxes to 'strip' naked and to parade her nudity before a roomful of drunken men.[53] Stripping naked against one's will is almost always a characteristic of sexual violence, stemming from the desire to exert dominance on vulnerable others.

In both cases of the Motswana woman at the taxi rank and Jesus, the victims were stripped naked. The stripping here can be viewed as not just stripping the victims of their clothes but of their dignity as well. As observed by Tombs, sexual violence is used to humiliate and degrade a victim and its meaning is socially and culturally constructed around gender and identity.[54] Gender injustice is clearly at play in the case of the Motswana woman and identity is at play in the case of Jesus. The Jews lived under the Roman Empire and Jesus' leadership was seen as a threat partly because he was a Jew. Thus he was crucified as 'King of the Jews',[55] which implies that he could incite his people to rebel against Roman imperial rule. Moreover, as argued by Carter, people were not crucified because they were spiritual but because they posed a threat to the Roman imperial system.[56] Plus the Roman Empire regulated all spheres of life, political, economic, societal and religious.[57] So although Jesus' mission was religious, it could not escape the totalitarian eyes of the Roman imperial power. Unlike other religious leaders in the land, namely, chief priests and scribes, Jesus was not an ally of the Roman Empire.[58] Consequently, he was viewed as a threat. Likewise in Botswana, women's lives are basically regulated by men; women have no acceptable choices. This is evidenced by the accusations of indecent dressing laid upon the woman stripped naked at the taxi rank and in the cases of intimate partner homicides rampant in the country. The dynamics of gender inequality are at play in all cases of gender-based violence in Botswana.

Sexual violence is one of the most humiliating means used by the powerful to render their victims completely powerless. As observable in the Motswana woman's case, the men insisted that she wanted to be raped by dressing as she did and that rape would teach her a lesson.[59] The implication being that sexual violence was the ultimate means of forcing submission from her. In the case of Jesus, an adult man was stripped naked and hanged with his hands spread and tied up at each end of the cross, implying that he was left helpless to do anything to protect his privacy.[60]

As maintained by Tombs, the sexual element of the abuse becomes clear and can only be controversial insofar as it is unconventional to the usual presentations.[61] A WCDA approach that juxtaposes the case of the Motswana woman stripped naked makes the usual presentation and the familiar story of Jesus' crucifixion quite unfamiliar. Although Gospel readers are familiar with the picture of Jesus half-naked on the cross and the division of his clothes among his crucifiers, they could pause to re-imagine what all those images mean. It is strange to imagine afresh for once that, as noted by Tombs, an adult man (Jesus) was stripped naked, flogged and displayed naked to die.[62] This resonates with sexual violence as observed in the stripping naked of a young Motswana woman at the taxi rank. As further argued by Reaves and Tombs, sexual violence can be used to display the power of the perpetrator and the vulnerability and defeat of the victim.[63] This is true in both Jesus' crucifixion and the ordeal of the young Motswana woman stripped naked at the taxi rank.

Insults and mockery: powerful tools used in sexual violence

In both cases under scrutiny, mockery is expressed through the power of spoken words. The mob of 'rapists' stripped the Motswana woman naked at the taxi rank and mocked her, saying she called it upon herself and was asking to be raped. In the case of Jesus, the mockers yelled that 'he saved others, let him save himself' (Matt. 27.37–44). Again, the words are loaded with power connotations that point to the anger and bitterness that arise when rotten power feels challenged and when there is hunger to dominate and subdue that which is seen as a threat. It is interesting too that even those crucified with him hurled insults at him (v. 44).

Similarly, it is reported that in the case of the Motswana woman, even other women heaped insults on her and participated in the violence. This is the power of dominance; the dominant other 'rapes' or conquers even the minds of the dominated. Batswana women live under oppressive patriarchal conditions; one would expect them to take the side of those like the woman at the taxi rank who are being brutally attacked. However, because their minds have been raped and brought under fatal submission by the menace of patriarchy, many have internalized and normalized their own oppression so that it does not matter any more. Those crucified with Jesus, too, have been exposed to the same humiliation and one would expect them to be in solidarity with him, which was not the case. Instead, they had accepted the unjust tradition of being shamefully killed through crucifixion. It was culturally encoded and, hence, was normalized. It is also important to remember that a clash with the powerful can be dangerous.[64] It is especially dangerous when the powerful are already enraged, as in the case of the men who stripped the Motswana woman at the taxi rank, and also in the case of Jesus' crucifiers. That might also explain why in both cases even those expected to show solidarity with the victims would rather join the powerful perpetrators.

Conclusion: can naming Jesus a victim of sexual violence be liberating?

The crucifixion of Jesus analysed from a WCDA perspective has revealed that the shame and denigrating treatment he received throughout the passion narratives constitute sexual violence and, notably, it resonates with the sexual violence suffered by contemporary real flesh and blood people. Juxtaposing the crucifixion ordeal with issues of gender-based violence in Botswana has uncovered the liberating message embedded in the reading that views Jesus as having suffered one of the most humiliating crimes against humanity.

The reading also brings to life Jesus' own words when he said, 'Truly I say to you, whatever you did for one of the least of these brothers and sisters of mine, you did it for me' (Matt. 25.40). Thus, if the 'least' of his brothers and sisters is understood within the contextual situation of those who have suffered sexual violence of whatever kind, naming him a victim of the crime affirms his solidarity with those victims and survivors.[65]

As already argued by Tombs, Christ identifies with the vulnerable, including the sexually abused.[66] Bearing in mind the link between the crucifixion and the Batswana women's ordeals of gender-based violence, the idea of seeing or naming Jesus as a victim of sexual abuse becomes a reality. The comfort of knowing that Jesus too experienced and continues to experience sexual abuse through the experiences of the victims and survivors can bring healing. It takes away self-condemnation from the survivors. As Elaine Heath argues, healing for survivors of sexual violence begins when they can hear their own stories in Jesus' suffering.[67] It then has the potential to ignite in the survivors the hope that, though once vandalized, they are neither trashed nor condemned, for Christ is in their corner and understands their pain from his own experience of it.

As for the perpetrators, the realization that Jesus literally suffered sexual abuse in the crucifixion ordeal, as well as metaphorically standing in solidarity with the victims and survivors of the crime, means that the perpetrators are his enemies. It also implies that they are continuing to crucify, rape, sexually vandalize, mock and brutalize him until they repent and cease from committing the crimes. If they could pause to reflect, sex scandals and gender-based violence should not be found in our societies, especially those that claim to be Bible-believing. Gender-based violence condemns the perpetrators as the accusers and crucifiers of the very Christ they claim to follow.

References

Agamben, G., *Pilate and Jesus*, Stanford, CA: Stanford University Press, 2015.

Agence de Presse Africaine, 'Botswana Child Rape Cases Rise During Lockdown – UNICEF', *Agence de Presse Africaine News*, 15 April 2020, http://apanews.net/en/pays/botswana/news/botswana-child-rape-cases-rise-during-lockdown-unicef.

Alao, A. A., and M. B. Molojwane, 'Childhood Sexual Abuse: The Botswana Perspectives', in *Child Sexual Abuse: Issues and Challenges*, Megan J. Smith ed., New York: Nova Science Publishers, 2008, pp. 9–18.

Botlhoko, P., 'Kuke Cop Charged with Wife's Murder', *Mmegi Online*, 16 April 2020, www.mmegi.bw/index.php?aid=85247&dir=2020/april/16.

Brintnall, K. L., 'Tarantino's Incarnational Theology: "Reservoir Dogs", Crucifixions and Spectacular Violence', *CrossCurrents* (2004), pp. 66–75.

Carter, Warren, *The Roman Empire and the New Testament: An Essential Guide*, Nashville, TN: Abingdon Press, 2006.

Cassidy, R. J., *Jesus, Politics, and Society: A Study of Luke's Gospel*, Eugene, OR: Wipf and Stock Publishers, 2015.

Chakamba, R., 'Botswana activists march in miniskirts to fight gender-based violence', in *News Deeply: Women and Girls*, 6 September 2017, www.newsdeeply. com/womenandgirls/articles/2017/09/06/botswana-activists-march-in-mini skirts-to-fight-gender-based-violence.

CIA World Fact Book, 'Religions: Botswana', www.cia.gov/library/publications/ the-world-factbook/fields/print_2122.html.

Daly, R. J., *The Atonement: The Origins of the Doctrine in the New Testament*, Philadelphia PA: Fortress Press, 1981.

——, 'The Expiatory Sacrifice of Christ', *Bulletin of John Ryland Library* (1979–80), pp. 454–75

Ellece, S. E., and C. Rapoo, 'Who Should Teach Our Boys How to Respect Life?: Theorizing Volatile Gender Identities in Botswana', *Marang Journal of Language and Literature* 23:1 (2013), pp. 59–73.

Exner, D., and W. E. Thurston, 'Understanding "Passion Killings" in Botswana: An Investigation of Media Framing', *Journal of International Women's Studies* 10:4, (2009), pp. 1–16.

Fairclough, N., 'Critical Discourse Analysis as a Method in Social Scientific Research', *Methods of Critical Discourse Analysis* 5:11 (2001), pp. 121–38.

——, *Analyzing Discourse: Textual Analysis for Social Research*, London: Routledge, 2003.

Fitzmyer, J. A., 'Crucifixion in Ancient Palestine, Qumran Literature, and the New Testament', *The Catholic Biblical Quarterly* 40:4 (1978), pp. 493–513.

Galvin, J. P., 'Jesus as Scapegoat?: Violence and the Sacred in the Theology of Raymund Schwager', *The Thomist: A Speculative Quarterly Review* 46:2 (1982), pp. 173–94.

Geisler, G. G., *Women and the Remaking of Politics in Southern Africa: Negotiating Autonomy, Incorporation, and Representation*, Uppsala: Nordic Africa Institute, 2003.

Green, J. B., 'The Death of Jesus', in *PB Handbook for the Study of the Historical Jesus*, Leiden: Brill, 2011, pp. 2383–408.

Heath, E. A., *We Were the Least of These: Reading the Bible with Survivors of Sexual Abuse*, Grand Rapids, MI: Brazos Press, 2011.

Hogan, Linda, *From Women's Experiences to Feminist Theology*, Sheffield: Sheffield Academic Press, 1995.

Inter-Agency Working Group on Reproductive Health in Crises (IAWG-RHC), *Inter-Agency Field Manual on Reproductive Health in Humanitarian Settings: 2010 Revision for Field Review*, Geneva: IAWG-RHC, 2010, www.ncbi.nlm. nih.gov/books/NBK305149/.

Jørgensen, M. W., and Louise Phillips, , *Discourse Analysis as Theory and Method*, London: Thousand Oaks, 2004.

Junior, Nyasha, 'Womanist Biblical Interpretation', in *Engaging the Bible in a Gendered World: An Introduction to Feminist Biblical Interpretation in Honour of Katharine Doob Sakenfeld*, Linda Day and Carolyn Pressler eds, Louisville, KY: Westminster John Knox Press, 2006.

Kamitsuka, M. D., 'Reading the Raced and Sexed Body in Colour Purple: Repatterning White Feminist and Womanist Theological Hermeneutics', *Journal of Feminist Studies in Religion* 19:2 (2003), pp. 45–66.

Kang'ethe, S. M., 'The Perfidy and Ramifications of Gender-based Violence (GBV) Meted against Women and the Girl Children in Botswana: A Literature Review', *Mediterranean Journal of Social Sciences* 5:23 (2014), pp. 1563–7.

Kebaneilwe, Mmapula Diana, 'This Courageous Woman: A Socio-rhetorical Womanist Reading of Proverbs 31:10–31', PhD Thesis, Murdoch University, 2012,
http://researchrepository.murdoch.edu.au/id/eprint/16159.

—, 'The Vashti Paradigm: Resistance as a Strategy for Combating HIV', *The Ecumenical Review* 63:4 (2011), pp. 378–84.

Kuhlmann, M., 'COVID 19 Lockdown: Are Domestic Abuse Victims Safe at Home
or Stuck at Home?', *Sunday Standard*, 13 April 2020, www.sundaystandard.
info/covid-19-lockdown-are-domestic-abuse-victims-safe-at-home-or-stuck-at-
home/.

Masenya, M., 'Proverbs 31:10–31 in a South African Context: A Reading for the
Liberation of African (Northern Sotho) Women', *Semeia* 78 (1997), pp. 55–68.

Modie-Moroka, T., 'Intimate Partner Violence and Poverty in the Context of
Botswana', *Journal of Psychology in Africa* 20:2 (2010), pp. 185–91.

Mookodi, G., 'Male Violence against Women in Botswana: A Discussion of Gendered Uncertainties in a Rapidly Changing Environment', *African Sociological
Review/Revue Africaine de Sociologie* 8:1 (2004), pp. 118–38.

—, 'The Dynamics of Domestic Violence against Women in Botswana', *Pula Journal of African Studies* 18:1 (2004), pp. 55–64.

Neufeld, T. Y., *Jesus and the Subversion of Violence: Wrestling with the New Testament Evidence*, London: SPCK, 2011.

Patterson, A., 'Critical Discourse Analysis: A Condition of Doubt', *Discourse:
Studies in the Cultural Politics of Education* 18:3 (2010), pp. 425–35.

Raditloaneng, W. N., 'An Analysis of Gender-based Domestic Violence and Reactions in Southern Africa', *Wudpecker Journal of Sociology and Anthropology* 1:5
(2013), pp. 60–71.

Reaves, Jayme R., and David Tombs, '# MeToo Jesus: Naming Jesus as a Victim of
Sexual Abuse', *International Journal of Public Theology* 13:4 (2019), pp. 387–412.

Rutledge, F., *The Crucifixion: Understanding the Death of Jesus Christ*, Grand
Rapids, MI: Eerdmans, 2015.

Shannon, Kate, Karen Leiter, Nthabiseng Phaladze, Zakhe Hlanze, Alexander C.
Tsai, Michele Heisler, Vincent Iacopino and Sheri D. Weiser, 'Gender Inequity
Norms are Associated with Increased Male-perpetrated Rape and Sexual Risks
for HIV Infection in Botswana and Swaziland', *Public Library of Science (PLoS)
One* 7:1 (2012), https://doi.org/10.1371/journal.pone.0028739.

Tombs, David, 'Crucifixion, State Terror, and Sexual Abuse', *Union Seminary
Quarterly Review* 53:1–2 (1999), pp. 89–109.

—, 'Honor, Shame and Conquest: Male Identity, Sexual Violence and the Body
Politic', *Journal of Hispanic/Latino Theology* 9:2 (2002), pp. 21–40.

—, *Crucifixion, State Terror, and Sexual Abuse: Text and Context*, Dunedin: Centre for Theology and Public Issues, University of Otago, 2018, http://hdl.handle.
net/10523/8558.

Tsai, Alexander C., Karen Leiter, Michele Heisler, Vincent Iacopino, William Wolfe,
Kate Shannon, Nthabiseng Phaladze, Zakhe Hlanze and Sheri D. Weiser, 'Prevalence and Correlates of Forced Sex Perpetration and Victimization in Botswana
and Swaziland', *American Journal of Public Health* 101:6 (2011), pp. 1068–74.

Tull, P. K., *Esther and Ruth*, Louisville, KY: Westminster Press, 2007.

Weatherall, A., 'Constituting and Responding to Domestic and Sexual Violence',
Gender and Language 12:2 (2019), pp. 149–52.

Wodak, R., 'What CDA is About: A Summary of Its History, Important Concepts and Its Development', in *Methods of Critical Discourse Analysis*, R. Wodak and M. Meyer eds, London: Thousand Oaks, 2001.

Notes

1 Jayme R. Reaves and David Tombs, '#MeToo Jesus: Naming Jesus as a Victim of Sexual Abuse', *International Journal of Public Theology* 13:4 (2019), pp. 387–412.

2 Reaves and Tombs, '#Me Too Jesus', p. 388.

3 Joseph A. Fitzmyer, 'Crucifixion in Ancient Palestine, Qumran Literature, and the New Testament', *The Catholic Biblical Quarterly* 40:4 (1978), pp. 493–513.

4 Joel B. Green, *The Death of Jesus: Tradition and Interpretation in the Passion Narrative* (Eugene, OR: Wipf and Stock, 2011), p. 2, citing Robert J. Daly, *The Atonement: The Origins of the Doctrine in the New Testament* (Philadelphia, PA: Fortress Press, 1981), which is an expansion of Daly's earlier article, 'The Expiatory Sacrifice of Christ', *Bulletin for John Ryland Library* (1979–80), pp. 454–75.

5 Ken L. Brintnall, 'Tarantino's Incarnational Theology: "Reservoir Dogs", Crucifixions and Spectacular Violence', *Cross Currents* (2004), pp. 66–75.

6 David Tombs, *Crucifixion, State Terror, and Sexual Abuse, Text and Context* (Dunedin: Centre for Theology and Public Issues, University of Otago, 2018), p. 10.

7 Rumbi Chakamba, 'Botswana Activists March in Miniskirts to Fight Gender-based Violence', *News Deeply: Women and Girls*, 6 September 2017, www.news deeply.com/womenandgirls/articles/2017/09/06/botswana-activists-march-in-mini skirts-to-fight-gender-based-violence.

8 CIA World Factbook, 'Religions: Botswana', www.cia.gov/library/publications/the-world-factbook/fields/print_2122.html.

9 Linda Hogan, *From Women's Experiences to Feminist Theology* (Sheffield: Sheffield Academic Press, 1995), p. 122.

10 Margaret D. Kamitsuka, 'Reading the Raced and Sexed Body in Colour Purple: Repatterning White Feminist and Womanist Theological Hermeneutics', *Journal of Feminist Studies in Religion* 19:2 (2003), pp. 45–66.

11 Madipoane Masenya, 'Proverbs 31:10–31 in a South African Context: A Reading for the Liberation of African (Northern Sotho) Women', *Semeia* 78 (1997), pp. 55–68.

12 Nyasha Junior, 'Womanist Biblical Interpretation', in *Engaging the Bible in a Gendered World: An Introduction to Feminist Biblical Interpretation in Honour of Katharine Doob Sakenfeld*, Linda Day and Carolyn Pressler eds (Louisville, KY: Westminster John Knox Press, 2006), pp. 37–47. Masenya shares the same concern as Junior and argues that the feminist approach is concerned with issues of gender but overlooks the real and intimate issues that black women and other women of colour are faced with such as racism, classism and sexism. See Madipoane Masenya, 'A Bosadi [Womanhood] Reading of Genesis 16', *Old Testament Essays* 11:2 (1998), pp. 271–87.

13 Norman Fairclough, 'Critical Discourse Analysis as a Method in Social Scientific Research', *Methods of Critical Discourse Analysis* 5:11 (2001), pp. 121–38; Annette Patterson, 'Critical Discourse Analysis: A Condition of Doubt', *Discourse: Studies in the Cultural Politics of Education* 18:3 (2010), pp. 425–35.

14 Norman Fairclough, *Analyzing Discourse: Textual Analysis for Social Research* (London: Routledge, 2003).

15 Ruth Wodak, 'What CDA is About: A Summary of Its History, Important Concepts and Its Development', in *Methods of Critical Discourse Analysis*, Ruth Wodak and Michael Meyer eds (London: Thousand Oaks), p. 2.

16 Marianne Jørgensen and Louise J. Phillips, *Discourse Analysis as Theory and Method* (London: Thousand Oaks, 2004), p. 9.

17 Fairclough, 'Critical Discourse Analysis', p. 117.

18 'Motswana' refers to a citizen of Botswana and is a singular form of 'Batswana'.

19 Inter-agency Working Group on Reproductive Health in Crises (IAWG-RHC), *Inter-Agency Field Manual on Reproductive Health in Humanitarian Settings: 2010 Revision for Field Review* (Geneva: IAWG-RHC, 2010), p. 157, www.ncbi. nlm.nih.gov/books/NBK305149/pdf/Bookshelf_NBK305149.pdf.

20 *Inter-Agency Field Manual*, p. 157.

21 See Wapula N. Raditloaneng, 'An Analysis of Gender-based Domestic Violence and Reactions in Southern Africa', *Wudpecker Journal of Sociology and Anthropology* 1:5 (2013), pp. 60–71. Raditloaneng postulates that the different forms of gender-based violence in Botswana include murder, rape, sexual harassment, incest, defilement, severe beatings and threats to kill.

22 Godisang Mookodi, 'Male Violence against Women in Botswana: A Discussion of Gendered Uncertainties in a Rapidly Changing Environment', *African Sociological Review/Revue Africaine de Sociologie* 8:1 (2004), pp. 118–38.

23 Mookodi, 'Male Violence against Women in Botswana', p. 119.

24 Mercy Machisa and Roos van Dorp, *The Gender Based Violence Indicators Study: Botswana* (Oxford: African Books Collective, 2012), p. 11.

25 Machisa and van Dorp, *Gender Based Violence Indicators Study*, p. 11. See also Raditloaneng, 'An Analysis of Gender-based Domestic Violence', p. 11.

26 Simon M. Kang'ethe, 'The Perfidy and Ramifications of Gender-based Violence (GBV) Meted against Women and the Girl Children in Botswana: A Literature Review', *Mediterranean Journal of Social Sciences*' 5:23 (2014), p. 1563.

27 Kate Shannon, Karen Leiter, Nthabiseng Phaladze, Zakhe Hlanze, Alexander C. Tsai, Michele Heisler, Vincent Iacopino and Sheri D. Weiser, 'Gender Inequity Norms are Associated with Increased Male-perpetrated Rape and Sexual Risks for HIV Infection in Botswana and Swaziland', *Public Library of Science (PLoS) One* 7:1 (2012), https://doi.org/10.1371/journal.pone.0028739.

28 Deinera Exner and Wilfreda E. Thurston, 'Understanding "Passion Killings" in Botswana: An Investigation of Media Framing', *Journal of International Women's Studies* 10:4 (2009), pp. 1–16. Also see Sibonile Edith Ellece and Connie Rapoo, 'Who Should Teach Our Boys How to Respect Life?: Theorizing Volatile Gender Identities in Botswana', *Marang Journal of Language and Literature* 23 (2013), pp. 59–73.

29 Raditloaneng, 'An Analysis of Gender-based Domestic Violence', p. 64.

30 Mpho Kuhlmann, 'COVID 19 Lockdown – Are Domestic Abuse Victims Safe at Home or Stuck at Home?', *Sunday Standard*, 13 April 2020, www.sunday standard.info/covid-19-lockdown-are-domestic-abuse-victims-safe-at-home-or-stuck-at-home/.

31 Agence de Presse Africaine, 'Botswana Child Rape Cases Rise During Lockdown – UNICEF', *Agence de Presse Africaine News*, 15 April 2020, http://apa

news.net/en/pays/botswana/news/botswana-child-rape-cases-rise-during-lock-down-unicef.

32 Pini Botlhoko, 'Kuke Cop Charged with Wife's Murder', *Mmegi Online*, 16 April 2020, www.mmegi.bw/index.php?aid=85247&dir=2020/april/16.

33 Exner and Thurston, 'Understanding "Passion Killings" in Botswana', pp. 7–8.

34 Godisang Mookodi, 'The Dynamics of Domestic Violence against Women in Botswana', *Pula Journal of African Studies* 18:1 (2004), pp. 55–64.

35 A summary of Matthew 27.32–56. All direct scriptural quotations are from the New International Version.

36 Pini Botlhoko, 'Hunt Begins for Bus Rank Stripping Thugs', *Mmegi Online*, 26 May 2017, www.mmegi.bw/index.php?aid=69098&dir=2017/may/26.

37 Chakamba, 'Botswana Activists March in Miniskirts to Fight Gender-based Violence'.

38 Exner and Thurston, 'Understanding "Passion Killings" in Botswana', p. 2.

39 Amos A. Alao and Maithamako B. Molojwane, 'Childhood Sexual Abuse: the Botswana Perspectives', in *Child Sexual Abuse: Issues and Challenges*, Megan J. Smith ed. (New York: Nova Science Publishers, 2008), pp. 9–18.

40 Fleming Rutledge, *The Crucifixion: Understanding the Death of Jesus Christ* (Grand Rapids, MI: Eerdmans, 2015), p. 498.

41 Thomas R. Yoder Neufeld, *Jesus and the Subversion of Violence: Wrestling with the New Testament Evidence* (London: SPCK, 2011), pp. 1–2.

42 Gisela G. Geisler, *Women and the Remaking of Politics in Southern Africa: Negotiating Autonomy, Incorporation, and Representation* (Uppsala: Nordic Africa Institute, 2003), p. 104.

43 John P. Galvin, 'Jesus as Scapegoat?: Violence and the Sacred in the Theology of Raymund Schwager', *The Thomist: A Speculative Quarterly Review* 46:2 (1992), p. 189.

44 Giorgio Agamben, *Pilate and Jesus*, Adam Kotsko trans. (Stanford, CA: Stanford University Press, 2015).

45 Agamben, *Pilate and Jesus*, p. 3.

46 David Tombs, 'Crucifixion, State Terror, and Sexual Abuse', *Union Seminary Quarterly Review* 53:1–2 (1999), p. 96.

47 Richard J. Cassidy, *Jesus, Politics, and Society: A Study of Luke's Gospel* (Eugene, OR: Wipf and Stock, 2015). p. 65.

48 Cassidy, *Jesus, Politics, and Society*, p. 65.

49 Cassidy, *Jesus, Politics, and Society*, p. 65.

50 Ann Weatherall, 'Constituting and Responding to Domestic and Sexual Violence', *Gender and Language* 12:2 (2019), pp. 149–52.

51 Mmapula D. Kebaneilwe, 'The Vashti Paradigm: Resistance as a Strategy for Combating HIV', *The Ecumenical Review* 63:4 (2011), pp. 378–84.

52 Kebaneilwe, 'The Vashti Paradigm', p. 378.

53 Tombs, 'Crucifixion, State Terror, and Sexual Abuse', p. 96.

54 David Tombs, 'Honor, Shame and Conquest: Male Identity, Sexual Violence and the Body Politic', *Journal of Hispanic/Latino Theology* 9:2 (2002), pp. 21–40.

55 Joel B. Green, 'The Death of Jesus', *PB Handbook for the Study of the Historical Jesus*, vol. 4 (Leiden: Brill, 2011), pp. 2383–408.

56 Warren Carter, *The Roman Empire and the New Testament: An Essential Guide* (Nashville, TN: Abingdon Press, 2007), p. x.

57 Carter, *The Roman Empire and the New Testament*, p. 2.

58 Carter, *The Roman Empire and the New Testament*, p. 2.

59 Botlhoko, 'Hunt Begins for Bus Rank Stripping Thugs', p. 6.

60 Tombs, *Crucifixion, State Terror, and Sexual Abuse: Text and Context*, p. 10.

61 Tombs, 'Crucifixion, State Terror, and Sexual Abuse', p. 104.

62 Tombs, 'Crucifixion, State Terror, and Sexual Abuse', p. 104.

63 Reaves and Tombs, '#Me Too Jesus', p. 397.

64 Patricia K. Tull, *Esther and Ruth* (Louisville, KY: Westminster Press, 2003), p. 12; cited in Mmapula D. Kebaneilwe, 'This Courageous Woman: A Socio-rhetorical Womanist Reading of Proverbs 31:10–31' (unpublished PhD dissertation, Murdoch University, 2012), p. 197, http://researchrepository.murdoch.edu.au/id/eprint/16159. In this work, I explain that we have to admit the predicament that may result from a clash with the powers that be. Vashti and all the women in the land got into trouble because of her bravery in challenging oppression.

65 Tombs, 'Crucifixion, State Terror, and Sexual Abuse', p. 109.

66 Tombs, 'Crucifixion, State Terror, and Sexual Abuse', p. 109.

67 Elaine A. Heath, *We Were the Least of These: Reading the Bible with Survivors of Sexual Abuse* (Grand Rapids, MI: Brazos Press, 2011), p. 9.

PART 4

Sexual Abuse, Trauma
and the Personal

14

Jesus: A Critical Companion in the Journey to Moving on from Sexual Abuse

BETH R. CRISP

Introduction

Over a number of decades, both as a friend and as a social worker, I have been privileged to hear the stories of women and men who have experienced sexual abuse. Some of these stories have been told by survivors themselves, some have been shared by third parties, and others I have read. While every story is in some ways unique, the experience of being silenced has been a frequently recurring theme. Furthermore, breaking that silence has been crucial to a resurrection of the self, after an experience which for many has been akin to a crucifixion of the soul.

This is also my story. Not only forbidden to speak, but lacking a vocabulary for speaking about my experiences, and in particular the issues I have been presented with as a woman of faith. Some of the issues I struggled with have been documented previously in scholarly articles as well as in a book of Lenten reflections.[1] Titled *Beyond Crucifixion: Meditations on Surviving Sexual Abuse*, it was critical that my story did not end at Good Friday but rather with the promise of resurrection that is Easter Sunday. It is not 'recovery', because I can never again be the person I was prior to the abuse, but as I write now, I have moved to a point where sexual abuse is no longer a central and defining part of my life.

Recently, I have experienced a considerable shift in Australian society in respect of its preparedness to listen and acknowledge the experiences of people who have experienced sexual abuse. Internationally, the #MeToo movement represents the refusal of survivors of abuse to remain silent any longer. Each story told has not only been testimony to the strength of one individual who has challenged the silence surrounding sexual abuse, but has also acted as an invitation to others to share their stories. The same could be said about the Australian Royal Commission into Institutional Responses to Child Sexual Abuse,[2] of which many of the inquiries and recommendations concerned churches and religious institutions. One of the consequences of the Royal Commission was that by listening and taking seriously the testimonies of survivors, a 'previously hidden subject became publicly discussable, and new forms of knowledge were produced'.[3]

Drawing on my own story as well as the stories of others, this chapter considers how these new forms of knowledge may influence our understandings of survivors of sexual abuse; of God; and of what it means to be church.

#MeToo

The #MeToo movement has highlighted the silencing of survivors of sexual abuse in two forms: forbidding experiences of sexual abuse being spoken of; and marginalizing the testimonies of those who nevertheless spoke out, either by refusing to hear and acknowledge what was being said or by denigrating the speaker. One reflection on the Royal Commission was that having been heard, survivors moved from being marginalized individuals to forming a shared voice which sought to bring governments to account for failing to act to support victims and prevent abuse occurring.[4]

Church authorities have also been confronted with their failure to care. For survivors of clerical abuse, giving evidence at the Royal Commission was not only an opportunity to share their stories, but for many the process of giving testimony. This was particularly so for those who had previously been provided financial compensation by the Catholic Church. Compensation cases were often settled with recipients agreeing to remain silent. However, as a public inquiry held on behalf of the state, a Royal Commission can hear evidence which parties have previously agreed to remain confidential. As such, in the process of participating in the Royal Commission, some survivors found the care with which they were treated was what they had expected but not found in the Church.[5]

It is not as if sexual abuse is new to Christianity. Indeed, the Bible includes many texts in which rape and sexual abuse are explicit, and other texts where such behaviour is implied.[6] Yet such texts rarely find themselves included in lectionaries, or when they are, the abuse tends to be overlooked by preachers by placing the focus elsewhere. As a result, for people of faith these texts told stories with which they might resonate, but they are texts which are unfamiliar.[7] Discovering these biblical texts for myself was in some ways a #MeToo moment, in that I saw myself not on the periphery of the faithful but as one whose experiences were shared with the women and men of faith recorded in Scripture. At the time I reflected that both those subjected to sexual abuse and their abusers who appear in the pages of Scripture were similar to their contemporary counterparts for whom rape is not confined to particular sections of society. Furthermore, sexual abuse tended to be inflicted on those known to the offender rather than strangers. As such the biblical texts challenge the myths about rape that have been allowed to permeate Western societies.[8]

One of the powerful moments in dealing with my own experiences of sexual abuse came as I listened to the passion narrative on Palm Sunday more than 20 years ago.[9] As I listened to the story, the many ways in which Jesus experienced physical and emotional abuse were very apparent. These included being jeered at and mocked by the crowds, rejected and turned over to the authorities by those who were supposedly his closest and most trusted friends, sentenced to death in a legal process that denied his human rights, being struck on the head, spat upon, stripped of his clothes, and nailed on a cross that would be an excruciating way to die. The abuse suffered by Jesus was not the same as what I had endured, but at that time I could see in him an ally who understood some of the consequences of sexual abuse. In particular, Jesus was someone who had experienced repeated rejection and denial of his humanity, rather than being treated with the respect which one might contend is a human right.[10]

Like many survivors of abuse, at times the painful image of the crucified Jesus on the cross is one that I have identified with. Being confronted with his wounds can enable survivors to recognize that they too have been wounded. In doing so, 'the Crucified becomes friend instead of stranger, and resurrection is God's raising of one's belief in Self in the face of powerful messages to the contrary'.[11]

Even before the growing canon of literature that has been published over the last two decades,[12] it was being suggested to me that Jesus was a victim of sexual abuse. I realize that this is important for some people, but for me whether or not this occurred has not been something I have ever felt the need to ponder. For me it was enough that Jesus had experienced abusive acts which, although not the same as the abuse inflicted on me, led to him experiencing a sense of despair and desolation with which I was all too familiar.

#YouToo

While there are times when it is appropriate, and even necessary, to place oneself as the focus, which is what #MeToo does, permanently placing oneself at the point of focus is narcissism. In contrast, a mature Christian faith requires the capacity to gaze on the mystery of God, in order that we might come to understand how God sees us.[13] While recognizing that we may see ourselves in the crucified Jesus, we need a theology in which God is not a super human who is better than we will ever be. Rather, we need to understand God as being 'indescribably different from us' and with whom 'every encounter . . . exposes our limits, even our capacity for self-deception', but who is loving and 'limitlessly generous, desiring only to give life'.[14]

At the same time as I was working through my experiences of sexual abuse, I was also exploring Ignatian spirituality, which dates back to the mid-sixteenth century. In the Ignatian tradition you are encouraged to learn about God not by reading Scripture as a rational and detached act but rather by imagining yourself in the midst of the biblical scene and reflecting on the experience.[15] Struggling with low self-esteem, I was encouraged by a spiritual director to read the parable of the man who found a pearl of great value and sold all of his possessions so that he could purchase it (Matt. 13.45–46).[16] While it had been hoped that I might see myself as this valuable pearl and God as the one who would give all to have me, I found myself having a long conversation with God. He told me that I was loved, and I asked how this could be, given what had happened. God responded by acknowledging my feelings, but it was not until I had spoken further and told God of all the hurt I had experienced that I was in a position to hear about the love of God.[17] As such, 'The imaginative work here helped me identify my anger and my distrust of God; had these been left unaddressed, my ability to bring my relationship with God to maturity would have been hindered.'[18]

Others too have found healing from sexual abuse through engaging in ancient spiritual practices. For one group of Catholic men in Australia who had experienced sexual abuse in church contexts, the road to healing involved reworking the Stations of the Cross to incorporate their experience. Their reflection for when Jesus is nailed to the cross was as follows:

There are many truths about abuse. The truths about the institutions that failed to comprehend, the truths about men who abdicated their responsibility for the care of the other, the truths that the Royal Commission has uncovered, and more. In this station we come to the truth of the subjective experience of abuse, naked to be seen, undeniable. Yet, here you are, tougher in this moment of contemplation of the unspeakable. How have you managed to be here? What have you had to come to know about yourself in order to stand here?[19]

While turning the gaze from oneself to God can lead to healing, this can only happen if those who have experienced abuse have sufficient agency to be able to choose to do so. Sexual abuse represents a fundamental denial of human rights in which victims are rendered powerless and their bodies, minds and souls denigrated and violated. Being told that one is like Jesus because both of you have experienced sexual abuse not only may be unhelpful, but can also act as a reminder of the lack of control that is integral to sexual abuse. Moreover, it may be very difficult to dispute such suggestions if they are being made by theologians who are recognized by many in the Church as the scholarly experts about all things relating to God. A woman who had been raped was attending a theological conference when a trainee priest asked 'about the interrelationship between the mystical body of Christ and the abused body of Jesus'. Appalled that such a question was being asked, she interjected that 'There is nothing mystical about being raped.'[20]

Many survivors of sexual abuse are assumed by the wider community to have both given up on God and given up on the Church. For example, the report of the 2009 Irish Commission to Inquire into Child Abuse comprises five volumes with more than 2,500 pages of text focusing on abuse that happened in 216 residential schools which were run by several Catholic religious orders.[21] In stark contrast to detailed accounts of physical, emotional and sexual abuse being inflicted on large numbers of girls and boys, and the impacts this has had particularly in respects of long-standing mental health problems or difficulties in making or maintaining relationships, there were just 133 words devoted to the topic 'Religion now practised' in this report.

It is not surprising that many survivors come to believe that the Church was allied with their abusers or that God neglected or betrayed them when they were in need.[22] However, there are also those of us for whom making sense of our experiences after sexual abuse has led to us actively engaging with questions of faith, often in church contexts. In my own case, I would go as far as claiming that Jesus was a critical companion in the journey to moving on from sexual abuse. Yet despite the right to a religion being enshrined in the *Universal Declaration of Human Rights*, I have sometimes felt that as a survivor I have needed to defend my right to be a woman of faith, whereas the right to hold a faith was not questioned of those who were not known to have experienced sexual abuse.[23]

#WeToo

Acknowledging Jesus as a fellow victim of abuse also challenges our ecclesiology, or what it means to be church. It means taking seriously the need to consider how power and authority can privilege some members of the Church while marginalizing others, including women, children and victims of sexual abuse. Moreover, it means finding a way of being church in which respect for all humanity is the lived reality.[24]

It is important that this quest for a new ecclesiology is not just a scholarly exercise that takes place in the academy. Rather, developing a new way of being church needs theologians to actively engage with the theological questions of those who sit in the pews and may have no formal theological education. As Anglican bishop Alison Taylor has noted, 'Ordinary non-academic Christians need to hear how they can place the tragedy of institutional child sexual abuse in churches into the story of God and his people and their ways in the world.'[25]

Like Peter who denied knowing Jesus, too often churches and religious communities have sought to deny experiences of abuse inflicted in their midst.[26] As such, we have sought Easter without experiencing the pain of Good Friday. To enter into Christ's suffering, the Church is called to journey with him to the cross. It is a journey to walk on a path that 'is covered by the broken bodies of victims and survivors; lives abused, humiliated and discarded, not only by the perpetrators, but also by our institutions, by our leaders, by us'.[27]

When I listen to media coverage of inquiries into sexual abuse in churches, the portrayal of churches at times seems to consist only of clergy. Discussions of 'the Church' often do not recognize the essential presence of the laity in being the body of Christ. Whether the laity have willingly ceded power to the clergy or had it forcibly removed, church structures that are not accountable to either their membership or the wider community need to change. However, this will not be without its challenges because many people have benefitted from church structures that have placed the responsibility for the Church in the hands of the few and demanded little more than tacit agreement from the remainder.[28]

In a #WeToo church, it is not only clergy but all of us who are called to be the face of Christ to others. This call invites each of us to show the same courage and persistence to walk in solidarity with all those who have been marginalized by the Church or wider society that Jesus showed in all his earthly encounters.[29] As Dr Julia Baird in her graduation address to the University of Divinity in Melbourne in 2018 noted, when this invitation is embraced, we are being what it truly means to be church:

Vigilantes of grace would be people who, even if leadership has failed, can model love and keep an eye out for danger. For many decades, we have failed to observe and be vigilant. There is much work to do, much grinding, important work lies ahead. Some will be done one heartbeat at a time, in your parish, your street, your home. And grace will always leak through the cracks.[30]

Yet how that grace is communicated may need careful consideration. People who have experienced sexual abuse may be too traumatized to deal with 'normal' practices. For example, some years ago I wrote about a priest whose practice it was to give me a formal blessing at the end of each conversation. For him it was offering a loving gesture that was part of his priestly practice. However, at the time it felt like another act being forced onto me to which I had not given consent. As such, it acted too painfully as a reminder of the control that had been stripped away from me many years earlier by my abuser. Eventually we came to an agreement that if I wanted a blessing, I would ask.[31]

A #WeToo church also has to rethink how it understands and uses Scripture. When we embody experiences of violence and abuse, we bring this to our reading of the biblical texts. While not usually interpreted in this way, it has been proposed that the book of Revelation could be read as an invitation to make a commitment to the Christian community for the opposing of sexual violence and supporting victims of abuse.[32] In so doing, reading and responding to Scripture can become an avenue for the expression of intense and excruciating feelings. This is an important step to recognizing past injustices and taking action to ensure that they do not occur again.

Furthermore, if we allow it to, Scripture can provide a framework in which the Church can express lamentation in response to abuse:

> The voice of lament is as primal as a child's need to cry. It is a way of bearing the unbearable. It is in essence supremely human, for it refuses to accept things the way they are. The voice of lament is not an end in itself, but is undergirded by the hope that God will act with mercy and compassion. It acknowledges that healing is required by all and for all.[33]

Jesus himself provided a model of what it means to lament in a world in which cruelty and marginalization are too often the norm. He spoke up for those who could not speak for themselves and challenged those he encountered to believe that a better way of life was possible. Thus if we profess that the Church is the body of Christ on earth, ought we not to follow his example and speak out for those who need care and protection, rather than push them further to the margins of church and/or society?[34]

Conclusion

For survivors of sexual abuse, being able to identify with Jesus as someone who has experienced suffering may be critical in what can be a struggle to retain one's faith. But rather than place all the burden on survivors, a #MeToo Jesus, together with a #YouToo Jesus and a #WeToo Jesus, invites all Christians to reconsider their understanding of the divine and of what it means to be church.

Survivors of sexual abuse are among the many who look to the God of our churches in their efforts to find healing. As such, the Church needs to be a space where stories of sexual abuse that need to be told can not only be expressed but heard. Furthermore, churches need to be places where the potential for resurrection can be glimpsed, not just on Easter Sunday but throughout the year.

In 2006, while visiting New Zealand, I came across the paintings of New Zealand artist Michael Smither. The exhibition of his work, entitled 'The Wonder Years', featured paintings of domestic life interspersed with those reflecting his Catholic faith.[35] The message was that faith and domesticity were not separate domains. For me, the most powerful image was that of *The Crucifixion* (1977), in which Jesus' face has been replaced by an empty shell.[36] In the notes presented alongside this painting, Smither reflected that he felt the Church has spent disproportionately too much time emphasizing the three days of Jesus' death compared to the resurrection. I realized that this belief that crucifixion endures and resurrection is something which at most can be glimpsed, is the predicament in which many survivors of sexual abuse find themselves. That is, unless they make a conscious decision to reject crucifixion as the final word and grasp the promise of resurrection.[37]

Therefore, if Smither is right and it is the Church that has failed to come to terms with resurrection, then survivors of sexual abuse who have glimpsed the potential of resurrection have something important to offer the wider Church.

Embracing resurrection does not mean assuming that past injustices can be regarded as not having happened. When Thomas met the resurrected Jesus, the latter had changed in that he now had wounds in his hands that bore testimony to the crucifixion.[38] So too, survivors of sexual abuse will often carry marks of the wounds inflicted on them, whether physical, psychological or spiritual, for the rest of their lives. As such, resurrection is not about the removal or ignoring of scars but of embracing a future that offers hope. However, resurrection is not about romanticizing or trivializing what are often devastating effects of sexual abuse.

At times we may be painfully aware of the wounds we carry, even feeling that we are drowning in our pain and despair. The faith of a resurrection church can help us to stay afloat, but that requires a church that has had the maturity to recognize the extent of the harms that have been inflicted on individuals and communities, been able to apologise, and will be there as a source of hope and support long into the future. To date, too few of our churches at an organizational level have demonstrated that they really understand that the promise of resurrection needs to be sustained, and it is not just for Easter Sunday. Thankfully, for some of us who are survivors of sexual abuse, the community of faith includes some individuals, albeit too few, who have recognized that survivors of sexual abuse, like everyone else, have the right to share in the promise of resurrection faith but need to have their experiences and concerns listened to and validated.

References

Australian Royal Commission into Institutional Responses to Child Sexual Abuse, 2020, www.childabuseroyalcommission.gov.au/.

Brock, Megan, 'Cultural Change and Renewal: Challenges for Religious Life and the Church', in *Health and Integrity in Church and Ministry Conference Papers*, Stephen Crittendon ed., Sydney: Franciscan Friars, 2019, pp. 36–40.

Byrne, Lavinia, 'The Spiritual Exercises: A Process and a Text', in *The Way of Ignatius Loyola: Contemporary Approaches to the Spiritual Exercises*, Philip Sheldrake ed., London: SPCK, 1991.

Cahill, Desmond, '"... And what would God think?" Rebuilding Pastoral Health and Integrity After the Royal Commission into Institutional Responses to Child Sexual Abuse', in *Health and Integrity in Church and Ministry Conference Papers*, Stephen Crittendon ed., Sydney: Franciscan Friars, 2019, pp. 2–12.

City Gallery, Wellington, 'Michael Smither: The Wonder Years', 2006, https://citygallery.org.nz/exhibitions/michael-smither-the-wonder-years/.

Commission to Inquire into Child Abuse [CICA], *CICA Investigation Committee Report*, Dublin: CICA, 2009, www.childabusecommission.ie/publications/index.html.

Crisp, Beth R., 'Reading Scripture from a Hermeneutic of Rape', *Theology and Sexuality* 14 (2001), pp. 23–42.

——, 'Spiritual Direction and Survivors of Sexual Abuse', *The Way* 43:2 (2004), pp. 7–17.

——, Ignatian Spirituality and the Rebuilding of Self-esteem', *The Way* 45:1 (2006), pp. 66–78.

——, *Beyond Crucifixion: Meditations on Surviving Sexual Abuse*, London: Darton, Longman and Todd, 2010.

Crittendon, Stephen, 'Introduction', in *Health and Integrity in Church and Ministry Conference Papers*, Stephen Crittendon ed., Sydney: Franciscan Friars, p. xi–xxii.

Crysdale, Cynthia S. W., *Embracing Travail: Retrieving the Cross Today*, New York: Continuum, 1999.

Fewell, Donna Nolan, 'Imagination, Method and Murder: Un/Framing the Face of Post-exilic Israel', in *Reading Bibles, Writing Bodies: Identity and the Book*, Timothy K. Beal and David M. Gunn eds, London: Routledge, 1997, pp. 132–52.

Goulding, Gill, *Creative Perseverance: Sustaining Life-Giving Ministry in Today's Church*, Ottawa: Novalis, 2003.

Govett-Brewster Art Gallery, n.d., 'Crucifixion, Michael Smither', https://govett brewster.com/collection/71-12.

Healing in the Stations Group, *Seminar Day: The Role of Public and Private Ritual in Healing After Abuse*, Australian Province of the Society of Jesus, 2015.

Isaacs, Joan, 'Time to Get Back on the Donkey', in *Health and Integrity in Church and Ministry Conference Papers*, Stephen Crittendon ed., Sydney: Franciscan Friars, 2019, pp. 13–15.

Kirkwood, Maria, 'Implementing a Company Structure for Catholic Schools: Some Early Learnings', in *Health and Integrity in Church and Ministry Conference Papers*, Stephen Crittendon ed., Sydney: Franciscan Friars, 2019, pp. 75–7.

Lennan, Richard, 'Moving the Church: A Theology of Possibility', in *Health and Integrity in Church and Ministry Conference Papers*, Stephen Crittendon ed., Sydney: Franciscan Friars, 2019, pp. 20–8.

McPhillips, Kathleen, 'A Social Science Perspective', in *Health and Integrity in Church and Ministry Conference Papers*, Stephen Crittendon ed., Sydney: Franciscan Friars, 2019, pp. 16–19.

Marsh, Robert R., 'Imagining Ignatian Spiritual Direction', *The Way* 48:3 (2009), pp. 27–42.

Niven, Alan, 'Supervision Reframed: An Offer of Pastoral Care by the Church and a Spiritual Discipline for the Practitioner', in *Health and Integrity in Church and Ministry Conference Papers*, Stephen Crittendon ed., Sydney: Franciscan Friars, 2019, pp. 115–25.

Pippin, Tina, '"And I will strike her children dead": Death and the Deconstruction of Social Location', in *Readings from this Place: Social Location and Biblical Interpretation in the United States*, Fernando Segovia and Mary Ann Tolbert eds, vol. 1, Minneapolis, MN: Fortress Press, 1995, pp. 191–8.

Pritt, Ann F., 'Spiritual Correlates of Reported Sexual Abuse among Mormon Women', *Journal for the Scientific Study of Religion* 37 (1998), pp. 273–85.

Reaves, Jayme R., and David Tombs, '#MeToo Jesus: Naming Jesus as a Victim of Sexual Abuse', *International Journal of Public Theology* 13:4 (2019), pp. 387–412.

Sherlock, Peter, 'Foreword', in *Health and Integrity in Church and Ministry Conference Papers*, Stephen Crittendon ed., Sydney: Franciscan Friars, 2019, pp. vii–viii.

—, 'Reflections from the Vice-Chancellor', in *Health and Integrity in Church and Ministry Conference Papers*, Stephen Crittendon ed., Sydney: Franciscan Friars, 2019, pp. 131–3.

Taylor, Alison M., 'The Ecclesiology of the Whole Community Must Be Called into Account', in *Health and Integrity in Church and Ministry Conference Papers*, Stephen Crittendon ed., Sydney: Franciscan Friars, 2019, pp. 29–35.

United Nations, *Universal Declaration of Human Rights*, 1948, www.un.org/en/universal-declaration-human-rights/.

Winkett, Lucy, *Our Sound is Our Wound: Contemplative Listening in a Noisy World*, London: Continuum, 2010.

Notes

1 Beth R. Crisp, 'Reading Scripture from a Hermeneutic of Rape', *Theology and Sexuality* 14 (2001), pp. 23–42; 'Spiritual Direction and Survivors of Sexual Abuse', *The Way* 43:2 (2004), pp. 7–17; 'Ignatian Spirituality and the Rebuilding of Self-Esteem', *The Way* 45:1 (2006), pp. 66–78; *Beyond Crucifixion: Meditations on Surviving Sexual Abuse* (London: Darton, Longman and Todd, 2010).

2 Details of the Australian Royal Commission into Institutional Responses to Child Sexual Abuse can be found at www.childabuseroyalcommission.gov.au/.

3 Stephen Crittendon, 'Introduction', in *Health and Integrity in Church and Ministry Conference Papers*, Stephen Crittendon ed. (Sydney: Franciscan Friars, 2019), p. xiii, https://vox.divinity.edu.au/wp-content/uploads/2019/07/health-and-Integrity-conference-papers.pdf.

4 Kathleen McPhillips, 'A Social Science Perspective', in *Health and Integrity in Church and Ministry Conference Papers*, pp. 16–19.

5 Joan Isaacs, 'Time to Get Back on the Donkey', in *Health and Integrity in Church and Ministry Conference Papers*, pp. 13–15.

6 Crisp, 'Reading Scripture'.

7 Donna Nolan Fewell, 'Imagination, Method and Murder: Un/Framing the Face of Post-Exilic Israel', in *Reading Bibles, Writing Bodies: Identity and the Book*, Timothy K. Beal and David M. Gunn eds (London: Routledge, 1997), pp. 132–52.

8 Crisp, 'Reading Scripture'.

9 Mark 14.1—15.47.

10 Crisp, *Beyond Crucifixion*, pp. 3–4.

11 Cynthia S.W. Crysdale, *Embracing Travail: Retrieving the Cross Today* (New York: Continuum, 1999), p. 10.

12 For an overview of this literature, see Jayme R. Reaves and David Tombs, '#MeToo Jesus: Naming Jesus as a Victim of Sexual Abuse', *International Journal of Public Theology* 13:4 (2019), pp. 387–412.

13 Robert R. Marsh, 'Imagining Ignatian Spiritual Direction', *The Way* 48:3 (2009), pp. 27–42.

14 Richard Lennan, 'Moving the Church: A Theology of Possibility', in *Health and Integrity in Church and Ministry Conference Papers*, p. 21.

15 Lavinia Byrne, 'The Spiritual Exercises: A Process and a Text', in *The Way of Ignatius Loyola: Contemporary Approaches to the Spiritual Exercises*, Philip Sheldrake ed. (London: SPCK, 1991).

16 Crisp, 'Ignatian Spirituality'.

17 The full conversation has been published in Crisp, 'Ignatian Spirituality', pp. 69–70, and Crisp, *Beyond Crucifixion*, pp. 63–4.

18 Crisp, 'Ignatian Spirituality', p. 71.

19 Healing in the Stations Group, *Seminar Day: The Role of Public and Private Ritual in Healing After Abuse*, Australian Province of the Society of Jesus, 2015.

20 Desmond Cahill, '"… And What Would God Think?" Rebuilding Pastoral Health and Integrity After the Royal Commission into Institutional Responses to Child Sexual Abuse', in *Health and Integrity in Church and Ministry Conference Papers*, p. 2.

21 Commission to Inquire into Child Abuse [CICA], *CICA Investigation Committee Report* (Dublin: Commission To Inquire Into Child Abuse, 2009), www.childabusecommission.ie/publications/index.html.

22 Ann F. Pritt, 'Spiritual Correlates of Reported Sexual Abuse among Mormon Women', *Journal for the Scientific Study of Religion* 37 (1998), pp. 273–85.

23 United Nations, Universal Declaration of Human Rights (1948), www.un.org/en/universal-declaration-human-rights/.

24 Peter Sherlock, 'Reflections from the Vice-Chancellor', in *Health and Integrity in Church and Ministry Conference Papers*, pp. 131–3.

25 Alison M. Taylor, 'The Ecclesiology of the Whole Community Must Be Called into Account', in *Health and Integrity in Church and Ministry Conference Papers*, p. 30.

26 Mark 14.66–72.

27 Peter Sherlock, 'Foreword', in *Health and Integrity in Church and Ministry Conference Papers*, pp. vii–viii.

28 Maria Kirkwood, 'Implementing a Company Structure for Catholic Schools: Some Early Learnings', in *Health and Integrity in Church and Ministry Conference Papers*, pp. 75–7.

29 Megan Brock, 'Cultural Change and Renewal: Challenges for Religious Life and the Church', in *Health and Integrity in Church and Ministry Conference Papers*, pp. 36–40.

30 Alan Niven, 'Supervision Reframed: An Offer of Pastoral Care by the Church and a Spiritual Discipline for the Practitioner', in *Health and Integrity in Church and Ministry Conference Papers*, p. 117.

31 Crisp, *Beyond Crucifixion*, p. 35.

32 Tina Pippin, '"And I will strike her children dead": Death and the Deconstruction of Social Location', in *Readings from this Place: Social Location and Biblical Interpretation in the United States*, Fernando F. Segovia and Mary Ann Tolbert eds, vol. 1 (Minneapolis, MN: Fortress Press, 1995), pp. 191–8.

33 Gill Goulding, *Creative Perseverance: Sustaining Life-Giving Ministry in Today's Church* (Ottawa: Novalis, 2003), pp. 138–9.

34 Lucy Winkett, *Our Sound is Our Wound: Contemplative Listening to a Noisy World* (London: Continuum, 2010).

35 *Crucifixion* (1977) displayed in 'Michael Smither: The Wonder Years' touring exhibition, details of which can be found at https://citygallery.org.nz/exhibitions/michael-smither-the-wonder-years/.

36 *Crucifixion* (1977) by Michael Smither can be viewed at the Govett-Brewster Art Gallery at https://govettbrewster.com/collection/71-12.

37 Crisp, *Beyond Crucifixion*, p. 105.

38 John 20.24–28.

15

Surviving Trauma at the Foot of the Cross

KAREN O'DONNELL

I wake up gasping for air, my stomach clenched in violent sobs. The room around me is dark and foggy. The distance between the world and me seems insurmountable. I reach out my hands to touch something solid but everything feels unreal. I am as helpless now as I was then.

The images play through my mind on a loop. I squeeze my eyes closed to block them out, covering my face with shaking hands, but still they play, flipping across my vision faster and faster. I can't stop them.

His broken body – naked, humiliated, abused, tormented, tortured – lingers in my mind's eye. I've seen Him since, of course, scarred but remade. But I can't stop this image of Him coming to me nightly, even as I struggle to assemble the events of those days into order. I'm missing something, I know I am. Something lies just beyond my grasp.

In the day, in the sunshine, with my friends, I remember He is risen.

But every night I can't help but remember that He died.

It is no stretch of the imagination to imagine these words coming from one of the group of family members and close friends who gathered at the foot of the cross as witnesses to the sexual abuse, humiliation, torture and eventual death of Jesus at the hands of Roman soldiers.[1] The Gospel narratives never tell us what the impact of witnessing such trauma was upon this group. Implicitly, these narratives point to the resurrection as the thing that 'glosses over' the horror of the cross. This is ironic because focusing on the resurrection as the remedy and healing for trauma is exactly what contemporary theologians and pastors do frequently. Indeed, Shelly Rambo notes:

> Insofar as resurrection is proclaimed as life conquering or life victorious over death, it does not speak to the realities of traumatic suffering. In fact, one must recognize the ways in which resurrection proclamations may gloss over and negate the difficult experience of life in the aftermath of death … The rush to life can belie the realities of death in life.[2]

In their rush to the resurrection narratives, the Gospels do not tell us of the ongoing trauma of those who were gathered at the foot of the cross. The membership of this group differs, depending on the choice of Gospel narrative. In Matthew, we have Mary Magdalene, Mary the mother of James and Joseph, and the mother of the sons of Zebedee (Matt. 27.55–56). In Mark, it is Mary Magdalene, Mary the mother of James the Younger and Joses, and Salome (Mark 15.40). In Luke, the group is described as 'all his acquaintances, including the women who had followed him from Galilee' (Luke 23.49). And finally in John, the group is Mary the mother of Jesus, her sister Mary – the wife of Clopas – Mary Magdalene and the Beloved Disciple (John 19.25). Regardless, in whichever Gospel tradition you prefer, it is safe to say that a group comprised predominantly of women, made up of Jesus' close family members and friends, witnessed his sexual abuse, torture and death.

In this chapter, I highlight the possibility that those who witnessed the abuse, torture and murder of Jesus might themselves have been traumatized by this event and the complex nature of communicating trauma from witness to witness. I posit that it is possible that the early Church was marked by the trauma of these witnesses in a collective sense. I will then consider the significance of witnessing sexual trauma in particular, in the context of the contemporary Church and theological responses to sexual abuse, and examine the concept of Jesus' solidarity with the abused as an insufficient response to sexual abuse.

Absence and presence of PTSD

It is often an error to read modern medical diagnoses back into ancient texts. Caroline Walker Bynum notes, in the case of medieval women mystics:

> One should not say that medieval women suffered from anorexia nervosa (or, for that matter, from hysteria or depression – since any such syndrome must be part of a particular culture and should not per se be transferred across cultures), [however] medieval women do show striking parallels to the modern syndrome – parallels that suggest psychological and social reasons for the fact that eating and not-eating are more central images in women's lives than in men's.[3]

This is a helpful example and a cautious note. Similarly, I do not wish to diagnose these women (and the Beloved Disciple) with post-traumatic stress disorder (PTSD). However, I do wish to suggest that were these close family and friends of Jesus to witness this event today, they would probably begin to meet the criteria for such a diagnosis.

The diagnosis of PTSD is outlined in the *Diagnostic Statistical Manual of Mental Disorders* published by the American Psychiatric Association, which is now in its fifth edition (DSM-V). In these diagnosis criteria, DSM-V begins with Criterion A:

Exposure to actual or threatened death, serious injury, or sexual violence in one (or more) of the following ways:

1 Directly experiencing the traumatic event(s).
2 Witnessing, in person, the event(s) as it occurred to others.
3 Learning that the traumatic event(s) occurred to a close family member or close friend. In cases of actual or threatened death of a family member or friend, the event(s) must have been violent and unexpected.
4 Experiencing repeated or extreme exposure to aversive details of the traumatic event(s) (e.g., first responders collecting human remains; police officers repeatedly exposed to details of child abuse).[4]

A detailed list of further criteria follows, highlighting behaviours and emotions, alongside frequency of PTSD symptoms – all of which are unknown to us in the context of the Gospel narratives. However, these further criteria rest on Criterion A and here we can easily see the basis for a potential PTSD diagnosis. For those who stood at the foot of the cross and witnessed the sexual abuse, torture and murder of their friend, we can easily say they fit into category 2, 'witnessing, in person, the event(s) [death, serious injury, or sexual violence] as it occurred to others'. Furthermore, we can see how even those followers who were not at the foot of the cross – Cleopas[5] and the unnamed disciple – may also have been traumatized because learning about the violent and unexpected death of a close friend also meets the criteria for category 3.

Witnessing trauma

Witnessing has always been a vital category in trauma studies. It is through being witnessed that the trauma survivor constructs a narrative of their trauma that can help make sense of their experience and bring life where death has reigned. In this sense, the one who witnesses – the listener – is part of the creation of knowledge of trauma. In his ground-breaking text on witnessing to trauma, Dori Laub – a Holocaust survivor, psychiatrist and psychotherapist – highlights the role of the one who witnesses: 'the listener to trauma comes to be participant and a co-owner of the traumatic event: through his very listening he comes to partially experience trauma in himself'.[6] For those who witnessed Jesus' violent abuse and death, witnessing takes on a complex relationship with trauma. Not only are those witnesses trauma victims themselves by the very act of having seen what happened to Jesus, but they are also involved in the complex transmission of trauma to those who were not there – those who witness, in turn, to the witnesses – through their testimony. Those of us who read the biblical narratives today see only the trace footprints of trauma in the text. Instead, we see the absence. Indeed, as Laub notes:

The victim's narrative – the very process of bearing witness to massive trauma – does indeed begin with someone who testifies to an absence, to an event that has not yet come into existence, in spite of the overwhelming and compelling nature of the reality of its occurrence.[7]

We testify to the absence of the event of trauma in the Gospel narratives. In the construction of this chapter – an imagined trauma narrative – we testify to the absence that marks the presence of trauma.

Early Church and trauma

In a previous publication, I argued that the reason the early Church does not seem to connect their celebrations of the Eucharist to the death of Jesus on the cross (in quite the same way that we do today) is because for the early Church the celebration of the Eucharist is not death-focused but life-focused, remembering the Annunciation-Incarnation event in a holistic manner.[8] However, liturgical scholar Dirk Lange argues that the absence of the cross from these early eucharistic liturgies is explained by acknowledging the lingering impact of trauma on the early Christian community. He writes:

> The return of something inaccessible in event is perhaps best witnessed in an early church document, the *Didache* ... The chapters that refer to an early Eucharistic celebration were probably recorded fifteen to twenty years after the event known as the crucifixion of Jesus. It is therefore astounding that the way in which Jesus is remembered in this liturgical document is not by images of the cross but by a sharing of bread and wine. In fact, the Eucharistic celebration in this document makes no (explicit) mention of the cross.[9]

Lange posits that this disruption of remembering in the liturgical event is due to the impact of trauma on the community. This ritual celebration points toward the inaccessibility of the traumatic event.

While I am unconvinced of Lange's explanation for the absence of the cross in these early Christian eucharistic celebrations, because I find the early Christian focus on life rather than death in these celebrations more compelling, it seems likely that we should expect to see some impact on the early Christian community of witnessing such a traumatic event. Various scholars have tried to identify this impact in different ways. For example, Serene Jones considers the story of Cleopas and the other disciple on the road to Emmaus to be a 'tale of trauma and survival'.[10] Similarly, Rambo situates Mary Magdalene as a trauma survivor in her experience at the empty tomb on Easter Sunday.[11]

The Gospel narratives are the narrative constructions of the early Church – a key element in post-traumatic remaking – based on what is necessary for life, rather than the true remembering of trauma and death. These narratives are born out of collective memory. Such memory is a collective social phenomenon and socially constructed.[12] Where cultural memory is acquired through social exchange, as in the oral tradition and community life of the early Church, so is cultural trauma. This cultural memory is not confined to those living in the immediate aftermath of the death of Jesus, but rather is passed along, with cultural trauma, through lines of religious inheritance. Sarat, Davidovitch and Albertstein note:

> Emphasis on social construction and the use of cultural narratives as a means to explain the self, produced a shift in trauma analysis by tying it to broad social structures (including structural violence) and moving it away from the individual as a primary unit of inquiry. Instead, collective identity becomes the unit of analysis and a group that shares an identity such as ethnicity, gender, or religion, is considered as the primary unit that experiences trauma.[13]

Does it do a disservice to those who experience horrific moments of trauma, or those who live in situations of complex, ongoing trauma, to argue that all Christians are traumatized through their religious inheritance of cultural trauma? Yes, I believe it does. And I do not wish to argue so. What I do want to recover, however, is twofold: first, the recovery (or uncovering) of the nature of the violence and sexual abuse in the torture that led to Jesus' death, and second, the impact this had on those who stood at the foot of the cross.

In relation to the first point, the uncovering of the nature of the violence and sexual abuse that Jesus suffered at the hands of those persecuting him allows a fresh consideration of the cross. This method of torture and crucifixion suffers from the contempt of familiarity. We are so accustomed to hearing the Gospel narratives – with all their absences and elisions – and so used to seeing the graceful body of Jesus on the crucifix that the cross has lost some of its power to shock and repulse us. Uncovering the sexual element of Jesus' abuse and torture helps us to consider the cross with fresh eyes, particularly from the vantage point of a society that is wrestling with experiences of sexual abuse and questions of belief in those who report it. As to the recovery/uncovering of the second point, I have already demonstrated that we should not assume that the group of relatives and close friends were unaffected by the experience of witnessing this torture and abuse as they stood at the foot of the cross.

If we allow these two ideas to impact us in the present day, what might it mean for us as contemporary Christians to witness the violent torture, abuse and death of Jesus from our perspective at the foot of the cross, both as those who are heirs to a cultural and religious inheritance that bears this memory within it, and as those who read, perform and experience this narrative through the biblical texts and the Church's liturgies? What might it mean to take seriously both the possibility of Jesus' own sexual abuse as part of his crucifixion and alongside it the possibility that those who witnessed his death were traumatized by the sexual abuse they witnessed?

The problem with solidarity

One possible theological response to the suffering and death of Jesus on the cross is to view it in terms of solidarity. We often hear it declared that Jesus suffered unimaginable pain, humiliation, anguish and distance from God, therefore we have a saviour who is able to empathize with our own experiences of suffering, pain, humiliation, anguish and despair. Jesus is in solidarity with us in these experiences. This is central to Jürgen Moltmann's thesis in *The Crucified God*, where he notes:

> In Jesus he [God] does not die the natural death of a finite being, but the violent death of the criminal on the cross, the death of complete abandonment by God. The suffering in the passion of Jesus is abandonment, rejection by God, his Father ... He humbles himself and takes upon himself the eternal death of the godless and the godforsaken, so that all the godless and the godforsaken can experience communion with him ... There is no loneliness and no rejection which he has not taken to himself and assumed in the cross of Jesus.[14]

Solidarity – between us and Jesus, through his suffering and death on the cross – is key. It is an argument taken up by many other theologians and those engaged in pastoral care, and an overview of literature indicates that some people do find the concept of solidarity to be powerful and comforting.[15] To an extent, I can agree. In the days following a miscarriage, I really valued the care and comfort of women who had experienced miscarriages themselves, who knew my pain and could grieve with me. In the moment of my loss, their solidarity was important.

However, I find the concept of solidarity alone to be insufficient for three reasons. In the first instance, I am unconvinced that the specificity of Jesus' suffering and death on the cross is a compelling enough argument to make for solidarity. If I were to say to victims of sexual assault and abuse that they should take comfort in the fact that Jesus too was sexually abused and assaulted, they may find comfort there, but what about all the other forms of suffering – the long-drawn-out illness, the pain and grief of a miscarriage, the complex trauma of domestic violence – that are not represented in their specificity on the cross? Where is the solidarity here? Surely Jesus' solidarity with us is revealed far more strongly through his life rather than his death? The location of redemption and Jesus' solidarity with us is challenged by a number of theologians, including Delores Williams, who reminds us that 'humankind is, then, redeemed through Jesus' *ministerial* vision of life and not through his death. There is nothing divine in the blood of the cross.'[16] Williams moves away from the cross as part of a resistance to the black woman's surrogacy experience. I am taken by a focus on the life of Jesus, over and above his death, as a place of any potential solidarity between Jesus and us. Not to say that Jesus experiences all of the specificities of suffering a human being can, but rather that if we are looking for solidarity of experiences, we are more inclined to see such solidarity (and redemption in Williams' terms) in Jesus' life lived – in friendships, in family relationships, in prayer, in celebration, in growth, in sadness, in laughter.

My second frustration with solidarity is that it makes too quick a turn to resurrection. Solidarity through Jesus' suffering on the cross is given significance because that same suffering is followed by the resurrection, which can give hope that our own suffering will be similarly followed by a relief from that suffering. As I noted at the outset of this chapter, trauma theologies resist too quick a turn to the resurrection because it does not do justice to the ongoing experience and realities of living with trauma. Rambo notes:

> The redemptive narrative of the cross and resurrection is often read in a linear fashion in which life (resurrection) is victorious over death. While this outlook can provide a sense of promise and hope, the linear reading of life over-and-against death runs certain dangers. It can gloss over difficulty, casting it within a larger framework in which the new replaces the old, and in which good inevitably wins out over evil. Death is concluded and new life is ushered in ... This thrust toward life can foster Christian triumphalism and supersessionism (sic). If redemption is depicted as a happy or victorious ending in which life wins out over death, or in which death is somehow concluded/ended, such a depiction runs the risk of glossing over a more mixed experience of death and life.[17]

Rambo's solution to this is to dwell in the liminal period of Holy Saturday where death has been experienced and there is not yet the hope of the resurrection. It is only from here that we witness to the experience of trauma and move towards the resurrection with all the promise and hope it may bring.

Finally, solidarity is insufficient. I find myself wondering 'so what?' What does it matter if Jesus knows what it is like to suffer in a way akin to my own suffering? Perhaps that might offer a moment of fleeting comfort to me. However, solidarity without any movement towards changing the circumstances that cause me to suffer is futile, especially if that one is able to enact change. Simply saying 'I know how you feel' and being able to empathize with someone's experience is a good starting point but it should not be the end point.

I am not rejecting the concept of solidarity. I am convinced that solidarity is an essential aspect of Christian life. As one committed to left-wing politics throughout my life, I am convinced that it is through solidarity with the other that progress is accomplished and society improved. I do not reject solidarity as a significant element to the purpose of the death of

Jesus on the cross. I simply find it insufficient in and of itself in this context. If I am to look upon the cross of Christ and find meaning there, solidarity alone is not enough.

Perhaps we could reframe solidarity as Diane Elam does, adopting the form of 'groundless solidarity' that she proposes in *Feminism and Deconstruction*.[18] Here Elam proposes that:

> Groundless solidarity is a possibility of a community which is not grounded in the truth of a prosocial identity. Solidarity forms the basis, although not the foundation, for political actions and ethical responsibility. That is to say, groundless solidarity is a stability but not an absolute one; it can be the object of conflict and need not mean consensus.[19]

Elam's proposal is helpful in that it moves us beyond the specificity of solidarity and the dichotomy that polarizes individuality from community. This solidarity is characterized as an alliance based on the notion of shared ethical commitment that recognizes differences between individuals and the other, but allows the other to partake in community. It is groundless because community is constantly shifting across nonessential commonalities. Individual singularities are ungrounded and unfixed, and separate from each other.[20]

Therefore an appeal to a 'groundless solidarity' might allow for a broader sense of solidarity that is not based on the commonality of similar traumas, but rather recognizes the constantly shifting nature of community and the differences between the individual and the other. For Elam, this solidarity leads to an ethical activism that recognizes that solidarity alone is insufficient but requires action to change the circumstances of injustice.[21]

This 'groundless solidarity' begins to address some of the concerns I have outlined with regard to the theme of solidarity in general. However, solidarity with Jesus on the cross falls short of this 'groundless solidarity' for me because it lacks the ethical activism essential to the outworking of such solidarity. What kind of ethical activism can there be in this dialogue of 'groundless solidarity'? We, in solidarity with Jesus, cannot change the circumstances of his abuse and death. He, in his death, cannot change the experience of sexual abuse that the sexual abuse survivor has experienced. Perhaps the ethical activism essential to this 'groundless solidarity' is to be found in the action of witnessing to the trauma survivor and, in love, making space for post-traumatic remaking.

Surviving trauma at the foot of the cross

Those who stood at the foot of the cross were witnesses to the humiliation, torture, abuse and murder of Jesus. They were then also witnesses to the wider world – their community of disciples in the first instance, but ultimately a much broader scope of witnesses – of what had happened to Jesus.

It is this term 'witness' that I want to draw upon as a helpful addition to 'groundless solidarity': an active, ethical response to the trauma survivor.

Witnessing is, as I have already noted, an essential concept in trauma studies. As a trauma survivor constructs their trauma narrative – a key element to post-traumatic remaking – it must be witnessed and believed by others. In trauma theology, this witnessing community has been much emphasized as a role that the Church can play in supporting survivors of trauma. Hearing and believing survivors of trauma – particularly survivors of sexual assault – is a topic subject to much contemporary discussion and debate.[22] Since the explosion of the #MeToo movement in 2017, hearing and believing survivors of sexual trauma has been the subject of much debate and angst. At one end of the spectrum is the 'due process' approach which does not believe a survivor's testimony of abuse without corroborating evidence (of which there is often very little in cases of sexual assault and abuse), with further arguments being made against the reliability of trauma survivors' memories.

The other side of this spectrum is the 'believe women' approach. The hashtag #believewomen rose to prominence at the time of the hearings for Brett Kavanaugh's nomination to the US Supreme Court. In those hearings, Christine Blasey Ford testified that Kavanaugh had sexually assaulted her and she was not believed.[23] The hashtag was meant to indicate that false allegations of sexual assault are far less common than true allegations and that no victim – facing the kind of backlash Blasey Ford experienced – makes such allegations lightly.[24]

Contemporary culture has begun to take seriously the idea of witnessing to trauma as an essential part of post-traumatic remaking. A recent Netflix series, *Unbelievable*, explored these issues with great sensitivity, reflecting powerfully on what it meant to be believed as a trauma survivor and the connections between belief, gender and socio-economic power.[25] Similarly, the podcast *Believed*, broadcast by NPR, explores the case of Olympic gymnastics doctor Larry Nassar, who abused hundreds of women and girls for decades, and the significance for these women and girls of being believed for their post-traumatic remaking.[26]

More than just solidarity between Jesus and ourselves, the humiliation, abuse, torture and death of Jesus calls us to witness. Recognizing those who stood at the foot of the cross and both witnessed and subsequently witnessed *to* these events as survivors of trauma themselves, we see the vital role that witnessing plays in post-traumatic remaking. To return to the work of Laub, witnessing is not simply speaking and listening, but rather the witness co-births the knowledge of the traumatic event in their relationship with the survivor. Being witnessed is, for Laub, imperative to survival.[27]

In her reflections on Mary Magdalene's experiences in the Johannine Gospel, Rambo explores Mary Magdalene's role as witness to the resurrected Jesus. She writes:

What *kind of presence* can witness to an absence? ... witness would demand a loving presence, the voice of love calling someone out of death. It is a love breaking into the scene of death, proclaiming life in the face of death. It is powerful and victorious, love that breaks the stranglehold of death ... Love itself is a remainder. It is a survivor. It does not break into the scene of death but is instead birthed through death and persists in the fractured *between* space, where life is an impossibility. It is a kind of *presence* birthed through absence. This is not just a narrative of human love persisting in the wake of violence; it is the narrative of divine love surviving a death.[28]

As ever, I want to resist a turn to any kind of victory as a necessary component of witnessing. While I appreciate that some people may experience the resurrection as a promise of future victory over their situations, this is not true of many trauma survivors who will probably bear the wounds of trauma in their bodies for a lifetime. Post-traumatic remaking in this context is not recovery. Indeed, I am careful to avoid the term 'trauma recovery' wherever possible as it does a disservice to the actual experience of putting oneself together in the aftermath of trauma. This rebuilding of the self will result in the construction of a new self rather than a recovery of the self that was.[29] The phrase 'post-traumatic remaking' is a far more accurate description of the activity of the survivor in the aftermath of trauma.

Entwined with *witness*, then, is *love*: a love that calls the trauma survivor out of death; a love that survives. Perhaps this is the hope a trauma survivor can see in the broken, tortured and abused body of Jesus on the cross – that love, or at least this love anyway, survives. And this love is strong enough to call the trauma survivor out of death.

In this love, I find a turn to *a* resurrection, but not *the* resurrection. Rather than Jesus' resurrection, I draw upon the resurrection of Lazarus (John 11). At the death of his friend Lazarus, Jesus is deeply upset by the distress of Lazarus' sisters Mary and Martha. The Gospel writer says '[W]hen Jesus saw her weeping, and the Jews who came with her also weeping, he was greatly disturbed in spirit and deeply moved' (John 11.33). Jesus weeps with those he loves after their loss and in that love calls Lazarus out from death. This resurrection is not a final, triumphant, glorious resurrection as in the case of Jesus' own resurrection (after all, we should assume that Lazarus did eventually die again), but of love witnessing to our suffering and distress, love calling us out from death, and love surviving. In this narrative we find a counter-narrative to both the triumphant resurrection narratives and to the insufficiency of solidarity. This love is the love of the community that pleads with God on behalf of the one in death. Both Martha and Mary, as well as the Jewish community around them, indicate that they believe Jesus could have prevented the death of their brother. Their distress greatly disturbs Jesus and he calls Lazarus out of death. The love that witnesses and acts on behalf of the trauma survivor is both the love of the community around them and the love of God.

Witness, love and survival are the three terms I offer as the ethical activism essential to the reframed idea of 'groundless solidarity'. Witnessing the cross of Christ calls us to witness to each other in our vulnerabilities and to recognize the cross itself as a form of witness, known only through the testimony of trauma survivors. And they are survivors. Older accounts of trauma define it as a missed encounter with death; an experience in which one should have died but did not.[30] For many reasons this definition is unhelpful and inaccurate but it does speak to the *survival* of those who have experienced trauma. They are not victims but survivors. Love survives trauma and the divine love is strong enough to call trauma survivors out of death.

Liturgical witness

The place where many Christians encounter the passion and death of Christ most regularly is in the eucharistic liturgy. The Eucharist has been of particular interest to trauma theologians because it is focused on memory and repetition ('Do this in remembrance of me'), which are also central elements to understanding trauma. Studies in Eucharist and trauma seem to be circling around the same ideas.

For the sexual abuse survivor (or a survivor of any other kind of trauma), an encounter with this liturgy – particularly in the context of Easter but similarly in the eucharistic liturgy around the year – could be a profound opportunity for liturgical witness to their trauma and offer a space for post-traumatic remaking.[31] I am reminded here of the wealth of creative feminist work in the realm of liturgy, not least that of Rosemary Radford Ruether in her text *Women-Church*, which encompasses a wide range of liturgical rites including a chapter on rites for overcoming patriarchal violence (of which sexual assault is one facet).[32] These rites take place in small groups, taking the experience of the body seriously and as central to the rite, and offering the survivor space to speak and be heard. They witness to the survivor's trauma and offer a loving response that calls the survivor out from death.

What would a eucharistic liturgy that offered the same opportunities look like? What might it mean to witness to each other's vulnerabilities in love through the breaking of bread and the pouring out of wine? I offer below an experiment in such a eucharistic liturgy. In this rite, I have drawn together research on trauma, understanding of post-traumatic remaking, the perspective of the sexual assault survivor, and my own work on witnessing, love and survival in dialogue with biblical texts, the materials of Christian ritual, and the familiar rubric of the liturgy. I suggest this liturgy, if it is ever used, is done in very small groups where all know and consent to exactly what will take place and that serious consideration is given to location, presider, witnesses, and even time of day. The goal of this liturgy is to aid and equip the sexual assault survivor for the task of post-traumatic remaking, and it is imperative that the survivor is not re-traumatized in the process.

A (Quite Feminist) Eucharistic Liturgy for Sexual Assault Survivors (according to the Church of England rubric)[33]

The Lord be with you. **And also with you.**

Lift up your hearts. **We lift them to the Lord.**

Let us give thanks to the Lord our God. **It is right to give thanks and praise.**

God of life, who breathes life-giving Spirit into our bodies, who wept for Lazarus and called him out of death, who weeps for us in our sorrow, with our sisters Dinah, Tamar, Hagar, Bathsheba and Bilhah, we ask why you have turned your face from us in the hour of our most need.

In our rage and sorrow, we wonder why you did not save us from pain and anguish, why you did not rescue us.

We stand with the unnamed women throughout history who know our pain and witness to our distress and we hear you, as Lazarus did, call us out of death and into remaking.

Though it pains our hearts, we give you thanks, with angels and archangels, and all the company of heaven who witness to our distress, singing the hymn of your unending praise.

Holy, holy, holy Lord, God of power and might.
Heaven and earth are full of your glory.
Hosanna in the highest.
Blessed is he who comes in the name of the Lord.
Hosanna in the highest.

Self-giving God, in the Eucharist we are brought near to the agony of the cross, to the torture, abuse, humiliation and death of your dear Son Jesus. We cry out 'Is there any sorrow like my sorrow?' and you witness our cry from the cross, in love that calls us out from death.

Come now, comforting Spirit. Remake us whole and one body in Christ. Open our graves, loosen our tongues, release our imaginations: remake all that has been lost to us, that we need not cling to our pain but be remade in love that is stronger than death.

The sexual assault survivor(s) stands. The presider sprinkles them with holy water saying:

You are clean and holy already. May this water, which brings life and quenches thirst, be for you a mark of your remaking.

The presider anoints the forehead of the sexual assault survivor(s) with oil saying:
Precious child, in the midst of darkness, you are loved.

The presider anoints the hands of the sexual assault survivor(s) with oil saying:
These hands are anointed for your remaking, remembering that you have a community with you that witnesses your anguish and joins in your remaking. Be blessed, be loved, and be part of this body.

Send down your Holy Spirit that this bread of sustenance and wine of joy may be for us the body and blood of your Son Jesus Christ. Who, at supper with his disciples, took bread, gave you thanks, broke the bread, and gave it to them, saying, 'Take, eat: this is my body which is given for us; do this in remembrance of me.' After supper, he took the cup. Again he gave you thanks, and gave it to his disciples, saying, 'Drink this, all of you: this is my blood of the new covenant, which is shed for you and for many in the forgiveness of sins. Do this, as often as you drink it, in remembrance of me.'

Great is the mystery of faith. **Christ has died; Christ is risen; Christ will come again.**

A Prayer to God

Our Mother who is within us
we celebrate your many names.
Your wisdom come; your will be done,
unfolding from the depths within us.
Each day you give us all that we need.
You remind us of our limits and we let go.
You support us in our power and we act with courage.
For you are the dwelling place within us,
the empowerment around us,
and the celebration among us,
now and for ever. Blessed be![34]

The Peace

We, who have no peace and desperately seek it, turn to you, our brothers and sisters, and to you, O Mother, that you might share with us the peace that passes all understanding.
We share the sign of peace by either making eye contact and blessing each other or by passing a flame around from small candle to small candle (avoiding physical contact with the other unless requested).

In the distribution of bread and wine the presider may say:
The body of Christ, witnessing your body.
Blood of Christ, keeping you in love.

Ever-present God,
You stand in solidarity with all those who suffer; may this shared meal join us with all who labour for justice.
You witness to our trauma in your vulnerability; may our memory of your death allow us to witness to our own vulnerabilities and begin the task of remaking ourselves.
You call us to remake ourselves in our anguish; may the bread and wine we share today nourish our spirits and give us strength for the task ahead.
Bless our bodies, broken and pained, as your body was, that we might become one body in Christ, reconnecting with our loved ones and rebuilding our lives.
Fill us with your peace and let us hear the call of love that brings us out of darkness, in communion with all those who witness to our vulnerabilities in love and compassion, through whom and with whom and in whom comes all comfort and peace, Creator, Sustainer, Comforter, one God, now and for ever. **Amen.**

Loving witness

Recovering or re-imagining sexual assault as part of Jesus' experience in the journey to his death gives us an opportunity to reconsider the cross in all its agony and horror once again and be horrified by it. This may have the first effect of putting us in solidarity with sexual assault survivors, but, as I have argued, solidarity alone is not enough. This solidarity is reframed as a 'groundless solidarity' that accounts for the shifting sense of commonality and the distinction between the individual and the other. As this 'groundless solidarity' establishes a claim for ethical activism, it must take a turn into loving witness – from both the Divine and the human community – that gives space for both the construction of knowledge about trauma and also the task of post-traumatic remaking.

Those who stood at the foot of Jesus' cross and witnessed his torture, humiliation and eventual death face a multitude of directions. They face the cross and witness the death of a close relative or dear friend. They face themselves as they are traumatized through their witnessing of this trauma. They face the world as they witness to the reality of Jesus' experience and the genuineness of his death (most important in the light of his subsequent resurrection). These women (and the Beloved Disciple) demonstrate to us what it might mean to witness to sexual assault survivors in our churches today. To witness not only their experiences but also to the vulnerabilities within each of us and to give space in our witnessing for the task of post-traumatic remaking. This space is the portal to the tomb of Lazarus – black and hopeless – into which the voice of God speaks and calls us out of death.

References

American Psychiatric Association, *Diagnostic and Statistical Manual of Mental Disorder*, 5th edn, Arlington, VA: American Psychiatric Association, 2013.

Brison, Susan J., *Aftermath: Violence and the Remaking of a Self*, Princeton, NJ: Princeton University Press, 2002.

Bruni, Frank, 'Christine Blasey Ford's Riveting, Persuasive Testimony', *The New York Times*, 27 September 2018, www.nytimes.com/2018/09/27/opinion/christine-blasey-ford-kavanaugh-testimony.html.

Bynum, Caroline Walker, *Fragmentation and Redemption: Essays on Gender and the Human Body in Mediaeval Religion*, 2nd edn, New York: Zone Books, 1992.

Caruth, Cathy, *Unclaimed Experience: Trauma, Narrative, and History*, Baltimore, MD: The Johns Hopkins University Press, 1996.

Cholodenko, Lisa, Michael Dinner and Susannah Grant, *Unbelievable*, Netflix, September 2019.

Doyle, Sady, '"Believe Women" Has Never Meant "Ignore Facts"', *ELLE*, 29 November 2017, www.elle.com/culture/career-politics/a13977980/me-too-movement-false-accusations-believe-women/.

Elam, Diane, *Feminism and Deconstruction*, London: Routledge, 1994.

Hess, Cynthia, *Sites of Violence, Sites of Grace: Christian Nonviolence and the Traumatised Self*, Plymouth: Lexington Books, 2009.

Jones, Serene, 'Emmaus Witnessing: Trauma and the Disordering of the Theological Mind', *Union Seminary Quarterly Review* (2002), pp. 113–28.

Lange, Dirk G., *Trauma Recalled: Liturgy, Disruption, and Theology*, Minneapolis, MN: Fortress Press, 2010.

Laub, Dori, 'Bearing Witness or the Vicissitudes of Listening', in *Testimony: Crisis of Witnessing in Literature, Psychoanalysis, and History*, Shoshana Felman and Dori Laub eds, New York & London: Routledge, 1992, pp. 57–74.

Llewellyn, Dawn, *Reading, Feminism, and Spirituality: Troubling the Waves*, London: Palgrave Macmillan, 2015.

Michigan Radio and National Public Radio, 'Believed', 2018.

Moltmann, Jürgen, *The Crucified God*, London: SCM Press, 2013.

O'Donnell, Karen, *Broken Bodies: The Eucharist, Mary and the Body in Trauma Theology*, London: SCM Press, 2018.

Rambo, Shelly, 'Between Death and Life: Trauma, Divine Love, and the Witness of Mary Magdalene', *Studies in Christian Ethics* 18 (2005), pp. 7–21.

—, *Spirit and Trauma: A Theology of Remaining*, Louisville, KY: Westminster John Knox Press, 2010.

Reaves, Jayme R. and David Tombs, '#MeToo Jesus: Naming Jesus as a Victim of Sexual Abuse', *International Journal of Public Theology* 13:4 (2019), pp. 387–412.

Riswold, Carolyn, 'Our Mother...', *Patheos*, 27 January 2014, www.patheos.com/blogs/carynriswold/2014/01/our-mother/.

Ruether, Rosemary Radford, *Women-Church: Theology and Practice of Feminist Liturgical Communities*, Eugene, OR: Wipf & Stock, 2001.

Sarat, Austin, Nadav Davidovitch and Michal Alberstein, 'Trauma and Memory: Between Individual and Collective Experiences', in *Trauma and Memory: Reading, Healing, and Making Law*, Austin Sarat, Nadav Davidovitch and Michal Alberstein eds, Stanford, CA: Stanford University Press, 2007, pp. 3–20.

Scarsella, Hilary Jerome, 'Belief: A Practice of Resistance to the Alchemy of Reality into Incoherence', in *Feminist Trauma Theologies: Body, Church, and Scripture in Critical Perspective*, Karen O'Donnell and Katie Cross eds, London: SCM Press, 2020, pp. 59–82.

Tombs, David, 'Crucifixion, State Terror, and Sexual Abuse', *Union Seminary Quarterly Review* 53:1–2 (1999), pp. 89–109.

Williams, Delores S., *Sisters in the Wilderness: The Challenge of Womanist God-Talk* 2nd edn, Maryknoll, NY: Orbis Books, 2013.

Yusin, Jennifer, 'Postcolonial Trauma', in *Trauma and Literature*, J. Roger Kurtz ed., Cambridge: Cambridge University Press, 2018, pp. 239–54.

Notes

1 For the purposes of this chapter, I will be drawing on David Tombs' and Jayme Reaves' argument that Jesus' torture and death included elements of sexual abuse in the naked exposure and public humiliation Jesus experienced on his way to the cross. Fuller accounts of this argument can be found in David Tombs, 'Crucifixion, State Terror, and Sexual Abuse', *Union Seminary Quarterly Review* 53:1–2 (1999), pp. 89–109; Jayme Reaves and David Tombs, '#MeToo Jesus: Naming Jesus as a Victim of Sexual Abuse', *International Journal of Public Theology* 13:4 (2019), pp. 387–412.

2 Shelly Rambo, *Spirit and Trauma: A Theology of Remaining* (Louisville, KY: Westminster John Knox Press, 2010), p. 7.

3 Caroline Walker Bynum, *Fragmentation and Redemption: Essays on Gender and the Human Body in Mediaeval Religion*, 2nd edn (New York: Zone Books, 1992), p. 140.

4 American Psychiatric Association, *Diagnostic and Statistical Manual of Mental Disorder*, 5th edn (Arlington, VA: American Psychiatric Association, 2013), p. 271.

5 Cleopas is named as one of the two disciples walking to Emmaus. The Gospel of John names his wife Mary as one of the women at the foot of the cross. It is easy to imagine a husband comforting a horrified wife as she returned home after Jesus' death to tell him of what had happened to their good friend (or possibly nephew) Jesus.

6 Dori Laub, 'Bearing Witness or the Vicissitudes of Listening', in *Testimony: Crisis of Witnessing in Literature, Psychoanalysis, and History*, Shoshana Felman and Dori Laub eds (New York & London: Routledge, 1992), p. 57.

7 Laub, 'Bearing Witness or the Vicissitudes of Listening', p. 57.

8 Karen O'Donnell, *Broken Bodies: The Eucharist, Mary and the Body in Trauma Theology* (London: SCM Press, 2018), pp. 56–7.

9 Dirk G. Lange, *Trauma Recalled: Liturgy, Disruption, and Theology* (Minneapolis, MN: Fortress Press, 2010), p. 9.

10 Serene Jones, *Trauma and Grace: Theology in a Ruptured World* (Louisville, KY: Westminster John Knox Press, 2009), p. 24.

11 Shelly Rambo, 'Between Death and Life: Trauma, Divine Love, and the Witness of Mary Magdalene', *Studies in Christian Ethics* 18 (2005), pp. 7–21.

12 Jennifer Yusin, 'Postcolonial Trauma', in *Trauma and Literature*, J. Roger Kurtz ed. (Cambridge: Cambridge University Press, 2018), p. 272.

13 Austin Sarat, Nadav Davidovitch and Michal Alberstein, 'Trauma and Memory: Between Individual and Collective Experiences', in *Trauma and Memory: Reading, Healing, and Making Law*, Austin Sarat, Nadav Davidovitch and Michal Alberstein eds (Stanford, CA: Stanford University Press, 2007), p. 7.

14 Jürgen Moltmann, *The Crucified God* (London: SCM Press, 2013), p. 286.

15 For positive evaluations of this divine solidarity for trauma survivors, see Jones, *Trauma and Grace*; Cynthia Hess, *Sites of Violence, Sites of Grace: Christian Nonviolence and the Traumatised Self* (Plymouth: Lexington Books, 2009).

16 Delores S. Williams, *Sisters in the Wilderness: The Challenge of Womanist God-Talk*, 2nd edn (Maryknoll, NY: Orbis Books, 2013), p. 167.

17 Rambo, *Spirit and Trauma*, pp. 6–7.

18 Diane Elam, *Feminism and Deconstruction* (London: Routledge, 1994), pp. 105–15.

19 Elam, *Feminism and Deconstruction*, p. 109.

20 Dawn Llewellyn, *Reading, Feminism, and Spirituality: Troubling the Waves* (London: Palgrave Macmillan, 2015), p. 61.

21 Elam, *Feminism and Deconstruction*, p. 105.

22 For an excellent account of the current debate around believing survivors of trauma and the psychological underpinnings at play in this debate, see Hilary Jerome Scarsella, 'Belief: A Practice of Resistance to the Alchemy of Reality into Incoherence', in *Feminist Trauma Theologies: Body, Church, and Scripture in Critical Perspective*, Karen O'Donnell and Katie Cross eds (London: SCM Press, 2020), pp. 59–82.

23 Frank Bruni, 'Christine Blasey Ford's Riveting, Persuasive Testimony', *The New York Times*, 27 September 2018, www.nytimes.com/2018/09/27/opinion/christine-blasey-ford-kavanaugh-testimony.html.

24 Sady Doyle, '"Believe Women" Has Never Meant "Ignore Facts"', *ELLE*, 29 November 2017, www.elle.com/culture/career-politics/a13977980/me-too-movement-false-accusations-believe-women/.

25 Lisa Cholodenko, Michael Dinner and Susannah Grant, *Unbelievable* (Netflix, September 2019).

26 Michigan Radio and National Public Radio, 'Believed' (2018).

27 Laub, 'Bearing Witness'.

28 Rambo, 'Between Death and Life', pp. 19–20. Italics in original.

29 For a fuller account of post-traumatic remaking of the self, see Susan J. Brison, *Aftermath: Violence and the Remaking of a Self* (Princeton, NJ: Princeton University Press, 2002).

30 Cathy Caruth, *Unclaimed Experience: Trauma, Narrative, and History* (Baltimore, MD: The Johns Hopkins University Press, 1996), p. 62.

31 I have previously outlined the ways in which eucharistic liturgy might have potential for post-traumatic remaking. See *Broken Bodies*, pp 179–80.

32 Rosemary Radford Ruether, *Women-Church: Theology and Practice of Feminist Liturgical Communities* (Eugene, OR: Wipf & Stock, 2001).

33 As a lay member of the Church of England, I feel free to construct new eucharistic liturgies that meet the needs of trauma survivors. I recognize, of course, the difficulties that ordained ministers may have in using such liturgies. I have tried to keep this reimagined liturgy broadly in the shape of a traditional Anglican eucharistic liturgy in order that some brave priests might be able to use it.

34 Prayer by Miriam Therese Winters, cited in Caryn Riswold, 'Our Mother …', *Patheos*, 27 January 2014, www.patheos.com/blogs/carynriswold/2014/01/our-mother/.

16

'This is My Body': A Womanist Reflection on Jesus' Sexualized Trauma during His Crucifixion from a Survivor of Sexual Assault

SHANELL T. SMITH

This is not your typical academic essay. With a more personal tone and style of writing, I unpack and reflect on difficult theological questions that arise for me when I think about sexual violence in general, and my own horrific experience with sexual violence, in particular. Using a womanist interpretive lens, I critically analyse Jesus' sexualized trauma during his crucifixion as found in Matthew 27.27–43 and Luke 23.34. This means that I begin with, and centre, the experiences of black women, namely mine, in my biblical analysis. It includes countering the tri-dimensional reality of racism, sexism and classism with the belief in God's solidarity with, and commitment to, black women's survival and wholeness, and to that of everyone. Employing a womanist lens is important because more often than not, it is the voices and experiences of black women that are left on the margins or simply ignored. As a womanist New Testament scholar, I aim to change that.

It is pertinent, at this point, that I make the following assertions. First, what follows is raw, honest, real and, most importantly, mine. Second, neither the trauma of survivors nor the ways in which we view Jesus' experience during his crucifixion are uniform. Third, seeing Jesus as a victim of sexual assault is problematic for some folk, including me.

Revisiting Jesus' sexualized trauma in the above Gospel passages exacerbates the pain and shame I feel as I relive my own. Yet, as always, for the sake of breathing deeply, bringing awareness to others, and for the love of scholarship, I write.

* * *

This is MY body! Yet, he took from it. Stripped and violated it. My body became a stranger to me. No longer *just* mine. Physically attached to it, yet mentally detached from it. My skin crawls from the ever-felt contact of years past. Dirty from being defiled. Ugly from his usage. It was MY body. It was not freely given. As if my body was the meal at the institution of his own Last Supper, my assailant's actions said to me: 'This is my body. Broken for me. I will take, and do what I want with it.'

I am an African American woman, a New Testament scholar, and an ordained Teaching Elder in the Presbyterian Church (USA). Despite my certifications, which lead folk to presume that I have special access to God, I continue to struggle with my faith because of the sexual trauma I experienced.[1] Why did God not do anything? Church folk who hear me question God about this often retort, 'Why *not* you? Even Jesus ...' STOP. Even Jesus what? Suffered? What does that have to do with me? Knowing that Jesus suffered does not make me feel better, or provide enough reason for me not to feel what I feel. I was sexually violated, and God did not stop it from happening. Full stop.

Interestingly enough, the response that Jesus suffered makes me consider if Jesus might have an inkling of what I experienced. I never thought about whether Jesus was sexually violated. Oh, no. It would be blasphemous for God to allow that to happen to God's own Son. Too troubling regarding the notions of Jesus' purity, and 'too human' in terms of the vile and disgusting experiences that we as sinful folk experience. Jesus is beyond that. *Right*? He was crucified. Yes. But sexually violated? No.

Oh, but he was. Jesus experienced sexual trauma. On his way to the cross.

Nevertheless, I struggle to find solace in Jesus as a Saviour regarding my own sexual assault. He is not a confidant. I do not feel solidarity with Jesus because I cannot relate to, or fathom, the ways in which he responded while undergoing his sexual violation. There are so many contradictions! '*This is my body ... Take ...*', followed by an agonized question of abandonment. '*My God. My God. Why ...?!*' Jesus' divinity and humanity, as if equally full proportions on a balanced scale, topple in varying degrees at different points during his crucifixion.

What can Jesus do for me as a survivor of sexual assault? I struggle with this. I am able to compartmentalize this particular disconnect with Jesus in terms of my sexual trauma; my faith in Jesus' salvific work on the cross remains intact. However, whenever I hear or read about Jesus' crucifixion – that is, the occasion in which his sexual assault occurs – I cannot help but interpret it through the lens of my own. Jesus becomes foreign. Unrelatable. Who, then, is my saviour during the times when I am triggered and remember ... when my assailant said, 'This is my body', in reference to his possession of mine.

Am I supposed to regard Jesus' resurrection as a form of his healing from his sexual trauma? I do not. It is quite difficult for me to find comfort in Jesus with regard to my sexual trauma, despite the fact that he is stripped naked and made vulnerable during his crucifixion. Am I supposed to forgive my assailant because Jesus asked God for forgiveness for his assailants *in the midst of* his sexual trauma? I have not. I am not there.

What about my relationship with God? Am I not supposed to be angry with God because it appears that Jesus was not? I do not understand Jesus' acceptance and love of God right after he cries out to God for abandoning him. Disregarding any theological notions of salvation: His. Father. Abandoned. Him. As a survivor of sexual assault, this is how I feel.

I do not take comfort in knowing that Jesus died with sexual trauma as a main component of his torture. Am I supposed to find solidarity with Jesus because he experienced sexual trauma like me? Where is the 'good news' in that?! Despite the fact that Jesus was raised on the third day, my third day – my deliverance – still has not come. It has been decades.

So, no. I do not feel better knowing that 'I am not alone' in my sexualized trauma. I wish that neither one of us experienced that! I cannot look to Jesus in this regard. I do not want to 'see' him on the way to the cross. It is triggering for me. It causes me to remember. I know how it feels to be vulnerable and violated. It sucks. I do not want to hear Jesus ask for forgiveness for his assailants. That is still a far notion for me. I want to hear Jesus be angry with God. I can relate to that. I fist-pump when he cries to God for abandoning him. *Tell it like it is, Jesus!* God abandoned me too. At least, that is how it felt.

Some say that Christians tend to rush through Lenten season and jump to Easter Sunday, because Jesus' suffering makes us uncomfortable. They say we need to 'ride it out' with Jesus, to remember and reflect on his sacrifice, and be thankful for the salvation we now have through him. *Well, I'm just gonna keep bunny hopping over to Easter.* I do not need to witness over and over again the sexual trauma that Jesus experienced. For me. There *had* to have been another way!

Jesus was sexually assaulted, but his experience and the way he responded does not help me deal with or understand my own. I did not say, '*This is my body. Take ...*' My body was not freely given. Jesus' body was. Several times in the Gospels, Jesus predicts his death by way of crucifixion to his disciples (for example, see Matt. 16.21; 17.22–23; 20.17–19; 26.26).[2]

Because of Jesus' divinity, I have to think that he knew what they would do to him. Crucifixion was common in antiquity. This extreme form of punishment signalled criminals, rebellious slaves and unruly foreigners. Oftentimes, these persons were naked. However, the humiliation doesn't stop with the public exposure of one's privates. In Jesus' case, it also includes having his masculinity snatched away by being penetrated, and by being the object of the crowd's gaze.

Masculinity was highly coveted during the first century. It represented power, dominance and control. It was not determined by one's anatomical make-up. Although looked down upon, a woman could be referred to as masculine. Notions of masculinity and femininity were related to one's actions. To be masculine means to be the penetra*tor* or the gazer. To be feminine means to be the penetra*ted* or the object of another's gaze.

Jesus' was triply humiliated. He was made naked. *They stripped him.* He was penetrated. *Not with a penis, but with nails.* He was a spectacle for the crowd's amusement. *They watched and mocked him.* When a man was penetrated in the first century, it was considered demeaning, effeminizing, and referred to him as having been conquered, overpowered.

Jesus' masculinity was snatched. In essence, he became first-century feminine. There is a big difference with regard to how these terms are understood then and now. Thus I choose not to expend energy considering the implications of Jesus becoming 'feminine' during his crucifixion, in which his sexual trauma occurred. Differentiating between men and women in terms of being survivors of sexual assault is unhelpful. No one's body should be violated.

The reverberations of my own sexual trauma are felt annually during the liturgical year when we remember Jesus' salvific work on the cross, and each time I teach the Gospel texts, particularly Matthew and Luke because of the authors' attention to details.

Jesus' crucifixion calls to mind my own experience with sexual trauma. In fact, I cannot view Jesus' experience without viewing it through my own. Can anyone? As a womanist biblical scholar, I interpret biblical texts through the experiences of African American women. In this case, mine. When I hear about Jesus' crucifixion, the vulnerable state of his nakedness, the penetration of his hands and feet, the forgiveness of his assailants, and the questioning of God's abandonment, I cannot help but be triggered.

Jesus was sexually violated. As was I. But somehow Jesus remains unrelatable to me in this regard. My disconnect with Jesus is a testament to the fact that sexual assault survivors may not be able to say #MeToo to other survivors. Details differ, and a feeling of one-upmanship may occur, especially when one is interrupted in the midst of sharing one's truth. Thus, the certainty with which one says, 'me too' should shift to one of uncertainty: 'me too?'[3]

All of this leads me to contemplate if Jesus can function as a source of hope for me. It evokes certain troubling theological inquiries such as whether the sexual violence against Jesus is justified because his crucifixion – in which his sexual trauma plays a major part – is considered salvific. Certainly, there had to have been another way! Am I supposed to forgive my assailant because Jesus did? #WWJD? How do I rectify a sexually abused Jesus with my own sexualized trauma? As a black female survivor of sexual assault, who is also ordained clergy, what are the contextualized implications and applications of seeing Jesus as a victim of sexual abuse?

The best way for me to answer the above questions is to give you a front-row seat to my thinking process as I read about Jesus' crucifixion. Jesus' crucifixion, although viewed as salvific in terms of what he afforded believers with his death – everlasting life – is difficult for me to swallow. I cannot think about the 'good news' of Jesus' death and resurrection without thinking about the stripping, spitting, beating and humiliation that comes with his sexual trauma. It is difficult for me to see Jesus' crucifixion ending in an Easter moment without some theological stretching and acrobatics. It takes work to move beyond the unwanted touching and probing that he suffered.

What follows is a womanist response – *mine* – to Jesus' sexualized trauma during his crucifixion as described in the Gospel of Matthew (27.27–43), in particular with a reference to his asking for forgiveness for his assailants in Luke 23.34. I chose to focus on these two Gospel texts because these are the two most read during the Lenten season. Very rarely have I heard some-one preach from the Gospel of Mark. With each reading of these texts, I find myself revisiting, reliving and re-traumatized by my sexual assault. This is what I think as a survivor of sexual assault while other folk are focusing on Jesus' redemptive death.

> Then the soldiers of the governor took Jesus into the governor's head-quarters, and they gathered the whole cohort around him. They stripped him and put a scarlet robe on him, and after twisting some thorns into a crown, they put it on his head. They put a reed in his right hand and knelt before him and mocked him, saying, 'Hail, King of the Jews!' They spat on him, and took the reed and struck him on the head. After mocking him, they stripped him of the robe and put his own clothes on him. Then they led him away to crucify him. (Matt. 27.27–31)

They stripped him. They did not ask him to disrobe. I imagine the soldiers pulling his clothes off him for everyone to see him. Naked. It was humili-ating and degrading. As they stripped him to put a scarlet robe on him, I am sure they did not have a garment to cover him up as they transitioned him into the robe. They paraded his penis. They did not even say that the robe was closed.

They mocked him. It had to be more than just calling him the 'King of the Jews'. Nay, they went beyond his supposed assumed political position. I bet they talked about the proportions of his privates. They made jokes about his sexuality. They spat on him. They sullied him. They struck him on the head with the reed. Swapping out his clothes again – revealing his genitals in the process – they led Jesus away to be crucified.

> [33]And when they came to a place called Golgotha (which means Place of a Skull), [34]they offered him wine to drink, mixed with gall; but when he tasted it, he would not drink it. (Matt. 27.33–34)

And when they returned from seeing an Alvin Ailey dance production,[4] he offered her something to drink. She drank it because she was thirsty, and because she trusted him. But soon after, she wished she had not drunk it, because she would remember no more.

> [35]And when they had crucified him, they divided his clothes among them-selves by casting lots; [36]then they sat down there and kept watch over him. [37]Over his head they put the charge against him, which read, 'This is Jesus, the King of the Jews'. (Matt. 27.35–37)

Almost 20 years later when my brain released parts of my trauma to me, I began to contemplate what actually happened. What else had he done to me? Had he removed the rest of my clothes, sat down next to me, and kept watch over me? Did he look me over from head to toe and say to himself, 'This is Shanell, the girl who is mine'?

> Then two bandits were crucified with him, one on his right and one on his left. Those who passed by derided him, shaking their heads and saying, 'You who would destroy the temple and build it in three days, save yourself! If you are the Son of God, come down from the cross.' In the same way the chief priests also, along with the scribes and elders, were mocking him, saying, 'He saved others; he cannot save himself. He is the King of Israel; let him come down from the cross now, and we will believe in him.' (Matt. 27.38–42)

Jesus is God's son! Why did he allow himself to be beaten, his flesh exposed, and his character to be mocked? Not many of us survivors are able to do this! Why didn't you save yourself?

Why did I not save myself? Did I scream? Did I just lay there and take it? Why didn't I sound the alarm right after it happened? Am I supposed to follow in the way of Jesus and *take it*, knowing that when it is all over – when my life is over, that is – God will return God's face to me and deliver me? It never happened.

> He trusts in God; let God deliver him now, if he wants to; for he said, 'I am God's Son'. (Matt. 27.43)

If Jesus was God's son, then why …? Was humanity – with all our sinfulness – worth the sexualized trauma he experienced? Did he still trust God when he hung on the cross bleeding and naked as the day he was born? Did he think that God would deliver him as the others were mockingly saying? What was going through Jesus' mind?

If God is all-knowing, all-powerful and all-seeing, then why did God not do something? Why did God allow my assailant to do those things to me? Why did God not deliver me from this man? This supposed God-fearing man? This church leader who to this day preaches and reads Scripture from the pulpit. I am a daughter of the Church! I am God's child. And yet … I laid there. Like Jesus hung there. There was no deliverance for me either. Not then. Not now. I want retribution, but Jesus …

> Jesus said, 'Father, forgive them; for they do not know what they are doing.' (Luke 23.34)

Forgive? Forgive?! How can Jesus forgive? After all that they did to him. After jostling his junk as they pushed him around. After placing a crown of thorns on his head, piercing his flesh and drawing blood. Jesus was penetrated! They actively twisted those thorns into a crown and placed it on his head. They intentionally stripped Jesus butt-naked and played dress-up in front of an audience. What do you mean, Jesus, that 'they do not know what they are doing'? Yes. They. Do!

How can I relate to Jesus when he asked for forgiveness for his assailants *while his sexualized trauma was occurring*? I still cannot comprehend forgiveness for my assailant and it has been over 20 years!

> From noon on, darkness came over the whole land until three in the afternoon. And about three o'clock Jesus cried with a loud voice, '*Eli, Eli, lema sabachthani?*' that is, 'My God, my God, why have you forsaken me?' (Matt. 27.45–46)

Finally! Jesus keeps it real! Yes, God, why did you forsake Jesus?! He is your one and only begotten Son, right? He is the One on whom the Holy Spirit descended like a dove during his baptism, no (Matt. 3.16)? Why, God? Why?! Jesus, who had healed the sick, made the blind see, made the deaf hear, and who taught the good news to the poor, was abandoned by God. And for what? For us? Having been a victim of sexual abuse, I say, 'No. No thank you!' There had to have been another way to achieve the same result!

This ... to this I can relate. Twenty years later, I still feel as if God had abandoned me. I still feel as if God were *all that*, if God were all that my Sunday school teachers, family and professors said God was, then why did God turn a blind eye to my sexual trauma? Why did God turn God's back and let me experience such a traumatic experience? I do not understand it!

Some folk, thinking they had the right theological answer, have said to me, 'If Jesus, then why not you?' Say what?! I wish that Jesus did not have to undergo sexual trauma either! Why was *that type* of trauma necessary?

Others might say that Jesus experienced sexual trauma so that survivors can have someone to whom they can relate. That is nonsense! Jesus' sexual trauma is still different from mine. In fact, each survivor's truth is different. So I do not find solidarity with Jesus other than the feeling of humiliation, defeat and devastation at being forgotten by the One I serve – God!

I once heard a sermon that said God turning God's back during Jesus' crucifixion is like a mother who cannot bear to watch her baby get their immunizations. He said that if God saw what Jesus was going through, then God would have intervened. Again, couldn't there have been another way?

God had forsaken me *and* Jesus. In that, we share a commonality. I have still not reconciled believing in a God that would 'allow' such a horrific act to occur. I do not understand why God did not stop it. I do not understand why my assailant is still active in the Church, reading Scripture and preaching from the pulpit, no less ... despite the fact that I 'sounded the alarm' to church authorities.

Then Jesus, crying with a loud voice, said, 'Father, into your hands I commend my spirit.' (Luke 23.46)

Into God's hands. I was raised thinking that God has the whole world 'in God's hands'. What happened, God? How am I to entrust myself to you again? Huh?

And yet … And yet, there is no one else to whom I can turn. It is quite paradoxical.[5] I have an ambivalent love of God. Perhaps Jesus did too? I mean, he was both fully *human* and fully divine.

* * *

The above are my thoughts as I hear or read about Jesus' crucifixion as a survivor of sexual assault. It is triggering. It is troubling. At times, it is paralysing.

Jesus was stripped. Naked. His privates were no longer private. His right to privacy was taken away from him. Jesus said, 'This is my body'; however, they treated his body as if it was their own, and that they had every right to do with it what they pleased. *Like what happened to me.*

In front of an audience, he dangled even as they dangled death before his eyes. This is not a happy story of salvation. This is not a joyful moment. It is a horrible one. One that I wish did not have to occur in order to save sinful humanity. *Why God? Was there no other way?*

While I am eager to quickly move from Jesus' sexual trauma in his crucifixion to Easter Sunday, I have several traumatizing 'hiccups' along the way. I cannot unsee what happened to Jesus. One does not have to be a primary witness to imagine his horrid ordeal. I cannot forget.

Jesus. Was. Stripped.

Jesus. Was. Put. On. Display.

Jesus. Was. Violated.

Just. Like. Me.

I do not want solidarity with Jesus with regard to sexual trauma. No one should have to experience this. Not even Jesus! Folk tell me, however, that it is a good thing because it makes Jesus relatable. So not true! I am supposed to be encouraged knowing that Jesus 'survived' his sexual trauma because in the end, he was raised from the dead. God had delivered him. I can say that if I had a choice as to *when* my sexual assault *had* to happen, it would be closer to my death date. Just like Jesus. That way, the suffering, the shame and the humiliation that I feel would be minimal.

Folk tell me to 'look to Jesus' for comfort when those bad memories are dredged up, but all I see is Jesus who suffered. Jesus who was stripped. Jesus who cried out and was ignored. Jesus who was traumatized. I wonder if Jesus asked his Father, 'Why?' when he saw God. I know I will.

Reading Jesus' sexualized trauma through the lens of my own raises difficult theological questions for me for which I do not have any answers. I still struggle with why that part was necessary – not that death was any better. I wonder how can I relate to a God who permits such sexualized cruelty? The argument of free will and sin does not work for me. God is more powerful than that. God is a God of love. To allow one to undergo sexual trauma is not love. Just because Jesus' crucifixion, death and resurrection made salvation available to believers, it does NOT justify the sexual violence that Jesus experienced. Again, were there no other options?

Sexual violence is NEVER justified.

This has been a difficult, triggering chapter to write. Seeing Jesus experience sexual trauma through the lens of my own is hard. Despite all of the questions, doubts and lingering anger I have toward God, I still love God. What a paradox, huh? Although I shake my head at some of Jesus' actions during his crucifixion – asking for forgiveness for one's assailant *as one's sexual assault* occurs, commending his spirit to God after having been forsaken by God – I still love him, and am grateful to him for making salvation available to believers.

Nevertheless, I do not know if Jesus can function as a source of hope and comfort for me as a survivor of sexual assault. He said, 'This is MY body', but he is a survivor himself. *I am sorry that you went through that, Jesus.*

I am not Jesus. This is MY body, which I do NOT freely give.

Notes

1 My monograph, Shanell T. Smith, *touched: For Survivors of Sexual Assault Like Me Who Have Been Hurt by Church Folk and for Those Who Will Care* (Minneapolis, MN: Fortress Press, 2020), speaks both to fellow survivors and caregivers. Based on my own experience with sexual assault, fellow survivors will find affirmation of their own truths, and caregivers will find ways to engage, care for and journey with survivors on their journey to their own form of healing.

2 One might suggest that Jesus did not willingly give up his body to be crucified, but that it was given by God, whom Jesus had to obey. I tend not to view Jesus' willing sacrifice this way because it removes or lessens Jesus' divinity and power.

3 This is my way of asserting the differences between survivors' experiences with sexual assault, and is in no way a critique of the #MeToo movement. Tarana Burke's work is amazing and has helped many a survivor, offering them solidarity, support and much-needed care.

4 See Alvin Ailey American Dance Theater, www.alvinailey.org.

5 See womanist biblical scholar Renita J. Weems, 'Reading *Her Way* through the Struggle: African American Women and the Bible', in *Stony the Road We Trod: African American Biblical Interpretation*, Cain Hope Felder ed. (Minneapolis, MN: Fortress Press, 1991). Weems notes the paradoxical relationship between the Bible and African American women. In particular, she highlights the fact that the Bible is very influential in African American religious life despite its use as a tool of oppression.

17

Seeing His Innocence, I See My Innocence

ROCÍO FIGUEROA AND DAVID TOMBS

Exploring responses to Jesus as a victim of sexual abuse

The article 'Crucifixion, State Terror, and Sexual Abuse' (1999) drew on Latin American liberationist hermeneutics for a reading of biblical texts with attention to both past context and present context.[1] As a new reading of crucifixion, it focused on presenting textual and contextual evidence for recognizing Jesus as a victim of sexual abuse.[2] It is not until its final pages that the theological and pastoral implications of this recognition are addressed.[3] Drawing on the parable of judgement (Matt. 25.31–46), it affirms the Christological connection between the suffering of the naked Christ and the suffering of those who are tortured and abused.[4] This connection might offer a liberating and healing approach to those who continue to struggle with the stigma and other consequences of sexual abuse.

This chapter focuses on how this pastoral response might be developed further, in response to survivor suggestions. It offers findings from qualitative interviews undertaken during 2019 to explore responses to naming Jesus as a victim of sexual abuse.[5] The participants are five female survivors of sexual abuse in Argentina, France, Germany, Peru and the Philippines. Four interviewees are former nuns, and the fifth is a current nun.[6] They are referred to here by the pseudonyms Dina (Germany), Franca (France), Lilian (the Philippines), Lucia (Argentina) and Maria (Peru). The participants discuss their responses with particular attention to the difference that seeing Jesus in this way makes to them personally as a survivor, and the difference they believe it might make to the wider Church.

Of course, Jesus' experience of crucifixion should not only be seen in terms of sexual abuse or sexual violence.[7] There was more to crucifixion than that. Recognizing sexually abusive elements in Roman crucifixions, and naming them properly for what they were, is not to limit the understanding of Jesus' crucifixion in any way. Rather, it is to ensure that sexual abuse as a historically important element is included in the overall understanding of the passion.

Our questions here were informed by two previous studies we had undertaken with a small group of male survivors of church-related sexual abuse in Peru.[8] The first study involved eight participants and investigated the impact of sexual abuse with particular attention to its impact on their spirituality and faith. This highlighted their feelings of betrayal and lack of trust, and the damage done to their faith in God and in the Church. The second study, which is much closer in purpose to this current study, explored responses to a reading of Jesus as victim of sexual abuse.[9] Five of the seven participants in the second study had also participated in the first study.[10] We asked whether they saw Jesus being a victim of sexual abuse was significant for them as survivors, and whether they saw it as important to the wider Church. Two findings from the work with male participants were specifically illuminating. First, the findings demonstrate that individual survivors respond to the abuse of Jesus in different ways. Two of the male survivors said it would not be helpful, and another said it would probably not be helpful, but the other four found it positive. This variety suggests that any proposals for a pastoral approach should be made tentatively and require further research. Further work should be undertaken into how Jesus' experience can be addressed in the most helpful way, and also into what should be avoided. Second, their responses indicated that Jesus' experience of sexual abuse should be seen as important for everyone within the Church, and not just survivors. In fact, both the earlier study and the findings presented here suggest that the issues are of even more pressing relevance to the wider Church than they might be for survivors.

To build on the earlier interviews with male victims, we wanted to speak to a group of female victims. We prioritized speaking to nuns for two reasons. First, in 2019 the sexual abuse of nuns in the Church had attracted global attention, and we wanted to learn more about their experiences.[11] Second, a 2013 study by Gloria Durà-Vilà, Roland Littlewood and Gerard Leavey had interviewed a group of contemplative nuns in Spain who had experienced sexual abuse within the Church. Some of the abused nuns had stated that they found it consoling to reflect on the suffering of Jesus.[12] They had 'felt that Jesus was with them while they were being abused, and was himself undergoing the abuse as well'.[13] We wanted to explore this further. The contemplative nuns had seen a connection with the suffering of Jesus, but appear to have understood Jesus' suffering in a more general way, rather than as a form of sexual abuse per se.[14] For our study, we wanted to name Jesus' own experience more explicitly as sexual abuse and then to ask our participants their thoughts on this.

Michael Trainor's book *The Body of Jesus and Sexual Abuse* is an important landmark in biblical work on this issue.[15] It offers a detailed book-length discussion of the presentation of sexual abuse in the four Gospels. As a biblical scholar, Trainor draws on textual criticism alongside his pastoral experience, as both an Australian Catholic priest and an educator, to discuss the portrayals of sexual abuse in the different Gospel accounts and to reflect on their significance.[16] Yet, despite Trainor's book, there is still much work to be done on the historical side. The longstanding silence around Jesus as a victim of sexual abuse has proved to be resilient. Detailed scholarly works on crucifixion published in recent years, which offer significant advances in scholarship on other questions, nonetheless typically neglect to address any sexual dimension in the stripping, the mockery and the cross.[17] As a result, when Jesus is described as a victim of sexual abuse it still requires careful explanation. In many cases it is received, at least initially, with scepticism and even hostility. There is still a need to repeatedly restate and explain the historical and textual evidence for why Jesus should be seen as a victim of sexual abuse.[18] Within the academy, the Church and wider society, the sexual abuse of Jesus typically remains 'hidden within plain sight'.[19] Further scholarly work to clarify and confirm the historical and textual insight that Jesus was a victim of sexual abuse is therefore needed. However, this should take place alongside a consideration of how and why this acknowledgement makes a practical difference.

As the subtitle to Trainor's book indicates – 'How the Gospel Passion Narratives Inform a Pastoral Response' – he is concerned with how his investigation might serve a positive pastoral purpose in his own Australian context.[20] He asks: 'what can authentic discipleship look like in one who has experienced sexual abuse, feels hurt and anger towards the church institution and its leaders, and struggles to believe in a God who cares?'[21] Trainor recognizes that survivors respond in different ways, and he is aware that some survivors argue against an identification of the abuse of Jesus with their own sexual abuse.[22] However, he believes that for others Jesus' experience can sustain and give hope, and can also help the Church to listen to the stories of others who have been hurt and abused.[23] Fortunately, these two areas of research, the historical and the pastoral, can support and illuminate each other.[24] Other research is underway on the historical and textual grounds for understanding Jesus in this way; in this chapter the focus is more directly on the practical issue of why this matters.[25] Taking up Trainor's commitment to a pastoral concern, our chapter considers how Jesus' experience of abuse might be addressed in a way that could be helpful to survivors and transformative for the wider Church.[26]

Over the years, a number of important questions have been asked about why the acknowledgement of this disturbing insight should matter. To what extent, if at all, might the acknowledgement of Jesus as a victim of sexual abuse really offer a sense of healing or hope? How can the dangers of a naive valorization of the suffering of Jesus be avoided? How might contemporary survivors of sexual abuse respond to Jesus as a victim? What positive meaning might it have for them? What relevance does it have to victim-blaming and stigmatizing attitudes in the wider Church?

Three developments in the social landscape since 1999 add to the urgency of responses to these questions. First, the extent of sexual abuses within churches has become much more widely known. These abuses were already known in the 1980s and 1990s, but became much more widely publicized especially in the light of coverage by the *Boston Globe* newspaper in 2002, followed by subsequent revelations in many other countries around the world.[27] Second, the prevalence of sexual violence during wars and political conflicts has been much more clearly documented and discussed.[28] Churches and faith organizations have shown a growing leadership at a global level in understanding and addressing conflict-related sexual violence, and in recognizing the devastation it leaves behind.[29] While the majority of this violence is directed against women and girls, there is also now much wider recognition that men and boys are often also targeted. Third, the #MeToo movement, taking on mainstream attention in 2017, publicized the extent of sexual harassment and sexual assault in wider society and has also shown how often these issues are normalized, trivialized, ignored and silenced.[30]

There can no longer be a question that a strong pastoral and theological response is needed to sexual abuse and sexual violence in its many different forms. If this response is to be adequate it will need to be courageous and honest. It must be willing to confront difficult issues, stigmas and taboos, and not fall back on platitudes or abstractions. The churches need a clear-sighted sense of the problem and an understanding of how its legacies continue to affect the lives of survivors long after the abuse itself.

The indirect impacts of abuse, as well as the often more obvious direct harms, also need to be considered. The indirect impacts include the victim-blaming and stigma. These are referred to as a 'secondary victimization'.[31] Many survivors report that they are left to carry these additional burdens with little help or support from the churches. In fact, in many cases, churches can reinforce the stigma and victim-blaming attitudes that add to the problems faced by survivors and contribute to isolation and abandonment.[32]

Following a summary presentation of the findings, a discussion section explores how the interviews might contribute to a more proactive and theologically grounded pastoral response to sexual abuse. We suggest that attention to the innocence of Jesus may challenge the victim-blaming that survivors often face in the wider Church. One of the most striking responses from participants was the significance of Jesus' innocence. In the words of Maria, 'the beautiful thing is that Jesus was innocent' because 'Seeing his innocence, I see my innocence.' We had not anticipated this particular response, but it shows how survivors might find value in acknowledging Jesus as victim of sexual abuse in creative and even unexpected ways. For some survivors, an identification with Jesus' innocence can help to resist destructive social and psychological pressures to self-judgement or self-blame. For the wider Church, this recognition might offer insight into the prevalence of victim-blaming and negative judgements.[33] The interviews encourage the conviction that the acknowledgement of Jesus as a victim of sexual abuse serves a positive role. However, identifying with the suffering of Jesus should not be seen as a simple or straightforward solution. It carries risks of misunderstanding and misappropriation and will need careful expression if it is to make a constructive contribution to the Church's response to sexual abuse.

Interview findings

After receiving ethics approval, we conducted structured individual interviews with our five participants.[34] The five participants now range in age from 35 to 70 years old but the sexual abuse took place when they were young adults or minors. Three of them were abused by priests as young adults during their religious life, and the other two experienced child sexual abuse by relatives. The abuse incidents disclosed ranged from penetrative sexual abuse (four participants) to non-penetrative sexual touching (all participants). We are very grateful to all the participants for their willingness to be interviewed. They were generous in their readiness to reflect on our questions and to share their thoughts with us and with a wider audience.

Prior to the interview, the participants agreed to read about sexual abuse in the crucifixion of Jesus. The reading was an abridged version of the 'Crucifixion, State Terror, and Sexual Abuse' article, which had been shortened in 2019 for publication in the Brazilian theological journal *Estudos Teológicos*.[35] The abridged version, entitled 'Crucifixion and Sexual Abuse', was provided to the participants in English, French, German or Spanish. Participants were asked to prepare for their interview by reading this work, or alternatively by reading a two-page summary, which was provided alongside it.[36]

Each individual interview generally lasted for about 40 minutes. Most were held over Skype but one of the interviews was written.[37] The interviews sought information on the impact of vocation and faith on participants' response to sexual abuse in general, as well as their more specific responses to seeing Jesus as a victim of sexual abuse. However, for brevity, it is only the questions relating to Jesus as a victim of sexual abuse that are presented here. The questions on their responses to Jesus as victim were grouped under four headings:

1 Whether the participant had previously viewed their abuse in light of the suffering of Jesus.
2 Whether the reading on crucifixion and sexual abuse was new to them, and whether they felt it was persuasive.
3 The significance (if any) that understanding Jesus as a victim of sexual abuse had for them.
4 Their views on the significance of this for the wider Church.

Previous identification with Jesus' suffering

This area of questions asked about any previous connection participants had made to the suffering of Jesus prior to their participation in our project. Only one participant, Franca, had made no connection between her own suffering and the suffering of Jesus. She said:

During the period of abuse, I made no connection between Jesus' sufferings and my own experiences. And when I started to free myself from my abusers, I went through a long period (15 years) of rejecting the mystery of the Incarnation and the person of Jesus, because I had been abused in Jesus' name.

The other four participants had each made some form of personal connection between their abuse and the suffering of Jesus, but they differed in how they saw this. For two of the participants (Maria and Lilian), the connection to the suffering of Jesus was positive and helpful, for one (Dina) it was mixed, and for one (Lucia) it was negative. As in the study of the Spanish nuns, those who made a connection to the suffering of Jesus saw this in terms of generic suffering, and had not thought of Jesus' experience in terms of his own sexual abuse.[38]

Maria had set her suffering alongside the suffering of Jesus. Her response shows the powerful effect that Jesus' innocence as a victim can have. His innocence had reinforced her own sense of innocence, and had helped her to resist feelings of shame and guilt:

One positive thing that helped me in the process of healing was the Cross of Christ. The idea of an innocent Jesus suffering for us helped me to understand that I was innocent. I felt guilt and shame. I felt powerless. Putting my experience alongside Jesus' experience helped me to assimilate it in my life.

For Lilian, although the image of Jesus as a victim of sexual abuse did not provide an answer to the question of why she suffered, nonetheless the sense of Jesus being with her in suffering had brought her great comfort. Like Maria, she saw particular significance in his innocence:

I saw how Jesus was mistreated, being innocent, and what he suffered during his life. Jesus was whipped; they spat at him; they used words that were very abusive and abused him as a person and they insulted him; they humiliated him. Jesus is an innocent person.

I asked the question why me? Why has this happened to me? The answer that came to me was the picture of the crucifixion. God cries for me; God also suffers with me. For me this is a great consolation.

Dina's response was more mixed. She had identified the suffering of Jesus with her own suffering, but she did not find Jesus' response to be helpful. She gave her response as both 'Yes and No'. On the one hand, Jesus' suffering was very present in her community's spirituality. This made it easy to identify her own suffering with the suffering of Jesus. Yet on the other hand, there were differences that created difficulties. Jesus' suffering was seen as heroic, and he was seen as accepting it and suffering in silence. This suggested that Dina should also suffer in silence. She said: 'The only feeling that I could allow was to bury it and not complain.' Dina also struggled with Matthew 5.39 where Jesus calls on followers to turn the other cheek. While this made sense to her as a response to a striking on the cheek, did this mean that Jesus expected you to allow someone to rape you again? She said:

> He would never say that. So, it made me think: what is the difference between striking on the cheek and sexual abuse? Somehow, I think it is not right to be silent, but I couldn't find any encouragement from Jesus to help me to speak out and defend myself. At least I understood Jesus' suffering, and I also suffered, so in one sense he was close to me, yet his suffering was so different to mine. At the same time my identification with Jesus helped the abusers to keep me silent.

Lucia also identified a connection to the suffering of Jesus, but she did not see it as helpful, at least not at the time:

> Each time during my time as a nun when I suffered something painful, or the abuse itself, I thought that Jesus suffered worse than me, and I had to offer my own suffering without complaining so much ... You couldn't complain because we asked God to suffer in this life and live in purgatory so it was good that these things were happening.

Both Lucia and Dina felt that if they suffered as Jesus suffered this meant that they therefore should not complain. They were expected to carry suffering in the same way as Jesus bore his cross. Rather than being helpful, Jesus' suffering worked to silence them as victims and suppress their cries for help.[39]

Response to the reading

The second area of questioning was their response to the reading, and how plausible they found the suggestion that Jesus was a victim of historical sexual abuse. Their answers to this question shared much in common. It was a new reading to most, with the exception of Franca who had come across it some months earlier. Furthermore, they all found it persuasive, and felt it allowed them to understand Jesus' suffering in a fuller way.

Lucia said: 'I believe that it is persuasive ... I never thought about it and it really touched me.' In a similar way, Lilian said it was new and persuasive:

> I think that the only type of abuse that I knew was the one I went through and when I thought about Jesus I just thought about the insults and the crucifixion. The idea of Jesus as a victim of sexual abuse is quite persuasive.

Maria also said that it was both new and persuasive, and explained:

> Sincerely I felt like: 'it makes sense'. At an intellectual level I thought it makes sense because these things happen. Why didn't I think about it before? When people are humiliated in a crucifixion or in a torture of that type, shame and sexual abuse happen.

Dina also saw it as convincing. She also commented on the strangeness of nobody having thought about it before.

> It is very clear that the stripping of a prisoner before execution was a humiliation and sexuality was involved. My first reaction is that it is a very interesting idea, it somehow makes sense and nobody has thought about it.

The participant who had previously heard that Jesus was a victim of sexual abuse was Franca. A few months before the interview she had heard the idea when listening to a lecture on the internet.[40] Franca explained that in Matthew 27, when Jesus is handed over to the soldiers, it is said that they 'mocked him' (verse 29). 'Mocked' is the expression used in Judges 19 to refer to the rape of the concubine.[41]

> For Matthew, Jesus is delivered to the soldiers and they stripped him of his clothes, even if it is not explicitly stated, there is a kind of rape in the passion of Christ ... When you throw a person, man or woman, in the middle of an unaccountable gang, who knows what could happen? I think that the passion of Christ echoes many stories of suffering.

For all the participants, the historical evidence and the idea of Jesus as a victim of sexual abuse made sense and was clearly persuasive. They did not see sexual abuse as bringing a forced or false external perspective on his experience. Rather, they saw it as helping to recognize and name Jesus' experience for what it was. Maria registered her surprise that she had not thought of it before. Dina commented on how strange it is that this is not more widely recognized or discussed, and saw it as a result of a victim-blaming culture:

> It is so strange that Jesus has not been considered a victim of sexual abuse: I think that it is because we have this whole victim-blaming culture and the idea that victims of sexual abuse have actually done something to provoke it. Picturing Jesus as a victim of sexual abuse makes it entirely clear that a victim is innocent.

In terms of their emotional response to the article, Lucia and Franca reported that thinking of Jesus as a victim of sexual abuse provoked strong emotions. Lucia said: 'I felt the same emotion as when I watched movies about his passion: a feeling of powerlessness, a rage ('*bronca*') that Jesus suffered like that.' Franca said: 'Jesus lived through the sexual abuse of so many children, so many men, so many women, including those who claim to be his disciples. This is a great comfort for me, a great consolation.' Dina spoke of her wish to know more: 'I also see Jesus and the Gospels as an object of study and research.' Lilian described a shift in her feelings:

> First, I had a feeling of resistance. I felt that Jesus' abuse was different from mine. But then I considered that the feelings were the same: feeling humiliated and people staring at him.

Maria spoke of her conflicted emotions. On the one hand, she felt it strengthened the bond between her own suffering and that of Christ, and says, 'I identified more with Christ.' If Jesus suffered sexual abuse she felt he could better identify with this human experience. On the other hand, however, this was also upsetting. It created a conflict for Maria because she recognized it as dehumanizing experience:

> I didn't want anybody living through an experience like that. I would not like him going through something like that because it is horrible [she cries]. The abuse deprives you of your own humanity and your own dignity. It is humiliating and it is horrible. Physically it is horrible. It is psychologically and spiritually very painful.

During the interviews Lucia, Maria, Franca and Lilian had a strong empathy towards Jesus as a victim of sexual abuse. They expressed compassionate concern for what had happened to him.[42] Lucia spoke of her rage that Jesus suffered in this way. Franca spoke of Jesus as present in the suffering of others, not just her own suffering: 'Jesus lived through the sexual abuse of so many children, so many men, so many women, including those who claim to be his disciples.' Maria said she found it hard to relate to God's power. By contrast, she felt a closer connection with the suffering of Christ.

> But a Christ who has suffered, who has been humiliated makes me feel that he is more connected with me. We have lived the same things. He understands what I have gone through. And I understand a little bit of what he lived.

Thinking of Jesus as a victim of sexual abuse gave her new insight into his suffering and his humanity.

> The abuse dehumanizes. Someone steals your humanity and the autonomy that you have over your own body, over yourself … Knowing this side of Christ's suffering was a relief … Jesus didn't give up just his divinity but his own humanity.

Maria said it was easier for her to have a relationship with Christ when she understood him this way.

Assessment of its value for participants

The third area of questioning was around whether participants felt the idea was helpful or unhelpful to them. Three participants (Franca, Lilian and Maria) said that recognizing this aspect of Jesus' experience was helpful for them. Franca explained the positive value she saw in it:

> Yes, this thought is a help, a comfort, a source of consolation for me. This in no way devalues my own painful experience, quite the contrary ...
> Knowing that Jesus Christ, Son of God and Son of Man, has really been the bearer of all our sufferings and all our diseases, even in the intimate and almost unspeakable area of sexuality, becomes, in my view, a source of comfort for the victims of abuse – especially for those who have been abused by priests and religious.

Franca also suggested that it 'could also, perhaps, help the victims who still suffer in silence, to speak. It can help them realize that they are not culpable.' Lilian also saw it as positive:

> I suppose that when you know that someone has gone through the same pain that you had experienced it is a kind of strength that you gain, knowing that Jesus suffered. You have a reason to live. You have a reason to stand up.

Maria said it helped her to see herself in a new way. At one level, she already knew her own innocence, but there are times when she is troubled by doubts and a temptation to self-blame.

> Despite saying to myself 'You are not guilty', one part of me, in my innermost part, maintains my guilt and leads me to accuse myself, 'You could have done something to avoid the abuse.'

She found that reading the article offered her reassurance on this. She explains:

> And then I have the experience and the knowledge that Jesus was innocent. That makes it easier to believe that I am innocent. It has been a beginning. Reading it has been like a relief. It is not just on a theoretical level. There is an emotional level that helps me to go into my heart. I love Jesus. I don't blame him. I don't say to him, 'You had to do something. You could have avoided it.' Seeing his innocence, I see my innocence.

Although Maria saw it as helpful personally, she acknowledged that other survivors might not find it helpful. Some might not feel that Jesus experienced the same as they experienced, because the abuse was different for them. However, speaking for herself, Maria felt a strong connection:

I have been raped and my reaction is that I feel Jesus' solidarity and I feel solidarity for him, and it feels good. Spiritually, I feel that I know Jesus better, that I understand Jesus more. I feel that he can walk with me more closely because he knows what I have gone through. Sincerely, I don't care to what extent he was abused because it is enough for me that he lived through some abuse and he can understand. That is how I feel. For someone who has suffered abuse it is a positive and deep way to interpret your own experience.

For Dina the answer was more mixed. She saw it as especially helpful for other nuns, seminarians, or other men who have been abused. And for people who have a strong faith and a strong connection with Jesus. However, when speaking about her own situation, Dina said that at an earlier time it would have helped her to resist guilt or blame, but she no longer struggles with this.

I think that the idea would have been very helpful for me back then. Now I feel that it makes no difference to me. I have realized that it was not my fault and whether or not Jesus was abused doesn't make a difference. It would have made a big difference back then.

Lucia did not see it as helpful, at least not at the present time. She also doubted that it would be helpful for the network of survivors of church abuse to which she belongs. She described the gap between their current faith outlook and what they once believed as 'a huge abyss'. In view of this, she said, 'At this stage I don't think that anyone will be touched, or I don't think that this idea will help them in their process of healing.' Instead, she suggests, 'We need to re-read and re-interpret our own story.'

The different answers to this question reflect the different ways that survivors respond to their experience and what they each find meaningful. To sum up, Franca, Lilian and Maria each said that the idea of Jesus as a victim of sexual abuse was helpful for them. Dina said that it would have been very helpful in the past but she has no need of it now. Lucia said she did not find it helpful, and nor did she see it as likely to be helpful to the survivors with whom she worked.

Significance for the wider Church

The final set of questions was on the significance of this reading to others. The focus of this final area of questions was on whether the participants felt it was helpful to the wider Church rather than to other survivors.[43] It is striking that all our participants indicated that viewing Jesus as a victim of sexual abuse would be positive for the wider Church. Even Lucia, who did not find the idea helpful for herself and doubted its relevance to the network of survivors she knew, said:

For the Church, of course. Because it can be a topic that usually is silenced. It would be like an alert … Imagine a prayer saying, 'Lord, you who were manipulated in your own sexuality, protect us' … I think it would be very helpful.

Franca said, 'It would be good if this idea is more valued and published in theological education and exegetically.' She suggested that it might prompt a more compassionate response, and help to address misplaced blame.

And it could also, perhaps, convince the members of the hierarchy of the Church that the victims are not blameworthy. Perhaps this idea would also help combat the ever-present tendency of the hierarchy to bury all these abuses in silence? And it would help the 'good Christian people', shocked by these revelations likely to harm the image of the Church, to walk towards the truth that alone can liberate us. It might also be an incentive for church members to take the suffering of victims seriously.

Maria suggested that recognizing Jesus as a victim of sexual abuse might actually have even more value for the wider Church than it does for survivors:

I think it would be more useful for those who have not been victims. I think there is a culture within the Church and also throughout society which fails to recognize victims of sexual abuse as victims. I think that if the people of the Church identify Jesus as a victim of abuse, they would be more able to see Jesus in those who are victims and love us more [crying].

She described the additional harm to survivors that comes from the negative attitudes in the Church.

I see such horrible things. That lack of identification with the victims by clergy, priests and bishops is so painful. They identify more with the perpetrators. Many of the perpetrators have been priests and the priests are 'other Christs'. But if you see Christ in this light, as a victim, it would be easier for them to feel solidarity with the victims, to be more understanding and be on their side.

Dina agreed that it could make a positive difference to the Church. However, she saw some risks in how it might be appropriated by church leaders:

I do see a danger here. Yes, it could be good if the wider Church owned this idea. But, on the other hand, I see that if the church leaders (who have been covering abuse for so long now) appropriate the concept that Jesus was a victim of sexual abuse and preach about it, the danger is that they could use it as a way of further silencing the victims: for example, like saying Jesus was the perfect victim. Perhaps there is a risk that church leaders could devalue survivors' stories with the icon of Jesus as a victim of sexual abuse. That might happen.

To counter this risk, she suggested that survivors rather than the Church should take the lead in charting the way forward:

I would prefer if the individual survivors appropriate this image of a victim of sexual abuse first, they should own it and then take it to the Church.

Lilian also agreed that it could help the Church, because 'if the Church sees Jesus as a victim, people would have sympathy for those who are victims'. However, like Dina, she warned that this also involved dangers and risks. Lilian stressed the need for great care when raising the idea with victims.

To sum up, the first area of questioning asked whether participants had made an identification with the suffering of Jesus at the time of the abuse, or in the aftermath. Four of the participants made some form of connection and one did not. For two of the participants the connection was helpful, for one it was mixed, and for one it was negative. The second area was whether the reading of Jesus as a victim of sexual abuse was new to participants, how they saw the evidence, and how they responded to this reading. The idea was new to them, with one exception. The historical evidence appeared persuasive to all of the participants. It provoked a range of emotional response, including empathy for Jesus. The third area was the significance they saw in the idea for themselves as survivors, and whether it was helpful or unhelpful. Three of the participants saw the idea as helpful for them. One replied that it would have been very helpful to her when she was abused, but it made little difference now. One stated that it was not personally helpful to her and nor did she see it as likely to be helpful to the survivors with whom she worked. All of the participants said that it was significant for the Church and offered an opportunity of positive change, albeit with some risks and dangers.

Discussion

The interviews offer survivor perspectives on how acknowledgement of Jesus as a victim of sexual abuse might help the Church to develop its pastoral approach.[44] It is not possible to discuss at length all of the issues that the participants address.[45] Instead, the discussion will focus on three points: the impact of Jesus' innocence; the relevance of these issues to the wider Church; the danger that Jesus' victimhood might be misappropriated.

First, acknowledging Jesus as innocent can help to address victim-blaming. Lilian and Maria both indicated that the innocence of Jesus was important to them. It reaffirmed and reinforced their own innocence. Likewise, Dina said, 'Jesus as a victim of sexual abuse makes it entirely clear that a victim is innocent.' Furthermore, Dina suggested that victim-blaming may help to explain the widespread silence on Jesus' own experience. She seems to suggest that, in the conventional view, Jesus cannot be named because he cannot be blamed. The consequence of this is that Jesus' sexual abuse has gone unnamed and the narratives have been distorted. Dina's comment suggests that there is much more at stake in Jesus' innocence than may first appear. Recognition or denial of Jesus as a victim is connected to deeply embedded cultural assumptions about blame, shame, guilt, innocence, purity, as well as masculinity, power, vulnerability and bodily integrity.[46] Acknowledgement of Jesus as victim of sexual abuse is likely to require a radical rethinking of attitudes rather than just a minor adjustment. This makes the naming of Jesus as a victim all the more important, especially for the wider Church.

The blame and stigma associated with sexual abuse help to explain the reluctance of the Church to confront the obvious. The perceived impurity of sex makes a discussion of Jesus in relation to anything sexual extremely difficult. Because the mistaken assumption that victims are to be blamed is so widespread, and the stigmatizing of victims is so prevalent, viewing Jesus as a victim of sexual abuse can scarcely even be suggested. A common reaction to the suggestion that Jesus was a victim of sexual abuse is to assume that if this were true, then Jesus would inevitably be less worthy and less pure. The implication of this line of thinking is that this would conflict with his status as a saviour.[47]

It is seen as offensive, even blasphemous, to associate Jesus with anything sexual in this way. In keeping with this outlook, despite being a victim of sexual abuse the default response encourages attitudes of blame and judgement. These assumptions and negative attitudes match the blame and stigma that sexual abuse survivors often report as being directed against them. Either explicitly and overtly, or indirectly and through judgemental silence, both wider society and the Church frequently convey blame and stigma against survivors. Opportunities for the recognition of these dynamics may prove to be where the idea has its greatest transformative potential.

One of the critical conversations that the acknowledgement of Jesus as a victim of sexual abuse should therefore open up is around widespread negative attitudes to survivors. These attitudes are close to the surface in many churches but are rarely named or critically examined. On the contrary, they are often denied or disowned if they are considered in the abstract. They therefore remain hidden most of the time. They can usually stay beneath the surface, but they readily emerge as a backlash that dismisses the claim that Jesus was sexually abused as self-evidently offensive.

The experience of Jesus can play a crucial role in exposing these dynamics. Resistance within the churches to seeing Jesus as a victim of sexual abuse reflects the confusion that still exists within churches and within wider society on where blame should rest in relation to sexual abuse. Recognizing that Jesus was a victim disrupts the circular reasoning of victim-blaming, and exposes its mistaken assumptions. Exposing and confronting this confusion, and the harmful behaviours it sustains within churches, should be a pressing priority for the Church as it seeks to affirm the irreducible dignity of all people.

The innocence of Jesus can thus strengthen survivors when they encounter negative and judgemental responses from others, or experience low self-esteem or self-blame. Of course, the innocence of victims should be recognized on its own terms without need for anything more to be said. However, within the Church the experience of Jesus can further support this truth. Saying the innocence of Jesus can make a difference is not to suggest that the innocence of survivors can only be recognized in light of the innocence of Jesus. The innocence of survivors is something that the Church should already fully embrace, and public statements are often made to this effect. Nonetheless, even though articulating the innocence of survivors should not be new or necessary, connecting the innocence of survivors to the innocence of Jesus can make the innocence of both more meaningful to some in the Church. It offers insight into how victim-blaming can undermine a survivor's sense of self even though the blame is obviously misplaced. A clear and uncontested statement of innocence can be an important support in reinforcing the truth.

Second, all the participants agreed that recognition of Jesus as a victim of sexual abuse is important for the wider Church and not just for survivors. Even Lucia, who felt that Jesus' experience was not directly helpful to herself, nonetheless saw it as important for the Church. Here, our interviews with both male and female survivors point in the same direction. Jesus' sexual abuse should not be seen as only a concern for survivors but as a concern for the whole Church. This raises important questions for future work. Why has the Church kept silent? Why has it ignored this important element of crucifixion for so long? Why is it not more widely addressed?

Third, some participants voiced concern that Jesus' experience might be misappropriated by the Church. For example, the troubling association of Jesus' suffering and silence was noted.[48] Concern was also voiced that survivors' actual experience might be displaced by an abstract icon of Jesus' experience. Another danger might be in how the experience is related to resurrection. From a theological perspective, reflection on Jesus' experience of crucifixion will be incomplete unless it also addresses resurrection. However, some interpretations of cross and resurrection may be unhelpful for survivors of sexual abuse. As feminist scholars have noted, there are potential dangers in presenting the cross as the glorification of suffering.[49] Attention to the cross and identification with the suffering of Jesus can be positive and offer helpful resources, but it also carries risks and is open to misinterpretation.[50] Some in the Church may wish to move too quickly from crucifixion to resurrection, and offer a cheap message of reassurance that denies the reality of suffering. A theology of resurrection has integrity only if it presents the full and painful truth of crucifixion. A message of resurrection cannot be a simplistic solution that evades what really happened, nor should it minimize the damage of abuse.[51] Rather, a theology of resurrection must be reconsidered in the light of the actual experience of Jesus attested in Scripture. Survivors of sexual abuse must be fully heard in this process.[52] This will be challenging work. Survivors do not always share the same views or the same experiences, and should not be seen as a uniform group. What some might find positive might be irrelevant, or even negative, to others.[53] Further work therefore needs to be done to investigate how and when the acknowledgement of the sexual abuse of Jesus can be helpful to survivors. A pastoral approach must include a commitment to listening to diverse experiences and avoid essentializing or over-simplifying the full range of experiences and views.

Conclusion

More work clearly needs to be done on how Jesus' experience of abuse might best help survivors, but there are several directions suggested here. The participants all agreed that recognizing Jesus as a victim of sexual abuse should be a concern for the whole Church and not just a concern for survivors. Furthermore, the participants warned against a number of risks and dangers that need to be avoided. In particular they warned against the superficial misappropriation of Jesus' experience to turn attention from, or undermine, the lived experience of abuse. Significantly, the innocence of Jesus might offer a resource to resist self-blame and confront victim-blaming by others. It might expose and challenge victim-blaming attitudes in the wider Church that continue to shape the lives of survivors many years after the abuse may have finished.

References

Allen, John, and Pamela Schaeffer, 'Reports of Abuse. AIDS Exacerbates Sexual Exploitation of Nuns, Report Alleges', *National Catholic Report*, 16 March 2001, https://natcath.org/NCR_Online/archives2/2001a/031601/031601a.htm.

Blyth, Caroline, Emily Colgan, Katie Edwards eds, *Rape Culture, Gender Violence and Religion*, 3 vols, London: Palgrave Macmillan, 2018.

Bongi Zengele, Patricia, *To Make Our Voices Heard: Listening to Survivors of Sexual Violence in Central African Republic*, Teddington, Middlesex: Tearfund, 2015.

Brock, Rita Nakashima, and Rebecca Ann Parker, *Proverbs of Ashes: Violence, Redemptive Suffering and the Search for What Saves Us*, Boston, MA: Beacon Press, 2001.

Brownmiller, Susan, *Against Our Will: Men, Women and Rape*, New York: Simon and Schuster, 1975.

Cavanaugh, William, *Torture and Eucharist: Theology, Politics and the Body of Christ*, Malden, MA: Blackwell, 1998.

Chibnall, John T., Ann Wolf and Paul N. Duckro, 'A National Survey of the Sexual Trauma Experiences of Catholic Nuns', *Review of Religious Research* 40:2 (December 1998), pp. 304–13.

Cooper-White, Pamela, 'Clergy Sexual Exploitation of Adults', in *When Pastors Prey: Overcoming Clergy Sexual Abuse of Women*, Valli Boobal Batchelor ed., Geneva: World Council of Churches, 2013, pp. 58–81.

Cozzens, Donald B., *Sacred Silence: Denial and the Crisis in the Church*, Collegeville, MN: The Liturgical Press, 2002, pp. 59–64.

Crisp, Beth R., 'Reading Scripture from a Hermeneutic of Rape', *Theology and Sexuality* 14 (2001), pp. 23–42.

——, 'Spiritual Direction and Survivors of Sexual Abuse', *The Way* 43:2 (2004), pp. 7–17.

——, 'Ignatian Spirituality and the Rebuilding of Self-esteem', *The Way* 45:1 (2006), pp. 55–78.

——, 'Spirituality and Sexual Abuse: Issues and Dilemmas for Survivors', *Theology & Sexuality* 13:3 (May 2007), pp. 301–14.

——, 'Beyond Crucifixion: Remaining Christian After Sexual Abuse', *Theology & Sexuality* 15:1 (January 2009), pp. 65–76.

——, *Beyond Crucifixion: Meditations on Surviving Sexual Abuse*, London: Darton, Longman and Todd, 2010.

——, 'Silence and Silenced: Implications for the Spirituality of Survivors of Sexual Abuse', *Feminist Theology* 18:3 (2010), pp. 277–93.

——, 'The Spiritual Implications of Sexual Abuse: Not Just an Issue for Religious Women?', *Feminist Theology* 20:2 (January 2012), pp. 133–45.

Durà-Vilà, Gloria, Roland Littlewood and Gerard Leavey, 'Integrating Sexual Trauma in a Religious Narrative: Transformation, Resolution and Growth among Contemplative Nuns', *Transcultural Psychiatry* 50:1 (2013), pp. 21–46.

Durà-Vilà, Gloria, Simon Dein, Roland Littlewood and Gerard Leavey, 'The Dark Night of the Soul: Causes and Resolution of Emotional Distress among Contemplative Nuns', *Transcultural Psychiatry* 47 (2010), pp. 548–70.

Du Toit, Louise, and Elisabet le Roux, 'A Feminist Reflection on Male Victims of Conflict-related Sexual Violence', *European Journal of Women's Studies* 22:4 (2020), pp. 412–27.

Edwards, Katie B., and David Tombs, '#HimToo – Why Jesus Should Be Recognised as a Victim of Sexual Violence', *The Conversation*, 23 March 2018, https://theconversation.com/himtoo-why-jesus-should-be-recognised-as-a-victim-of-sexual-violence-93677.

Edwards, Katie B., and Meredith J. C. Warren, '#MeToo Jesus: Is Christ Really a Good Model for Victims of Abuse?', *The Conversation*, 14 February 2018, https://theconversation.com/metoo-jesus-is-christ-really-a-good-model-for-victims-of-abuse-91812./

Figueroa, Rocío, and David Tombs, 'Lived Religion and the Traumatic Impact of Sexual Abuse: The Sodalicio Case in Peru', in *Trauma and Lived Religion: Transcending the Ordinary*, Ruard Ganzevoort and Srdjan Sremac eds, London: Palgrave Macmillan, 2019, pp. 155–76

——, 'Recognising Jesus as a Victim of Sexual Abuse: Responses from Sodalicio Survivors in Peru', *Religion and Gender* 10:1 (June 2020), pp. 57–75.

Fortune, Marie, *Sexual Violence: The Unmentionable Sin: An Ethical and Pastoral Perspective*, Cleveland, OH: Pilgrim Press, 1983.

——, 'Is Nothing Sacred? The Betrayal of the Ministerial or Teaching Relationship', *Journal of Feminist Studies in Religion* 10 (1994), pp. 17–26.

Gafney, Wil, 'Crucifixion and Sexual Violence', *HuffPost*, 28 March 2013, www.huffingtonpost.com/rev-wil-gafney-phd/crucifixion-and-sexual-violence_b_2965369.html.

Ganzevoort, Ruard, and Srdjan Sremac eds, *Lived Religion and the Politics of (In)tolerance*, Palgrave Studies in Lived Religion and Societal Changes, London: Palgrave Macmillan, 2017.

——, eds, *Trauma and Lived Religion: Transcending the Ordinary*, Palgrave Studies in Lived Religion and Societal Changes, London: Palgrave Macmillan, 2019.

Harley-McGowan, Felicity, 'Picturing the Passion', in *Routledge Handbook of Early Christian Art*, Robin M. Jensen and Mark D. Ellison eds, New York and London: Routledge, 2018, pp. 290–307.

Harries, Richard, *The Passion in Art*, Ashgate Studies in Theology, Imagination and the Arts, Aldershot, Hampshire: Ashgate, 2004.

Heath, Elaine A., *We Were the Least of These: Reading the Bible with Survivors of Sexual Abuse*, Grand Rapids, MI: Brazos, 2011.

Jenkins, Philip, *Paedophiles and Priests: Anatomy of a Contemporary Crisis*, New York and Oxford: Oxford University Press, 1996.

Jensen, Robin Margaret, *Understanding Early Christian Art*, New York and London: Routledge, 2000.

Jones, Serene, *Trauma and Grace: Theology in a Ruptured World*, Louisville, KY: Presbyterian Publishing Corp., 2009.

Kelly, Liz, *Surviving Sexual Violence*, Cambridge: Polity, 1988.

Keshgegian, Flora A., *Redeeming Memories: A Theology of Healing and Transformation*, Nashville, TN: Abingdon Press, 2000.

Lembo, Makatamine, *Relations Pastorales Saines et Matures entre Femmes Consacrées et Prêtres: Un Analyse Qualitative de cas d'abus de femmes consacrées par des prêtres*, Roma: Pontificia Università Gregoriana, 2019.

McGarry, Patsy, 'Church Sources Puzzled by Claims about Nuns', *Irish Times*, 21 March 2001.

Murray-Swank, Nichole A., and Kenneth I. Pargament, 'God, Where Are You?: Evaluating A Spiritually-integrated Intervention for Sexual Abuse', *Mental Health, Religion & Culture* 8:3 (September 2005), pp. 191–203.

O'Donnell, Karen, *Broken Bodies: The Eucharist, Mary and the Body in Trauma Theology*, London: SCM Press, 2018.

O'Donnell, Karen, and Katie Cross eds, *Feminist Trauma Theologies: Body, Scripture & Church in Critical Perspective*, London: SCM Press, 2020.

Pargament, Kenneth I., and Curtis R. Brant, 'Religion and Coping', in *Handbook of Religion and Mental Health*, David H. Rosmarin and Harold G. Koenig eds, Cambridge: Academic Press, 1998, pp. 111–28.

Pellauer, Mary D., Barbara Chester and Jane A. Boyajian eds, *Sexual Assault and Abuse: A Handbook for Clergy and Religious Professionals*, San Francisco, CA: Harper & Row, 1987.

'Pope Acknowledges Scandal of Priests Sexually Abusing Nuns', *The Guardian*, 5 February 2019, www.theguardian.com/world/2019/feb/05/pope-francis-acknowledges-scandal-of-priests-sexually-abusing-nuns.

Rambo, Shelly, *Spirit and Trauma: A Theology of Remaining*, Louisville, KY: Westminster John Knox Press, 2010.

——, 'Theology After Trauma', *Christian Century* 136:24 (20 November 2019), pp. 22–7.

Reaves, Jayme, and David Tombs, '#MeToo Jesus: Naming Jesus as a Victim of Sexual Abuse', *International Journal for Public Theology* 13:4 (2019), pp. 387–412.

Rudolfsson, Lisa, and Inga Tidefors, 'I Have Cried to Him a Thousand Times, But It Makes No Difference: Sexual Abuse, Faith, and Images of God', *Mental Health, Religion & Culture* 17 (2014), pp. 910–22.

——, 'The Struggles of Victims of Sexual Abuse Who Seek Pastoral Care', *Pastoral Psychology* 64 (January 2015), pp. 453–67.

Scarsella, Hilary J., 'Victimization via Ritualization: Christian Communion and Sexual Abuse', in *Trauma and Lived Religion: Transcending the Ordinary*, Ruard Ganzevoort and Srdjan Sremac eds, London: Palgrave Macmillan, 2019, pp. 225–52.

Segovia, Fernando H., 'Jesus as Victim of State Terror: A Critical Reflection Twenty Years Later', in *Crucifixion, State Terror, and Sexual Abuse: Text and Context*, David Tombs ed., Dunedin: University of Otago, Centre for Theology and Public Issues, 2018, pp. 22–31, http://hdl.handle.net/10523/8558.

Sipe, Richard A. W., *Sex, Priests, and Power: Anatomy of a Crisis*, New York: Brunner/Mazel, 1995.

Slee, Nicola, *Seeking the Risen Christa*, London: SPCK Publishing, 2011.

Tearfund, *Silent No More: The Untapped Potential of the Worldwide Church in Addressing Sexual Violence*, Teddington, Middlesex: Tearfund, 2011.

——, *Breaking the Silence: Sexual Violence in South Africa and the Role of the Church*, Durban: Tearfund SA, 2013.

Thistlethwaite, Susan Brooks, *Sex, Race, and God: Christian Feminism in Black and White*, New York: Crossroad, 1989.

Tombs, David, 'Crucifixion, State Terror, and Sexual Abuse', *Union Seminary Quarterly Review* 53:1–2 (1999), pp. 89–109, http://hdl.handle.net/10523/6067.

——, 'Lived Religion and the Intolerance of the Cross', in *Lived Religion and the Politics of (In)tolerance*, Ruard Ganzevoort and Srdjan Sremac eds, London: Palgrave Macmillan, 2017, pp. 63–83.

——, 'Abandonment, Rape, and Second Abandonment: Hannah Baker in *13 Reasons Why* and the Royal Concubines in 2 Samuel 15–20', in *Rape Culture, Gender Violence and Religion: Biblical Perspectives*, Caroline Blyth, Emily Colgan, Katie Edwards eds, London: Palgrave Macmillan, 2018, pp. 117–41.

——, *Crucifixion and Sexual Abuse*, Dunedin: Centre for Theology and Public Issues, University of Otago, 2019, http://hdl.handle.net/10523/9834 (English); http://hdl.handle.net/10523/9843 (Spanish); http://hdl.handle.net/10523/9846 (French); originally published as Tombs, 'Crucificação e Abuso Sexual', *Estudos Teológicos* 59:1 (June 2019), pp. 119–32.

——, 'Confronting the Stigma of Naming Jesus as a Victim of Sexual Violence', *Enacting a Public Theology*, Clive Pearson ed., Stellenbosch: SunMedia, 2019, pp. 71–86.

——, 'The Stripping and Mocking of Jesus: Reading Crucifixion as a Text of Terror', in *Terror in the Bible: Rhetoric, Gender, and Violence*, Robyn Whitaker and Monica Melanchthon eds, International Voices in Biblical Studies Series, Atlanta; Society of Biblical Literature Press, forthcoming.

——, *The Crucifixion of Jesus: Torture, Sexual Abuse, and the Scandal of the Cross*, London: Routledge, in preparation.

Trainor, Michael, *The Body of Jesus and Sexual Abuse: How the Gospel Passion Narrative Informs a Pastoral Approach*, Eugene, OR: Wipf & Stock Publishers, 2014.

Voices of Faith, 'Women's Voices in the Abuse Crisis', 27 November 2018, www.youtube.com/watch?v=su4_LqYElZs.

West, Gerald O., *The Academy of the Poor: Towards a Dialogical Reading of the Bible*, Sheffield: Sheffield Academic Press, 1999.

—, 'Reading the Bible with the Marginalised: The Value/s of Contextual Bible Reading', *Stellenbosch Theological Journal* 1:2 (2015), pp. 235–61.

Williams, Delores S., *Sisters in the Wilderness: The Challenge of Womanist God-Talk*, Maryknoll, NY: Orbis, 1993.

Williams, Joyce E., 'Secondary Victimization: Confronting Public Attitudes about Rape', *Victimology* 9 (1984), pp. 66–81.

Williams, Joyce E., and Karen A. Holmes, *The Second Assault: Rape and Public Attitudes*, Westport, CT: Greenwood Press, 1981.

Notes

1 David Tombs, 'Crucifixion, State Terror, and Sexual Abuse', *Union Seminary Quarterly Review* 53:1–2 (1999), pp. 89–109.

2 It investigated the dynamics of state terror and sexual abuses in Latin American torture practices in the 1970s and 1980s and used these as a vantage point to re-examine Roman crucifixion practices that might shed light on the biblical narratives. It sought to illustrate the value of reading from present to past as well as from past to present. A guiding hermeneutical principle was that state terror and sexual abuse are not just relevant current concerns that the crucifixion narratives might address, but recent reports on torture provide an insightful lens through which to see the first-century context and the biblical text in new ways. Understanding the use of torture for state terror and the prevalence of sexual abuse in torture practices provides new insights into what is clearly present within the texts but is often unrecognized or ignored. Attention to torture practices helps to re-read the texts on the stripping and exposure of Jesus as an instrument of sexual humiliation and as a form of sexual abuse. Torture reports also raise the possibility of further sexual assault, which may have taken place in the praetorium. In the intervening years, torture reports from Sri Lanka, Libya, Syria, Democratic Republic of Congo, South Sudan, Myanmar and other contexts have underlined and reinforced this understanding of sexual abuse and prisoner mistreatment as a global issue.

3 Tombs, 'Crucifixion, State Terror, and Sexual Abuse', pp. 108–9.

4 Tombs, 'Crucifixion, State Terror, and Sexual Abuse', p. 109. William Cavanaugh's excellent work on torture and Eucharist had only recently been published. Had there been more opportunity it would have been useful to further explore Cavanaugh's insights on torture and the body of Christ. Even though Cavanaugh does not give sustained attention to sexual abuse within torture, his work demonstrates the practical difference that addressing torture can make to an understanding of Christ, the Church and liturgy. See William Cavanaugh, *Torture and Eucharist: Theology, Politics and the Body of Christ* (Malden, MA: Blackwell, 1998).

5 The initial findings were published in a longer discussion paper as Rocío

Figueroa and David Tombs, 'Seeing His Innocence, I See My Innocence: Responses from Abused Nuns to Jesus as a Victim of Sexual Abuse' (Dunedin: Centre for Theology and Public Issues, University of Otago, 2020).

6 In this context, the term 'nun' is used for brevity for religious sisters and consecrated women who belong (or formerly belonged) to Roman Catholic orders, congregations, or new religious communities. Technically the term 'nun' refers to women belonging to enclosed orders, but we use it slightly more inclusively, extending it to all orders. The common denominator in this more inclusive sense is that all of them made the vows of celibacy, poverty and obedience within a religious community. Unless stated otherwise, we use the term nun for all five of the women.

7 On viewing sexual violence as a form of power and control, see Liz Kelly, *Surviving Sexual Violence* (Cambridge: Polity, 1988).

8 Rocío Figueroa and David Tombs, 'Lived Religion and the Traumatic Impact of Sexual Abuse: The Sodalicio Case in Peru', in *Trauma and Lived Religion: Transcending the Ordinary*, Ruard Ganzevoort and Srdjan Sremac eds (London: Palgrave Macmillan, 2019), pp. 155–76.

9 Rocío Figueroa and David Tombs, 'Recognising Jesus as a Victim of Sexual Abuse: Responses from Sodalicio Survivors in Peru', *Religion and Gender: Special Issue on Gendering Jesus* 10:1 (2020), pp. 57–75.

10 Five of the group had also featured in Pedro Salinas, *Mitad monjes, mitad soldados: Todo lo que el Sodalicio no quieres que sepas* (Lima: Planeta, 2015), and we used the same pseudonyms for them in our studies.

11 Associated Press, 'Pope Acknowledges Scandal of Priests Sexually Abusing Nuns', *The Guardian*, 5 February 2019, www.theguardian.com/world/2019/feb/05/pope-francis-acknowledges-scandal-of-priests-sexually-abusing-nuns. See also Makatamine Lembo, *Relations Pastorales Saines et Matures entre Femmes Consacrées et Prêtres: Un Analyse Qualitative de cas d'abus de femmes consacrées par des prêtres* (Roma: Pontificia Università Gregoriana, 2019). For earlier revelations, based on concerns raised by Irish nuns Maura O'Donohue and Marie McDonald, see John Allen and Pamela Schaeffer, 'Reports of Abuse: AIDS Exacerbates Sexual Exploitation of Nuns, Reports Allege', *National Catholic Report*, 16 March 2001; Patsy McGarry, 'Church Sources Puzzled by Claims about Nuns', *Irish Times*, 21 March 2001. See also John T. Chibnall, Ann Wolf and Paul N. Duckro, 'A National Survey of the Sexual Trauma Experiences of Catholic Nuns', *Review of Religious Research* 40:2 (December 1998), pp. 304–13.

12 See Gloria Durà-Vilà, Roland Littlewood and Gerard Leavey, 'Integration of Sexual Trauma in a Religious Narrative: Transformation, Resolution and Growth among Contemplative Nuns', *Transcultural Psychiatry* 50:1 (2013), pp. 21–46; see also Gloria Durà-Vilà, Simon Dein, Roland Littlewood and Gerard Leavey, 'The Dark Night of the Soul: Causes and Resolution of Emotional Distress among Contemplative Nuns', *Transcultural Psychiatry* 47:4 (2010), pp. 548–70.

13 Durà-Vilà et al., 'Integration of Sexual Trauma in a Religious Narrative', p. 38.

14 See also Figueroa and Tombs, 'Lived Religion and the Traumatic Impact of Sexual Abuse: The Sodalicio Case in Peru', pp. 167–8.

15 Michael Trainor, *The Body of Jesus and Sexual Abuse: How the Gospel Passion Narrative Informs a Pastoral Approach* (Eugene, OR: Wipf & Stock, 2014). Other important work on the issues include Elaine A. Heath, *We Were the Least of These: Reading the Bible with Survivors of Sexual Abuse* (Grand Rapids, MI: Brazos, 2011); Wil Gafney, 'Crucifixion and Sexual Violence',

HuffPost, 28 March 2013, www.huffingtonpost.com/rev-wil-gafney-phd/crucifixion-and-sexual-violence_b_2965369.html; Chris Greenough, *The Bible and Sexual Violence Against Men* (London: Routledge, 2020).

16 See Michael Trainor's chapter in this volume for further detail.

17 See David W. Chapman, *Ancient Jewish and Christian Perceptions of Crucifixion* (Grand Rapids, MI: Baker Academic, 2008); Gunnar Samuelsson, *Crucifixion in Antiquity: An Inquiry into the Background of New Testament Terminology* (Tübingen: Mohr Siebeck, rev. edn 2018 [orig. 2011]); John Granger Cook, *Crucifixion in the Mediterranean World* (Tubingen: Mohr Siebeck, 2014); David W. Chapman and Eckhard J. Schnabel, *The Trial and Crucifixion of Jesus* (Tübingen: Mohr Siebeck, 2015).

18 Katie B. Edwards and David Tombs, '#HimToo – Why Jesus Should Be Recognised as a Victim of Sexual Violence', *The Conversation*, 23 March 2018, https://theconversation.com/himtoo-why-jesus-should-be-recognised-as-a-victim-of-sexual-violence-93677.

19 David Tombs, 'Hidden in Plain Sight: Seeing the Stripping of Jesus as Sexual Violence', *Journal for Interdisciplinary Biblical Studies* 2:1 (2020), pp. 224–47.

20 Trainor, *The Body of Jesus and Sexual Abuse*, p. 6. In November 2012, the establishment of a Royal Commission of Inquiry to investigate institutional responses to allegations of child sexual abuse was announced. The Commission (which ran January 2013–December 2017) was in its early stages as Trainor's book was written, and sexual abuses in church settings are a key concern for his work; Trainor, *The Body of Jesus and Sexual Abuse*, p. 245.

21 Trainor, *The Body of Jesus and Sexual Abuse*, p. 247.

22 Trainor, *The Body of Jesus and Sexual Abuse*, pp. 9–11.

23 Trainor, *The Body of Jesus and Sexual Abuse*, p. 275.

24 More work is also needed on the depiction of crucifixion in art. See, Richard Harries, *The Passion in Art*, Ashgate Studies in Theology, Imagination and the Arts (Aldershot, Hampshire: Ashgate, 2004); Robin Margaret Jensen, *Understanding Early Christian Art* (New York and London: Routledge, 2000); Felicity Harley-McGowan, 'Picturing the Passion', in *Routledge Handbook of Early Christian Art*, Robin M. Jensen and Mark D. Ellison eds (New York and London: Routledge, 2018), pp. 290–307.

25 See David Tombs, *The Crucifixion of Jesus: Torture, Sexual Abuse, and the Scandal of the Cross* (London: Routledge, in preparation).

26 On how religion can offer important resources for coping and resilience, see Kenneth I. Pargament and Curtis R. Brant, 'Religion and Coping', in *Handbook of Religion and Mental Health*, David H. Rosmarin and Harold G. Koenig eds (Cambridge: Academic Press, 1998), pp. 111–28.

27 For early literature, see Richard A. W. Sipe, *Sex, Priests, and Power: Anatomy of a Crisis* (New York: Brunner/Mazel, 1995); Philip Jenkins, *Paedophiles and Priests: Anatomy of a Contemporary Crisis* (New York and Oxford: Oxford University Press, 1996); Donald B. Cozzens, *Sacred Silence: Denial and the Crisis in the Church* (Minnesota, MN: The Liturgical Press 2002).

28 See especially the early work by Susan Brownmiller, *Against Our Will: Men, Women and Rape* (New York: Simon and Schuster, 1975), pp. 31–113. More recent work includes: Christina Lamb, *Our Bodies, Their Battlefields: What War Does to Women* (London: William Collins, 2020); Elaine Storkey, *Scars Across Humanity: Understanding and Overcoming Violence Against Women* (London: SPCK, 2015). On male victims, see Marysia Zalewski, Paula Drumond, Elisabeth

Prügl and Maria Stern eds, *Sexual Violence Against Men in Global Politics* (New York: Routledge, 2018). For wider literature on law and policy on conflict-related sexual violence, see *International Review of the Red Cross* 96:984 (Summer 2014).

29 Since 2010, Tearfund and other faith agencies have worked to engage and resource faith leaders and faith communities to prevent and respond to sexual and gender-based violence. In partnership with the Anglican Communion and UNAIDS, they have launched an international coalition called 'We Will Speak Out' (www.wewillspeakout.org), which has included significant attention to sexual violence during conflict.

30 On the relevance of #MeToo for the Church, see Ruth Everhart, *The #MeToo Reckoning: Facing the Church's Complicity in Sexual Abuse and Misconduct* (Downer's Grove, IL: InterVarsity Press, 2020). On #MeToo and the Bible, see Johanna Stiebert, *Rape Myths, the Bible, and #MeToo* (London: Routledge, 2019). See also Jayme R. Reaves and David Tombs, '#MeToo Jesus: Naming Jesus as a Victim of Sexual Abuse', *International Journal of Public Theology* 13:4 (2019), pp. 387–412; and Caroline Blyth, Emily Colgan, Katie Edwards eds, *Rape Culture, Gender Violence and Religion*, 3 vols (London: Palgrave Macmillan, 2018).

31 See Joyce E. Williams, 'Secondary Victimization: Confronting Public Attitudes about Rape', *Victimology* 9 (1984), pp. 66–81. Secondary victimization in this sense has been described as a 'second assault': 'For women who are raped, the essence of the second assault is skepticism, blame, and even condemnation, emanating from society at large, from one's own community, from one's own self-blame (an internalization of the attitudes of others), from family, and from significant others', in Joyce E. Williams and Karen A. Holmes, *The Second Assault: Rape and Public Attitudes* (Westport, CT: Greenwood Press, 1981). On the related idea of 'second abandonment' in secondary victimization, see David Tombs, 'Abandonment, Rape, and Second Abandonment: Hannah Baker in *13 Reasons Why* and the Royal Concubines in 2 Samuel 15–20', in *Rape Culture, Gender Violence and Religion: Biblical Perspectives*, Caroline Blyth, Emily Colgan, Katie Edwards eds (London: Palgrave Macmillan, 2018), pp. 117–41.

32 Tearfund, *Silent No More: The Untapped Potential of the Worldwide Church in Addressing Sexual Violence* (Teddington, Middlesex: Tearfund, 2011); Tearfund, *Breaking the Silence: Sexual Violence in South Africa and the Role of the Church* (Durban: Tearfund SA, 2013); Patricia Bongi Zengele, *To Make Our Voices Heard: Listening to Survivors of Sexual Violence in Central African Republic* (Teddington, Middlesex: Tearfund, 2015).

33 For discussion of negative judgements and stigma, see David Tombs, 'Confronting the Stigma of Naming Jesus as a Victim of Sexual Violence', in *Enacting a Public Theology*, Clive Pearson ed. (Stellenbosch: SUNMeDia, 2019), pp. 71–86.

34 University of Otago Human Ethics Committee, Approval 13 September 2019, Reference 19–112. We are especially grateful to Dr Tess Patterson, Department of Psychological Medicine, University of Otago, for her assistance with the ethics approval and for her advice as consultant on the project.

35 The abridged version was first created in English, and then translated into Portuguese for publication in Brazilian Portuguese as David Tombs, 'Crucificação e Abuso Sexual', *Estudos Teológicos* 59:1 (June 2019), pp. 119–32. It was then translated into Spanish, French and German to facilitate the interviews, and published under Creative Commons as David Tombs, *Crucifixion and Sexual Abuse* (Dunedin: Centre for Theology and Public Issues, University of Otago, 2019), http://hdl.han

dle.net/10523/9834 (English); http://hdl.handle.net/10523/9843 (Spanish); http://
hdl.handle.net/10523/9846 (French); http://hdl.handle.net/10523/9924 (German).

36 The use of the abridged article, rather than the fuller version, was to reduce
the time we were asking participants to offer us, and also to reduce the overall cost
of the translation work. In the 2018 interviews with male survivors it had only been
necessary to translate the article into Spanish, and the full article was used for this.
Since the group of nuns spoke French and German, as well as Spanish, it was more
practical to use the newly abridged article to reduce the translation work. We do
not believe that the use of an abbreviated article makes a significant difference to
the responses offered, but it should be noted that the version was slightly shorter
for the nuns than it had been for the male survivors.

37 The Skype interviews were recorded on a digital audio system. The tran-
scriptions of the interviews were anonymized and the pseudonyms were assigned
to maintain the confidentiality of the five participants. The interviews were then
translated into English.

38 The answers to the next question confirm that Maria, Lilian, Dina and Lucia
had not thought of Jesus suffering sexual abuse prior to their involvement with the
project. On the Spanish study, see Durà-Vilà et al., 'Integration of Sexual Trauma
in a Religious Narrative'.

39 The negative use of Jesus' suffering to silence victims of sexual abuse and
assault is discussed in Katie B. Edwards and Meredith Warren, '#MeToo Jesus:
Is Christ Really a Good Model for Victims of Abuse?', *The Conversation*, 14
February 2018, https://theconversation.com/metoo-jesus-is-christ-really-a-good-
model-for-victims-of-abuse-91812; see further Rita Nakashima Brock and Rebecca
Ann Parker, *Proverbs of Ashes: Violence, Redemptive Suffering and the Search for
What Saves Us* (Boston, MA: Beacon Press, 2001).

40 The lecture by Father Philippe Lefebvre OP was part of the conference 'Violence in the Church, Violence by the Church, Violence in the Eyes of the Church:
What Perspectives, Particularly for Europe and Francophone Africa?', Strasbourg,
5 April 2019.

41 See further David Tombs, 'The Stripping and Mocking of Jesus: Reading
Crucifixion as a Text of Terror' in *Terror in the Bible: Rhetoric, Gender, and
Violence*, Robyn Whitaker and Monica Melanchthon eds (International Voices
in Biblical Studies Series Atlanta, GA; Society of Biblical Literature Press, forthcoming).

42 The women were much more explicit in voicing concern for Jesus than
the participants in the previous study. This difference may, however, be because
the interview questions in the previous study did not focus in the same way on
emotional response.

43 We did not want to ask our participants to speak for other survivors, as
this would place an unreasonable burden upon them. However, in answer to the
previous question about their own experience as survivors, some of them also
commented on whether they saw it as helpful or unhelpful to other survivors. These
answers were included in the previous section.

44 Works which might further shape this approach include: Marie Fortune,
Sexual Violence: The Unmentionable Sin: An Ethical and Pastoral Perspective (Cleveland, OH: Pilgrim Press, 1983); Marie Fortune 'Is Nothing Sacred? The Betrayal of
the Ministerial or Teaching Relationship', *Journal of Feminist Studies in Religion*
10 (1994), pp. 17–26; Mary D. Pellauer, Barbara Chester and Jane A. Boyajian eds,
Sexual Assault and Abuse: A Handbook for Clergy and Religious Professionals (San

Francisco, CA: Harper & Row, 1987); Kenneth I. Pargament and Curtis R. Brant, 'Religion and Coping', in *Handbook of Religion and Mental Health*, David H. Rosmarin and Harold G. Koenig eds (Cambridge: Academic Press, 1998), pp. 111–28; Nichole A. Murray-Swank and Kenneth I. Pargament, 'God, Where Are You?: Evaluating a Spiritually-integrated Intervention for Sexual Abuse', *Mental Health, Religion & Culture* 8:3 (September 2005), pp. 191–203; Pamela Cooper-White, 'Clergy Sexual Exploitation of Adults', in *When Pastors Prey: Overcoming Clergy Sexual Abuse of Women*, Valli Boobal Batchelor ed. (Geneva: World Council of Churches, 2013), pp. 58–81; Lisa Rudolfsson and Inga Tidefors, 'I Have Cried to Him a Thousand Times, But It Makes No Difference: Sexual Abuse, Faith, and Images of God', *Mental Health, Religion & Culture* 17 (2014), pp. 910–22; Lisa Rudolfsson and Inga Tidefors, 'The Struggles of Victims of Sexual Abuse Who Seek Pastoral Care', *Pastoral Psychology* 64 (January 2015), pp. 453–67.

45 For example, we did not attempt further discussion of the similarity or dissimilarity of Jesus' experience and the experience of the nuns, nor the significance of Jesus' gender as a male victim for the experience of the nuns as female victims. On the complexity of responding to male victims alongside female victims, and how male victims in conflict-related sexual violence might be best understood from a feminist perspective, see Louise Du Toit and Elisabet le Roux, 'A Feminist Reflection on Male Victims of Conflict-related Sexual Violence', *European Journal of Women's Studies* 22:4 (2020), pp. 412–27.

46 For an insightful perspective on men's experience of conflict-related sexual trauma and its meaning, see Ruard Ganzevoort and Srdjan Sremac, 'Masculinity, Spirituality, and Male Wartime Sexual Trauma', in *Interdisciplinary Handbook of Trauma and Culture*, Yochai Ataria, David Gurevitz, Haviva Pedaya, Yuval Neria eds (Cham, Switzerland: Springer, 2016), pp. 339–51.

47 Tombs, 'Confronting the Stigma of Naming Jesus as a Victim of Sexual Violence', pp. 71–86.

48 On the dangers of silence and the virtue of speaking out, see further Edwards and Warren, '#MeToo Jesus: Is Christ Really a Good Model for Victims of Sexual Abuse'.

49 For example, Marie Fortune, 'Religious Issues in Family Violence', in *Sexual Assault and Abuse: A Handbook for Clergy and Religious Professionals*, Mary Pellauer et al. eds (San Francisco, CA: Harper & Row, 1987), pp. 72–5; see also, Delores S. Williams, *Sisters in the Wilderness: The Challenge of Womanist God-Talk* (Maryknoll, NY: Orbis, 1993); Brock and Parker, *Proverbs of Ashes*; Serene Jones, *Trauma and Grace: Theology in a Ruptured World* (Louisville, KY: Presbyterian Publishing Corp., 2009), pp. 75–83.

50 See especially the careful and nuanced work on this complexity by Beth Crisp in her chapter in this book and in her past work. Beth R. Crisp, 'Spiritual Direction and Survivors of Sexual Abuse', *The Way* 43:2 (2004), pp. 7–17; 'Ignatian Spirituality and the Rebuilding of Self-esteem', *The Way* 45:1 (2006), pp. 55–78; 'Spirituality and Sexual Abuse: Issues and Dilemmas for Survivors', *Theology & Sexuality* 13:3 (May 2007), pp. 301–14; 'Beyond Crucifixion: Remaining Christian After Sexual Abuse', *Theology and Sexuality* 15:1 (January 2009), pp. 65–76; *Beyond Crucifixion: Meditations on Surviving Sexual Abuse* (London: Darton, Longman and Todd, 2010); 'Silence and Silenced: Implications for the Spirituality of Survivors of Sexual Abuse', *Feminist Theology* 18:3 (2010), pp. 277–93; 'The Spiritual Implications of Sexual Abuse: Not Just an Issue for Religious Women?', *Feminist Theology* 20:2 (January 2012), pp. 133–45.

51 Insights from feminist trauma theology are especially useful here. See Flora A. Keshgegian, *Redeeming Memories: A Theology of Healing and Transformation* (Nashville TN: Abingdon Press, 2000); Jones, *Trauma and Grace*; Shelly Rambo, *Spirit and Trauma: A Theology of Remaining* (Louisville, KY: Westminster John Knox Press, 2010); Rambo, 'Theology After Trauma', *Christian Century* 136:24 (20 November 2019); Karen O'Donnell, *Broken Bodies: The Eucharist, Mary and the Body in Trauma Theology* (London: SCM Press, 2018); Karen O'Donnell and Katie Cross eds, *Feminist Trauma Theologies: Body, Scripture and Church in Critical Perspective* (London: SCM Press, 2020).

52 See especially Heath, *We Were the Least of These*.

53 Susan Thistlethwaite has discussed her concerns over the negative messages that might be conveyed by Christa figures, but also notes that many survivors see their own suffering represented in a positive way in Christa figures. See Susan Brooks Thistlethwaite, *Sex, Race, and God: Christian Feminism in Black and White* (New York: Crossroad, 1989), pp. 92–108. On responses to Christa figures, which show a woman crucified or in a crucifix shape, see further Nicola Slee, *Seeking the Risen Christa* (London: SPCK Publishing, 2011), and also her chapter in this volume. On negative responses of survivors to communion, see Hilary J. Scarsella, 'Victimization via Ritualization: Christian Communion and Sexual Abuse', in *Lived Religion and the Politics of (In)tolerance*, Ruard Ganzevoort and Srdjan Sremac eds, Palgrave Studies in Lived Religion and Societal Changes (London: Palgrave Macmillan, 2017), pp. 225–52.

Acknowledgements

Many people have made the publication of this collection possible and we are very grateful for the many hands who have been a part of this piece of work. First, and foremost, we wish to thank our contributors for their willingness to share their scholarship, thoughts and their writing. We also owe a great debt to our three academic reviewers, Hannah Strømmen, Emily Colgan and Johanna Stiebert, who were extraordinarily generous in the time and energy they offered us in their feedback and their advice as the collection seen here took shape. The paper by David Tombs that is re-published as Chapter 1 in this volume was first presented in the Contextual Biblical Hermeneutics Section at the Society of Biblical Literature international meeting in Krakow in 1998. Co-chairs Fernando Segovia and Jeremy Punt offered generous encouragement at the time of presentation and they have remained gracious and supportive colleagues in the years since.

We would also like to extend our gratitude to our colleagues and our respective institutions, Sarum College (Salisbury, UK), Te Kupenga – Catholic Theological College (Auckland, New Zealand) and University of Otago (Dunedin, New Zealand), who supported the process from start to finish in different ways. Finally, we would like to say that it has been a particular pleasure to work with David Shervington, Rachel Geddes, Kate Hughes, Hannah Ward and the team at SCM Press who have been supportive of this project from day one.

Acknowledgement of Sources

Index of Biblical References

Old Testament

New Testament

Index of Names and Subjects

Part 3: Parsing Culture, Context and Perspectives

Part 4: Sexual Abuse, Trauma and the Personal

Contents

'come celebrate
with me that everyday
something has tried to kill me
and has failed.'

excerpt from 'won't you celebrate with me?' by Lucille Clifton,
from *The Book of Light* (Copper Canyon Press, 1993)

For those who have found a way to survive, in life or in death,
and for those who bear witness to their stories

© The Editors and Contributors 2021

Published in 2021 by SCM Press
Editorial office
3rd Floor, Invicta House,
108–114 Golden Lane,
London EC1Y 0TG, UK
www.scmpress.co.uk

SCM Press is an imprint of Hymns Ancient & Modern Ltd
(a registered charity)

Hymns Ancient & Modern® is a registered trademark of
Hymns Ancient & Modern Ltd
13A Hellesdon Park Road, Norwich,
Norfolk NR6 5DR, UK

British Library Cataloguing in Publication data

A catalogue record for this book is available
from the British Library

978-0-334-06032-1

Typeset by Regent Typesetting
Printed and bound by
CPI Group (UK) Ltd